People of Rimrock

People of Rimrock

A STUDY OF VALUES IN FIVE CULTURES

edited by Evon Z. Vogt and Ethel M. Albert

HARVARD UNIVERSITY PRESS
Cambridge · Massachusetts · 1966

IN MEMORIAM

Clyde Kluckhohn

Preface

THE "Comparative Study of Values in Five Cultures" Project of the Laboratory of Social Relations, Harvard University, was planned in 1948–1949 and formally initiated in June 1949. It was supported by the Rockefeller Foundation, through its Social Science Division, which made two three-year grants to the project, terminating in 1955. All publications of the Values Study, by which brief term the project has come to be called, have been based on field observations made during the six years of the formal duration of the project. The present volume is among the terminal publications; Appendix I lists other publications.

Field research was carried out in the Rimrock Area of western New Mexico, where the late Clyde Kluckhohn had been doing field work among Navahos since 1936. Nearby were communities of Zunis, Spanish-Americans, Mormons, and Texan homesteaders. The area thus provided five contrasting cultures for comparative study. Pseudonyms have been used for all persons named and for all local place names except Zuni pueblo.

Field headquarters were maintained from the summer of 1949 through the summer of 1953. From headquarters in Rimrock, Homestead, or Railtown, the field director supervised the research of individual field workers, who lived in the area. Problems of rapport with and adjustment to the local cultures varied with community and with observer. Professor Kluckhohn's long acquaintance with the Rimrock Navaho minimized problems with this group. Zuni pueblo, on the other hand, has always been difficult of access to outsiders, including perhaps especially anthropological observers, and we were not exceptions. Generally, research workers interested in Zuni lived in Railtown or Rimrock and made intermittent visits to the pueblo or worked with informants away from Zuni. The Texan homesteader community presented few special problems, if observers could avoid becoming embroiled in factional disputes. To those who went to church and manifested some interest in Mormon theology, the Mormon community also proved to be friendly. Not infrequently they attempted to convert project field workers. Adjustment to the Spanish-American communities depended chiefly upon good command of the Spanish language and sympathetic understanding of their customs and special problems in the area.

Data in the form of field-note diaries and reports of formal interviews were sent to the project office at Harvard University. There they were processed into files that followed the Human Relations Area Files categories but with additions suitable for data on observations and informant statements related to values. Such specialized data as questionnaire results and tape recordings on small group interaction were not entered in the files but were stored in the project office. All research results were available to all participants in the project.

John M. Roberts served as Coordinator and Evon Z. Vogt as Deputy Coordinator of the project from 1949 to 1953. These men alternated between Cambridge and New Mexico on a yearly basis, the one in New Mexico serving as field director. They made policy decisions in consultation with an Advisory Committee consisting of Professors Talcott Parsons, J. O. Brew, and the late Clyde Kluckhohn. Ultimate responsibility rested with the Director (the late Professor Samuel A. Stouffer), the then Associate Director (Professor Richard L. Solomon), and the Executive Committee of the Laboratory of Social Relations of the Department of Social Relations. The Department of Anthropology and the Peabody Museum collaborated informally in the planning and direction of the research, and the project office and files were located in the Peabody Museum from 1949 to 1952, when they were moved to a newly acquired Laboratory of Social Relations building.

Katherine Spencer served as Research Fellow during 1949–50 and Ethel M. Albert as Research Associate from 1953 to 1955. The office coordinators were Edward I. Fry (1950–51) and Irving Telling (1951–52). Twenty-nine individuals served as analysts of data in the project office at Harvard. During the six-year period of the research, thirty-seven field workers, representing the disciples of anthropology, sociology, social psychology, personality psychology, political science, philosophy, history, and geography, participated in the field work. Papers in the present volume are chiefly anthropological, but these are in most cases combined with concepts from other disciplines. Responsibility for bibliographic references rests in each paper with its author or authors.

The reader, it is hoped, will gain from the papers of the volume an appreciation of the role of values in various social institutions and processes, a general view of the five cultures of the Rimrock area, and insights into the variations of socio-cultural phenomena disclosed by comparative analysis. It should be remembered that the papers were prepared between 1955 and 1960. They therefore do not take account of more recent work, nor do they necessarily reflect the authors' present views.

We should like to express our deepest gratitude to the late Professor Clyde Kluckhohn, who was the moving spirit behind the Values Study Project from start to finish. He provided much of the intellectual inspiration for the research, created the basic design of the project, contributed ideas for its organization, and served untiringly on the Advisory Committee for six years. We dedicate this volume to his memory.

Professors J. O. Brew and Talcott Parsons served on the Advisory Committee with Professor Kluckhohn to establish basic policy and advise on the various complexities of the project's operation. We should especially like to express our gratitude to Professor Brew for his guidance on field operations in the Southwest and for making available to us the facilities of the Peabody Museum. Professor Parsons contributed countless theoretical ideas, both in Cambridge and in the Southwest when he visited us in the field, and also gave us strong administrative support. It was a pleasure for us to work with this effective Advisory Committee.

We should like to acknowledge the assistance of the Rockefeller Foundation, and especially the interest and attention of Dr. Leland C. DeVinney of the Social Sciences Division, for the support of the project during the years 1949 through 1955. The late Professor Samuel A. Stouffer, then Director of the Laboratory of Social Relations, maintained a lively interest in our research operations at all stages and never failed to give us the benefit of his vast wisdom. The Associate Director of the Laboratory, Professor Richard L. Solomon, gave equally warm support and advice on many points. Other members of the Harvard Faculty who were not formally attached to the Project but who maintained an interest in our research and engaged us in helpful discussion about our problems include Professors Gordon W. Allport, Robert F. Bales, Jerome S. Bruner, Cora DuBois, Frederick Mosteller, Henry A. Murray, Douglas L. Oliver, Benjamin D. Paul, John Pelzel, and Robert W. White.

The editors are also grateful to the Center for Advanced Study in the Behavioral Sciences at Stanford, California, where we had the opportunity as Fellows during 1956–57 and 1957–58 to work on earlier drafts of the chapters of this volume.

In the Southwest we are indebted to many who with patience and dignity gave us hospitality in their homes, answered our often foolish questions, and helped us in ways that we all remember and appreciate. Our gratitude runs deepest to Mr. and Mrs. Major Bruton, John Chatto, Mr. and Mrs. Paul Davis, Jose Garcia, Bailey Henio, Mr. and Mrs. Marvin Lewis, Mr. and Mrs. Wilson Link, Mr. and Mrs. Paul Merrill, Robert Pino, David Skeet, Mr. and Mrs. Edward Vanderwagen, and Mrs. Shirley Vogt.

Contents

TABLES

ILLUSTRATIONS
(following page 80)

OLD ZUNI PUEBLO
(photos courtesy of Peabody Museum Collection, Harvard University)
The Caciques of Zuni, headmen of a former era. Most present-day Zunis wear Southwestern rancher-style clothes. (Hillers photo)
View in Zuni looking southeast, showing sacred mesa (Corn Mountain) in the extreme left background and the dance plaza at left center. (Hillers photo)
View in Zuni from a rooftop, showing chimneys made of Zuni pots, beehive ovens, and strands of drying chilies. (Hillers photo)
Old Mission Church. A contemporary photograph would show weathering of church and surrounding wall. (T. H. O'Sullivan photo)

NAVAHO SCENES
(photos courtesy of Leonard McCombe)
Navaho girl with dog, herding sheep.
Navaho man smoking hand-rolled cigarette.
A portrait of wrinkles and character.
Hair-combing, Navaho-style.
Young girl wearing a velvet blouse embellished with coins.
Baby in cradleboard is easily transported by horseback and able to view family activities.

SPANISH-AMERICAN SCENES
(photos courtesy of David DeHarport)
Catholic church and schoolyard in Atrisco.
The altar of the Catholic church.
A rancher's sons.
A Hereford cow wanders by deserted Atrisco houses.

ILLUSTRATIONS

THE MORMONS
(photos courtesy of David DeHarport)

A Rimrock Mormon hoes beans in his irrigated garden.

A Mormon house in Rimrock village.

Seen in the background, the Rimrock reservoir lies one mile southeast of the village.

The school principal helps to construct the new high school.

TEXAS HOMESTEADERS
(photos courtesy of David DeHarport)

The Baptist church stands unused since the decline in Homestead population.

White-faced Herefords graze on range lands.

Texas Homesteaders at rodeo grounds near the town center.

Log house and outlying sheds amid pinyon and juniper trees.

Homesteader on tractor cultivating bean fields.

People of Rimrock

The "Comparative Study of Values in Five Cultures" Project

EVON Z. VOGT and ETHEL M. ALBERT

THE RIMROCK AREA of New Mexico is well suited to cross-cultural study. Within reach of the visitor in a day's driving are the Rimrock Navaho reservation, the Zuni Indian pueblo, the Spanish-American village of Atrisco, a homesteader community of Texan and Oklahoman farmers and some ranchers, and the Mormon village of Rimrock for which the region is named. Selected as the site of the Values Study research, the Rimrock area was a rigorous proving ground for the thesis that values can be studied by the methods of the social sciences. The research results have added materially to our knowledge of values, and, equally important, have led to reformulation of some of the basic concepts and aspirations of empirical, comparative values research.

In a statement drawn up by the late Clyde Kluckhohn, the aims and general framework of the Values Study were outlined:

> There is general agreement among thoughtful people today that the problem of "values" is of crucial importance, both practically and from the point of view of scientific theory. There has been much talk among social scientists, and a number of suggestive essays have been published. However, there has been very little sustained empirical research. These problems urgently need further exploration, both theoretical and empirical.
>
> Since questions of culture (anthropology), social structure (sociology), the psychology of groups (social psychology), and individual motivation (clinical psychology) are all inextricably interwoven in the matter of values, it is likely that an approach from the angle of any single one of these sciences would prove to be highly incomplete, if not sterile. The research must be interdisciplinary and can, in part, take off from

hypotheses developed by other studies in the Laboratory of Social Relations.

Five distinct cultures co-exist in the same relatively small ecological area in New Mexico. For two full generations four of the groups involved have been in continued face-to-face contact. They have also been subject to approximately the same historical process, influenced by the same streams of cultural diffusion. The number of individuals in each cultural group is small enough to permit convincing workmanship in detail with relatively small resources in personnel. All five societies must meet the problems of gaining subsistence under environmental conditions which present the same challenge and hazards to all groups. Today all of these societies have available essentially the same technology.

The research design is premised upon the possibility of using the methods of agreement and difference (and of replication) in five different life-ways co-existing in the same external environment. Some of the same values are probably current in all five groups, perhaps even held by a majority of the members of each group. The degree to which this is true can be settled only by intensive and systematic investigation. Demonstration of similar values would have important theoretical implications. Likewise, the extent of variation among values held by individuals within a group has never, to our knowledge, been carefully described. Finally, the fact that some values continue to be distinctive of each separate culture, in spite of the common environmental setting and historical contact, requires explanation.

Each group will be studied in terms of its own internal mechanisms. For example, how does each group handle the scapegoat problem? The non-Indian groups (and the Indian to an increasing extent) export their young men to urban areas. How are the pressures handled in these altered situations? To what extent do the original values persist after protracted residence away?

Some Primary Questions:

1. What values characterize the five distinct cultures in this area?
2. What is the place of each value system in the total structural-functional economy of each culture?
3. By what processes of formal and informal teaching and learning are the value systems perpetuated in each culture?
4. What changes in value have occurred (a) in the period for which satisfactory documentation is available? (b) in the period of the project?
5. In terms of what situational pressures have such changes occurred? In what ways has each group reacted differently to roughly similar pressures because of (a) different cultural traditions, (b) different social structures?

2

6. To what extent is the range and incidence of distinct personality types various for the five cultural groups? If such variation exists, what is its relation to the perpetuation of the several value systems, the resistance of each to change, the distinctive patterning of the changes which are occurring in each culture?

7. What do value systems mean to individuals in each group?

8. To some degree each of the above-listed questions is merely a special phase of a more general problem:

Why do different value systems continue to exist in five cultures all having to meet similar problems of adjustment and survival in the same ecological area, all having been exposed by actual contact and by stimulus diffusion to each other's value ideas and practices? [1]

Kluckhohn's statement initiated a type of values research not previously undertaken. It involved a complex methodological design: research was to be simultaneously a ground-breaking empirical study, hence exploratory; to be carried out in five cultural groups, hence comparative and cross-cultural; and approached from different theoretic and methodological standpoints, hence interdisciplinary. Exploratory research does not aspire to definitive results. Its principal task is to test initial assumptions and theory so that the way can be cleared for future research. In both cross-cultural and interdisciplinary inquiry, aims, methods, and theories are diverse, sometimes divergent, despite a common focus on a single subject. When that subject is values, a concept with a notoriously long and involved history, research problems become more acute.

The results of the frankly exploratory research of the Values Study project, carried out by representatives of a dozen different specializations over a period of six years and dealing with five cultures, cannot be summarized in a brief, neat, conclusive statement. Some of the negative aspects, however, lend themselves all too easily to generalization. It was to be expected that the initial theory would require correction, that some of the aims would have to be modified, and that problems would arise that were unforeseen in the original design. Evaluation of the over-all project design, methods, and theory is a part of the project research report, and our discussion will be governed by a policy that considers candor to be in the best interests of future inquiry.

The problems to be examined are in part related to the complex design of the Values Study, in part to the problematic history of the values concept. By far the deepest difficulties of method and theory,

3

however, are shared with social-behavioral science inquiry generally in the state of the science as it existed in the 1950's and early 1960's, the period of the research and subsequent writing up of results.

PROBLEMS OF METHOD AND THEORY

Decisions concerning the organization and design of the Values Study project had to be made for which little precedent existed but which would have a critical effect on field work and the resultant published record. Should a single definition of "values" be established for use by all fieldworkers, or should variations and innovations be permitted? Should a uniform method be laid down for studying values in the field, or should fieldworkers be free to use different methods and to devise new ones? Should each fieldworker be assigned to the study of a single culture, or should each concentrate on some aspect of values to be studied comparatively in two or more of the five cultures? Should topics of field-work research be determined by a fixed, prearranged design, or be left to the discretion of the individual fieldworkers?

In each case, the alternative that allowed the individual fieldworker freedom of choice was elected. As a consequence, diverse definitions of "values" and a wide variety of methods were used. Some fieldworkers specialized in a single culture, others in some aspect of values in two, three, four, or all five. Some of the work focused on values, some on the relationship of values to selected aspects of environment, personality, or culture.

The consequences of a permissive policy in an exploratory research project can be seen in certain characteristics of the total results. Because each fieldworker, predoctoral or postdoctoral, had full scope for individuality, field work was carried out with a degree of intellectual excitement and discovery not likely to have accompanied externally imposed tasks. New ways of conceptualizing values and new techniques and methods were devised that probably would not otherwise have been developed. There were several collaborative ventures, but each was at the initiative of the researchers involved in them. Individuals were free to write up their research results when they were ready, thus avoiding the frustrations of delay and loss of individuality characteristic of collaborative analysis and publication. As a result, there has been a relatively large volume of publication over an extended period (see Appendix I). A more limited, hence more limiting, design would have resulted in less scholarly growth and development and less publication for the individual participants.

Predictable disadvantages also accrued from the permissive policy. The data produced are not uniform for all aspects of the five cultures and their values, nor did a unified theory or set of methods emerge. From this point of view the project as a whole paid a fairly high price for the scope and creativity enjoyed by its individual participants. Some of the disadvantages are convertible into gains. Where individually designed research ventures converge on uniform results, the outcome is more reliable than it could have been if all the work had sprung from the same definition, theory, and methods. It is noteworthy and reassuring that there is general agreement as to what the values of the five cultures are.

DEFINITIONS OF "VALUES"

The term, "values," represents a diverse body of data and concepts, not a uniform field of inquiry. This is evident from a review of the literature on the subject, both that used by Values Study researchers and that produced by them.[2] By far the greatest number of general treatises devoted to the social scientific study of values are in fact programmatic, quasi-philosophical, and quasi-scientific. In many cases, theory consists primarily of a priori arguments for or against the view that values are naturalistic phenomena that can and should be studied empirically. Much attention is claimed by disagreements about similarities or differences between facts and values, by relativism and absolutism or universalism in respect to values, and by other issues on the borderline between philosophical and social scientific value theory. The role of values in the observer's perceptions, which presumably affect all inquiry, is often confused with methodology for studying values as a distinct class of phenomena. These issues become entangled in disputes over basic and applied science. Continuation of implicit or explicit dialogues with earlier theories keeps alive problems of values that may not be relevant to empirical research or resolvable by it.

In the metalinguistic periphery of value theory, definitions frequently serve as weapons of metaphysical polemic. An important

5

impetus to empirical research, most of the classic statements are too general to be of use to the social scientist in the field. Examples of such influential and stimulating but excessively general definitions include Ralph Barton Perry's definition of values as "any object of any interest"; Köhler's identification of values as an undifferentiated "vector" quality of experience; Max Weber's *Werttheorie*; the positivist interpretation of values as subjective, emotive expression; and John Dewey's view of values as cognitive phenomena.[3] The latter, modified by Charles W. Morris' behavioral refinement of the pragmatist conception of values, is at the basis of Clyde Kluckhohn's effort at formal definition: "A value is a conception, explicit or implicit, distinctive of an individual or characteristc of a group, of the desirable which influences the selection from available modes, means, and ends of action."[4]

Kluckhohn's definition was used by a number of the Values Study fieldworkers in a variety of ways. An attempt was made to combine it with empirical indices suggested by Kluckhohn and others and to introduce the concept of systematic relations into the definition:

> Values, positive and negative, are (1) elements in the effective definition of the situation of action that designate desirable and undesirable modes, means and ends of action, i.e., normative orientations related in varying ways to cognitive and affective processes; (2) may be explicit or implicit, i.e., given directly in value judgments or inferred from verbal and non-verbal behaviors that involve approval, blame, praise, reward, punishment, support and suppression; (3) are persistent through time and manifest directionality, i.e., there is observable consistency of response to recurrent situations; and (4) are interrelated as elements in culturally or individually distinctive patterns or systems, i.e., as differentiated but interdependent parts of a whole.[5]

Generally, verbal definitions of "values," concise or extended, are not satisfactory guides to field work. This is in part revealed by the presence of a vast, unexplored conceptual space between definitions proposed by theorists and the considerable body of empirical descriptive literature on values. Descriptive studies of values usually either offer no definition at all or adopt a verbal definition that does not make effective contact with the data. Any other definition might have been cited without affecting the description. Such "ritual" use of a definition of values does not contribute to stabilizing the concept.

6

The difficulties created by the excessive generality and vagueness of verbal definitions of "values" are aggravated by the ambiguity of the term. An indication of the variety of phenomena to which the "values" label has been attached is supplied by the guide to a bibliography on values that was part of the work of the Values Study.[6] A sample of the nearly fifty topics listed suggests the range of variability in values research and theory and hence in the underlying definitions of values: administration, children's values, conflict, decision-making, game theory, ideology, international relations, kinship, language, law, mental health, morals, personality, planning, political behavior, relativism, social control, social stratification, socialization, and universals. Area studies report on the values of societies in every corner of the globe, but they are neither systematic nor parallel in coverage. The relation between science and values is a substantial subdivision in the literature that connects, or divides, empirical values study and philosophical issues of values. Preoccupations in this area include: the possible biological bases of values; value problems of applied science, natural and social; the relation of facts and values; science as an ethic; and value judgments in relation to scientific method, especially the issue whether science is value-free.

A complicating factor is the obvious similarity of some conceptions of values to phenomena studied under other labels, for example, motivation, attitudes, opinions, ideology, choice, policy-making, mores, law, and taboos. Since these, too, tend to be ill-defined or subject to a multiplicity of competing definitions, any attempt to relate them to values is likely to be merely a verbal exercise.

From the point of view of operational definition, methods and techniques reveal or determine definitions. Here, as in attempts at verbal definition, pluralism prevails. In some studies of values, methods are unspecified. Sometimes they are described as impressionistic or as empathetic identification. There has also been extensive use of quantitative techniques, content analysis, questionnaires, scales, inventories, tests, experiments, and mathematical and formal models. To the extent that different operations define different phenomena, each of these methods defines a distinct variety of values. Lacking generally accepted ground rules, "values" constitute a loose federation of meanings, not yet integrated for the field as a whole.

We must agree with Aristotle that a reliable definition is the

7

hoped-for result, not the starting point of empirical inquiry. A tentative working definition must suffice to indicate what we are looking for and to communicate information about what we have found. In the course of the Values Study research, the policy of permissiveness as to definitions and methods turned out to be a realistic acceptance of pluralism as appropriate to exploratory study of values.

METHODS AND TECHNIQUES OF DATA COLLECTION, ANALYSIS, AND REPORTING

A large part of the spectrum of methods available in the 1950's for the study of human behavior was utilized by the fieldworkers and analysts of the Values Study project. The papers in this volume are typical of the full list of research reports in their combined use of a variety of techniques for collecting, analyzing, and reporting fieldwork data. The methods and techniques utilized to obtain data on the value systems and other characteristics of the five cultures can be classified generally as follows: (1) formal and informal interviews to elicit statements from informants; (2) field observations of both routine behavior and of responses to recurring problem situations; (3) eliciting value choices in formal questionnaires; (4) eliciting responses to standardized stimuli, such as color charts, tachistoscope images, and projective tests; (5) tape recordings of small group interaction; and (6) recording, by appropriate techniques, oral literature, music, and art. Statistical analysis, thematic and content analysis, ethnographic description, and theoretic concepts from most of the social sciences were employed to interpret the data.

A standard ethnographic method, eliciting statements from informants in formal and informal interviews was used to some extent by all fieldworkers. Illustrations of its application as a major technique are: Ladd's (1956) study of Navaho ethics; Rapoport's (1954) investigation of Navaho religious values; Edmonson's (1957) study of Spanish-American institutional values; the study of Zuni law by Smith and Roberts (1954); O'Dea's (1957) study of the Rimrock Mormons; Vogt's (1955) study of Texan homesteaders; and Untereiner's (1953) comparative study of "self" and "society" orientations of Texan homesteaders and Zuni.

Interviewing was almost always supplemented by field observations of individuals and groups. Observations of routine behavior in

8

selected settings is exemplified by Roberts' (1956) study of *Zuni Daily Life*. The data, collected by systematic observations and dictated into an audiograph, were directed to specific behavioral acts of the members of three Zuni households and two Zuni sheep camp groups during the course of five different days in 1951. Observations were continued throughout the waking day in each case. The published results provide a more complete description of the flow of Zuni daily life than has ever been reported. Focusing observation on behavioral responses to recurring problem or crisis situations as a special application of field observation is found in Vogt (1955), who systematically recorded responses to recurring problem situations in the Texan homesteader community over a period of eighteen months; Smith and Roberts (1954), who collected responses of Zunis to "trouble cases" for their study of Zuni law; and Vogt and O'Dea (1953), in a comparative study of the role of values in the Texan homesteader and Mormon community organizations.

Systematic use of a formal questionnaire to elicit value choices is exemplified in the work of Florence Kluckhohn *et al.* (1961). A value-orientations questionnaire was devised to test a theory of systematic variation in value orientations. It was administered to a sample of approximately twenty informants in each of the five cultures and the results subjected to intensive statistical analysis.

Standardized psychological tests were utilized by a number of fieldworkers: the Rorschach Test by Kaplan (1954) in his study of Navahos, Zuni, Spanish-Americans, and Mormons; the Magic Man Test, by Whiting, Chasdi, Antonovsky, and Ayres (see Chapter 4) in their study of the socialization process among the Zunis, Mormons, and Texans; color charts by Lenneberg and Roberts (1956) in their study of Zuni color categories; and tachistoscope images by Michael (1953) in his field study of closure.

Tape recordings of small group interaction were used to advantage by Von Mering (1961), who developed a technique for "theme-controlled discussion"; by Strodtbeck (1951) in his study of husband-wife interaction in three cultures; and by Roberts (in press) in his study of *Four Southwestern Men*. Studies of oral literature and of musical and art forms utilized, in addition to conventional recording methods, special techniques of thematic and content analysis to relate them to values, for example, Spencer's (1957) study of Navaho Chantway Myths; McAllester's (1954) study of the social and aesthetic values expressed in Navaho Enemy Way Music; and Mills's (1959) study of Navaho art forms. Logico-semantic techniques for content analysis of descriptive data were employed by Albert (1957) for ordering the contents of the five value systems. The inventory of concepts and methods also includes an adaptation of geographical methods in Landgraf's (1954) study of land use in the Rimrock area, and special historical methods by Telling (1952) for his study of the social history of the principal market town in the region. In Chapter 7, Pauker has adapted concepts and methods from political science for his comparative study, and Edmonson, in Chapter 5, has supplemented his ethnographic account of kinship systems in the five cultures by conceptual apparatus from linguistics.

Diversity in methods of observation and analysis of values intensifies the disconcerting versatility of the values concept in the very process of enriching research. In this, as in respect to diversity of definitions, the publications of the Values Study reflect the general state of social science inquiry. Sharp disagreement persists as to methodological principles. Values research reveals the persistent dichotomy of humanism and science in the social sciences. Development of a scientific theory of values is as much a matter of philosophy of science as of method and theory. Rigorous techniques have been used successfully with certain aspects of values, and this promises well for continuing experimentation with methods designed to achieve scientific control of the subject. However, there are objections on principle and open disdain for the results of values studies that aspire to scientific rigor. It seems that the more precise the method, the more minute and limited the results; and, the more grand the theory, the more vague and impressionistic the methods.

In the same historical shift that redirected attention to values, investigation of other "subjective" phenomena was reopened. Studies of values, however, have not followed the same course as research on perception, concept formation, language processes, and related subjects. "Language" and "thought" are not intrinsically more "objective" than values. Unlike so-called cognitive phenomena, however, values are often a symbol of a humanistic stand taken against real or seeming scientific philistinism. Advocates of both scientific and humanistic methodologies may agree that values are in their very nature unobservable, thus unsuited to scientific inquiry. For one side this is a positive judgment that calls for special, nonscientific methods; for the other, it is a condemnation of values to limbo. A methodological commitment to scientific method for the study of values must reject the view that values are intrinsically and inalterably different from other verbal and intellectual phenomena. While the humanist-scientist dichotomy — or the facts-values dichotomy in any other guise — persists, values will be a misleading symbol, to the detriment of inquiry, used to separate the humanistic sheep from the scientific goats.

DESCRIPTION AND COMPARISON OF VALUES

Some of the most acute methodological problems of the Values Study research appeared where they might have been least expected — at the seemingly elementary level of description and comparison. Ethnographic description and comparisons based on them are deceptively simple modes of reporting fieldwork observations. Here again, the difficulties that beset the Values Study represent problems that extend beyond the boundaries of any single research project and of any single research topic.

One of the most perplexing problems in contemporary social scientific attempts to describe social structures, or cultural patterns, or values can be phrased as follows: should the descriptive models be derived from the culture or subculture described or from the observer's culture, hence, normally, from traditional Western European thought? If models are derived from the cultures being described, the social scientist has an array of noncomparable cases. If a single model is used, derived from Western culture or any other, the descriptions may be comparable, but they will be culture-bound distortions of the originals. The conception of the uniqueness of each culture pattern appears to challenge the utility, if not the validity or even the possibility, of comparison. Yet, the comparability of human institutions and behavior follows from the assumed unity of the species and calls into question the conception of each culture as in all respects unique and distinctive. A review of the models devised for description and comparison of values in the Rimrock area will give specific substance to the paradox.

Specialized schemata to describe the values of a single culture or to compare pairs of cultures were developed by Ladd (1957), Mills (1959), and Von Mering (1961). Ladd's approach, derived from con-

11

temporary Western philosophical value theory, was applied to Navaho ethics. Mills developed a set of propositions relating art to culture and used them to analyze and interpret Navaho and Zuni art forms. Von Mering, concerned with both culturally distinctive processes of evaluation and with the content of values, obtained fruitful results from application of his schema to data on the Rimrock Mormons and Texan homesteaders. Not so much on these efforts as on attempts to deal with the total value systems of all five cultural groups is the full impact of the conflict of unique description and cross-cultural comparison felt.

Three approaches to the description and comparison of the values of the five cultures of the Rimrock area were developed by participants in the Values Study project: Ethel Albert's (1956) classificatory scheme for value systems, which explicitly adapts categories of Western European philosophy for use with nonliterate, non-European cultures; Florence Kluckhohn's (1961) sociological value-orientations scheme, based upon tripartite alternatives of five common human focal points in the conceptualization of experience; and Clyde Kluckhohn's (1956) scheme for the comparison of value-emphases, based on a series of binary oppositions derived from linguistic theories of contrastive analysis of distinctive features.

Each of the schemata, reflecting its author's particular theoretical and methodological bent, has certain advantages and represents marked gains in the study of values. Aware of the risks, all nevertheless use European-derived categories for both European-based and non-European cultures. Use of a single framework for the five cultures unavoidably flattens cross-cultural contrasts in some ways and to some extent. None of the models offers a decisive method for preserving cultural uniqueness in the framework of cross-cultural comparison. Consequently, all are caught in one way or another on the horns of the dilemma posed by the conflicting demands of description and comparison.

Value Systems in Ethnophilosophical Context. In Ethel Albert's schema, the categories of the Western philosophical tradition form a conceptual framework within which the values system fits as one subsystem. The threat of violating culture context was mitigated by the mixed cultural heritage of Western traditional philosophy, particularly its unspecialized inclusion of "all knowledge." Ancient Greek naturalism provided an unexpectedly apt vocabulary and

12

model for phrasing and ordering parts of the Navaho world-view and values. Hebraic and Christian elements in the tradition were ready-made for the three European-based cultures. The Spanish-American system incorporated elements from general Mediterranean culture. Mormonism, as a matter of explicit policy, involves a return to the Old Testament. The ancient Hebraic pattern was easily adaptable to description of Zuni values, with their emphasis on piety, vigilant attention to morality, and high esteem for prosperity as a reward of religion. The Texan homesteaders are the sole representatives in the Rimrock area of dominant Anglo-American culture. For them and for the Mormons, the New Testament tradition and the secular tradition of Western thought, especially as represented by science, are relevant.

Despite these convenient approximations, penetration beneath the surface of the broad categories of Western philosophy — metaphysics, epistemology, logic, and values—revealed that the model was an externally imposed construct for all five cultures. It proved no better or worse suited for illiterate Hispanic-American herders or unread Anglo homesteaders than for Zunis or Navahos:

> The terminology employed in the construction includes terms that are patently unfamiliar to the members of the culture to which the value system is ascribed; it is frankly the observer's language that is used, not the informant's. Nevertheless, both reported and constructed concepts are supported by data on both verbal and non-verbal behavior which indicate that the beliefs and values are held by individuals in the culture.[7]

Neutrality was more nearly achieved for the model used to describe and compare the cultural value systems than for the ethnophilosophic context. In lieu of content categories, the model for the value system incorporated "centrality" and "organization" from Kluckhohn's (1952) list of "dimensions" of values. Values were located in the cultural system according to level of generality and logical function.[8]

By avoiding content categories, the schema for the values system effectively blocked at least one variety of contextual violation, assuming comparability solely on the basis of presence of a specific value. To say that "health" is a value for all the cultures is only superficially true. For Navahos and Mormons, it is a focal value; for Hispanic-Americans, it is a relatively unimportant valued entity,

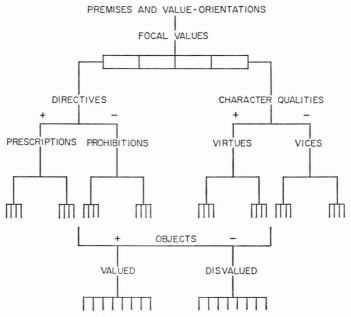

Figure 1. Schematic representation of the structure of a value system.

given or withheld by God or destiny. Specific definitions of "health" and its relation to other values and to behavior are so different among the several cultures as to falsify a generalization that "health" is commonly valued. The same would apply to other such content-specific terms as knowledge, wealth, or religion. Some of the difficulties entailed in tracing a specific content category through the different contexts of the five cultures are discussed in the introduction to Chapter 9, "Expressive Activities."

The description of each value system aspired to report a totality distinctive of each culture — as well as a general model permitted. Relating cultural logic and symbolic systems to values produced a paired comparison that placed the European-based cultures on one side, the American Indian on the other. When social organization was selected as a basis of comparisons, a marked shift in the alignment occurred. The Zuni and Mormon were together on the "society-oriented" side, the Navaho and Texan homesteaders on the "individual-oriented" side, and the Spanish-Americans in an intermediate position. In checking out the full inventory of components of the five value systems some interculturally common values and some culturally unique values were found. The culturally unique values appeared to be "symbolic values," such as a preference for a particular food, that functioned as tokens of group identification. For example, an outsider might be warmly welcomed despite ignorance of the Spanish-American *costumbres* if he liked hot chili.

The conflict between faithful description and cross-cultural comparison finds at least a partial solution in the distinction between the descriptive content of a value system, which is unique, and the structural, relational, and functional aspects of value systems, which are comparable. A residual limitation of the schema used by Albert is implied in her choice of the designation, "normal operating base," for the descriptions of the cultural value systems:

> The construction of a cultural value system, as it is here understood, is not intended as a description of the value system of any or each individual in the culture at every moment in time. No individual encompasses in his experience the entire content of his culture or any considerable part of it. Moreover, even in a relatively homogeneous culture, there are individual differences in viewpoint. Changes in beliefs and values occur in the course of history, and temporary adjustments are made in response to short-term circumstantial pressures. Further, especially in the case of values, there is usually some discrepancy between what is believed and what is said and done, between what is asserted and what may be consciously or unconsciously believed. The inclusion of all these factors in the description of a cultural value system would produce an impractically unwieldy result, even if the data were avilable. The illustrative description which follows the proposal of the classificatory scheme has therefore been scaled down to what may be called the "normal operating base" of the cultural value system. This is conceived as a summative construct or cultural consensus, envisaged as a point of reference for the description and discussion of individual differences in beliefs, behavioral deviations from verbalized norms, historical and acculturative changes, and other factors in the dynamics of value systems.[9]

By contrast, attention to intracultural variation and change through time is built into Florence Kluckhohn's theory of value-orientations.

Variations in Value-Orientations. Florence Kluckhohn's theory of value-orientations is directed both to systematic ordering of variations within cultural systems and to cross-cultural differences. It also has potential predictive utility for describing changes through time in value-orientations. Bringing the methods and objectves of soci-

15

ology to bear upon the data and problems of anthropological values study, she has said:

> In large part the difficulties encountered in the understanding and use of the cultural anthropologists' concepts are attributable to the failure to organize these concepts into a systematic and analytic theory of cultural variation . . . In both formulation and application they have been too particularized to single cultures to permit systematic comparisons *between* cultures and analysis of variations *within* cultures.

The treatment of the problems of comparative study starts from the assumption that:

> *there is a limited number of common human problems for which all peoples at all times must find some solution.* This is the universal aspect of value orientations because the common human problems arise inevitably out of the human situation. The second assumption is that *while there is variability in solutions of all problems, it is neither limitless nor random but is definitely variable within a range of possible solutions.* The third assumption . . . is that *all alternatives of all solutions are present in all societies at all times but are differentially preferred.* Every society has, in addition to its dominant profile of value orientations, numerous *variant* or *substitute profiles.*[10]

The classificatory scheme of value orientations consists of five problems, tentatively singled out as crucial and as common to all human groups. Stated as questions, these are: (1) What is the character of innate human nature? (2) What is the relation of man to nature (and supernature)? (3) What is the temporal focus of human life? (4) What is the modality of human activity? (5) What is the modality of man's relation to other men? The ranges of variability are given in Table 1.

Statistical analysis of the questionnaire results substantially confirmed the hypothesis that all alternatives for the five value-orientations would appear in each culture, but that their order would be distinctive for the culture. Given the brief temporal span of the research, it was not possible to establish with assurance that the order of preference of each value-orientation would be the order of culture change, from first-order to second-order to third-order value-orientation. Future development of the schematism anticipates the addition of other fundamental value-orientations, for example, spatial orientations.

Table 1. The five value orientations and the range of
variations postulated for each.

Orientation	Postulated range of variations					
Human nature	Evil		Neutral	Mixture of good and evil	Good	
	mutable	immutable	mutable	immutable	mutable	immutable
Man-nature	subjugation-to-nature		harmony-with-nature		mastery-over-nature	
Time	past		present		future	
Activity	being		being-in-becoming		doing	
Relational	lineality		collaterality		individualism	

Source: F. Kluckhohn and Strodtbeck, *Variations in Value-Orientations*, p. 12.

The problems posed by using Western cultural categories, even those as general and fundamental as the value-orientations, to describe and compare non-Western cultures may be viewed now in a different light. The objectives and methods of sociology, which in the past collided so forcibly with the objectives and methods of history, may here be seen as conflicting with the dominant methods and objectives of ethnographic description. Early twentieth-century methodology of social science and history crystallized in its own terms much the same problem faced by the Values Study: cultural anthropology, like history, has been oriented to what is distinctive and individual in its subject matter, and it has tended to report its finding in narrative description. Sociology, past and present, has been directed toward the search for general laws which necessarily concern what is common or universal, and it has increasingly resorted to socio-statistical and other non-narrative methods of inquiry. Comparison, in sociological analysis, is a device for building theoretical generalizations, not a means of contrasting descriptively unique patterns.

In the history of anthropology, comparative method has gone in and out of style with perplexing frequency. Opposition to the various forms it has taken tends to be phrased as a radical relativism

17

that defines each culture pattern as unique and each item of culture as meaningful only in its own cultural context. Thus phrased, devotion to faithful description automatically reduces all comparison to naught or at best relegates it to some other level or branch of inquiry. Stated in these extreme terms, there is a conflict that requires a choice: either each culture and its contents are to be described exclusively in their own terms, or generalizations about cross-culturally common phenomena will be sought. The obverse is a choice between surrendering the possibility of generalizations inherent in radical relativism or accepting the necessity to violate cultural context in one way or another for the sake of generalization. A new perspective on the dilemma is suggested by examination of the third model.

Binary Oppositions. An adaptation of linguistic concepts was proposed by Clyde Kluckhohn as a possibly fruitful way of dealing with the problems of relating and reconciling descriptive and comparative studies of values. He phrased the dilemma as follows: "How can we compare with minimal ethnocentrism the more general or thematic value-tones or value-emphases that constitute the structure-points of whole systems of cultural values?"

Kluckhohn evaluates the approach of linguistics in the following terms:

> Some linguists in their elegant analyses of one aspect of culture have found it extremely useful to set up a series of distinctive contrasts or oppositions, usually binary, which serve to identify each separate phoneme. A "lump" or "bundle" of such "distinctive features" defines a phoneme. In its simplest form the process is like a specialized and sophisticated version of the "twenty questions game." Thus one may ask, "Is the phoneme vocal? Yes or no." "Is the phoneme strident? Yes or no." . . . There seem to me to be grounds, both theoretical and empirical, for suspecting that a similar approach might yield good results in the realm of value culture . . . In working out a first sketch of suggested "distinctive features" or cross cultural core value-emphases, I shall not hesitate to draw upon the broadest categories of human experience as revealed in history, philosophy, psychology, and the arts.[11]

His preliminary list of "binary oppositions" was based on three value-orientations, each involving a yes-no response for each cultural value component.[12]

18

Cluster 1: Man and Nature
   1a. Determinate-Indeterminate
   1b. Unitary-Pluralistic
   1c. "Evil"-"Good"
Cluster 2: Man and Man
   2a. Individual-Group
   2b. Self-Other
   2c. Autonomy-Dependence
   2d. Active-Acceptant
   2e. Discipline-Fulfillment
   2f. "Physical"-"Mental"
   2g. Tense-Relaxed
   2h. Now-Then
Cluster 3: Both Nature and Man
   3a. Quality-Quantity
   3b. Unique-General

These "distinctive features" were applied on a trial basis to the five cultures of the Values Study research. Subsequently, additional pairs such as "skepticism-credulity" and "sober-humorous" were considered. Additions to the list and some refinements as well as extensions to a larger sample of cultures have been made.[13]

Application of this linguistically based model produced new and interesting insights into the values of the five cultures. However, the clusters of paired opposites that make up the model are culture-bound in much the same way as the categories employed in the descriptive-comparative schemata criticized above. The conflict between description and comparison was not really settled.

On the descriptive side, there was no satisfactory solution of the problem of eliciting and representing crucial cultural distinctions which do not fit into any of the categories provided by the three comparative schemes. A dramatic example was provided during the field work of John M. Roberts during the summer of 1959. Pursuing a Zuni distinction between "raw" and "cooked" which has been known to ethnographers for many years,[14] Roberts was interviewing an elderly Zuni informant who spent more than an hour, without further prompting, explaining this nice distinction. From the informant's point of view, a significant and interesting question had been posed, and he explained how Zunis, who regard themselves as "the cooked ones," differ from other people in the world who are "raw." He went on to describe how the contrast effectively differentiates young Zunis, who are still "raw," from mature Zunis, who are "cooked," and from senile Zunis, who have become "raw" again. The terms also differentiate the core members of the matrilineal household as "cooked" from those affinally related men who marry into the household and are considered "raw." There is probably a distinction here of great importance in Zuni culture, but it would be difficult to fit it into any category provided by the three comparative schemes.[15]

Navaho culture provides a similar example. The Navaho make a basic conceptual distinction between states or events, using terms usually translated as "harmonious" and "disharmonious." The positive concept is expressed by the root -Žó. It is difficult to translate even approximately the sense of this term. Although the usual translation is "harmony," the word could just as correctly be rendered as "beauty," or "happiness," or "equilibrium." The term occurs with great frequency in Navaho myth and ceremonial chants, suggesting that it is of crucial importance for the culture. However, none of the comparative schemes has an appropriate place for it, although Albert's discussion of the Navaho value vocabulary attempts to communicate the complexity and centrality of the concept.

In the 1950's and 1960's methods have been developed which promise to achieve closer approximations to culturally faithful description. These rigorous techniques are specifically directed to the intricate and subtle contrasts and discriminations made by different cultures. Were we now, in the middle 1960's, to undertake another values study, we could proceed quite differently. Our approach to data collection could be based upon a type of elicitation and analysis that utilizes models for determining significance and distinctive characteristics explicitly derived from each culture. After describing the value systems for each culture, we would then, and only then, undertake comparative analysis of the basic conceptual systems of each culture. As Hymes has remarked of linguistics, "One need not stop with the individual systems, but one must pass through them." [16]

The methods we have in mind are those developed by linguists and ethnographers who specialize in "componential analysis" or "ethnoscience." [17] These new methods depend upon thorough knowledge of the language spoken by informants. In this, they are like the linguistic-model approach of Clyde Kluckhohn which has been described. However, selection of paired opposites follows a very different principle. The new methods require rigorous semantic analysis of native terms to locate "distinctive features" of maximal significance to the native informants. The use of systematic discovery procedures and such concepts as "levels of contrast," has made it possible to construct folk taxonomies of various domains of a number of cultures. These methods provide a sound basis for describing and understanding the conceptual principles of cardinal importance in the culture under investigation.

The first applications of componential analysis and related methods were to kinship terminology and to such domains as plants, diseases, colors, firewood, and numeral classifiers. Procedures have been suggested to make possible their extension to the analysis of settlement patterns and to ritual.[18] Data collected by methods like those in use between 1949 and 1953 are not adaptable to analysis by these new methods, for they involve radically different field operations. In principle, however, the newer methods can be extended to the study of cultural systems of beliefs and values. Explorations of the possibilities are being written into the designs of new studies of values.

Values and Other Socio-Cultural Variables

Concern with the external relations of values — as distinguished from concern with their definition, description, comparison, or internal relations in value systems — leads the investigator away from values as such to specific behavioral and institutional forms and toward problems germane to such inquiry. There is in effect a figure-ground reversal that makes values subservient or accessory to other variables. Some of the contributors to this volume have elsewhere treated problems of definitions and methods, but these are peripheral here. In the context of the objectives of the Values Study, as in the wider field of research, values cannot be kept in splendid isolation from other aspects of culture.

Taken as a unit, the papers of this volume present a view of the relations of values to the principal institutions of society. Oriented to different specific research objectives, they are nonetheless individually and collectively a contribution to our knowledge of values.

In addition, they supply materials for evaluating and correcting some of the underlying assumptions of the Values Study. In many instances, the impact of the research results was negative, contradicting or radically modifying the starting points of the project. This is to be welcomed rather than deplored, for such corrections are among the prime objectives of exploratory research. Differences in theories of social institutions and processes are reflected in interpretations of values. Indeterminacy and disagreements remain, but some reasonably secure conclusions have been reached.

It may be assumed that there are critically important relationships between values and the institutional structures developed by human groups over time for dealing with the common problems of the "human situation." There is disagreement about such fundamental issues as whether or not such structures are in equilibrium or continually in disequilibrium; whether they are functionally interrelated in all respects or only partly so; and what constitutes the precise inventory of "common human problems." It has been firmly established that there is patterned behavior in respect to the way in which biological relatedness is reckoned and behavior towards relatives governed. The way in which the helpless human infant is brought to adulthood in the patterns of the society in which he is socialized is increasingly well understood. There is growing consensus about the ways in which order is maintained and power distributed and used in the governing of society; social provision for getting a livelihood and defining property; the ways in which relations between humanity and suprahuman powers are conceived and a system of beliefs and values maintained that provides a context of meaning for ultimate concerns; and the ways in which recreational, aesthetic, and other activities channel play and other expressive tendencies.

The patterned solutions may be given different names and the problems they must solve may be phrased or classified in different ways, but problems and their patterned solutions are always present. Values, understood in Clyde Kluckhohn's terms as "conceptions of the desirable," are crucial ingredients of these patterned solutions. Since the solutions persist in the form of different institutional structures, it is not surprising that different value systems persist. If the term "values" is used to designate the system or pattern of solutions to the problems posed by the demands of societal order, and if different societies are observed to pattern their solutions differently, then the general assumption of the Values Study is established by definition. As a guide to empirical research, the assumption answers part of the generic question the Values Study research poses: why different value systems persist. However, interpretation of some specific initial assumptions have been revised by results of the research.

Environment, History, and Value Systems. The key question of the Values Study research was: Why do different value systems continue to exist in five cultures all having to meet similar problems of adjustment and survival in the same ecological area, all having been exposed by actual contact and by stimulus diffusion to each other's value ideas and practices?

As phrased, the question assumes that the persistent variability of the values of the five cultures is a consequence of the inertial, self-perpetuating tendencies of cultural patterns. The persistence of the different value systems appeared especially significant because it was assumed that the environment was uniform and that the exposure of each culture to all the others and to the larger surrounding American culture was uniform. Evidence to the contrary was produced by the Values Study research, as previously unappreciated geographical and historical characteristics of the area were uncovered. Whatever factors account for the persistence of the main lines of the value systems of each culture and for major and minor changes in them, environmental and historical variations cannot be omitted from the theoretical representation.

The general geologic and geographical characteristics of the Rimrock area are described in Chapter 2, and the general history of the area and intercultural relations in Chapter 2 and Chapter 3. Close study of the ecology was crucial to the analysis of the economy of the cultures and of the relation of ecology and economy to values, the concerns of Chapter 6. Study of the area revealed that, while the ecology is generally the same for all five groups, important microvariations in ecological niches within the area greatly affect adjustments to the natural environment. For example, although altitude, rainfall, and flora and fauna are in general the same, there are significant local variations in the availability of water, both in permanent springs and in reservoir sites, for irrigation agriculture. The Zunis and Mormons control these sources of water supply, and they are not available to the Spanish-Americans (except in limited degree), to the Navahos, or to the Texans. As Vogt shows in Chapter 6, these microvariations in ecological niches within the general ecological setting were of critical importance in the history of settlement in the area. They are also among the determinants of the type of settlement pattern and economic system each group established.

Each type of ecological adjustment in the Rimrock area is related in a complex manner to distinctive value assumptions about the most desirable way or ways of making a living. The interrelation between ecological and value factors appears to be a two-way process. The features of the natural environment set hard limits, but within these limits, a given ecological niche provides certain opportunities and stimulates certain types of adaptation. At the same time, cultural groups develop over time certain value assumptions about their ecological niches which also set limits and stimulate and then continually re-enforce the adaptations.

Diverse value systems persist in the Rimrock area in part because each cultural group has carved out a different ecological niche for itself and has maintained different settlement patterns and economic systems, the ecological and cultural factors and values interacting to re-enforce the general culture pattern. These observations are not novel; an astute social science investigator, perhaps even a layman, could have predicted them. We have to go beyond them and ask: What factors in the Rimrock area led the five cultural groups to carve out these niches, to develop and maintain different institutional structures and different value systems? Part of the answer lies in the events of history. But instead of recounting the unique series of events that led to settlement and subsequent developments in the Rimrock area, we can conceptualize the significance of historical uniqueness in a more general way. A hypothesis suggested and borne out by research indicates that diversity in values is in part a result of the differential relations that the local cultural groups have with the outside world and in part a result of intercultural dynamics within the Rimrock area.

Two distinct aspects of the relations of the five communities with the world beyond the Rimrock area have been noted. First, the Zuni, although they have some important ties with other Pueblo Indians, are the only group whose total society is located within the area. The other communities are local manifestations of cultures whose centers of power and influence are elsewhere. The Rimrock Navaho are geographically and in some respects culturally at some distance from the main body of Navaho society, located principally to the north and west on the Navaho Reservation in New Mexico and Arizona. The tribal council meets at the tribal headquarters at Window Rock, Arizona. Local Navaho communities have in the past functioned more or less autonomously, but in recent times, they have been functioning as local branches of an increasingly cohesive Navaho tribe. The Spanish-American communities in the area look for their main cultural affiliations to the centers of Spanish-American population and influence in the Northern Rio Grande Valley of New Mexico. The Mormon community of Rimrock is one "ward" of the St. George "stake," which is in turn a unit of the Mormon church organization that has its control center in Salt Lake City. The Texan community of Homestead maintains contacts with its parent communities in the Texan Panhandle and in Oklahoma, although the ties are not close. Important stimuli to maintain distinct cultural identities are continually reaching the different local communities from the larger centers of population and power of each cultural group outside the Rimrock area.

Second, the Texans and Mormons are much more an integral part of general American society than are the Spanish-Americans, Zunis, or Navahos. The influences that impinge upon the Texan and Mormon communities are diffusions from urban to rural segments of the same general culture. The same streams of cultural diffusion, in order to reach the Spanish-Americans, Zunis, and Navahos must cross linguistic and cultural boundaries. Therefore, the historical process is decidedly not the same for the non-Anglo cultures as it is for the Texans and Mormons. Since the Spanish-American, Zuni, and Navaho communities each speaks a different language and has a different culture, the influence of cultural diffusions, as of other potential sources of change, must be unique for each community. In Chapters 2 and 3, the relevant historical and contemporary data are presented and interpreted.

A previously unsuspected facet of the social system of the Rimrock area was revealed in the course of field work. The five cultures, different though each is from the others and despite primary orientations outside the area, form a *de facto* intercultural system, with important dynamics of its own. The details are presented in Chapter 3, "Intercultural Relations, Historical and Contemporary." The intercultural system can be described on two levels, structural and cognitive. It is structural in the sense that each cultural group maintains special intergroup role networks with each one of the others. The result is a complex series of relationships and pressures which sometimes leads to changes in the cultures, but perhaps more often to resistance to change. Each group seeks to maintain its own cultural identity, in part because it is constantly confronted by others that are quite different. Sometimes this reaches a level of a nativistic trend — Navahos determined to be more Navaho because Mormons are trying to convert them into Mormons. At the cognitive level, each cultural group has its own conception of the other groups. These cognitive maps are derived only in part from observation data. Rarely flattering to the originals, they block full understanding and appreciation of the ways of life of the neighbors. For example, the Mormon Bishop, a very knowledgeable man who had lived all his life near a Spanish-American community, did not have the slightest idea what a "patron saint" is or that the fiesta, which he regularly attended, was always scheduled on the day of the patron saint.

Although propinquity generally leads to some intercultural borrowing and to some pattern of intercultural communication, it is also a first-rate preservative of uniqueness and difference. The intercultural dynamics of the Rimrock area appear to lead to a tenacious retention of distinctive values. The self-image of each cultural group is ethnocentrically flattering. All refer to themselves in terms that define them as "persons" or "people," and to the others as excluded from or inferior to true humanity. The Navahos call themselves *dineh,* which literally means "the people," and the Zunis call themselves *ashiwi,* literally "the flesh" or "the cooked ones." The Mormons, in keeping with their Old Testament restoration, have adopted the ancient Hebraic title, "the chosen people." More tolerant in their views of outsiders, the Spanish-Americans nevertheless think of themselves as *la gente,* "people," in the honorific sense. The Texans share the self-congratulatory vision of the "real" or "super" American, figuratively the only really "white men."

In 1951–52, Vogt interviewed a sample of informants in each culture to elicit information as to the extent to which understanding and appreciation of the customs of other groups in the Rimrock area had developed, putting the following question:

Suppose there was a ten-year drought in this area. The land all dried up and all the kinds of people who are living here now had to move away. Then after another few years, it began to rain again and the country got green and nice again. God (or the gods, or the Holy People) decided it was time to put people in this area again, but he wanted to build up a new and very good community with just one kind of people in it, instead of several kinds of people like there are now around here. God (the gods, or the Holy People) knew everything about the ways of living of the different peoples who live in this area now, and so he could decide just what things, what ways of making a living, what customs, what languages, and what religions he would put into this new and very good community. Now suppose that you are God (one of the gods, or one of the Holy People) and you have to decide what to put in this community. What kind of community would you put up? What ways of making a living, what customs, what language and what religion would you set up for this new and very good community?

The responses were generally to the effect that each cultural group would re-establish its own members in the Rimrock area. Rather than selectively adopting customs and values from neighboring groups, the informants strongly emphasized their own distinctive way of life as by far the most desirable for the Rimrock area.

A typical Zuni response:

I would pick the Zunis because a long time ago there *was* a drought in this area according to the stories my grandfather told me. But the Zunis worshiped and prayed for rain and good country and made the country good again. So if the Zunis moved away, I would tell them to come back again and to renew their old religion and to make them a good people and to follow their ways and customs.

A typical Navaho response:

If I was a Holy People, I would first build a good hogan. When the hogan is already up, next will be a sweat house. Then the men would go in the sweat house. When they were inside the sweat bath, they would be talking to each other. They want to get in mind what else they should have besides a hogan and sweat house. They talk in the sweat bath and say how we should have nice grass and lots of water to make the country look pretty again. That's all.

A typical Spanish-American response:

I would try to make a community with my own people, with Catholic religion, raising livestock, and speaking Spanish. I would just give them the *costumbres* [customs].

27

Mormon responses gave even stronger expression to their own values:

> I've often commented to myself that I'd like a newly man-made community. I think we ought to have a big reservoir the first thing to take care of the water supply. I believe I would put it under the United Order [of the Church of Latter-Day Saints, i.e., Mormons]. And then we should have some good ranches with some cattle and sheep, but they should be separated because cattle and sheep don't go together. There would be just one people, all of one belief, where they treat everybody equal, no injustice to any of them, each looking out for the other's welfare. I think that used to be done in years back. This one belief would be Mormonism, and we would have a good church and good recreation facilities, where we could take care of all that comes, because Mormon people like to dance, and that's one way we hold our young people together.

The typical Texan response, predictably ambitious and expansive:

> In the new community each family would have some ranch land, six sections for each family. And we'd take some of that Mormon irrigated land for around headquarters. That's for hay. And part of the ranches would have Mexican sheep. And we'd have quite a bit of rug weaving to sell when the highway comes through. Boy, Mamma [turning to his wife], wouldn't we have a place — six sections, a few beans, and hay. Rugs like your grandmother wove and the girls could make a little jewelry for sale. And cows on the range. The people would be Protestants, and we'd have a good school, dances, and a movie house.

Substantial modification has been made in the initial assumptions about the relations of variations in values to environment and history in the Rimrock area. Viewed as a single area, it is uniform by contrast with other types of environment. However, variations within it encourage and reinforce variations in culture, including values, and, at the same time, values that develop around ecological and economic variables reinforce the adaptations that develop. Interpretation of the historical positions of the five cultures has been much more markedly altered than the assumptions about ecology. The persistence of cultural variations in values is in part due to the history of differential relations with the surrounding American culture, with "parent cultures" outside the area, and within the intercultural system that developed in the area.

Values and Socio-Cultural Variations. Cultural variability in values has numerous facets. Chapters 4–9 are addressed to some specific aspects of the place of values in culture and in some instances use data from outside the Rimrock area to justify generalizations. There is ample evidence from the studies of Whiting *et al.*, reported in Chapter 4, "The Learning of Values," that cultural variations in the socialization process are associated with the inculcation of different values. The young of each cultural group are socialized to the institutions and values of the parental culture, and, once firmly inculcated, values tend to persist tenaciously in adult personalities. The fact that they can and do sometimes change provides a theoretical and behavioral link between socialization and the historical processes of cultural transmission and change.

Whiting and his associates have made a valuable contribution to our understanding of cultural variations in methods of socialization and have also taken a significant step in relating socialization to historical analysis. Whiting presents a novel and intriguing interpretation of the relation between social structure, child-rearing, and key values in the Zuni, Texan homesteader, and Mormon communities. Historical data are combined with current ethnographic data on family structure and the socialization process in the three cultures, and cross-cultural data from the HRAF files are added, to produce the following generalizations about historical shifts as the sources of change to contemporary value emphases:

ZUNI: Shift from nuclear to extended households and isolated settlements of the past to compact pueblos required the strict control of aggression and an emphasis upon *harmony* as a dominant value.

TEXAN HOMESTEADER: Shift from Elizabethan extended family to nuclear family after arrival of Anglo immigrants in America required a shift from obedience to independence, from group responsibility to individualism, and an emphasis upon *success* as a dominant value.

MORMON: Shift from Elizabethan family to polygynous family between 1840 and 1890 led to exclusive mother-infant sleeping arrangements and the postpartum sex taboo, which in turn required rigid sex impulse control (to prevent mother-son incest) and an emphasis upon *virtue* as a dominant value.

From this type of analysis, the authors proceed to a general theory that certain crises may require a society to modify its social structure, particularly its living arrangements and family organization. These in turn may require extraordinary control of such impulses as aggression, dependence, and sex. Child-rearing practices would then

29

have to be developed to insure that these impulses are controlled. These instill the acceptance and elaboration of dominant values — for example, harmony or success or virtue — as protection against impulses viewed as dangerous in the new conditions of family life. The data and theory, interesting in themselves, also supply answers to the third question listed by Kluckhohn as to the perpetuation of values through teaching and learning, and at the same time are an unexpected bonus in elucidating the process of value change. Chapters 2–9 are at the same time informative individual studies and relevant to answering Kluckhohn's broad second question, "What is the place of each value system in the total structural-functional economy of each culture?"

In Chapter 5, "Kinship Systems," Edmonson attempts to distinguish features of kinship systems due to value choices from features determined by economic or social structural factors. The Zuni inclusion of in-laws in the kinship system and their exclusion by the Navaho, and the Zuni extension of kinship to the gods are interpreted as dictated by and expressive of values. The loose and open-ended structure of Navaho mate-selection seems also to be determined by values. This view is strengthened by comparisons with semi-nomads of Asia and Africa, peoples with economic structures very similar to the Navaho's. Unlike the Navaho, however, they have highly structured lineage systems and specific rules of preferential marriage. The concept of concentric generations among the Navaho, the patrilineal emphasis of the Spanish-Americans, the hyperindividuality of the Texans, and the group-mindedness of the Mormons all appear to be linked to central values in these cultures and to be strongly expressed in the various kinship systems.

In Chapter 6, Vogt suggests that an appreciation of the role of values in vis-à-vis economy and ecology requires a distinction between location and land settlement pattern. The specific geographic location of each cultural group within the region seems to have been determined by a combination of geographical, historical, and political factors. However, the types of settlement pattern established within the ecological niches were strongly influenced by the value systems of each group. Similarly, land-use patterns, types of occupations, and the development of mechanisms for the social management of economic enterprises were found to be influenced by value factors. Values are not regarded as the sole or overriding determinants. Rather, existing social structures and cultural patterns are viewed as resulting from a complex interaction of many determinants.

Guy Pauker, in Chapter 7, on "Political Structure," takes up the problem of the relationship between the political process and the value systems in the five cultures. A number of variations in political structure appear to be related to variations in values. For example, openly seeking for power and authority is disvalued by the Zuni and Navaho, and candidates must show reluctance to assume positions of leadership. In the groups of European descent, political ambition is considered normal and acceptable, although in differing forms and intensities. This contrast in values has had an important effect upon the differential development of political institutions in the various cultures. There is also an important contrast in the decision-making process. Navaho and Zuni prefer to operate through lengthy and patient confrontation of opinions, debate continuing until unanimous consent is reached. The mechanism of majority decision, regularly used by Mormons and Texans, is imperfectly understood by Navahos and Zunis. Similarly, in all three groups of European descent, political representation is normal, whereas in the two Indian groups, there is a tendency to regard decisions as valid only when they have been made by the primary groups as a whole. Linked to the concept of representation is the meaning of voting to the members of the five cultures. Pauker points out that the underlying philosophical premise of the electoral process as practiced in the West is the conception of free will. It permits and even requires choices that originate in the citizen's own free volition. Neither Navaho nor Zuni ethics includes this doctrine. It is not surprising that, when this value premise is absent and has no functional equivalent, the Western conception of voting is not a highly respected procedure. Hence, the development of political representation and the electoral process characteristic of the surrounding American polity has been a slow and uneven process among the Navaho and Zuni, as among other American Indian tribes.

In Chapter 8 on "Religious Systems" Robert Bellah defines the most important function of religion as the provision of a context of meaning for the central values of a society. Not only is a society's morality based on its religion, but also religion relates values to an ultimate source of power. Bellah describes the critical religious symbols of the five cultures and traces in some detail the ways in which they rationalize and sanction the values and moral norms of the five societies. Both subtle and striking cross-cultural variations are found. Harmony, balance, and equilibrium may be seen as the central value in both Zuni and Navaho cultures. Although they share a great number of religious symbols, their religious conceptions reflect their radically different social organizations: the Zuni have a strongly centralized system, the Navaho one that is diffuse. Their religious behavior is geared to the problems of people living in two quite differently structured societies: the Zunis live in a compact pueblo and are self-contained in language, culture, and religion. This is reflected mythologically in the Zuni designation of their pueblo as "The Middle Place," and all the universe is ordered by orientation to it. If the Navaho can be said to have a "middle place," it is the hogan, and there are as many "middle places" as there are hogans. The construction of the hogan and the placing of its contents are related to imperatives in the mythology. Navaho ceremonials must be conducted within the hogan, and many ritual directions depend on the hexagonal plan of this structure. Bellah contrasts the two Indian cultures, where the answer to the problem of the meaning of life lies in an all-embracing harmony, with the three Christian cultures, in which the answer lies in the idea of salvation. However, he deals with these as three different versions of Christianity, the Catholic Spanish-Americans, the Mormons, and the Texans.

Chapter 9 deals with "Expressive Activities." In it Clyde Kluckhohn set himself the task of describing the forms of art, play, dance, music, and other expressive activities valued in the five cultures. His data reveal that, while there is much common content in the expressive activities in the Rimrock area, they have varied styles and fit in different ways into each total way of life. Dancing provides an apt example. For the Navahos and Zunis, dancing is associated with religious ceremonials. Mormon dances are often held in the church, opened and closed with a prayer, and sanctified by the church as a manifestation of community solidarity, but they are not in themselves religious or ceremonial. Among the Texan homesteaders, dances are completely secular. They are held in the schoolhouse and accompanied by much drinking of alcoholic "salty dog" and often by fist-fights. For the Spanish-Americans, dancing is also primarily secular, though it is often incident to a religious fiesta. The *baile,* chiefly a social occasion, has more aesthetic overtones in itself and in the expressions it brings of the courtship patterns and of social formalities than dances in the other European-based cultures. The description of the expressive activities in the Rimrock area is preceded by an introduction by Ethel M. Albert which reviews the problematic status of the concepts of aesthetic, emotive, and expressive values.

Geographical and Cultural Setting

EVON Z. VOGT

T HE RIMROCK AREA (see Maps 1 and 2), located on the southern edge of the Colorado Plateau in western New Mexico, is approximately forty miles square. It lies south of Railtown, the closest town in the research area on the Santa Fe Railroad and on U.S. Highway 66, southwest of the Zuni Mountains.

LANDSCAPE

From a comparative physiographic point of view, the Rimrock area is placed in the Datil section of the Colorado Plateau province.[1] Located just south of the Rocky Mountains, this province is characterized by high plateaus formed of relatively horizontal strata cut into deep semiarid drainages. Scattered over the province are ocasional great synclines and anticlines that give local tilts to geological structures. The Datil section contains one of these major tilted structures, known as the Zuni uplift, or Zuni Plateau. It is an elliptically shaped anticline with its axis oriented northwest and southeast, whose present larger surface remains are known as the Zuni Mountains. The section is also characterized by extensive basaltic surface lava flows. The Rimrock area lies within the northern part of the Datil section on the southwest slopes of the Zuni uplift. The major land forms are based primarily on the sedimentary beds lifted up by the Zuni anticline in late Cretaceous or early Tertiary Time, and secondarily on the more recent igneous flows.

Looking southwest from the summit of the Zuni Mountains, at approximately 9200 feet, it is possible to view in panorama almost the entire Rimrock area. Down through the pine-covered slopes of the mountains, one sees first the "Upper Valley" wedged between

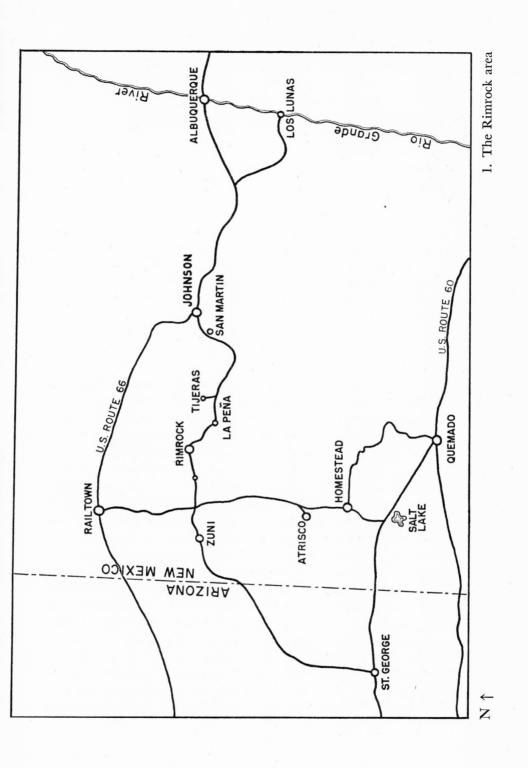

1. The Rimrock area

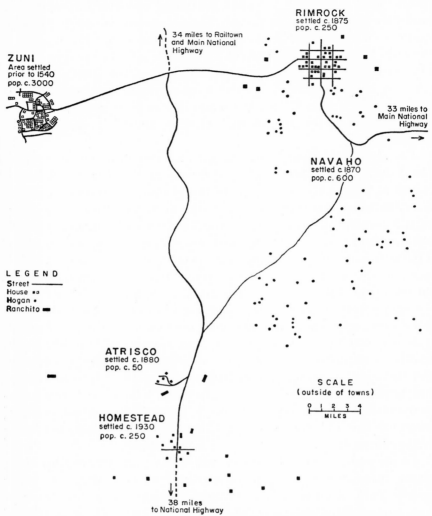

RIMROCK
settled c. 1875
pop. c. 250

34 miles to Railtown
and Main National
Highway

ZUNI
Area settled
prior to 1540
pop. c. 3000

33 miles to
Main National
Highway

NAVAHO
settled c. 1870
pop. c. 600

LEGEND
Street ———
House ▪▫
Hogan •
Ranchito ▬

ATRISCO
settled c. 1880
pop. c. 50

SCALE
(outside of towns)

0 1 2 3 4
MILES

HOMESTEAD
settled c. 1930
pop. c. 250

38 miles
to National Highway

N ↑

2. A close-up of the Rimrock area
(Adapted from Kluckhohn and Strodtbeck,
Variations in Value-Orientations)

the mountains and a majestic line of red-and-white banded mesas
composed of sandstones that were tilted up by the Zuni uplift and
originally extended across the mountains. Erosional processes later
removed the sandstones from the Zuni Mountains and cut the "Upper Valley" down to a level of 7500 feet.

The same erosional processes cut sheer canyons through these sandstone mesas at several points. These canyons, running west and southwest away from the mountains, form the upper headwaters of the Zuni River, a tributary of the Little Colorado. In the days before the Zuni Muntains were denuded of much of the Ponderosa pine cover by logging operations, there were permanent streams running through the canyons. Now the streams flow only in the spring, when the snow pack in the mountains is melting, and after heavy summer rains.

The three most important canyons in this drainage system are Jose Pino Canyon (named after the former headman of the Rimrock Navaho), Rimrock Canyon (where the Mormon irrigation reservoir is located), and Nutria Canyon (where one of the Zuni farming villages is located). Looking first to the left from our vantage point on top the mountains, we see the small Spanish-American settlement of Tijeras situated near an important spring which emanates from the base of the Zuni Mountains. From Tijeras the drainage flows through Jose Pino Canyon and into the Rimrock Valley. Across the valley from Tijeras is El Morro, or Inscription Rock, the sandstone mesa which was an important landmark on the old Spanish trail between the pueblos of Zuni and Acoma and on which the Spanish conquistadores left their inscriptions in the seventeenth and eighteenth centuries. Immediately before us is Rimrock Canyon, and beyond the green Rimrock Valley and village of Rimrock immediately below the reservoir. From Rimrock the drainage flows westward past the Zuni farming village of Pescado and on toward the pueblo of Zuni.

To the right is Nutria Canyon, which also contains an important spring that (along with melting snows) furnishes irrigation water for the Zuni farming village of Nutria. From Nutria the drainage flows toward Zuni and joins the Rio Pescado east of Zuni pueblo to form the Zuni River. Zuni pueblo is not visible from where we stand, but the mesas which flank Zuni Valley, especially Towayalane (the sacred "Corn Mountain" of the Zunis) and Kwiayalane (the "Twin Mesas" of the Zunis) are clearly in view as they rise a full 500 feet above the valley floor. Most of the elevations in view are 7000 to 7500 feet, but the Zuni Valley stands at 6500 feet, below our line of vision. Nor can we quite see the third Zuni farming village, Ojo Caliente, situated near another spring among some smaller sandstone mesas twenty-two miles south southeast of Zuni pueblo at an elevation of 6000 feet.

Beyond this panorama of sandstone mesas and canyons, the character of the country changes. Off to the south and east is an impressive volcanic zone, dotted with a row of extinct volcanic cones and covered extensively with lava flows. The highest cone is *Cerro Alto* (high peak), which forms a major landmark for the area. Both more ancient and more recent lava flows extend from this volcanic zone toward Rimrock and Zuni and southward toward Homestead. The more ancient flows are now eroded and covered with grasses to the point where they can be used for grazing. The recent flows, especially near *Cerro Bandera* (flag peak), are dotted with pines and firs but have no grass cover and are complete wastelands. West of the volcanic zone and near the center of the Rimrock Navaho country, one can see a series of parallel ridges covered with pinyons and junipers with wash valleys in between.

Finally, on the far horizon to the southwest is the Atrisco region in a wide shallow canyon with red cliffs on one side and a black basalt ridge on the other. The scattered bean farms of Homestead are on a low, gently rolling mesa just beyond Atrisco. To the south of Homestead is a high escarpment, known locally as "the rim," which rises about 1000 feet above the Salt Lake Valley to the south and forms the southern border of our research area. Salt Lake, situated in another extinct volcanic crater, provides salt for livestock and, for the Zunis and Navahos, also almost all of the table salt.

The surface soils produced from these various geological formations are highly susceptible to erosion by wind and water, but they are moderately to well developed, ranging in texture from sandy to clay loam. These soils generally provide excellent conditions for plant growth, the limiting factors being temperature and precipitation, rather than soil fertility.

FLORA AND FAUNA

Almost all of the Rimrock area is located within the pinyon-juniper belt, known as the Upper Sonoran Zone which extends from Colorado and Utah south to central Arizona and New Mexico, and reaches to some extent on the west into Nevada and eastern California and on the east into western Kansas, Oklahoma, and Texas.

The altitudinal range of this zone is from about 4500 to 7500 feet. and its limits vary with differences in exposure and moisture conditions.

In the Rimrock area the mesa heights and raised portions of the flats and valleys are covered with pinyon and juniper trees with underlying short grasses. The drainage ways and the larger part of the flats are covered with sparse, short grasses and short to waist-high perennial composite shrubs. On the northern slopes of canyons, on the higher elevations on the ridges, and on the Zuni Mountains, there are stands of Ponderosa pine, Gambel oak, and even some intrusions of Douglas fir and Englemann spruce that are characteristic of a higher plant zone. The most common types of shrubs are sagebrush, rabbitbrush, and snakeweed. The most important grass is the blue grama grass, which is excellent forage for livestock. Other common plants filling the natural "niches" of this plant zone include two varieties of yucca (the broad-leafed and narrow-leafed), the prickly pear and the buckhorn cholla, and many species of flowering shrubs and herbs that are characteristic of the Upper Sonoran Zone and grow profusely in rainy years — the Indian paintbrush, Rocky Mountain beeplant, scarlet bugler, Mariposa lily, larkspur, long-flowered gilia, locoweed, and Pingüe. The larkspur, the locoweed, and the Pingüe are poisonous range plants — the larkspur affecting cattle, the locoweed affecting horses, and the Pingüe affecting sheep, horses, and cattle. When the land is overused, it tends to become covered with Russian thistle, or "tumbleweed"; if gramagrass is destroyed beyond recovery, less palatable woody composite shrubs like sagebrush may become dominant. Vestal has identified a total of 469 plant species in the Rimrock area.[2]

The native fauna of the Rimrock area are also typical of the Southwestern Upper Sonoran Zone. Mule deer are found in the Zuni Mountains and in the more inaccessible mesa and canyon country. Mountain lions, though rare, occasionally invade the region to feed upon the deer. Other predaceous animals, especially the coyote and two species of wildcats, were once common in the area but have become rare since the New Mexico Bureau of Biological Survey carried on a vigorous campaign to eliminate them.

Although the large herds of prong-horned antelope are generally found in the lower, more open country to the south and west, they also graze, in small herds, in the southern part of the Rimrock area

39

and are occasionally hunted. The smaller forms of mammalian fauna are more conspicuous. Jack rabbits and cottontails, abundant until they were killed by the "plague" a few years ago, have begun to reappear. The prairie dog population was heavy throughout the region in the early days of settlement, but the efforts of the Biological Survey combined with the recent "plague" have virtually eliminated this rodent from the natural setting. Porcupines live in the pinyon groves and make summer raids into the fields of corn. The striped skunk is common and often feeds on chickens. Badgers, chipmunks, rock squirrels, kangaroo rats, and gophers are also observed frequently. Pack rats build nests in the woodlands and gather pinyon nuts, and in good years their nests form an important supply of nuts for pinyon-pickers.

It is unnecessary to list all of the many species of birds found in the Rimrock area. By far the most numerous are the pinyon jays, which travel in large flocks and often completely consume a pinyon crop before the nuts can be gathered. Two types of hawks are common, the desert sparrow hawk and the red-tailed hawk. There are also two types of owl, the burrowing owl and the western horned owl. Golden eagles nest in the cliffs, especially at El Morro. Crows and turkey vultures are observed occasionally. The most conspicuous smaller species include the western robin; the Arkansas kingbird, which chatters incessantly in the pinyon trees all summer and is "mocked" by the western mockingbird; the flocks of western mourning doves, which feed in the fields; the red-shafted flicker, which feeds largely on ants; and the nighthawk, which startles one with its whirring dives in the late afternoon and evening.

The Rimrock area is relatively free of pestiferous insects. Few mosquitoes are found, but there is a two to three week "gnat season" in June and early July which drives people to cover.

CLIMATE

The general climatic patterns of the Southwest are now noted for both the "eastern" and "western" zones that are demarcated by the Rocky Mountain chain.[3] Because the Rimrock area is in the western zone, the following discussion will center on the climatic patterns characteristic there and the variations in the patterns that are found locally.

Climatologists find that there are five principal source regions of air masses contributing to the climate of the Southwest: cold, dry, Polar Continental (Canada and northward); cool, moist, Polar Pacific (northern Pacific Ocean); hot, dry, Tropical Continental (Mexico, extreme southwestern United States); warm, moist, Tropical Gulf (Gulf of Mexico and Caribbean); and warm, moist, Tropical Pacific (southern Pacific Ocean). Although the weather at any given place may be influenced in many ways by the movement and interaction of these air masses, the normal directional movements have a particular pattern for each of the seasons.

In the western zone the summer type of storm usually develops when moist, warm, Tropical Gulf air enters southern Arizona from Old Mexico and moves northward into northern Arizona and New Mexico. Alternatively, the moist, warm air may move into western New Mexico more directly from the Gulf of Mexico, rather than following the more circuitous route through Arizona. Although Tropical Pacific air does not invade the Southwest except under unusual circumstances, when this type of invasion does occur, periods of excessive and widespread rainfall result. During the winter months precipitation ordinarily occurs when moist Polar Pacific air encroaches on the western zone from the north, northwest, or west. Alternatively, some winter moisture reaches the western zone of New Mexico with air masses from the east or southeast, but this is not as regular an occurrence.

Dry periods result in the summer months when Tropical Continental air is developed over the Southwest from the heating of an air mass present in the area that has already lost its original characteristics. The weather during such periods is characterized by high temperatures, low humidity, and an almost complete lack of precipitation. This condition is particularly prevalent in western New Mexico during the late spring and early summer. During the winter Polar Continental air may invade the Southwest from the north or northeast. This air mass brings intense cold and its extreme dryness usually precludes precipitation unless other sources of moisture are available.

Like the rest of the western zone, the Rimrock area has two rather distinct rainy seasons, one during January–March and the other during July–September. The first is due to the activity of the Polar Pacific air, the second to the Tropical Gulf air. During the dry months of April–June, the activity of the Polar Pacific air is greatly lessened and the invasions of moist Gulf air have not yet begun. From September to December the invasions of Gulf air diminish in intensity and frequency and the activity of Polar Pacific air is not great. During the summer dry period the weather is controlled by the Tropical Continental air; during the winter dry period there are frequent invasions of the dry Polar Continental air.

At the prevailing elevations of 7000 feet, winter storms usually come in the form of snow, which sometimes accumulates to a depth of over two feet. The deepest snowfall (30 inches) was recorded on November 22, 1931, in what is known as "The Winter of the Big Snow." Summer storms typically are scattered thundershowers, but occasionally there are general rains over wide areas.

Although these are the characteristic climate patterns of the Rimrock area, great variations may occur from year to year, month to month, and from place to place within the area. As indicated in Table 2, although the average rainfall in the Rimrock area is 13.35 inches, over a twenty-eight-year period, it has varied between 6 and 23 inches. Furthermore, there is always variation in any given year within a small locality — summer showers have been known

Table 2. Average rainfall for the Rimrock area.

Year	Amount (inches)	Year	Amount (inches)
1923	20.48	1939	8.28
1924	10.51	1940	17.55
1925 and 1926	—	1941	19.01
1927	18.73	1942	9.14
1928	8.86	1943	11.06
1929	14.97	1944	8.02
1930	6.71	1945	7.12
1931	—	1946	10.63
1932	16.82	1947	15.19
1933	14.77	1948	12.67
1934	14.69	1949	10.95
1935	23.00	1950	6.00
1936	21.33	average*	13.35
1937	11.88		
1938	15.47		

* Averages for Zuni (at lower elevation) are less; 12.43 inches rather than 13.35.
Source: Data for 1923–1940 from Landgraf, *Land-Use in the Ramah Area of New Mexico;* for 1941–1950 from Vogt, *Modern Homesteaders.*

literally to "stop at a barbed-wire fence." The factors which account for these variations are immensely complicated and have to do with the fluid interaction of the various air masses, the topographic relief, the changes in elevation, and location with reference to storm movements. As local people say, "you don't have to be crazy to be a farmer in these parts, but it sure helps."

While the average growing season in most of the area is 120 days, the time between killing frosts in the late spring and the autumn has varied between 82 and 169 days. Killing frosts have occurred as late as June 18, and as early as September 8. The mean temperature is 52.7 degrees Fahrenheit. The monthly average temperatures vary from 25 degrees during January to 66.2 in July, but winter temperatures have been known to reach 48 degrees below zero, and summer temperatures have been recorded as high as 116 degrees. However, the extremes are rarely above 95 or below minus 30 degrees. Although secondary threats are posed by killing frosts, wind erosion, and occasionally too much snow, the major geographical problem for human settlement in the Rimrock area is the limited and fluctuating rainfall.

NEIGHBORING TOWNS AND COMMUNICATIONS

Beyond the five groups of settlements in the immediate Rimrock area lie various market towns and county seats which form the principal links with the outside world. The most important of these is Railtown, forty-three miles northwest of Rimrock village. Founded in 1882 as a division point on the Santa Fe Railroad which came through western New Mexico at that time, Railtown has become the principal market and trading center for a large area of northwestern New Mexico and northeastern Arizona. It is the self-styled "Indian Capital of the World" and the county seat of Cleveland County. The ethnic composition of its approximately 10,000 people is diverse: the town contains groups of South Europeans (principally Slavs and Italians), Spanish-Americans and Mexicans from Old Mexico, Navahos and Zunis who have moved into town, and "Old American" families from the Middle West.[4]

Seventy-nine miles from Rimrock, across the state line in Arizona, is St. George, a half Mormon and half Spanish-American community of approximately 1500. Some grocery shopping is done in this community, but it is especially important to the Spanish-Americans, who have relatives living there; to the Mormons, who see it as the head-quarters of the Stake in which the Rimrock ward is located; and to the Homestead Texans, who buy their tractors and other farming equipment from dealers located there.

South of Homestead thirty-eight miles is Quemado, a mixed Texan and Spanish-American ranching town of approximately 400 people. Quemado is especially important for the Homesteaders as a secondary shopping center. About fifty miles to the east across the Zuni Mountains is Johnson, another railroad town and second-ary shopping center. Uranium ore was recently discovered near Johnson, and the town, which contained about 2500 people in 1950, has grown enormously in population and importance. Still further east, about one hundred thirty-five miles from the Rimrock area, is the county seat of Verona County. While Zuni and Rimrock are in Cleveland County and look toward Railtown, the communities of La Peña, Tijeras, Atrisco, and Homestead are in Verona County, and their residents must travel a much greater distance to transact their business at the county seat.

Farther yet beyond these neighboring towns, the people of the Rimrock area have connections with the larger urban centers of Albuquerque and Santa Fe in New Mexico, and, to a more limited extent, with Phoenix, Arizona. Of more importance, both symbol-ically and in terms of travel and various economic, religious, and political transactions, are special centers for particular cultures. The Mormons travel frequently to Mesa, Arizona, to have their marriages "sealed" in the Mormon temple there; they send their children to Brigham Young University located in Provo, Utah; and they often visit Salt Lake City, the center of the Mormon world. The Texans favor Amarillo, Plainview, Lubbock, Fort Worth, and San Antonio, Texas. The Navahos have special connections with Window Rock, Arizona, the headquarters of the Navaho Tribal Council to which the Rimrock Navahos send a delegate. The Zunis have many trading and visiting relationships with the Rio Grande pueblos. And the local Spanish-Americans have close relationships with San Martín, an almost wholly Spanish-American village near Johnson.

The communication network in the Rimrock area has its most important connections with Railtown. An Indian Service telephone line runs from Railtown to Zuni, to Rimrock village, and to La Peña. Atrisco and Homestead have no telephones. The major north–south road also leaves Highway 66 at Railtown and runs south to Homestead. It was paved as far as the cross-junction with the east–west road running from Johnson through La Peña, Rimrock, Zuni, and on to Arizona, but unpaved the rest of the way to Homestead and Quemado. The east–west road is partially paved east of La Peña, but unpaved over the rest of the route.

Mail is delivered daily by a truck which starts at Railtown and goes to Rimrock and Zuni. From Rimrock, another line takes mail to Homestead on Mondays, Wednesdays, and Fridays; on Tuesdays and Thursdays, Homestead receives mail from Quemado. Thus, all of the communities which have post offices receive daily mail service. Beginning in 1949, the Rimrock area was serviced by Rural Electrification power lines, which now reach all communities but the scattered Navaho hogans.

The television station at Albuquerque reaches only a limited part of the Rimrock area, and there were no more than six television sets (all in Rimrock and Homestead) by the end of our field work in 1955. Radio programs are more important and are listened to by people of all five cultures. The Railtown stations now has programs in four languages: English, Spanish, Navaho, and Zuni. Reception from radio stations located in Albuquerque, Holbrook, and Winslow is also easy to pick up in the area.

45

Intercultural Relations

EVON Z. VOGT

with the assistance of MALCOLM J. ARTH

HOW LONG THE ZUNIS as a separate and identifiable cultural unit have lived in their present territory along the banks of the Zuni River and its tributaries is not known. Certainly they were there when the Spanish conquistadores arrived in 1540, and archaeological evidence indicates that their cultural ancestors occupied the region for some hundreds of years earlier, extending back at least into Pueblo III times (A.D. 1050–1300) and probably much earlier.[1]

It appears that the Zunis are one of several Western Pueblo cultures that developed over a long time span from earlier Basket Maker roots in the Colorado Plateau country. A few Basket Maker sites and many later Anasazi sites are found in the area. Although few of these have been excavated, the indications are that they were abandoned and the people concentrated in the historic six Zuni villages[2] before any of the other present-day groups entered the region. By 1705 the six Zuni villages had been reduced to one main village. Later three outlying farming villages were established: Nutria ("beaver" in Spanish), so named because there used to be beaver dams near this village at the base of the Zuni Mountains; Pescado ("fish"), named for the fish found by the early Spanish explorers in the stream emanating from the springs near the village, which is located six miles below Rimrock; and Ojo Caliente ("hot spring"), twenty miles southeast of Zuni, where a warm spring bubbles up. The Zuni population on the Reservation in 1950 was 2486.

Compared to the Zuni, even the Navahos and early Spaniards are newcomers to western New Mexico. The Navahos may have had

46

sporadic contact with the Zunis before the Civil War, but they did not arrive in any great numbers until later. Early accounts of raids against the Zuni cite Apache de Navajo or Navaho and/or Apache raiders. Whether the Navaho as a differentiated group engaged in such attacks is contingent on such disputed issues as when differentiation of Navaho from Apache occurred. It is probable that the raiders were generalized Apache. In the two decades before their removal to Fort Sumner in 1864, Navahos hunted in the Rimrock area and cultivated a few fields. After their release from captivity in 1868, a few related families came to the Rimrock region instead of settling on the Reservation to the north. They selected the well-watered valley which is now mostly covered by the Rimrock reservoir built by the Mormons, and later spread south and east into less desirable lands in the lava country. In 1950 the Rimrock Navaho population was 625.

The Spanish conquistadores were in the Rimrock area as early as the Coronado expedition, which arrived at the Zuni villages in 1540. Several later Spanish expeditions passed through the region, including that of Don Juan de Oñate, the colonizer and first governor of New Mexico, who left his inscription on the side of El Morro in 1605. The ancestors of the present Spanish-American inhabitants did not enter the Rimrock area until the early 1860's, when they began to migrate west from older settlements across the Zuni Mountains. By 1865 Tijeras was established as a frontier *ranchería*. Later, as other families came to settle and use the land, the winter sheep range was extended southwestward toward the Arizona line, where there were broad grassy plains. Along the route from Tijeras to the southwest several small *rancherías* were built, usually by one or two families who located in a canyon where a dam could be built and gardens cultivated. The larger settlement of Atrisco was founded in 1882. The Spanish-American population has decreased markedly in recent decades and in 1950 was only 89.

In 1876, Mormon missionary scouts first appeared in the region, visiting the Zunis at Zuni pueblo and at Pescado, and the newly settled Spanish-Americans at Tijeras. Eventually a site for colonization was selected at the base of the Zuni Mountains about five miles from the present village. In 1877, the colony was virtually wiped out by a smallpox epidemic. In 1882 a new band of Mormons settled, this time near the missionary establishment in the lower valley. The

47

new settlement was first called Navajo and later Rimrock; by 1950 its population had expanded to 241.

Although a few Texan ranchers established cattle ranches in the area around the turn of the century, the main migrations from Texas occurred in the 1920's and 1930's. After World War I, Texans began to take up homesteads in the La Peña area. The number was much augmented during the depression of the early 1930's, when the community of Homestead was established near a rain-filled natural lake which the Spanish-Americans had fenced and had used for watering sheep and cattle since the 1880's. In 1950 the population of the Texan Homestead settlement was 232.

THE SPANISH CONQUEST

In the 1530's Cabeza de Vaca and three companions including the Moorish slave, Estevan, traveled across what is now south Texas and northern Mexico after surviving a shipwreck on the Gulf.[3] When they finally reached Mexico City in 1536, they brought stories to Viceroy Mendoza of an "El Dorado" land north of the route they had traveled. As a result of these reports, a small party with Fray Marcos de Niza as leader and Estevan as guide was sent north in 1539 to look for the fabulous "Seven Cities of Cibola." Estevan, marching ahead of the main party, was killed by the Zunis at Hawikuh. It is not certain that Fray Marcos ever reached the Zuni pueblos, although he may have seen them from a distance as he reported. At any rate, he returned to Mexico with glowing tales of what he had seen and heard, and these stories helped spur on the organization of a larger expedition led by Coronado which did reach the pueblos in July 1540. Hawikuh was taken by the Spanish in a pitched battle which lasted only an hour but nevertheless broke organized Zuni resistance. The ruins of the village of Hawikuh are near the present Zuni farming village of Ojo Caliente.

After Hawikuh's conquest, the leaders of the other Zuni villages brought gifts and held lengthy conferences with Coronado. According to Spanish reports, the Zunis promised to become Christians and subjects of the king of Spain. However, after the conferences they packed up their property and with their women and children deserted their villages and took refuge on Corn Mountain, a high mesa which served as a refuge for them throughout the centuries

48

of Spanish control. The Indians were finally persuaded to come down from the mesa, and Coronado and his troops made their headquarters in the Zuni villages and supplied themselves with Zuni food during the next few months while smaller expeditions were sent west to the Hopi pueblos and east to Acoma and the Rio Grande pueblos. In September 1540, the main army with sheep and cattle reached the Zuni country, and Coronado shifted his headquarters to Tiguex on the Rio Grande. In the spring of 1542, Coronado and his army passed through Zuni on their return to Mexico, having failed to find the gold, silver, and turquoise they had set out to discover.

The impact of Coronado's visit did not cease when he departed from Zuni. He left behind him three Catholic Mexican Indians, domesticated animals (sheep, cattle, horses, and mules), some Catholic paraphernalia, and possibly some wheat seeds. The Zunis also presumably retained vivid memories of the superior power of Spanish arms and of the potentiality of Corn Mountain as a sanctuary. For the next forty years the Zunis were not visited by any major Spanish expeditionary forces, and it was not until the 1580's that even small groups of Spaniards again reached Zuni. Chamuscado in 1581 and Espejo in 1583 found there the three Mexican Indians left by Coronado. However, Zuni did not feel the full force of Spanish power again until Governor Juan de Oñate, the colonizer of New Mexico, arrived in 1598. It was then that the Zunis formally made vows of allegiance and vassalage to Spain.

The first Catholic missionaries were established in 1629, at Halona and Hawikuh. Three years later Fray Francisco Letrado was killed at Hawikuh when he urged the Indians too strongly to attend Mass. The Zunis fled to the top of Corn Mountain where they remained for about three years. In the 1640's missionaries were re-established in Zuni, but in the general Pueblo Rebellion of 1680,[4] the Zunis killed Fray Juan de Bal and once more took refuge on Corn Mountain. By 1680, the number of Zuni inhabited villages had been reduced to four. It was on Corn Mountain that General Diego de Vargas found and conquered them in 1692. After De Vargas' conquest missionaries were again placed at Zuni. However, in 1703, the Indians killed three Spaniards who were living in the Zuni villages and returned to Corn Mountain. When they descended, the Zunis consolidated into a single pueblo which has remained to the present.[5] From the time of construction of the church at Zuni (in the late 1600's or early 1700's) until the mission was abandoned in 1821, resident missionaries were maintained more or less continuously in the Zuni country.[6]

Parsons cites the danger from Navaho attacks and poor church attendance as the two main reasons for the abandonment of the mission. The factor of outside pressures, particularly the raids, has been of great importance in Zuni life, no doubt influencing the pueblo type of construction and the progressive consolidation of the villages. Bandelier has suggested that the Zunis offered little initial resistance to Spanish power and control because they hoped that the Spanish would serve as an unwitting ally against the continual Navaho-Apache attacks; they hoped the coalition would prove enough to counteract the raiders.[7] Similar considerations probably played a role in their later acceptance of American power which did effectively end Navaho-Apache raids in the late nineteenth century.

These early contacts between the Zunis and the Spanish, extending over three centuries (1540–1846), have a number of significant features. There was only one major battle with Spanish troops, that between Coronado's men and the Zunis at Hawikuh in July 1540. Subsequent encounters between the two groups involved the isolated killings of Spanish priests when soldiers were not around to protect them, usually followed by attempts to evade Spanish retaliation by fleeing to Corn Mountain. At no time during these centuries did the Spanish establish settlements in the area. Contacts were limited to three specific types: Spanish expeditions coming to establish religious missions; Spanish expeditions passing through on their way elsewhere; and the resident Catholic missionaries.

Although the Zunis adopted elements of Spanish material culture, such as wheat and domestic animals, they were from the outset resistant to adopting the religious system. They looked particularly with hope to the Spanish religion, probably less as substitute for their own than as powerful magic which would help them "beat" the much dreaded "war-medicines" of their enemies. The early feelings of hostility over religious matters seem to be the historical root of the Zuni prohibition, still in force, that prevents Spanish-Americans from witnessing any of their ceremonials. On their side, the Spanish were motivated primarily by the hope of finding another

Mexico or Peru with great riches and only secondarily by the desire to convert the natives. Neither goal was achieved. Closer and more enduring relationships between Zunis and Spanish-Americans were not established until the latter actually settled in the Rimrock area in the late nineteenth century.

THE NAVAHO ARRIVAL

Specialists are still debating the questions of when and by what routes the Athapascan-speaking peoples entered the Southwest and when differentiation into separate cultural groupings such as Navaho, Western Apache, and Jicarilla Apache occurred. Dates of arrival ranging from 1000 to 1500 have been proposed, and whatever dating is adopted, it is still an open question whether the Navaho entered the Southwest as Navaho or as generic Apache.[8] These questions are intimately bound up with the historical reconstruction of early Navaho-Zuni contacts. For example, it is known that seventeenth-century Zuni life was punctuated by periodic raids. In discussing the raid on Hawikuh in 1670, in which the Spanish priest was killed and the mission burned, Bandelier states specifically that it was a raid by Navahos; Hodge disputes this, saying it is more likely to have been Apache raiding in 1670.[9] In any event, there was general Athapascan (possibly Navaho) pressure on Zuni during the seventeenth century, and probably earlier, which was maintained intermittently until the middle of the nineteenth century. This external pressure is credited with reducing the number of Zuni villages from the original six or seven in 1540 to four in 1680, and finally to one site in 1705. Not only is the increasing consolidation of the Zunis attributed to Apache (or Navaho) attacks, but also the very architectural and settlement patterns which the villages took. The Zuni word, "apachu," meaning "enemies," applied to all Navahos and Apaches, seems aptly chosen.

Actual Navaho settlement in the immediate vicinity of Zuni is not recorded previous to the 1840's and 1850's.[10] During the decade preceding the confinement of the Navahos at Fort Sumner, the Zunis were concentrated mainly in the central village, while the Navahos occupied the Pescado and Nutria valleys. When the Navahos were placed in captivity, the Zunis took advantage of their

51

absence to establish Nutria, Pescado, and Ojo Caliente. When the Navahos returned, they settled in the Rimrock Valley and eastward along the southwestern base of the Zuni Mountains.

Looking at the two cultures for evidence of contacts, it may be seen that, although there is much in Navaho culture that appears to have derived from the Pueblo peoples generally, there is little that can be traced specifically to historical contacts with Zuni. Several local Navaho traits seem directly attributable to Zuni influences. At least four older men among the Rimrock Navahos speak Zuni and one knows the Zuni myth which "goes with" the Shalako. A few items of technology appear to have been acquired, such as outdoor bake ovens and painted pottery. The belief that Zuni gods and Zuni witches are able to influence events in Navaho life is further indication of contact.[11] There is evidence of absorption of some Navaho traits by the Zunis, for example, hand-trembling techniques and the Yeibichai dance, as well as the speaking of Navaho by many Zunis.

The historical sequence of Navaho-Zuni interaction seems to fall into two main stages, one of hostility and the other of relative harmony. The first lasted from some time in the seventeenth century to the middle of the nineteenth; the second, characterized by permanent Navaho residence near Zuni and subsequent social and economic interaction, resulted in the transmission of most of the cultural elements noted.

SPANISH-AMERICAN SETTLEMENT

The next phase of intercultural relations opens with the arrival of the Spanish-Americans at Tijeras in the 1860's. They did not enter Navaho country as settlers until the Navahos had been brought under control by the United States government. Before then, the principal westernmost Spanish-American settlements were at Cebolleta and Cubero (at the base of Mount Taylor), outposts at the edge of Navaho country for over a century.[12]

During the 1860's, Spanish-Americans began to expand westward. In 1866 one family moved with its sheep from Cubero to Concho, Arizona. By 1869, several families had settled at Ojo del Gallo and founded the village of San Martín. Two families which settled at San Lorenzo (later called Tijeras) were joined by two more in 1870;

from this small village, herds of sheep were grazed across the open country between Zuni and the Zuni Salt Lake. Atrisco, the second Spanish-American village in the area, was founded in 1882 by members of two related families from Cubero.[13]

Since the Spanish-Americans occupied an area considerably east and south of the Zuni grazing lands, early contacts were few. Superficial contact occurred when the Zunis passed through Atrisco on their way to the Salt Lake on salt-gathering expeditions, but such journeys were infrequent. There was some intergroup trading, especially between Tijeras and Pescado and Atrisco and Ojo Caliente. The Spanish-Americans began quite early to make pilgrimages to the *Santo* at Zuni, an image of the Infant Christ of Our Lady of Atocha that was one of the items of Catholic religious paraphernalia retained by the Zunis after the mission was abandoned in 1821.[14] Although at this time Spanish-Americans were welcome to visit the *Santo,* the taboo against their witnessing any Zuni ceremonials was strongly in force. Cushing, who lived at Zuni from 1879 to 1884, reports:

> There is one race, however — the Mexican — toward whom the Zuni, preserving an outward calm, keeps up an inward and undying hatred. He so heartily despises and abhors these inoffensive representatives of a priesthood who persecuted the gods of his forefathers that any white man who resembles one of them even, will meet with but tardy welcome in the town of Zuni. The Zunis would as soon think of imbibing poison as of permitting man, woman, or child of that detested race to witness one of their festivals or sacred dances. If Don or "Greaser" chances to heave in sight while any of the tribal ceremonies are going on, he is met by watchful subchiefs and amicably but firmly escorted to such quarter of the town as is most remote from the scene of celebration, and then locked up. He may rave and swear and call down the vengeance of "El Gobierno" on the Indians for detaining him, but so long as that festivity lasts, be it one day or four, he will be held strict prisoner. Yet so stringent are the customs of hospitality that the unhappy captive is supplied with every delicacy the Zuni cuisine can produce, his horses and donkeys are fed and watered, and nothing which a favored guest might anticipate is left undone.[15]

For their part, the early Spanish-American settlers regarded the Zunis with uneasiness. Florence Kluckhohn reports that when Atrisco was first settled, many people in the village, especially the women and children, feared the Zunis, for it was not known whether or not they would attack.[16]

Despite mutual mistrust, the Zunis permitted some Spanish-American families to live in their villages. In the 1880's, Frank Montaño's great-grandfather lived in the pueblo, making his living as a smith, and later establishing a ranch north of the Zuni reservation. In the 1890's, three Spanish-American families, including Trinidad Marez's maternal grandfather, lived for a few years in Pescado, one of the outlying farming villages; they did smithing and were allowed to farm small plots of Zuni land while they resided there.

After the *patrón* of Atrisco went bankrupt in the late 1920's, the Spanish-American people of this village began trading more often at stores in the Zuni pueblo and interaction with Zunis became frequent and more important. The women of Atrisco started going to the government doctor in Zuni for delivery of their children, thus necessitating their living in the pueblo for a time. However, they usually stayed with one family, the Eriachos, the head of which is reputed to be half Mexican Yaqui Indian in origin. At least one Atrisqueño engaged the services of Zuni witch doctors during this period, though her community expressed disapproval.[17]

The question of how the Zunis perceive the early Spanish conquerors' relation to the much later Spanish-American settlers is interesting. Linguistically they differentiate the early Spanish whom they call *Cipolo** from the Spanish-Americans whom they view, accurately, as a mixture of *Cipolo* and *Mehikukwe,* Mexican people. However, they also perceive the continuity between the two, a fact demonstrated by their refusal to allow Spanish-Americans to witness their ceremonials.

For Spanish-Americans in the Rimrock area, early contacts with Navahos were more important than those with the Zunis.† The Spanish-Americans moved directly into Navaho territory when they settled at Tijeras, and Atrisco has had Navaho neighbors living within ten miles of the village. There is evidence that the Navahos at first may have been predisposed to steal Spanish-American livestock. However, the relationship soon reached a somewhat more reciprocally trustful level, with the Spanish-Americans actually carrying out *patrón* functions, and providing the Navahos with credit in their stores and in their saloons. Thus, from the beginning, Spanish-

* This term is probably derived from the historical search of the Spaniards for the Seven Cities of Cibola.

† The Navaho term for "Mexicans" and "Spanish-Americans" is *Na-Kai.* Unlike the Zunis, the Navahos do not differentiate between "Spanish" and "Mexicans."

Americans were a main source of the Navaho liquor supply. In return, the Navahos worked as herders for them. Reciprocal trading and visiting relationships were established at both Tijeras and Atrisco. The Spanish-Americans engaged in some proselytizing in Tijeras.

As a result of this early interaction, many Navahos acquired Spanish names, learned to speak some Spanish, and copied Spanish-American techniques of handling sheep. There was relatively little conflict over land, such as occurred later when Mormons and Texans entered the Rimrock area. Spanish-American *patróns* made little fuss over the small Navaho herds that grazed in the open range. This was in part due to the fact that the range was still unfenced and uncrowded, but it no doubt also stemmed partly from the traditional Spanish attitudes of permissiveness and easygoingness. It seems unlikely that Texans or Mormons in the same situation would have responded to Navaho use of their land for grazing — or more literally have failed to respond — as did the Spanish-Americans. During this period there emerged an ecological balance among the Navahos, Spanish-Americans, and Zunis.

MORMON COLONIZATION

The Mormon entry into the Rimrock area was part of a purposeful church program to establish a missionary outpost to convert the Zunis and Navahos of the region to Mormonism. The first two missionaries arrived at Zuni in 1876.[18] Later that year, Brigham Young "called" two additional missionaries to carry on the work, and they settled with their families at the Spanish-American ranching village of Tijeras. In 1877 seven families founded a settlement in the upper Rimrock Valley at the base of the Zuni Mountains. By that October it was reported that the mission numbered 116 Zunis and 34 Navahos who had been baptized. In the late autumn nearly a hundred converts from Arkansas arrived, placing such a strain on the food supplies that most of them were sent on to Mormon settlements in Arizona.

A smallpox epidemic broke out in Tijeras and Zuni, forcing the Mormon families to leave Tijeras and give up missionary work at Zuni. The disease spread to the upper Rimrock Valley and nearly a dozen Mormons died during the winter of 1877–78. One of the missionaries at Zuni "administered," according to Mormon doctrine, to over four hundred Indians in the pueblo, reputedly with great success. (This act of faith-healing is still stressed by Mormon missionaries and by Zuni converts to Mormonism in the contemporary missionary program.) By 1880 only one Mormon family remained in the area. To prevent complete failure of the colony, the church authorities "called" several families from Sunset, Arizona, to revive the New Mexican outpost, and in 1882 they moved to the Rimrock Valley. The new settlement established down the valley at its present site, a townsite laid out, a dam and irrigation ditches constructed, and an irrigation company formed.

By 1884, Rimrock had become a full-fledged Mormon community, ready to fulfill the purpose for which it had been created — to convert the Indians to Mormonism. Missionary work was emphasized by church authorities until 1900 when all those who had been "called" to Rimrock as missionaries were officially "released" and allowed to go elsewhere if they so desired. At this point a goal which had emerged earlier now became prominent, that of "making the desert bloom like a rose." Missionary work continued, but the prime emphasis was placed upon building a permanent Mormon settlement.

The early relationships which the Mormons established with the Zunis, Navahos, and Spanish-Americans were heavily influenced by their definition of these groups as "Lamanites." The Mormons believe that all American Indians are descendants of Israelites who crossed the Pacific from the Old World and settled on the North American continent. According to the Mormons, the apostasy of these ancient Hebrews led to the degeneration of their religion and to the darkening of their skins; their conversion and "return to God," it is believed, will whiten their skins again. The Spanish-Americans are included in the category of "Lamanites" because of their mixed Spanish-Indian ancestry.

The Mormons who arrived in the Rimrock area, had a sincere desire to convert the "Lamanites," and the figures cited indicate considerable early success with both Zunis and Navahos. Among the 150 Zunis and Navahos baptized by the fall of 1877 were the headman of the Rimrock Navahos and a Zuni who later became governor of the pueblo.[19] The formal acts of conversion and baptism may

56

not have affected the value systems of those converted, but it is an indication that relationships between the Mormons and Indians were relatively friendly in these early decades.

A small group of Zuni families, including the convert who became governor, lived in Rimrock for a few years, helped the Mormons build the dam for their irrigation reservoir, and farmed a small plot of land the Mormons had promised them in exchange for their labor. Many of the Zunis from Pescado traded wheat in exchange for grinding services at the Mormon gristmill and lumber at the Mormon sawmill in Rimrock. Later, beginning in the 1920's, several Mormons worked for the Indian Service at the Zuni agency and developed close contacts with Zunis.

The difficulties between Mormons and Navahos began after 1900, when the Mormon emphasis shifted from missionary work to the task of building a permanent community at Rimrock. As the Mormon population increased, greater pressure was placed upon the lands that were being used by the Navahos. Eventually the Mormons gained control of much of the best Navaho land, and the resulting ecological conflict was not resolved until the Indian Service made allotments to the Navaho families in the 1920's. The situation has been legally stabilized, but the Navaho continue to feel that the Mormons, while talking about religion, have been taking the best Navaho lands. More recently the Mormons have also gained control of all of the local trading posts which handle most of the Navaho trade. This combination of developments has been at the root of the contemporary uneasy and mistrustful relationships between the two groups.

Like the early Mormon-Zuni contacts, the early relationships between Mormons and Spanish-Americans were free of the ecological conflict that emerged between Mormons and Navahos. Some early proselytizing was attempted by the Mormons, especially when they were living at Tijeras, but no successful conversions have been effected in the Rimrock area. Whereas the Navaho and Zuni traditions allowed them simply to add the Mormon religious label and such of the practices as they liked to their old religion, the Spanish-Americans could not become Mormons without renouncing Catholicism, and this they were unwilling to do. There were also some early economic arrangements between the Mormons and Spanish-Americans. Trade was carried on, and Mormons with technical knowledge were hired by the Spanish-Americans to build two dams in the Atrisco area.

TEXAN MIGRATIONS

The last of the five cultural groups to arrive was the Texan. This group came in three migrations: the first immigrants, a small number of cattle ranchers, arrived in the area around the turn of the century; the second, predominantly farmers, took up homesteads near La Peña in the early 1920's; and the third wave in the early 1930's established the community of Homestead. The Texans never developed close contacts with the Zunis, but relationships with the Mormons, Navahos, and Spanish-Americans have become important.

Contacts with the Mormons were initiated when the Texans traveled through Rimrock on their way to and from Railtown. At first there was a sense of relief when the Texans found that they were not the only "white folks" in the area. They wanted to believe that the Mormons were the same type of rural people that they were, held the same values, and were social equals. However, Rimrock had a longer and better established place in the region, higher material standards of living, and more community activities — qualities which made the Mormon community "superior" in the homesteaders' minds. Nevertheless, the Mormon religion was, from the first, considered very peculiar by the Texans, and the compact village pattern offended the Texan taste for privacy and wide-open spaces. For their part, the Mormons regarded their own way of life as distinctly superior. The Texan communities are usually considered "rough" and "immoral," because of the drinking, smoking, and fighting which take place and what is regarded as disorganization in Texan community life.

Before migrating to western New Mexico, most of the Texans had never seen an Indian, except in the movies, and they arrived with pioneer-type attitudes toward them: Indians were "wild and uncivilized" and "dangerous" if not closely watched, but they were destined to disappear as the land was settled by "superior" white people. The first contacts were established when Navahos were hired to work in the bean fields. Texan-Navaho relations in the La Peña area had developed on a markedly friendly and equalitarian basis.[20]

A number of the Texans in the La Peña area made "corn liquor" in homemade stills during Prohibition days and engaged in an active bootleg liquor business with Navahos. With Homestead, however, Navaho contacts have always been characterized by more aloofness and less friendly interchange. In neither Texan settlement was there serious ecological conflict with the Navahos. The Texans settled on lands that were peripheral to those held by the Navahos, and unlike the Mormons, have never gone in heavily for trading posts oriented toward the Navaho trade.

Before the Texans migrated to New Mexico their only contacts with Spanish-speaking peoples were with the migratory workers who came in small numbers to the Panhandle each year to assist in the cotton harvest. These Mexican laborers occupied a depressed position within the social and economic structure. As one of the Texans expressed it: "Down in Texas, Mexicans are considered as niggers, and niggers are pretty low." This stereotype was reinforced through school lessons on Texas history and by folklore about the battle of the Alamo in which the Mexicans are pictured as treacherous villains and Texans as courageous and righteous heroes. It is not surprising, then, that the Texans were distressed when they settled in the Rimrock area to discover that almost all of the county and many of the state officials were "Mexicans" and that they would be living next to "Mexican" villages where their children had to attend school. From the beginning, the homesteaders manifested a distrust and fear of the Spanish-Americans.

The Spanish-Americans, on the other hand, had developed a modus vivendi with the older settlers in the area in which there were relatively tolerant and respectful relations among the groups. Although the Spanish-Americans made overtures of friendship to the *Tejanos,* many of whom they pitied because of their utter poverty, they stopped such gestures after being rebuffed. The Spanish-Americans were quick to sense the hate, prejudice, and superiority which the *Tejanos* felt toward them. The *Tejanos* soon posed a serious economic threat to their village, for the homesteaders began to acquire title to, and fence in, land which the Spanish-Americans had been grazing as open range for almost fifty years.

In the Homestead area there have been two important outbreaks of hostility between the two peoples. The first occurred in the fall of 1934 when a Spanish-American teacher (a son of one of the most respected families in Atrisco) was sent by the county to the newly constructed grade school in Homestead. This met with violent objections from the homesteaders. During the first few weeks of school, windows were broken at night and signs appeared on the door of the school which read: "We Don't Want Any Chile Pickers for Teachers." Finally, one night the schoolhouse burned down. Both Spanish-Americans and some of the homesteaders now claim that it was set on fire by one of the more rabid Mexican-hating homesteaders.

These events increased tension on both sides, but over the years as the older Homestead children went to high school in Atrisco, and as the homesteaders went to Atrisco to pick up their mail, the groups were brought into closer contact. However, most of the homesteaders continued to object to sending their children to high school in Atrisco, and talked openly of attempting to take both the school and the post office away from Atrisco. They looked forward to the day when their numbers would bring them political control over the Atrisco district. Eventually most of these things came about. By 1936, Homestead had its own post office, although a small post office was still maintained in Atrisco. In 1938 the high school was shifted to Homestead, and a few years later the grade school in Atrisco was closed and the Spanish-American children had to go by bus to grade school in Homestead.

In the meantime, however, closer individual ties were developed between the two communities. Friendships between individuals were formed, and, despite objections from friends and relatives, two of the Texans married daughters of the former *patrón* of Atrisco; these families continue to reside in Homestead. One of the Spanish-Americans set up a bar in Homestead which in due course was well patronized by many homesteaders.

Just when it appeared that better relations between the two groups were developing, a second important outbreak of open conflict occurred in 1947. It began with a fight at one of the dances in Homestead and eventually involved almost all of the Spanish-American men and many of the Texans who were at the dance. The fighting continued off and on for several days, as one of the young Texans who was beaten in the first fight sought revenge on all of the young Spanish-Americans who had taken part in the fight. Although the open fighting stopped after a week or so, and many

60

Homestead families who were not present at the dance regretted the incident (which they named the "Spanish-American War"), the conflict was another tension-producing event affecting adversely the relations between the two communities. It seems unlikely that these events will soon be forgotten by either group.

Thus, intercultural relationships in the Rimrock area during the period of the research had their roots in Southwestern history. From the arrival of the Coronado expedition at Zuni in 1540 to the most recent Texan influx during the depression of the 1930's, the successive entries of different groups have gradually filled all the ecological niches in the region and have sharply reduced the amount of life space available to any one people. By 1955, each of the cultures had had a substantial history of contact with each of the others and had developed patterned ways both of viewing and of interacting with its neighbors.

The Contemporary Intercultural System

Analysis of contemporary intercultural relations will focus on the generalized cognitive orientations which each group has developed to each of the others, and the intercultural role network which, paradoxically, provides both effective lines of communication and limits on the degree of intimacy between cultures. The term cognitive orientations refers to the ways in which one group perceives another: the symbols and elements of the other way of life which are selected, often unconsciously, to characterize it — the "cognitive map" each has of its neighbors. The cognitive orientations are independent of the facts of the perceived group's behavior or symbols. They designate what their neighbors *think* they do, and it is to their cognitive orientations that they adjust their own behavior.

The concept of an intercultural role network is needed, since whole cultures as such do not meet, but individuals as culture carriers do.[21] Out of intercultural contacts, a complex but limited number of roles are developed which establish a precedent for future meetings. Ultimately these roles achieve the status of channels through which the content of cultural systems *must* be communicated and transmitted one to the other. Like their internal counterparts, intercultural roles may be conceptualized as constellations of behavior patterns appropriate to particular situations, and, since

61

they presuppose a social context, each calls for its complement if either is to be sustained. In an intercultural system, such reciprocal behaviors are paired cross-culturally; the performance of an act by a member of one cultural group evokes certain actions from a member of another. Underlying each set of actions in a paired set is a complex of beliefs and values. The pair constitutes a cross-cultural unit of mutually understood expectations founded upon a definition — probably implicit — of reciprocal rights and obligations.[22]

ZUNI-NAVAHO RELATIONSHIPS

Zunis and Navahos are definitely cognizant of a bond between them. They recognize their cultural similarity — that both are American Indian tribes with many common customs. They are also aware that they have a long history of contact. Many Zunis and Navahos now believe that the ancestors of both people emerged from the underworld at about the same time. In the words of one Zuni:

> They [Zunis and Navahos] had contact when they first came up from the underworld. Just after they came up. The Navahos and Zunis actually came out of the underworld together, that's what the Zunis describe. The Navahos and Zunis went around looking for the middle place. When it came to the distribution of animals, the Navahos qualified to get the horse. So that's why the Zunis say the Navahos like to wrestle with horses a lot.

Another view is expressed by a Navaho informant who states: "The Zunis and Navahos came up separately from the underworld, and right after that is when they came in contact with one another." Not only are both groups aware of the early contacts, but they have definite ideas of what those contacts were like. The Zunis particularly recall that their early meetings with the Navahos were hostile. Navaho raids on livestock and stealing of crops are frequently cited. Only after the Navahos were placed in Fort Sumner were they finally "tamed" and transformed into peaceful neighbors. The Zunis still tend to look down on the Navahos as "crude" and "unsophisticated" people living in rude hogans scattered in the woods, rather than in "good" houses clustered in a pueblo. A Zuni woman expressed this general attitude at Shalako time in the following way: "Navahos who come can be fed on the floor or any place, but our fancy friends from Laguna have to be fed at the table with plates and knives and forks."[23]

In other ways Navaho power is respected. For example, the Zunis believe that Navaho witches are effective against them in the same way that Zuni witches are. The Navahos hold similar beliefs about the power of Zuni witches. However, the Zunis do not hold that Navaho gods can affect the course of events in Zuni life, a position contrary to the Navaho belief about Zuni gods.*

The Navahos, acknowledging that they were the aggressors, also view the early interaction with the Zunis as hostile. (Their name for Zunis is *na·št'éži,* which means "blackened enemies.") This stage of hostile interaction was superseded by peaceful relations, which persist to this day, with even a few cases of intermarriage. Navaho attitudes toward Zunis are marked by ambivalence. On the one hand, they consider the Zunis as a people with a superior technology and a more sophisticated, elaborate ceremonialism; here the Zunis represent a kind of ideal model. On the other hand, Zunis are "big witches," and all contacts with them must be handled with care. Ambivalence finds another expression in the conflict between the Navahos' admiration for Zuni industriousness and their feeling that Zunis are "soft" and slightly effete compared with the "tougher" Navahos, who spend more time on horseback and withstand long periods of cold and hunger. Yet Navaho life is seen as more desirable, permitting more freedom of movement and providing an easier daily pace.

Among the key intercultural roles in the Zuni-Navaho interaction system are guest-host, employer-employee, and intermarriage. The guest-host relationship is based on mutual hospitality and gift exchange. Unlike the ordinary trading situation, it involves no bargaining. Each Navaho family visiting Zuni, especially during the Shalako ceremonial but at other times as well, has one or more Zuni families regarded as "friends." Upon entering the pueblo, they go at once to the house of the "friends," where they leave gifts of mutton, rugs, pinyon nuts, or jewelry. The Zuni family in turn is expected to house and feed them throughout the visit and to return gifts of bread, corn,

---

* This difference may be related to differentials in power and prestige between the two cultures, but it seems more likely to be related to the fact that, while Navahos have pregnancy taboos against attending ceremonials, the Zunis do not. Hence, a pregnant Zuni woman cannot (in Zuni belief) harm her baby by attending a Zuni, Navaho, or any other kind of ceremonial.

melons, or hay when they depart. Behavior during such visits is highly structured: there is handshaking upon arrival and again upon departure; there are mutual inquiries about the state of health of families, and about the condition of crops and herds. Communication is usually in the Navaho language rather than Zuni. Later in the year, the Zuni family may return the visit at the hogan encampment of the Navaho "friends." They are then expected to bring gifts, and it behooves the Navahos to house, feed, and give gifts to them when they leave.

Such guest-host "friendships" sometimes persist for several generations. However, they may be severed if one party fails to reciprocate with the expected hospitality or gifts. Though nothing is said at the time, the following season will find the family that was slighted either looking for other "friends" or merely failing to bring gifts to the same one.[24]

The employer-employee roles reflect the socio-economic hierarchy of the Rimrock area and show the superior position of the Zunis. Navahos work as sheepherders and occasionally as field hands for the wealthier Zuni families. The reverse, Zunis working as hired hands for Navahos, almost never occurs. As herders, the Navahos live at the Zuni sheep camps and are especially in demand during spring lambing time and also during the fall Shalako season when the Zunis prefer the pueblo to the open range.

In the last half century there have been thirteen cases of Zuni-Navaho intermarriage. (These cases include intermarriages with *all* Navaho communities, not just with Rimrock Navaho.) There may have been other cases before 1900 but we have no data on them. Of the thirteen cases, ten involved Zuni men married to Navaho women, three Zuni women married to Navaho men. The marriages were of varying degrees of success and lasted for variable periods of time, ranging from a few months to several years. Since both tribes have structurally similar matrilocal residence patterns and similar roles for sons-in-law living matrilocally, it might be presumed that intermarriage might work out well. But there have been two major difficulties. The Zunis do not practice the mother-in-law avoidance pattern, and when Zuni men live matrilocally but do not avoid their mothers-in-law, the situation is laden with tension. Furthermore, the Zuni men are accustomed to a much higher standard of living — stone houses with beds, tables, chairs, and other comforts of life —

and are reluctant to spend their lives in a Navaho hogan. The result has been that most Zuni men have insisted upon living in Zuni, thereby taking their wives away from their Navaho families and traditional matrilocal pattern and creating great strain for the wives. Comparable difficulties arise when Navaho men live matrilocally in Zuni. They feel uncomfortable not observing the mother-in-law avoidance pattern, and they feel restricted by loss of the customary Navaho freedom of movement in the confines of settled Zuni life. In no case has a Navaho man moved his Zuni wife away from her matrilineal household and relatives in Zuni to live in a hogan with his Navaho relatives.

When differences in language, custom, and ceremony are added to these structural strains, it is rather astonishing that as many as thirteen marriages have occurred and have lasted as long as they did. When divorce occurs, the Navahos frequently attribute the difficulty either to witchcraft practiced by the Zunis[25] or to a belief that a Navaho should not have married into a Zuni "animal clan," such as badger or eagle. To marry into a "vegtable or food clan" of the Zunis, such as corn or pumpkin, is regarded as good, but not to marry into the "animal or bird clans." We know of no comparable Zuni belief concerning differences among Navaho clans with respect to intermarriage. The children of divorced parents almost always stay with the mother and are reared as Zunis or Navahos, as the case may be.

Indian–Spanish-American Relationships

The orientation of the two Indian groups toward Spanish-Americans have much in common, since both feel a kinship with the Spanish-Americans who are also a subordinated group vis-à-vis the Anglos in the Southwest. The three groups share the guest-host intervisiting pattern and have common witchcraft patterns which extend across the cultural boundaries. But there is considerably more ambivalence in the Spanish-American–Zuni relationship than in the Spanish-American–Navaho relationship. A few cases of Zuni–Spanish-American intermarriage indicate a closeness of relationship, but the Zuni prohibition against Spanish-Americans attending their ceremonials indicates very ancient feelings of hostility. The prohibition is now glossed over with mythological justifications[26] and is most commonly expressed by Zunis as "protecting" their Spanish-American friends from suffering supernatural harm. In the Spanish-American view, it is an arbitrary singling out of one group, and, while they generally accept the situation, they do not like it. Nevertheless, the Spanish-Americans feel a certain cultural kinship with the Zunis, especially since many of the Zunis are now nominally Catholic and live in the kind of houses and type of compact village settlement that are much like Spanish-American houses and villages. The Navahos, they say, "live in hogans in the woods" and are *muy tontos* (very stupid).

The key intercultural roles are: guest-host, employer-employee, bootlegger-customer, and intermarriage. The guest-host pattern described for the Navahos and Zunis is much the same in the relationships between the Spanish-American and these Indian groups. Spanish-Americans are frequently fed and housed by their Zuni friends when they come to trade or to visit the *Santo*.[27] Spanish-Americans feed and house Navaho and Zuni friends, but, due to the differential in living standards, they seldom stay all night in Navaho hogans, even though they do have meals with their Navaho friends. The Spanish language is the primary medium of communication between Spanish-Americans and the two Indian groups.

With respect to employer-employee relationships, Zunis hire Spanish-Americans to herd sheep and do other work for them. Spanish-American ranchers employ many Navahos as herders and ranch hands, but the reverse almost never happens. Navahos are regarded as potential laborers for both well-to-do Zunis and Spanish-Americans, and rich Zuni families also employ poor Spanish-Americans as laborers.

Before the repeal of Indian prohibition in 1953, the bootlegger-customer intercultural role was of crucial importance in relationships between the Spanish-Americans and Indians. It was clear that the best source of supply of liquor for the Indians was from Spanish-American saloonkeepers or storekeepers who sold liquor (without benefit of license) to both Navahos and Zunis. The mutual role expectations were that Indians could buy liquor from Spanish-American saloonkeepers by going to the back door or arriving under cover of darkness. In return for these bootleg services, it was understood that higher prices would be charged for the liquor. It was also understood that the Indians would not communicate news of the transaction to Anglos, who, it was thought, would be likely to report the Spanish-Americans in question to the law-enforcement officials. Since 1953, the law has changed, but it is significant in terms of cultural continuity of occupational role that the only saloonkeepers in the Rimrock-Zuni area are still Spanish-Americans who are now doing a good legal business selling liquor to both whites and Indians.

Some intermarriage between Indians and Spanish-Americans has taken place. We have data on five cases of Zuni–Spanish-American and on two Navaho–Spanish-American marriages. In the marriages between Zunis and Spanish-Americans, four have involved Zuni men and Spanish-American women. Three of these couples do not live in Zuni (except during visits) but live in Railtown where their husbands have jobs. The fourth couple lives in the pueblo where, despite the close affinal kinship tie, the Spanish-American wife is still prohibited from witnessing Zuni ceremonials. The children, however, are permitted to attend the ceremonials, although it is not clear whether or not they will be inducted into Zuni ceremonial positions when they grow up.

The fifth case is a special one and requires some explanation. The husband was a Yaqui Indian from Old Mexico who, in his youth, was captured by the Apaches. He escaped from the Apaches and came to Zuni where he spent the remainder of his life. He married a Zuni woman by whom he had several children and became a successful stockman and a governor of the pueblo. He later married a Navaho woman and had a large number of children by her in the Rimrock Navaho country.[28] This polygynous family situation, involving persons from three cultural backgrounds, lasted for many years and was altogether a remarkable development. Many of the offspring (who were both biological and cultural hybrids) have had notably successful careers, especially in the livestock business, in both the Zuni and Navaho communities. One of the Zuni children later became the governor and a prominent leader of one of the political factions in the pueblo; one of the Navaho children became a large sheepowner, a "star" rodeo performer, leader of a large Navaho "outfit," and the father of at least seventeen children by two wives and countless "affairs" with other Navaho women until his career was prematurely ended when he died of typhoid fever in 1943. (It is perhaps questionable as to whether these marriages should be classed with the other intercultural marriages between Spanish-Americans and Indians, for the husband was biologically and culturally Yaqui rather than Mexican or Spanish-American.)

The only other record we have of a Spanish-American–Navaho marriage in the Rimrock area was that between the Spanish-American bartender in Homestead and his second wife, who was reputedly half-Navaho. If so, she highly acculturated to Spanish-American culture; hence, the marriage was not of the same character as one between a full-blooded, traditional Navaho woman and a Spanish-American. There have been many cases of extramarital relationships and a number of children fathered by Spanish-American men in the Navaho population, but no other cases of intermarriage involving social recognition and the full assumption of family responsibilities.

A few minor points of structured intercultural contact should be mentioned. When the Spanish-Americans first settled in the region some lay proselytizing among the Navahos and Zunis took place. Resultant baptisms involved the extension of the Spanish-American godparental pattern across cultural boundaries. More recently, Spanish-Americans have expressed little concern with missionary work, although one Zuni couple are godparents of a Spanish-American child.

There is some incidence of native "curers" crossing cultural boundaries, especially with cures for witchcraft ailments. Spanish-Americans employ Zuni curers, even though the Zunis believe that curers should not practice on anyone who is not a Zuni. Sometimes the Spanish-Americans go to Zuni for treatment; on other occasions, the Zuni "witch doctor" is brought to the Spanish-American villages. There are also cases in which Navaho "singers" have recommended the use of certain plants to Spanish-Americans for curing ailments — with good results, according to our informants. There is also one instance of a Zuni going to a Spanish-American "curer" for witchcraft, but none of Navahos going to Spanish-American "curers."

Certain important witchcraft beliefs are shared by Zunis, Navahos, and Spanish-Americans, and witches in each culture can effectively work across boundaries and bewitch persons in the other cultures. The techniques for curing can be effective across these cultural boundaries. This is especially important in the case of Zuni–Spanish-American relationships. Spanish-Americans hire Zuni curers to "suck out" objects shot into the body by witches, or to use the "smoke treatment" in which green boughs are burned in a room with door

68

and windows shut, or to place various herbs on the body. Another patterned context for intercultural contact between these three cultures is the occasional taking of Navaho sweat baths with Navaho friends by certain Spanish-American and Zuni men.

INDIAN-MORMON RELATIONSHIPS

Both Zunis and Navahos recognize Mormons as a special class of Anglo-Americans; there are words in both languages designating them. The Zunis call them *Mumankwe* (Mormon people), the Navahos *Gamali*. Members of both Indian groups clearly remember the coming of the Mormon group to the Rimrock area. They view the Mormons both as missionaries and as important economic agents (traders, farmers, and ranchers). The conflict between the missionary and the economic aims of the Mormons reaches more intense form in their relationships with the Navahos than in their relationships with the Zunis, since the Mormons have replaced the Navahos on their best lands while no Zuni land has passed into Mormon hands. In terms of both the amount of contact and the economic and emotional investment involved, the Navaho-Mormon relationship is one of the most important points of intercultural contact in the whole region.

The Mormon view of the Indians is strongly colored by their conception of them as "Lamanites." The aims of the Mormons with respect to the Indians have been explicitly stated in many of the writings of their church. Talmage writes: "The Lamanites, while increasing in numbers, fell under the curse of divine displeasure; they became dark in skin and benighted in spirit, forgot the God of their fathers, lived in wild nomadic life, and degenerated into the fallen state in which the American Indians, their lineal descendants, were found by those who rediscovered the western continent." [29] In keeping with this conception of their origin, the Mormons believe that it is wrong to destroy the faith of the Indians, which is viewed not as a false but as a degenerate form of the "true" religion. Mormons allow Indians to practice their own ceremonials and even attempt to relate elements of Indian religion to elements in the Bible and the Book of Mormon. They tend to interpret the Zuni *koyemci*, or "mudheads," who function partly as ceremonial clowns, as representations of the twelve apostles of Christ. (Since the *koyemci* are only

69

ten in number and their ceremonial behavior is often obscene, establishing the connection takes a great deal of imagination.) Similarly, the Shalako ceremonial is viewed as a Zuni version of Christmas.

Missionary zeal to convert the "Lamanites" to Mormonism has been reawakened in recent years. Not only has the official missionary program been stepped up in tempo and numbers, but the establishment of a Nazarene Church among the Rimrock Navahos in 1954 has been a stimulus for local Mormon missionary activity.[30] The missionary emphasis has also been important in stimulating Mormons to learn about Indian customs and to learn to speak Navaho and Zuni, although English is now the usual language of communication. As a result, the Mormons know far more about Indian culture than the Texans do.

While the official missionary view of the Indians has been of crucial importance in intercultural relations over the years, two other features of the Mormon "cognitive map" of Indians often offset the missionary attitudes. The Mormons share many of the general Anglo-American attitudes of superiority toward peoples who are different in language and customs, who are "dirty" and "uncivilized." Indians are not regarded as social equals when it comes to intermarriage, interdining, and other forms of close social interaction. There is some difference in attitudes toward Zunis and Navahos in these respects. The Mormons regard the Zunis as "a higher type of Indian," "an agricultural home-loving people," whereas "the Navaho is more of a nomad; stays where night overtakes him, in a little brush shelter." There is some speculation in Rimrock as to whether the Zunis might not be "Nephites" rather than "Lamanites." Further, the successful operation of the Mormon economic system depends upon Indian laborers and Indian customers, especially Navahos, in the local trading posts.

While the Zunis and Navahos perceive the conflicting attitudes and aims of the Mormons in their relationships with them, the Mormons do not perceive this conflict at all realistically and are often surprised by the negative responses they receive to their missionary efforts. The Mormon bishop expressed astonishment when we asked how he expected to convert the Navahos when he and his kinsmen had taken their lands in the past and were currently treating them as dependent laborers and customers in the Mormon economic system.

The key intercultural roles between the Mormons and Indians are missionary-potential convert, trader-customer, and employer-employee. The local missionary work is directed by the head of the Stake Missionary Board, who lives in Rimrock and is the largest landowner and wealthiest Indian trader in the village. He was later chosen to be First Councilor of the President of the Mission Board for the whole Mormon church, a choice which seems strange considering his reputation for "exploiting" the Indians economically. The actual missionary work is done by local Rimrock people and by mission teams of young men sent in from other areas who work in pairs. The work is done by visiting Navaho hogans and Zuni homes, talking to the Indians, and urging them to come to church on Sunday. A mission church has been established for Sunday services in the Navaho area. The Zunis have rejected Mormon efforts to establish a mission chapel in the pueblo. The missionary efforts with the Navahos have been relatively successful in recent years. The local ward now carries some 112 Navahos on the rolls; one Navaho has been elevated to the Melchizedek priesthood, a second is a member of the Aaronic priesthood. The program has met with more resistance in Zuni. As of 1952, only five nuclear families had been converted and one man made a member of the Melchizedek priesthood.

The Mormon trader-Indian customer is the key intercultural role in the operation of both the Mormon and Navaho economic systems. The large trading post in Rimrock (with two smaller stores, one at La Peña and the other at the Navaho Day School) sells goods for a profit to the Navahos and buys Navaho wool, lambs, rugs, pinyon nuts, and other products, reselling them at a profit in the outside market. The trader advances credit to Navaho families for the purchase of food, clothing, automobiles, and other commodities. When an account becomes too large, the trader announces that there will be no more credit until some of the debt is repaid and, in his role as a recruiting agent for the railroad, urges the Navaho to go off and work on the railroad until he can pay his bill. Or the trader may accept a mortgage on the Navaho's sheep or on his automobile as a guarantee that the debt will be paid. The trader also controls sources of income coming into the Navaho community. He has strict control of the funds paid to the Navahos for the products they sell him; he also has matters arranged so that state welfare checks and off-season railroad unemployment checks come to the Navahos addressed in care of the trading post. By such measures the trader insures that bills are paid within a reasonable time — a fact of crucial importance to him since he usually pays cash each month to wholesale houses in Railtown that sell him the goods he resells to the Indians.

The two-way profit and the tight control over income and credit are standard operating procedures throughout Navaho country. Given the obligations which the trader has to the outside market and to the outside banks which finance him, the system is probably necessary for the successful operation of a trading post. But it has the effect of keeping the Navahos in a dependent economic status and of stifling their initiative to learn about and assume more economic responsibility.*

The employer-employee relationship takes the form mainly of Mormons hiring Navahos to work by the day on farms and ranches, especially at harvest time, and to do various kinds of work on construction jobs in the village of Rimrock. In these wage-work situations, the Navahos are seldom fed and housed with the families of the Mormon employers; they either camp out at the edge of town or are given a small outlying shack or shed to live in. (This is in striking contrast with Spanish-American and Zuni employers who often feed and house the Navahos in their own homes.)

The guest-host relationship shared by Zunis, Navahos, and Spanish-Americans is by and large absent from intercultural contacts between Indians and either Mormons or Texans. Occasionally an Indian will be given a meal in a Mormon home (usually fed separately) and sometimes will be invited to stay all night. On rare occasions, Mormon men eat meals in Navaho hogans. But the usual day-to-day contact takes place in the missionary situation, in the trading post, or in the wage-work situation.

Other minor forms of patterned intercultural contact occur sporadically. Mormons have been known to seek advice on herbal treatments for certain disorders from Navaho curers; one or two Mormon men have taken sweat baths with Navahos; there have been a number of illicit sexual affairs involving Mormon men and Navaho women. No intermarriage has occurred between the local Mormon and

* The trading system in Zuni pueblo operates in much the same way, except that the traders are Anglos rather than Mormons.

Navaho populations, and the sanctions are strong against such an occurrence. The Mormons frequently bury dead Navahos, a task which the Navahos, with their fear of the dead, are delighted to turn over to the Mormons.

INDIAN-TEXAN RELATIONSHIPS

The Zuni-Texan relationship is the most tenuous of the intercultural connections in this area. Most of the Zuni informants failed to characterize the Texans as a special group of Anglos, and it is apparent that contacts have been slight. The Zunis recognize that there is a group of people living in Homestead, a community they pass through on their way to Salt Lake to gather salt, who live by growing pinto beans. One Zuni family has come to know a number of Texan homesteaders who went to them for help when they were stuck in the mud near the Zuni ranch. The Navahos have had much closer contacts with the Texans, especially at La Peña, but also at Homestead. They designate the Texans as a separate group whom they call *Tejanos,* following the Spanish usage. Their image of them involves most centrally the fact of their engaging in bean-farming.

In the Texan group there is considerable variation in the image held of the Indians. Many informants in Homestead, after twenty years of residence in proximity to these two Indian cultures, could not clearly distinguish between Zunis and Navahos, but tended to think of them all alike as "Indians." Thus, although the dress styles of Zuni and Navaho women are distinctly different, the informants could not distinguish between them when they saw them on the streets of Railtown. Others could distinguish between the two tribes, usually thinking of the Zunis as a "higher type of Indian" and speaking of them as "more industrious farming people" who live "in better houses than the Navahos." The Navahos were commonly regarded as the "poorest and most ignorant people on earth." Finally, there were two Texan families who had previously lived in very close proximity to Navahos in La Peña area and had depended upon them as their closest neighbors. These Texans learned to speak the Navaho language — unlike other homesteaders, who speak neither Navaho nor Zuni — and continue to maintain close relationships with the Navahos. They not only employ them on their farms, but also the Navahos eat with them and have close and warm contacts with them.

73

The other Texans single out these families for special comment, generally failing to understand how they "can stand to have Indians eating at their tables and sitting in their houses."

The most important role in the Navaho-Texan relationship is that of employer-employee. In years when the bean crop promises to be good and when the weeds threaten to take over the crop, large numbers of Navahos are hired to hoe the fields and help with the harvesting operations. But these relationships are (except for the two families mentioned above) strictly economic and highly formalized. Generally, the Navahos camp in the woods near the fields where they are working and contacts with the Texan families are slight.

It is highly significant that the trader-customer role and the missionary-potential convert role are unimportant in the Navaho-Texan relationship. Although a few Navahos trade at Homestead stores, the Homestead storekeepers have never encouraged their business. They do not like the idea of having Indians in their stores which are "for white folks," and they have never learned the language and the trading habits of the Navahos as the Mormons have. Nor is there any attempt on the part of the Homestead churches to do missionary work among the Indians. However, Homestead itself is regarded as a mission area by the churches and there is still much missionary work to be done among the homesteaders.

The homesteader-Navaho relationship is undergoing an important change. With the shift from federal to state responsibility for Indian education, large numbers of Navaho children are now enrolled in the Homestead school system. The Texan community is ambivalent about this development. They do not like the idea of having Indian children in their classrooms; but the increased enrollment makes it possible to maintain the school system in the face of decreasing Texan population. This development is likely to have a strong influence on relations between these two groups.

MORMON-TEXAN RELATIONSHIPS

The Texans' contacts with Mormons back on the Plains were limited to acquaintances with a few missionaries. For the most part, they held the familiar stereotype of Mormons as people who had a "peculiar religion" and "more than one wife." In the Rimrock area, the Texans came to admire and envy the Mormons' economic organization, their irrigated land, and more promising prospects for crops each year. Although denominationalism is rife in the Texan communities, they do not regard the Mormon religion as an acceptable variety of Christianity. It was a shock for the Texans to discover that the Mormons dance in their church and that they open and close their dances with a prayer. In recalling the first time he attended a Mormon dance, one of the Texans commented:

> We didn't know anything about Mormons. Never been around them much. Well, we went to that dance and directly they said a prayer. All of our women were sitting around talking, yackety-yackety, and somebody tapped them on the shoulder and said, "they're prayin." And you should have seen the look on them women's faces when they saw them Mormons prayin' to start a dance!

The Texans also tend to regard the Mormons as "cliquish" and somewhat "unfriendly" and fail to understand why anyone "wants to live all bunched up the way them Mormons do."

The Mormons consider their way of life superior to that of the homesteaders. They commonly call them "Tejaners," a Mormon version of the Spanish usage *Tejano*. Some Mormons will admit that the Texans have the virtue of being more friendly, of "mixing more with others," and the Texan efforts in the face of severe farming risks are admired, but in general the Texan way of life is regarded as "rough" and "immoral." The Mormons have attempted to persuade the Texans to take up the "better" Mormon way of life. For a time they gave almost monthly sermons in the Homestead Community Church. There have been no converts in Homestead, the only two Mormons in the community being Mormon wives married into the group, but one family has been converted in the La Peña community. This conversion is a particularly interesting case, since the man has an earlier record of making "bootleg corn likker" and selling it illegally to the Indians. But he gave up his "evil ways," became a good Mormon, and in fact, did missionary work for the Mormons among the Navahos. One Texan woman from the La Peña group was also converted when she married a Mormon husband from Rimrock.

Although there is some trading in livestock, feed, and other crops, the most important contacts between the two groups are not economic but social and recreational. The recreational contacts take the form of baseball games scheduled between the two village teams

75

and attendance at each others' dances and rodeos. But considerable strain in the relationship is evident; many "good Mormons" hesitate to attend Texan dances, because they risk coming into close contact with the drinking parties which are inevitable aspects of these affairs. Most Mormons who attend Texan dances regularly are "Jack Mormons" who enjoy the opportunity to escape the watchful eyes of their elders and have a good time at the Texan "hoedowns." And the Mormons dislike having too many Texans at their dances in Rimrock because they always bring liquor and not only get "likkered up" themselves but generously provide liquor for the "Jack Mormons."

The closest social contacts are maintained by the teenagers of the two communities who interdate. These courtships have led to eight intermarriages: four Mormon girls married Texan men, and four Mormon men married Texan girls. One of the latter type ended in divorce after a few years, but the others have been relatively successful. Although there has been considerable pressure on them to do so, the Texan husbands have not joined the Mormon church; one of the Texan women has joined the Mormon church but not the others. In almost all cases the children of these mixed marriages have been "blessed" and will probably become Mormons.

A ninth intermarriage has occurred between a Mormon girl from Utah and a Texan in Homestead. In this case the wife was previously married to a Mormon who was a Marine "buddy" of this homesteader. Before the Mormon was killed at Iwo Jima, his "buddy" promised to look after the wife if anything happened to him. After the war, the Texan went to Utah to call on the widow and later married her and brought her back to New Mexico. The intercutulral strains in this marriage epitomized the conflicts between Mormon and Texan values. The Mormon wife (and her family) tried to persuade the Texan to become a Mormon and give up drinking and smoking. She was also worried by the fact that she was "sealed" to her first husband "for all eternity"; yet she loves her second husband more than the first. Meanwhile the Texan husband scoffs at the drinking and smoking taboos and the Mormon beliefs concerning the afterlife. The difficulties were finally resolved after ten years, when in 1956 the husband became a Mormon and the family moved to the Mormon community of Bluewater, New Mexico.

76

Anglo–Spanish-American Relationships

From the point of view of the total populations involved, the Anglo–Spanish-American relationship is the most important intercultural boundary in the contemporary Southwest. The state of New Mexico is about 40 percent Spanish-American in population, and Spanish is still an "official" state language in the sense that legal notices must be printed in both English and Spanish.

Various segments of the Anglo population have reacted quite differently to contacts with Spanish-Americans. This contrast is sharp with respect to the two varieties of Anglo-American culture represented in the Rimrock area, the Mormons and the Texans. The Mormons define the Spanish-Americans as "Lamanites," hence important potential converts. They are also thought to be in need of conversion in order that they might acquire the "good living habits" of the Mormons. The Mormons are bothered by the fact that the Spanish-Americans have been the main source of supply of liquor to the Indians. The Spanish-Americans are recognized as being strongly Catholic and the difficulty of persuading them to change churches is considered realistically. But, just as the Mormons have considerable knowledge of Indian culture stemming from their missionary interests, they have considerable knowledge of Spanish-American culture, and many Rimrock Mormons speak some Spanish, a few fluently. The knowledge of Spanish-American and Mexican culture is particularly impressive in the Rimrock families who lived in Chihuahua, Mexico, for a number of years before they settled at Rimrock.

The Spanish-American image of Mormons is less clear than their image of Texans. Few items stand out as characteristic Mormon symbols, except the fact that the Mormons attempt to proselytize them. The general picture is one of a rather distant and neutral relationship, from the Spanish-American point of view. The key intercultural roles are focused around economic trade, especially in livestock and in employer-employee situations: Spanish-Americans have worked in Mormon fields and Mormons have occasionally been hired by the richer Spanish-Americans. There have been no intermarriages in the Rimrock area.

In contrast, the Texan–Spanish-American relationship is characterized by affect on both sides, and both groups have well defined and explicit ideas of what they think the other is like. What is perhaps most persistent in the Texan cognitive orientations is their cultural "opaqueness." Despite close contacts with Atrisco for over twenty years, they know almost nothing about the essential elements of Spanish-American culture. Only a handful of the Texans speak more than a few words of Spanish. The Texans frequently attend the dances accompanying the annual fiesta, but none of the informants (other than the two Texans married to Spanish-Americans) had any conception of why the fiesta was held on a certain day each autumn, nor did they know that San José is the patron saint in whose honor the fiesta is given. The Texans manifest more intolerance towards the "Mexicans" than any group in the area and tend to think of them as "chile-pickers" or "greasers."

The Spanish-Americans, by contrast, are one of the most tolerant cultural groups in the region. They think of the other groups as having different *costumbres*. While they prefer their own *costumbres,* they feel that the others have a right to maintain their own customs. Almost all Spanish-Americans speak English which they have learned at school. They know more about *Tejano* culture than the Texans know about Spanish-American customs.

The key intercultural roles are storekeeper-customer, employer-employee, recreational (especially attendance at dances), teacher-pupil, and intermarriage. The stores in Homestead are owned and managed by the Texans, and, since Atrisco no longer has a store, the Spanish-Americans do a great deal of their trading there. They often stay to loaf and visit with the storekeeper and the Texan customers. The bartender-customer role is similar, except that in this case a Spanish-American owns the bar and his customers are both Spanish-Americans and Texans. In quantity of contact, the intercultural situations in the store and bar are the most important day-to-day contacts between the two groups. There is another economic intercultural role, for each year Texans employ Spanish-Americans to work in the bean fields. The Spanish-American fieldhands usually live at home and travel to and from work each day, but they may be fed by the Texan employer in his home at noon.

The most important intercultural recreation in the contemporary scene is provided by the dances which used to be held in both Atrisco and at La Peña. For the most part, the males who choose dancing partners from the other group are a few Texans who are either married to Spanish-American women or are for other reasons more tolerant in their attitudes toward other cultures, and a few of the most acculturated Spanish-Americans, such as sons of the former *patrón* of Atrisco, who may dance with Texan women. A more common Spanish-American response is that the Texan girls are *muy orgullosas* (very proud or haughty) and do not want to dance with a *Mexicano*. The political battle for control of the school system was finally won by the Texans as the Spanish-American population declined, and all Spanish-Americans of school age now attend school taught by Texan teachers in Homestead. The Spanish-Americans accept it as inevitable that their children will be attending a Texan-controlled school.

Despite the deep antagonism between the two groups, three intercultural marriages have taken place. One of these occurred between the daughter of a Texan schoolteacher and a young Spanish-American. This couple did not remain in the area, and there is little data on the success of the marriage. The other marriages occurred between Texan men and two daughters of the former *patrón* of Atrisco. These marriages have been successful, and the families are still living in the Homestead area. One couple is childless, but the other couple has four children, all of whom are being reared as Catholics, and the Texan husband has also joined the Catholic church. There is much discussion of these two marriages on the part of both groups. On the whole, the Texan husbands, as would be expected, are more fully accepted in the Spanish-American community than are their wives in the Texan community. Although the four children of the Texan–Spanish-American marriage are fair-skinned and brown or blonde in hair color, there is a tendency of both groups to consider them as racial mixtures. The Texans think of the children as "half-breeds"; the Spanish-Americans call them *coyotes,* with the connotation that although they are good children now, they may not turn out well in the long run.

Over and above the special historical events which have characterized the intercultural contacts in the immediate Rimrock area, there are many dimensions to the potential or actual conflict between Texans and Spanish-Americans in the Southwest which make long-range adjustments extremely difficult. There is important ecological conflict in the question of which group dominates the land base in this area, which was originally under Spanish and later under Mexican control but has become increasingly Texan. This conflict is especially acute when the traditional rancher-*versus*-farmer antagonism is added. In many areas, such as Homestead, the Spanish-Americans are predominantly Republicans, whereas the Texans are Democrats. The religious conflict between Catholics and Protestants is also involved. Racial and ethnic differences, real and supposed, have deep roots in Mexican and Texan history and are being perpetuated in the Southwest. Finally, the value-orientations of the two cultures are diametrically opposed at most points, with the Texans emphasizing future-time, mastery over nature, individualism, and a high degree of intolerance and opaqueness in intercultural relations, the Spanish-Americans emphasizing present-time, subjugation to nature, hierarchical and lineal social relationships, and a relatively high degree of tolerance in intercultural relations. It is not surprising that the local scene has been characterized by a great deal of difficulty between the "Mexicans" and *"Tejanos."*

INTERCULTURAL HIERARCHIES

In three important respects these interacting groups are segments of a larger system of relationships:

(1) From the point of view of the American national economic and political system, the five cultures must be regarded as subcultures. Each is related significantly to the prices, markets, factory goods, credit structures, and so on of our national economic system, and each is a segment of a political order in which the ultimate control of force is in the hands of the United States Government.

(2) Except in the case of Zuni culture, which exists only in our research area, the populations of each of the cultures studied are localized manifestations of cultural groups that have significant extensions outside the Rimrock area — the Rimrock Navaho are one band of the Navaho tribe; the Spanish-Americans in Tijeras and Atrisco form outlying communities of the Spanish-speaking population centered in the northern Rio Grande Valley; the Rimrock Mormons are a southwestern outpost of the intermountain Mormon "empire"; and the Texans are scattered from Texas itself westward to the Pacific Coast and elsewhere.[31]

(3) In varying degrees the five groups are bound together in an

80

Zuni

Former Caciques of Zuni

Looking southeast, Corn Mountain in left background

Zuni

View from a Zuni rooftop

Old Mission Church

A Navaho girl herds sheep

Navaho

Man smoking hand-rolled cigarette

A portrait of wrinkles and character

Navaho

Hair-combing, Navaho-style

Baby in cradleboard

Navaho

Girl in a velvet blouse embellished with coins

Spanish Americans

Catholic church and schoolyard in Atrisco

The church altar

Spanish Americans

A cow wanders by deserted houses

A rancher's sons

A Mormon hoeing in his irrigated garden

Mormons

House in Rimrock village

Rimrock reservoir in background, a mile from the village

Principal helping to construct new school

Texas Homesteaders

This church stands unused since Homestead population decline

White-faced Herefords grazing

Texas Homesteaders

House and sheds amid pinyon and juniper trees

Rodeo grounds near the center of town

Texas Homesteaders

Homesteader cultivating bean fields

internal areal system of relationships. Each tends to occupy one or more roles vis-à-vis the others, and a disturbance in intercultural relations between two of the groups will affect the relationships which each has with the other three cultures. For example, an increase in Mormon pressure upon the Navahos to join their church might result in more Navahos becoming Mormons, thereby disturbing the liquor business which the Spanish-Americans do with the Navahos and also disturbing Navaho-Zuni guest-host relationships (Zunis disapprove of Navahos joining the Mormon church).

Are the five cultures arranged in a social rank or prestige and power hierarchy? The answer is complicated because the cultures vary as to their definition of the nature of the hierarchical arrangements, but there are two basic interpretations. The Mormon and Texan view is that the rank order of the cultures in terms of both prestige and power is, in descending order: Mormons — Texans — Spanish-Americans — Zunis — Navahos. The Zuni and Navaho interpretation would tend to follow these lines:

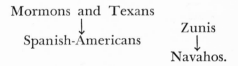

$$\begin{array}{ccc} \text{Mormons and Texans} & & \\ \downarrow & & \text{Zunis} \\ \text{Spanish-Americans} & & \downarrow \\ & & \text{Navahos.} \end{array}$$

They see the Anglo Mormons and Texans, undifferentiated in this respect, as "superior" to the Spanish-Americans; but they think of themselves as off to one side in a separate hierarchy with Zunis above Navahos and with Zunis ranking on a level with, or perhaps higher than, Spanish-Americans.

The Spanish-American interpretation is similar to that of the Mormons and Texans, except that, like the Indians, they do not clearly differentiate Mormons from Texans in a rank order and they often feel the Spanish-Americans are as "good" as the Mormons and Texans. They do, however, agree in placing the Zunis above the Navahos. There is general agreement that the Navahos are at the bottom of the rank order in both power and prestige in the Rimrock area.

One of the crucial bodies of evidence for this intercultural hierarchy is the over-all pattern of intermarriage. Going down the hierarchy, Mormons marry Texans but not Spanish-Americans or Indians; Texans marry Spanish-Americans but not Indians; Spanish-

Americans marry Zunis but not Navahos (except for the two quite special cases described); Zunis marry Navahos.

This finding is buttressed by the data on employer-employee relationships. Going up the hierarchy this time, Navahos frequently work for the members of all the other groups; Zunis are employees of Spanish-American, Mormon, and Texan employers, but almost never work for Navahos; Spanish-Americans work for Mormons and Texans, rarely for Zunis, never for Navahos; Texans are frequently employed by Mormon employers, occasionally by Spanish-American employers, but never by Indians; Mormons sometimes work for Texans, in rare instances for Spanish-Americans, but never for Indians.

The Learning of Values

JOHN W. M. WHITING,
ELEANOR HOLLENBERG CHASDI,
HELEN FAIGIN ANTONOVSKY,
and BARBARA CHARTIER AYRES

CERTAIN DOMINANT VALUES of a culture influence the way in which a parent responds to her child. If love and warmth are an important positive value for social interaction, this may govern a mother's behavior toward her child, even though at the same time she may believe she is spoiling him. In those societies where parents believe that their own actions, rather than fate or heredity, have some effect upon the moral development of their children, the value system of the culture will be an important part of what is consciously and intentionally transmitted to the child. Certain aspects of the child-rearing process seem to have the effect of, if not creating, at least strengthening values far beyond the conscious intent of the agents of socialization.

In the summers of 1950 and 1951, research teams[1] from the Laboratory of Human Development of the Harvard Graduate School of Education carried out a research project focusing on socialization in three of the groups under consideration in this volume — the Texans, the Mormons, and the Zuni. The field work consisted of ethnographic and standardized interviews, participant observation, and various pencil and paper tests given to a sample of children in each society. The sample, consisting of all the children in the third through the sixth grades in the Mormon and Texan communities, and from the fourth, fifth, and sixth grades of the Zuni Country Day School, is described in Table 3.

All the mothers of the children tested in the two Anglo groups were interviewed on their child-rearing practices. Since several

mothers had two or more children in school, there were fewer interviews with mothers than children tested — fifteen Mormons and
sixteen Texans. Since it was not feasible to interview all the Zuni
mothers of the child sample, fifteen were chosen, on the basis of
their knowledge of English and their willingness to cooperate, ap-

Table 3. Sample of children tested in the summer of 1950.

Group	Number of boys	Number of girls	Age range (years)	Mean age
Mormon	8	15	8–14	10.5
Texan	13	12	9–13	10.8
Zuni	32	43	10–14	12.4

proximately the number in the other two groups. The sample of
Zuni mothers is thus somewhat biased toward acculturation. Although their children were in no way strikingly different in their
responses to the tests from the remaining Zuni children tested, this
bias should be kept in mind.

The interviews were standard only in that the same topics were
covered, and generally, but not invariably, in the same order. Questions were not asked in standard form, nor were standard probes
employed. Although a few Mormon interviews were electrically recorded and transcribed verbatim, most were dictated from notes
directly after the interview and consisted of from eight to twelve
pages of single-spaced typescript.

The tests used, all of the paper and pencil variety, were administered to the children in groups. This was done in the school at Zuni,
but since school was not in session in the two Anglo communities,
the children had to be brought together especially for the purpose.
The details of those tests will be described when their results are
reported.

THE SETTING

Since socialization takes place in the context of the total society, it
is necessary to review certain elements of the cultural setting which
have particular relevance to child-rearing: the size and type of
dwelling; the membership and authority structure of the household;

the economic responsibilities of each parent and the place where each carries on his or her tasks.

The flat-roofed Zuni houses vary considerably both in size and in number of rooms. We have no information on the number of rooms for the houses of our Zuni sample but they are similar to the three dwellings described by Roberts which had three, six, and eight rooms respectively, occupied by six, ten, and twenty regular household members and three, five, and three "associate" members.[2] The Mormon houses vary in size from two to six rooms, the modal size being four. The average number of members of the nuclear Mormon household is between four and five. The typical Texan house consists of three rooms, and the size of their nuclear household also approximates five members. The modal number of persons per room is one for the Mormons, two for the Texans, and three for the Zuni. The Texans are considerably more crowded than the Mormons, but less so than the Zuni. All but one of the Texan mothers living in a three-room house volunteered the information that they were planning to add a room since they desired more privacy.

The Zuni house is occupied during the day not only by all adult female members and by children not attending school but also by the majority of the men. Where sheepherding is a major economic pursuit, the adult males take turns, two at a time, in tending their combined flocks.[3] Most Zuni men are therefore free to remain at home all but a few months of the year to work on silver and jewelry, which is done in the house. It is rare, however, that one would find either a Texan or a Mormon man in the house during a weekday, except at mealtime, and for the Texans, when the bean crop must be attended to, the whole family may be in the fields.

In each group as many rooms as possible are set aside exclusively for sleeping. However, this is not always possible. A living-room-bedroom combination is frequently resorted to by the Texans. In no instance in the Anglo groups is space used for sleeping also used for cooking and eating, although this may be done in Zuni households. This functional division of rooms leads to unusually crowded sleeping arrangements. Although one Mormon mentioned with pride that each of her children had his or her own bedroom, this is the exception rather than the rule for any of the groups. In both Anglo groups there is a tendency for the parents and the younger

85

children to sleep in one room and the older children, separated according to sex if possible, to occupy the other bedroom or bedrooms. Among the Zuni, the pattern is for each nuclear family in a house to have a sleeping room of its own. Thus, the grandparents, with perhaps some of the younger grandchildren, occupy one bedroom, and each married daughter with her husband and children, if possible, has her own room. The youngest married daughter is the last to get a room of her own and may share a bedroom with her parents.

The three groups differ in the authority patterns within the household. The Mormon father is ideally the patriarch, and in most of the households of our sample, he is considered the final authority in all family matters. The Texan husband and wife are supposed to discuss and come to common agreement on matters of policy; although either may be dominant, in the majority of the families studied, authority is shared. Among the Zuni, the authority pattern is much more complex. Usually neither of the parents of young children is in a position of final authority. Decisions regarding household matters are made by the matrilineal grandparents, particularly the mother's mother who is the owner of the house. Before making any major decision, however, she would generally consult her husband and, more particularly, her brother who, although he does not live in the house, is an important associate member and frequent visitor. The typical Zuni household, therefore, would have a hierarchy somewhat as follows: (1) the grandmother, (2) her brother, (3) the grandfather, (4) the mother, (5) the mother's brother, (6) the father, and (7) the child.

The mothers of our sample were asked whether they or their husbands had primary responsibility for policy decisions with respect to child-rearing. Their answers are summarized in Table 4. Unfortunately, the Zuni informants were not asked about the au-

Table 4. Responsibility (in percentages) for child-rearing policy as reported by mothers.

Responsibility assigned to	Mormons	Texans	Zuni
Primarily mother	11	11	42
Both parents	22	67	50
Primarily father	67	22	8
N =	15	16	15

thority of grandparents which would have been a more pertinent question. Their answers nevertheless indicate the relatively high responsibility of Zuni mothers in contrast to the other two societies.

There are also clear differences in the economic systems of the three groups. The Mormon and Zuni economic system may be described as bureaucratic, whereas the Texans' is entrepreneurial. The Morman Land and Development Company and the Zuni Sheep Camp groups bring together the heads of households in joint economic enterprise involving the differentiation of authority, whereas each adult Texan male is his own boss, and works his own land, sharing his profits only with his wife and children.

In sum, children in the three societies are born into contrasting physical and social settings. The world of the Zuni child consists of a medium-sized house, whose occupants, in addition to his own parents and siblings, are his matrilineally related aunts, uncles, and grandparents. Final authority in this group is jointly held by his grandmother and her brother, the latter being an associate member of the household generally living elsewhere. The Mormon child is born into a patriarchal, nuclear family household living in a moderate-sized house. The Texan child is born in a small, crowded house whose members consist of the nuclear family with authority shared between mother and father. Mormon and Zuni fathers work with other men in joint economic enterprises; the Texan father works on his own.

INFANCY

Mormon and Texan infants generally sleep in the same bed with their parents as long as they are nursing. The reasons given for this, however, are quite different in the two societies. Mormon informants explain that they do this to keep their babies warm. As one mother whose infant slept in the parental bed for eighteen months put it: "It's very cold out here and we were in a cold house and he couldn't keep warm sleeping alone, so he slept with me. And you know, every time I'd touch the baby he'd wake up and want to nurse, and sometimes I'd go off to sleep and he'd nurse for two or three hours." None of the Texan informants mentioned the cold, and their rationalizations were more varied. Two said that they were afraid that the infant would roll off the bed if he were alone, and one of them

87

claimed that it was easier to nurse the infant if he were sleeping with her. Crowded living conditions, however, seem in fact to be the reason. All Texan families living in houses with three rooms or less took their infants into the parental bed, whereas three of the four families who had four rooms or more did not do so. From this, and from the fact that several Texans complained of the lack of privacy, it appears that their ideal would be for the infant to sleep alone, even though this was not possible for the majority of families. By contrast, the Mormon ideal seemed to be for the infant to share the parental bed. Even though their houses are larger, only one Mormon informant clearly indicated that an infant should sleep in his own crib. Zuni infants usually sleep bound in a cradleboard which at night is placed next to the parental bed. Thus, although, as in the other two groups, the Zuni infant sleeps near its parents and may be nursed during the night with ease, he is not in physical contact with the mother as is the Mormon and Texan infant.

With rare exceptions, in all three groups the infant shares the bed with or is close to not only the mother but also the father. Of course, the Zuni father is sometimes away for several months at a time performing his sheepherding duties and may from time to time stay at his sister's place. In at least one Texan family, the husband had an out-of-town job which kept him away during the week. In this instance, the mother slept with her two-year-old son while he was away, and the father slept with him during the weekends, when the mother shared a bed with her ten-year-old daughter. In another Texan family each parent slept with one of the children, the mother with her nine-year-old daughter and the father with a four-year-old son.

During the day, Zuni infants have the most constant attention from a wide variety of caretakers. This is well illustrated in Roberts' observations of the activities of a Zuni household. From 7:00 A.M. until 8:30 A.M. a Zuni boy of eighteen months was held, carried, played with, and walked by the following members of the household: grandmother (age fifty-one), grandfather (age fifty-eight), aunt (age nineteen), aunt's husband (age twenty-seven), aunt (age fourteen), aunt (age forty), uncle (age eight), and cousin (age three). During all but five minutes of this period he was either held or closely attended by someone. During this time the mother finished her breakfast, cleared the table, washed the dishes, and started on her silver work. At 8:30, the infant began to fuss and cry, whereupon the mother got up from the bench, came and took the baby, strapped him in a cradleboard, nursed him, changed his diapers, and rocked him to sleep.[4]

The daily life of the Texan infant is quite different. Although we do not have the detailed observational record to make exact comparison with the Zuni, there are a number of obvious differences. Early in the morning the father usually leaves for work and, except in the summer, the older children go off to school, and the mother is left alone to do the housework and care for her infant and younger children. In addition, most Texan mothers feel that they have to aid in the economic support of the family, and therefore, assume responsibility for a home garden. It is usually near the house, so that as soon as the mother has finished the housework she can go outside to work in it, leaving the infant inside but able to hear if he sounds disturbed. During planting and harvesting she may also help her husband in the bean fields, in which case she may either leave the infant in the care of an older daughter or take him with her and leave him bedded in the truck. Although older daughters of the family help the mothers with housekeeping and baby-tending whenever they are not in school or working in the fields, the Texan nuclear household cannot approach the manpower for infant care found in the Zuni extended household. Of necessity, the Texan infant learns to be alone and to fend for himself at a very early age.

The nuclear household of the Mormons is in many respects similar to that of the Texans. Here again, the father generally leaves for work in the morning, and the mother must do the housework. Two factors, however, make the Mormon situation quite different from the Texan. In the Mormon value system baby care ranks first as a woman's duty. Furthermore, according to Mormon ideals and church doctrine, a Mormon mother is not expected to do outside work. A pamphlet put out by the Church describing the ideal role of a mother begins with the following statement: "A good wife and mother is not expected to do any grand works outside her home. Her province lies in gentleness, contented housewifery, and management of her children." [5] The Mormon mother is encouraged to and does devote considerably more time and attention to the care of her infants. Every Mormon mother in our sample who had children under two and a half years of age held her child in her lap during most of the interview. In contrast only one of the Texan mothers with small children did so, most of them leaving their infants in charge of an older sibling, or letting them play by themselves. A typical comment of a Texan mother when a small child called for attention during the interview was: "Don't bother me. Can't you see I'm talking with Miss Z?" — a comment never made by a Mormon mother.

Texan fathers are more likely to take responsibilities for the care of infants than fathers in the other two groups. Of eleven cases, three fathers helped a great deal, four helped some, and four assumed no responsibility for infant care. Only one Mormon mother reported that her husband helped appreciably in infant care, and no Zuni mothers did so. It should not be inferred from this that fathers who did not feel responsible for feeding or changing the diapers of infants ignored them. The typical father in all three groups would hold infants and play with them from time to time, but except among the Texans, the responsibility for infant care was felt to be exclusively woman's work.

Breast feeding is practiced by the majority of mothers in all three societies. Two Mormon and two Zuni mothers of our sample did not breast-feed one of their children for medical reasons. They did, however, breast-feed all the others. This was also true of three of the Texan mothers, but in addition there were two Texan mothers with three and four children who bottle fed all of their children, apparently from preference. Table 5 indicates the frequency with

Table 5. Frequency of various methods of infant feeding.*

Method	Mormon	Texan	Zuni
Breast to cup	34	27	62
Breast and bottle to cup	4	12	7
Breast to bottle to cup	10	12	1
Bottle to cup	2	10	2

* Figures indicate the number of infants reported to have been fed in the manner listed. Many of these children are members of the same families.

which four methods of infant feeding were practiced by mothers in the three societies: breast feeding followed by weaning to the cup, breast feeding followed by bottle feeding before weaning to the cup, breast feeding supplemented by concurrent feeding with the bottle before weaning to the cup, and bottle feeding only before weaning to the cup. Eighty-six percent of the Zuni children were entirely breast fed, as were 68 percent of the Mormons and 44 percent of the Texans.

Texan and Mormon mothers who breast-fed their children gave different reasons for doing so. Some Texan mothers commented that it was cheaper or more convenient than bottle feeding, but most of them claimed that it was more natural and healthy for the child. A number of Mormon mothers expressed similar sentiments. The typical Mormon response, however, which was not made by any of the Texan mothers is illustrated by the following quotation: "Oh, yes, it's much better to breast feed your children. Then you're closer to them, you have to hold them and love them up and show them a lot of affection. With the bottle you can just lay them down and give them the bottle — you don't have the closeness, the feeling of warmth and affection that you do when you breast feed them. It's very important to be close and warm to your children."

Half of our Texan mothers reported having fed their infants on a fairly strict schedule as compared with two of nineteen Mormon mothers and no Zuni mothers. One of the Texan mothers apologized for feeding her children on a self-demand schedule by saying, "I know it's thought best nowadays to follow a strict schedule, but that just isn't my temperament." Several mothers mentioned either that the "doctor" recommended a schedule or that they had read it was best.

The Texans wean their children earlier than Zuni or Mormon mothers. The median age of weaning for those Texan mothers who breast-fed their children was nine months, with a range of six to thirteen months. For the Mormons the median age was eleven months, with a range of from eight to seventeen months. The median age of weaning for the Zuni was two years, although there was an essentially bi-modal distribution, with nearly 40 percent of the sample stating that they had weaned their children at the age of twelve months. A few Zuni mothers reported having nursed at least one of their children for considerably longer than the median age, the extremes being four years reported by one mother and five by another. One of these mothers claimed that nursing was necessary because she could not afford to buy milk.

91

Bottle-fed Texan children were weaned somewhat later than their breast-fed peers, the median age being twelve months as against nine months. This was true also for the Mormon girls, but not for the boys. The median age of beginning weaning from the bottle for the Mormon girls was eighteen months, in contrast to twelve months for their breast-fed peers. Some informants from both the Texan and Mormon groups reported using the bottle as a pacifier until the child was two years old or more. One five-year-old Mormon girl still was taking the bottle to bed with her.

Most Texan parents reported that they had little difficulty weaning their children, but many Mormon and Zuni parents reported that their children were quite disturbed by the process. This confirms the finding of previous studies that weaning between the ages of one and two years is more disturbing to children than either earlier or later.[6] Texan and Mormon children who were weaned before twelve months and Zuni children who were weaned after two years caused less trouble than children in any of the groups weaned between twelve months and two years.

The pattern for toilet training is similar to that for weaning. The Texans begin earliest (the median age is nine months) and complete the training earliest (with median age between twelve and fifteen months). The Mormons begin when the child is a year old, and complete the process between eighteen months and two years. The Zuni start last, typically at eighteen months, and complete training when the child is between two and three years old. Twelve of eighteen Texan mothers and nine of fourteen Mormon mothers reported that they had considerable difficulty in training their children and had to resort to punitive measures, most frequently shaming the children by telling them they were dirty. Only three of sixteen Zuni mothers reported any difficulty in training and they used scolding, spanking, and not letting the offenders go out to play as punitive techniques.

During infancy, then, Zuni child-rearing is characterized by diffused and constant care and late training, the Texan by the least caretaking and the earliest training, and the Mormon by emphasis upon the warmth of the relationship between mother and infant, the timing of socialization falling between that of the other two groups.

92

EARLY CHILDHOOD

From the time children are weaned until they go to school, roughly between the ages of two and six, the main pressure upon them in each of the societies is to learn to take care of themselves, amuse themselves, and not expect the kind of attention they received as babies. Much of their time is spent playing with siblings in the house or close by in the yard. Mothers keep an eye on their children during this period and tend not to let them out of their sight or hearing unless they are in the care of an older person, generally an older sibling.

The transition from the almost complete dependence upon care-takers which has characterized infancy to the self-reliance and re-sponsibility expected in later childhood is often difficult for the child, and is managed differently in each of the three societies. For the Zuni child the shift is the most dramatic. Whereas before wean-ing someone always responded to him, now the same people ignore him unless they consider that he really needs help. One Zuni in-formant put it as follows: "By the time a child is two or three years old, he should know better than to be spoiled. You have to teach them differently then. They can't come around and want to climb in your lap. If you let them do that, they'll get in the habit of want-ing attention all the time. That isn't good because when you're busy working they'll always be next to you, wanting something or other. You have to stop paying attention to them. Just send them outside to play or have one of the older children take them out of the house. Maybe you have to scold them a lot, but they have to learn." There is no such sharp break in caretaking for either of the Anglo groups. The transition to independence is characterized rather by a gradual reduction in the amount of attention paid them by their mothers. In absolute terms, the Mormon toddler probably gets the most at-tention. His mother will often still take him on her lap or lie down with him at nap time. The busy Texan mother has less time to do this, but several informants commented that they would like more time to cuddle and play with their children.

Although toddlers are kept track of by older siblings, parents, or relatives in all three groups, Mormon mothers were most protective in this regard and several parents reported that they had punished children of this age for running away or wandering off without telling them where they were going. None of the informants of the other two societies showed such concern.

Early childhood is a time for play, and playfellows become important to toddlers. Children of this age get along fairly well, although minor tiffs and squabbles are not unusual. Young children like to play with older children, but this is often not reciprocated unless the older child is willing to assume a caretaking role or the game being played permits a wide discrepancy in skills. In the extended Zuni households, the probability of having a cousin or two of approximately the same age to play with is high. In one of the households observed by Roberts there were six children between the ages of two and six who spent much of the day of observation playing with one another in various groupings.[7] A child in a nuclear household is not so lucky. Only two of eleven children of this age grade among the Texans, and three of eleven young Mormon children had siblings in their own age grade. Mormon mothers make up for this to some extent by having the children of neighbors or relatives in or permitting their own children to visit next door. For the isolated Texan households, however, this is not possible. Except for an occasional Sunday picnic, Texan families cannot afford either the time or the gasoline to arrange to have playmates for their young children, and, especially when the older siblings are at school, the young Texan child is left pretty much to his own devices.

Toys, all bought from the same commercial sources, do not differ much among the three groups. Dolls, doll houses, and toy dishes are the favorites of the girls, and toy trucks, tractors, and automobiles are preferred by the boys. Texan children are also likely to make pets out of the farm animals — dogs, cats, calves, and chickens making up for their lack of playmates.

When children of this age do play together it is generally not long before a squabble starts and the first lessons in the control of aggression occur. Although Texan parents often allow fighting and quarreling with playmates in children of this age, they keep them under reasonable control and will separate and sometimes punish the children if things go too far. As one informant put it, "they are not old enough to know any better." Mormon parents are nearly as tolerant but they are more apt to step in earlier and more likely to use distractions or reasoning to stop the fighting. The following incident illustrates the reaction of a Mormon mother to fighting among siblings. "During the interview, Jane (age five) and Mary (age two) were at first playing outside. Mary came in after a while and crawled up in her mother's lap for a few minutes, then went out again. Shortly both girls came in and Mary started playing with a doll house. Jane came up to Mary and pushed her aside, whereupon she started to cry and then to hit her older sister fairly hard five or six times on the arm. Jane retaliated with some not very well aimed blows. Both girls by this time were crying and screaming at each other. The mother then got up with a big smile on her face, laughed and said, 'Now, Jane, you know that Mary was there first, so you'll have to let her play.' This made Jane very angry and she started to prance around crying. She was soon distracted, however, and then stopped. The mother resumed the interview."

Zuni parents consider fighting a serious matter and believe that children should be taught to control their tempers at an early age. Reasoning is the technique usually employed. This is well-exemplified by the following statement from a Zuni informant. "My husband tells them not to fight. He tells them that fighting between brothers and sisters is not a good thing. He says that if brothers and sisters fight and are mean to each other, they'll be the same way when they grow up. They'll be mean to each other. Then if one brother or sister wants help from the others when he is in trouble, the others won't help them. All of us tell the children that. I tell it to them and so does my mother. Another thing I tell them is, 'how would you like it if your grandfather and father started to fight? Would you like that? Then there would be trouble in the family. Nothing would work right. You might not even have a father or a grandfather because one of them would get mad and maybe leave the house for good.' Then I show them by example. I tell them about their uncle. He likes to drink. He often gets caught when he drinks and gets fined. Then he comes to his brothers and sisters and asks for help, for some money. Well, they help him out. I tell the children if the family didn't get along well with each other, no one would help the uncle when he needed it. We try to teach them that way. We tell them it is a good thing when all the family get along well." If such reasoning is unsuccessful, some families resort to spanking, others to bringing in the "scare Kachina," a masked impersonator of a god carrying a stone knife. One informant who used the latter device explained it as follows: "Once when my son and daughter were younger they used to fight and quarrel and would not stop, so one day my brother called out one of the dancers and he told them not to fight any more and be good children, that a brother should love his sister and the sister her brother. The children were very scared and the girl started to cry. Before he left, the dancer said that if they didn't mind and stop fighting he would come back and cut their ears off. I guess the children were pretty scared. After that there was no fighting." Only two of the fourteen Zuni informants admitted having called in a scare Kachina. Six reported spanking, six claimed reasoning was enough, and one reported that she tied the children in chairs facing one another until they promised not to fight again.

Lest the above description of Zuni methods for teaching aggression control give an exaggerated impression, it should be noted that Roberts reported three different squabbles among children of this age. Two of them were ignored and in the case of the third, which involved a little girl of three who threw an apple at her eighteen-month-old baby cousin and then slapped him, the mother scolded her daughter. When she started to cry her grandfather took her on his knee and talked to her.[8] One informant expressed this more permissive attitude as follows: "Many parents around town, when their children fight each other get mad and stay mad. That's all wrong. Children will fight together one minute and play together the next. They never hold any grudges or stay mad at each other the way adults do." Despite this evidence, the Zuni are more concerned than either of the other groups about the expression of aggression in young children.

The children of each group during this age get some training in modesty. The Zuni parents are the most casual; children up to the age of four or five are often permitted to run about both indoors and out without clothes on. The Mormon parents are the most modest, believing that even young children should not expose their bodies, and parents should certainly not be seen naked by their children. The Texans vary. Some mothers reported that they went to considerable pains, even in the crowded quarters in which they lived, to maintain standards of modesty, whereas others treated the matter quite casually. None of them, however, permitted children of this age to be seen nude in public.

Since each group was living in close contact with sheep and cattle, all young children acquired a practical knowledge of the reproductive process. Although a few parents attempted to promote the stork story or its equivalent, few of them made any attempt to discuss theories of human reproduction with their children.

Finally, it is at this age that children learn to dress themselves, wash their faces and hands, and comb their hair, and, in the Anglo groups but not in Zuni, to perform such household chores as bringing in chips for the fire, feeding the chickens, gathering the eggs, and helping to wash and dry the dishes. In Mormon households, these tasks are defined as "helping," and the mother and child do them together. Texan children, by contrast, are urged to do these little tasks by themselves, and are praised when they succeed. One mother reported with pride that her son started working in the fields at the age of three, as soon as he could hold a pitchfork. Although young Zuni children sometimes help with housework, they are not urged or expected to do so. With them it is a matter of play rather than of duty or achievement.

LATE CHILDHOOD

Going to school, which occurs when the child is about six years old, marks a dramatic change in the life of children in each group. Zuni and Mormon children walk to school, but most Texan children have to take a long bus ride. For the Zuni child, this is the greatest change from his previous life, for he has to learn a strange language and his teacher is a member of a different society.

Although the children of each of the three societies have been given some knowledge of the religious beliefs and practices of their parents in early childhood, serious formal training does not begin until the child is five or six years old. Zuni children have already overheard their parents discussing witchcraft, and some have been visited by the kachina impersonators; the young Mormons have heard their parents discuss church affairs and have participated in prayers with their families; children of the more religious Texan families may have been to Sunday School.

97

Formal religious training for the Zuni boys, and, in rare cases, girls, is focused on their initiation into one of the religious fraternities. The initiation comes at the end of a long and elaborate ceremony that generally takes place once every four years, in the spring. The ceremony emphasizes the relation of men to the gods and is meant to insure the fertility of the seeds to be planted. At one point in the ceremony, the boys, riding on the shoulders of a "godfather," are whipped with yucca branches by adult males dressed to impersonate the same Kachina gods who may have disciplined the boys during early childhood. The ritual beating is said to prevent bad luck. Despite the explanation that it is "for their own good," according to most reports, the boys are terrified by the experience. Following the whipping, each boy is given an eagle feather to wear and some kernels of corn to plant. For four days following the whipping the initiates are not permitted to eat meat. At the end of this period they exchange bowls of stew with their ceremonial parents and the ceremony is at an end.

From the age of four Mormon children are expected to go to Church School twice a week. There they are taught the tenets and values of Mormon religion, and the importance of the Church as an organization is transmitted to them. Although in any one session, only about half of the children attend, most children go to Church School at least once a week. Some school-age Texan children attend Sunday School, but attendance is small and the meetings are held only once a week. By comparison with both the Zuni and Mormons, there is much less emphasis on sacred subjects or concepts. The Sunday School teacher tells the children simplified versions of Bible stories, and, although there is some attempt to draw moral lessons from these stories and from Biblical quotations, the teacher is generally more concerned that the children behave and enjoy themselves.

In all three societies, the routines of housework and farmwork are learned during this period of late childhood by both observation and participation. Girls learn to wash dishes, to make beds, to clean and to sweep, to cook, and to sew. Boys learn to milk and herd cattle or sheep, care for chickens, drive tractors and cars, operate farm machinery, and do carpentry. Before they reach their teens, most children have mastered all the routine skills required of adults. Texan families exert the strongest pressure on their children to perform these tasks early. One mother reported proudly that her daughter was milking two or three cows a day at the age of six; another that her six-year-old son had as a regular daily duty the feeding and watering of the chickens and seeing to it that the light in the incubator was turned on every night. Another mother "admitted" that her six-year-old son, although he helped with the chores, had no responsibilities of his own as yet. Believing that seven or eight was early enough, she criticized her neighbors for starting to give responsibilities too young. The Texan ideal was expressed by the mother who said, "I want each child to feel he has to pull his own weight in the world. I gave them responsibilities as soon as they could understand the word."

Whereas individual responsibility is emphasized among the Texans, helpfulness and obedience is stressed among the Mormons. Mormon girls "help" their mothers with the housework, and the boys "help" their fathers with the farmwork. Regular tasks were not allotted to them until a much later age than the Texan average. A Mormon mother with girls of thirteen and eight said: "We haven't given them definite responsibilities yet. Lots of times the girls will do different things around the house like watching the fire, making the beds. One of them will help with the dishes in the morning and the other with the dishes at night . . . As they grow older I think they should have definite responsibilities each day so that they'll have something to do and something to look forward to each day." Another mother considered her eight-year-old daughter too young to be given too much responsibility: "After all, she's only eight." The attitude toward work is perhaps best summarized by the following statement: "I think when they learn together for the common good there's more of a spirit of cooperation."

Zuni children are not expected to do as much during this age period as those in either Anglo group. There are many hands to do the housework in the extended family household. Farmwork and herding are generally carried out by matrilineally related kin groups involving several nuclear families so that here, too, there are many hands. Thus, girls do not make a serious contribution to housework until they are in their teens, nor do boys help materially with the herding until this age. The youngest boys who actually helped with the herding in Roberts' observation of the sheep camp were twelve, thirteen, and fourteen. An idealized but somewhat deviant statement

99

was made by one Zuni informant on training boys to herd sheep: "I'm going to tell you how we train our boys. It is better to train our own boys while they are just about seven years old, because the older they get, they won't want to be trained I guess. They may start something else instead of getting to be a good sheepherder . . . That is why we keep our boys here with us, and so we can always put them in different work so that they can do different work and see different ways of handling sheep in the bunches . . . So we always train our boys out here. It is a good place to train them . . . We could instruct them like the white man does with the books, but they still wouldn't learn too well — it would be better to take them out to where the sheep are so we could show them just what they should know and just what they should do if they want to be good sheepmen . . . You might say that you think all Zuni boys would know how to handle the sheep, but then it is not the way. Very few Zunis are good sheepherders, and the rest are just ordinary Indians." [9]

Many Mormon mothers reported that trying to keep their children from quarreling was their worst problem. One said: "I can't stand to have children fight. I just put a stop to it. If that doesn't work, I tie their hands behind their back and make them sit down." Another mother: "Quarreling among children annoys me most. It happens in most families. You can't expect children to be sweet and pleasant to one another all the time, but it sure does upset me when the children argue. I try to get them interested in something else at a time like this." Another: "The two older girls, twelve and nine, fight most of the time but I get after them with a strap." Still another of her two girls, twelve and eight: "Oh, no, they don't fight, they just love each other! They just try to kill each other . . . I don't know what's wrong with them. Last night they made me so mad I had to end up by pulling the younger one's hair." Only two Mormon mothers reported they had no trouble, and one of them had children spaced ten years apart.

Although most Texan mothers also considered fighting and quarreling a problem, they seemed less concerned about it than the Mormons. The opinion was often expressed that if children were quarreling they should "fight it out," or "settle it themselves," or "get it out of their systems." As one mother put it: "If I feel angry, I express myself. If the children are angry, let them express them-

100

selves. When I'm mad I want to be left alone. I assume it is the same way with the children, so I ignore them and it passes." Even these more permissive parents, however, would "step in" if things got too rough or if a smaller child was being picked on unjustly. One family used an extreme form of fighting-it-out pattern in a distinctive way. When two of the daughters were fighting the father gave each of them a strap and forced them to hit each other until they were quite upset. Then he told them that the next time they wanted to fight, to come to him and he'd show them how. One group of Texan mothers who were upset by quarreling admitted that they "didn't know what they could do about it." They reported that they would shout and threaten but that it seldom did any good and they seldom carried out their threats. Only a few families were strict about fighting and stopped it effectively by separating the children, taking away their privileges, or strapping them.

Only two Zuni mothers reported problems with aggression in their children. Since by contrast eleven Mormon and thirteen Texan mothers did so, it might seem that Zuni culture was indifferent to the expression of aggression in children of this age. This, however, was far from the case. Rather, most Zuni children had, by this age, learned not to be "mean." Furthermore, to prevent possible backsliding, moral lectures on the subject were given by both parents and uncles. The initiation rite described above further emphasized the importance of controlling aggression. The Kachina gods that played a central part in this ceremony were the same gods that came to the houses of many of the children to warn them against aggression when they were little.

When the mothers of the three societies were rated on a scale measuring intolerance of aggression among peers, 77 percent (N = 17) of the Zuni and 69 percent (N = 19) of the Mormon mothers scored above the median for the three groups, whereas only 6 percent (N = 17) of the Texan mothers scored as high. The difference between the Texans and the other two groups is highly significant statistically (P < 0.001). There was a tendency for each society to be more intolerant of aggression in girls than in boys. This difference was slight and not statistically significant among the Texans and Zuni, but it was marked and significant (P = 0.047) among the Mormons.

Attitudes relative to aggression toward parents in the form of disrespect, "sassing," or defiance show much the same pattern as those towards peer quarreling. Most Zuni and Mormon families do not permit and severely punish such behavior, whereas in Texan families a considerable amount is tolerated. Whereas the Zuni stress the control of aggression between siblings, particularly between brother and sister, the Mormons stress respect for parents, and particularly the father, as the following quotation from a Mormon tract indicates: "The first form of authority before the child is that of the parent, and to the parent he has to be subject. The child is bound to obey his parent without hesitation or reply. There must be respect for age and experience, and a sense of the great sacrifices a parent has made for his children's welfare." Most Mormon and Texan mothers reported that their children were more obedient and respectful of their fathers than of them. Although one Texan father required his children to call him "Sir," most fathers in this group were casual in demanding such signs of respect from their children, compared to the typical Mormon father.

ADOLESCENCE

At adolescence pressure to assume responsibility for adult roles in society is important for most children. For girls, this consists of thinking about and preparing for marriage, and for boys, starting to make money, first for self-support and then for the support of a family. Only a few Texan and Mormon children thought of higher education, and few of them progressed beyond high school. Most of the boys, therefore, either sought outside jobs or took their places as serious contributors to the economic endeavors of their fathers. The girls had already become responsible helpers to their mothers in the home. Although some tried to earn money, there were few paying jobs available for them, and their main preoccupation was getting a husband. The average age of marriage for girls in each group was lower than the average for the United States as a whole. Of the sixty-five children of the mothers of our Mormon sample, there were seven girls over seventeen. All but one of them were married, and most of them already had children of their own. All but three of the nine girls over eighteen in our Texan sample were also married. Of the six girls of the middle generation (between eighteen and thirty) in the three Zuni households described by

Roberts, all were married or had been married, and all of them had children. Dating and courtship, therefore, are a major preoccupation among the adolescents in the three groups, but the rules governing these forms of behavior vary.

The Mormons keep the most rigid control over courtship. The following quotation from a Mormon tract states some of the values by which Mormon parents attempt to govern their adolescent girls during this period:

> The dominant evil of the world and one of the gravest dangers to human welfare are lawless sex gratification. We believe . . . that sexual sin is second only to the shedding of innocent blood in the category of personal crimes; and that the adulterer shall have no part in the exaltation of the blessed.
>
> Love does not spring from lust. Virtue is youth's dearest possession; and chastity is the strongest bulwark against the many temptations of life. Of all earthly possessions, virtue should be cherished most . . . one must enter the married state with an unstained, unviolated body.
>
> Young women should help young men keep pure. By their actions they may restrain their male friends from improper suggestions and behavior.
>
> It is far more wise that our girls of immature growth should be escorted where necessary to and from evening sociables by their fathers and brothers than that they should be attended only by boyfriends.
>
> Parties exclusively for boys or for girls may be commended as postponing the coming of that day which will arrive all too soon, despite all we can do as parents to retard its coming, when our children will seek companionship among those of the opposite sex in the possible jeopardy of their morals and in the certain lessening of their efficiency in schoolwork and in other necessary employments.
>
> Many religious people regard dancing as one of the most pernicious practices that can be indulged in. The Latter-Day Saints, on the other hand, have defended this amusement when carried on under proper conditions as innocent and promotive of culture. Dancing is an ancient art, and practically a universal one.
>
> There is a crying demand that mothers know more about the amusements of their daughters. An honorable man will find out before he begins inviting a girl to dances, theaters, or other amusements, that his attentions are agreeable to her parents. He will also be ready to have her mother or some other lady friend accompany them.[10]

Although the ideals stated above by no means represent actual practice, there is a strong attempt by the Mormon Church to organize the social life of adolescents so as to keep firm control over

children until they are married. This is not to say that these affairs are joyless. Dancing is favored and even kissing games are
sponsored by adults, but there is a strong feeling that all cross-sex
interaction among adolescents should occur in the presence of the
parental generation. In actuality there is some unchaperoned dating. As one informant put it: "Girls start dating when they are
about fourteen or fifteen years old. This usually involves riding
around for a short while after a dance or going to the movies in
town with a boy-friend. They may ride around a bit after the movies.
Almost always they go out two couples at a time. Once in a while
kids go into Railtown on dates. This doesn't happen until the girls
are about sixteen. A couple never goes in alone. They usually have
some of their friends along. I guess this is the form of chaperonage
out here."

The Texans disapprove of premarital sexual behavior, particularly
in girls, but nevertheless keep much less close control over their
adolescent children than the Mormons. Although explicitly disapproved, it was tacitly assumed that the boys would "sow their wild
oats," but the Texan informants agreed that it was an exceptional
girl who was not a virgin when she was married. Dancing and dating
were much less carefully chaperoned by the Texans. Drinking was
not uncommon, particularly among the older boys, an indulgence
strictly taboo for the Mormons.

Trysting is an accepted Zuni pattern, and premarital sexual intercourse is expected as a part of the culture. Courtship is often initiated by the girl and premarital affairs take place in her home.
According to one male Zuni informant: "If a girl asks you to her
house, you just sleep with her, and you leave before morning several times. Then one day you stay later and you're seen, and then
everyone knows you're married." In the old days, boys and girls of
different clans would carry on preliminary courtship and make
arrangements at the well where the girls went to get water. Nowadays the school provides an opportunity for young people of different clans to get to know one another.

Comparatively speaking, the Mormons are more severe than the
other two groups in their control of adolescent sexual behavior.
A rating on the severity of sex training taken from interviews with
mothers showed 57 percent (N = 19) of the Mormon mothers to
be above the pooled median on this scale, in contrast to 35 percent

(N = 14) for the Texans and 33 percent (N = 9) for the Zuni. In each of the three societies, boys marry later than girls, and there is a general feeling, especially in the two Anglo groups, that a boy should not get married until he is able to support a wife. In Zuni also, a boy should give promise of being a good provider before he is accepted by a girl and her parents.

SUMMARY OF CHILD-REARING PRACTICES

The main emphases on child rearing for each of the three societies may be summarized as follows: (1) The Zuni infant is indulgently treated by many caretakers. This indulgence comes to an abrupt end at about the age of two or three, at which time he is taught to keep his temper and not to fight. Little is expected of him in the way of performing economic tasks until he approaches adolescence. (2) The Texan infant receives much less care from his busy mother who weans him and starts his socialization at an early age. During childhood, the emphasis is on assuming individual responsibility for the performance of tasks. Relatively little pressure is exerted against fighting. (3) The Mormon infant is indulged nearly as much as the Zuni, but differs from the Zuni infant in that the mother is mainly responsible for caretaking. Mormon children are weaned later than the Texan, but earlier than the Zuni children, and the Mormon mother continues to be more nurturant and protective of her child for a longer period than in either of the other two societies. Dependency weaning is late and gradual. Mormon children are expected to perform tasks very similar to those expected of a Texan child, but these tasks are defined as helping the mother or the father, who remains responsible for them rather than as the individual responsibility of the child. Obedience and helpfulness are stressed rather than individual achievement and responsibility. The main pressure against emotional expressiveness is in the area of sex, which is considered by the Mormons as one of the worst sins.

RESULTS OF TESTS

To determine some of the effects of the differences in child-rearing methods described above, tests were given to samples of children in each of the three societies. The *Magic Man* test was intended to obtain an estimate of a child's motives, conflicts, and preferences. This test consisted of three questions; the instructions stated that there were no wrong answers:

1. Once upon a time a magic man met a child and said, "I'm going to change you into something else. You can be any kind of person you like." If you were this child, what kind of person would you want to be? Write down what this person would be like.

2. Suppose that you could be changed into a father or a mother or a sister or a brother. Which would you want to be? Put a line under the one you would want to be.

3. If the magic man could make you just as old or as young as you wanted to be, how old would you want to be?

A method of scoring this test for achievement has been validated by Mischel. He showed in a study of Trinidadian Negro children that responses to the question that involve the choice of an occupation (nurse, schoolteacher, farmer, or rancher) or of a personal quality clearly indicating achievement (a successful man, a wealthy woman) were significantly related to achievement scores derived from TAT, using the procedure developed by McClelland and his associates.[11] Using the same scoring procedure, we found that 57 percent of the Texan children gave scores indicating achievement, whereas only 38 percent of the Mormon children and 20 percent of the Zuni children responded with this type of imagery. Although the difference between Texans and Mormons was not statistically significant, that between Texans and Zuni was ($P = 0.001$).

This Texan preoccupation with success and achievement is strikingly shown by the answers of the Texan children to the first question of the test. One Texan boy stated that he wanted to be "a great doctor in the Mayo Clinic in Minneapolis, Minnesota, who had done many things toward man's health," another stated, "I want to be a rancher and raise beef cattle so I can get some money," another that he wanted to be "a great Yankee baseball player; I will be the pitcher." By contrast, the most popular choices for the Mormons were to be good, kind, or happy as exemplified by the following: "good, honest, and kind to everyone I meet," or, I would "fish, run around on the hills, and go swimming." The most popular Zuni choice was to be a man or a woman, without specific qualification, or, simply, to be a Zuni.

Although they did not occur frequently, when cross-sex choices

106

on this part of the test did occur they gave insight into the relative status of men and women in the three cultures. The egalitarian Texans made no cross-sex choices, whereas 10 percent of the Zuni boys chose to be females, and 23 percent of the Mormon girls chose to be males. No Mormon boys or Zuni girls made cross-sex choices. These responses reflect the relatively high status of women in Zuni and of men among the Mormons. Three Zuni girls said that they would like to be white; one Mormon boy expressed the wish to be changed into an Indian; another Mormon boy and a Mormon girl chose to be animals. Perhaps the cross-sex, cross-race, and cross-species choices indicate a need to escape from a culturally defined status that is felt to be unsatisfactory.

The intent of the next Magic Man question was to obtain the preference for roles within the family. The results of this part of the test are shown in Table 6. As can be seen, the majority of boys in

Table 6. Choices of family roles in the Magic Man test.

Role	Boys			Girls		
	Mormon	Texan	Zuni	Mormon	Texan	Zuni
Father	2	4	6	0	0	0
Brother	6	9	24	3	1	5
Mother	0	0	0	3	7	3
Sister	0	0	0	5	1	35

all three groups prefer the role nearest their sex and age. The girls show considerably more diversity. Only the Zuni girls show a pattern similar to the boys in the popularity of the status nearest their sex and age (sister). Both the Texan and Mormon girls reflect the values of their culture in their votes. That seven of nine Texan girls thought it best to be a mother rather than a sister is consonant with the Texan emphasis on achievement and growing up. The three Mormon girls who chose to be brothers indicate the patriarchal emphasis in their culture.

The third Magic Man question was designed to measure status preference in terms of age alone. Answers reflect the importance of both sex and culture as determinants. The mean age desired by the girls was 19.4 for the Texans, 15.8 for the Mormons, and 12.3

for the Zuni. Remembering that the median age of these girls was eleven years, these choices seem to reflect the relative emphasis on achievement and success in the three societies, the Texan girls showing the greatest wish to grow up, and the Zuni girls the strongest satisfaction with the status quo. They are consonant with the results of the previous Magic Man question. The results for the boys on this question, however, were somewhat unexpected. Zuni boys, like their sisters, are satisfied with the status quo, their mean desired age being 11.9. The Mormon and Texan boys, however, show a reversal, the former having a mean desired age of 19.7, the latter, 15.7. This may reflect the relatively high status of Mormon men as compared with Texan men as overriding a simple wish to grow up.

To summarize, the results of the Magic Man questions are for the most part consonant with our knowledge of the social structure and socialization practices of the three groups. They reflect the high status of Mormon men and of Zuni women and the relative equality of the statuses of the sexes among the Texans. They indicate the Texan value for success, achievement, and growing up, and Zuni satisfaction with the status quo. The Mormon emphasis on virtue and control is reflected only by inference in the frequency of the choice of the children of this culture for carefree freedom.

Conflict and Anxiety Test. In order to estimate the major source of conflict and anxiety in each society, the children were asked what they felt was the worst thing that could happen to them. Answers to this question can be scored in two ways, by the nature of the injury or by its agent or source. The responses classified by type of injury are presented in Table 7. The most common fear for both the Mormon and Texan boys and for the Texan girls is death or injury, but, within this category, dismemberment — breaking an arm or a leg, or getting it cut off — is the most frequent response by the Mormon boys. In the light of Mormon emphasis on the control of sexual behavior, this may well indicate the presence of castration anxiety as an underlying fear of these four boys. The Texans seem more preoccupied with death or with some accident whose consequences are unspecified.

The most common fear of Mormon girls and of Zuni children of both sexes is punishment. For the Zuni it is most commonly spanking, whereas for the Mormons it is to be put in jail, scolded, or denied privileges. The relatively high frequency among the Zuni,

Table 7. Injuries described by children in answer to the question "What is the worst thing that could happen to you?"

Worst thing	Mormons		Texans		Zuni	
	Boys	Girls	Boys	Girls	Boys	Girls
Death or injury:						
Death	1	2	3	1	3	2
Accident	2	0	4	2	4	8
Dismemberment	4	2	0	1	2	1
Total	7	4	7	4	9	11
Punishment:						
Physical	1	1	1	2	7	15
Other	1	4	0	0	3	6
Total	2	5	1	2	10	21
Separation:						
Ostracism	2	4	0	2	1	0
Death of family	0	0	2	1	0	0
Total	2	4	2	3	1	0
Wrongdoing:						
Fighting	0	0	0	0	9	3
"Go to Devil"	0	0	0	1	0	0
Total	0	0	0	1	9	3

particularly the boys, of the response that fighting is the worst thing that could happen is consonant with the strong taboo on aggression in this society. The relative frequency of fear of separation from the family is striking for the Mormons, particularly the girls, and this is consistent with the culture's emphasis on the importance of the family.

An analysis of the agent of injury is presented in Table 8. To

Table 8. Children's identification of agents of injury.

Agent	Mormons		Texans		Zuni*	
	Boys	Girls	Boys	Girls	Boys	Girls
I	7	7	4	2	7	9
It	1	0	3	4	2	7
They	3	6	3	5	22	22

* Responses from three Zuni boys and one Zuni girl were unscorable.

construct this table the responses were coded as follows: if the response indicated that the subject was responsible for the injury, such as "if I fell down and broke my arm," or "if I die," it was scored under the "I" category, whereas responses such as "They will spank me," or "to be put in jail," were scored as belonging in the "they" category. When the agent was an animal or something impersonal, such as a car or a tractor, the agent was scored as "it."

The modal response for both Mormon and Texan boys and for the Mormon girls is "I." This is consonant with the emphasis on individual responsibility in the Anglo groups. The modal response for the remaining groups is "they." The most striking is the great preponderance of the "they" category for Zuni children of both sexes. This is consonant with the hypothesis that severe punishment for aggression of Zuni children leads to its projection and a consequent paranoid fear of others. Since in all three societies girls were more severely punished for aggression than were boys, it is interesting to note that among the two Anglo groups, nearly twice as many girls as boys fear others.

There are at least two possible explanations for the popularity of the "it" category for the Texans. It may be a consequence of their lack of nurturance during infancy: the relation of this factor to the fear of the supernatural has been established.[12] Or, the isolated conditions of living in a scattered land settlement pattern and the earliness with which children are forced to cope with their environment may make it seem dangerous so that they would be more apt to have a fear of being eaten by bears or tipping over on a tractor than of "I" or "they" agents of harm.

Affirmative Values Test. The final question asked that is relevant to the content of values was: "What is the nicest thing that could happen to you?" The responses, shown in Table 9, were scored according to four categories. The first, "goods," included money, candy, toys, clothes, and so on. "Status" included being rich, famous, or powerful. "Fun" included playing, going on trips, and being happy. The "security" category included not being sick, not being punished, and not being separated from the family.

It can be seen from the table that Zuni children are predominantly concerned with consumable goods: candy, clothes, or money to buy something from the store occurred in protocol after protocol. The Texan children, particularly the boys, were most concerned

Table 9. Children's responses to the question "What is the nicest thing that could happen to you?"

Nicest thing	Mormons		Texans		Zuni	
	Boys	Girls	Boys	Girls	Boys	Girls
Goods	2	1	1	2	19	24
Status	4	2	7	5	2	2
Fun	1	5	1	3	6	7
Security	2	5	1	0	2	4

with status gain. Status gain was also the modal response for the Mormon boys, although not to so marked a degree. Mormon girls desired either fun or security, again reflecting the tight family organization considered by some girls to be an asset and by others as something from which to escape.

SOCIAL STRUCTURE, CHILD-REARING, AND VALUES

Although there are many similarities, some striking differences are apparent in the child-rearing practices of these three groups and in the responses of the children to the tests given them. By way of illustration, and frankly oversimplifying the problem, we shall select one aspect of socialization for each of the three societies that seems to contrast most strongly with the other two, and which also is most discrepant from the mean for socialization practices the world over. We would like to speculate as to why each society came to adopt such extreme practices, what effect they have upon the personalities and conflicts of the people living in the Rimrock area, and what cultural adjustments each society has made to reduce or relieve these conflicts. For the Zuni we have chosen the rigid training for the control of aggression as the child-rearing variable, and harmony as the relevant value; for the Texans we have chosen early weaning and early and strong pressure on self-reliance and individual achievement as the child-rearing variables and success as the value; for the Mormons we have chosen the warm and seductive relationship between mother and infant followed by the severe control of sexual impulses and behavior in later childhood and

111

adolescence as the child-rearing variables, and virtue as the dominant value.

Because each of these groups lives in the Rimrock area under comparable ecological conditions, neither the child-rearing practices nor the adult values produced by them can be explained in terms of adjustment to the current environment, and we shall seek an answer in the historical past of each society. Inasmuch as little is known about the details of socialization of these societies in the past, and, since it would be inappropriate to the scope of this chapter to search for or document in detail whatever may be available as to past values, we intend to be selective and interpretative in piecing together information that seems to be relevant and to lend some plausibility to our hypothesis.

Since the Zuni were the earliest inhabitants of the area, we will begin with them. Before A.D. 1000 the Rimrock area was inhabited by farming peoples who lived in scattered villages and dwelt in small single family pit houses. As Chang puts it: "On the whole, the household is the basic social unit throughout, and domestically self-sufficient and independent. This is evident in Basket Maker II and Pueblo I periods when each house was separate and had its own living quarters, workshop, fire pit and storage bins and granaries. This isolation disappeared superficially with the conjunction of houses which began in Pueblo II. Nevertheless, domestic self-sufficiency is still indicated by the partitions between neighboring houses, the functional self-sufficiency of each house is shown by its material content and the arrangements of doors." [13] About this time archaeological evidence indicates that a dramatic change occurred in household structure and by A.D. 1300 the small isolated households had been replaced by the great pueblos. This change in settlement pattern was dictated by the need for defense and must have been the consequence of some military crisis. Whether it was the result of internal strife, arising from a rapid rise in population, or of invasion of Apache bands from the north has not been definitely determined, but a drastic shift from nuclear to extended households and from isolated homesteads to compact pueblos occurred in a relatively short period of time. Many of these multiple-dwelling pueblos failed and were abandoned, but the Zuni pueblo was one of the few which were successful.

It is our hypothesis that this shift had a profound effect upon both values and child-rearing practices. Specifically, we presume that crowded living conditions required an emphasis on harmony and strict control of aggression. We believe this to be a consequence, not so much of the sheer number of people living under one roof, as of the requirement that several women share in the running of the household. To check the reasonableness of this intrepretation, we have made a cross-cultural test. We have taken a world-wide sample of societies which have been scored in Whiting and Child on the severity with which children are punished for aggression and which have been typed as to household by Murdock.[14] We have grouped Murdock's categories of stem, lineal, and extended families under the single heading of extended families. The association between punishment for aggression and household type is presented in Table 10.

Twenty-five of thirty cases, approximately 80 percent, confirm our expectation. The two-sided 99 percent confidence limits of this association vary from 65 to 97 percent.[15] Perhaps a more striking way of putting the relationship is that 92 percent of the extended families are above the median in the severity with which children's aggression is punished, whereas but 22 percent of the societies with nuclear family households are equally severe. The Zuni are in the list of societies above the median in the severity with which they punish aggression.

How long after they moved into the extended family pueblos it took the ancestors of the modern Zuni to discover that aggression must be controlled is, of course, impossible to say. It is our thesis that this adaptation occurred very rapidly, and that a significant change in child-rearing came as a consequence. The value system of the pre-crisis Zuni is lost in the past, but we presume that the emphasis of the modern Zuni on harmony as one of their essential values was developed as part of a pattern which included severe control of aggression and the extended family.

Since we have a long tradition of written history for the two Anglo cultures we do not have to rest our case on an interpretation of archaeological remains to gain historical perspective. For the most part, the forebears of both the Texans and the Mormons were British, and we can obtain information about their common culture in the British Isles before and during the early days of migration to America. Here again, we find a dramatic change in family and

Table 10. Relation between the severity with which children are punished
for aggression and contrasting household structures in thirty societies.*

Severity of aggression training	Households	
	Nuclear	Extended
High		Hopi 18
		Jivaro 17
		Kwakiutl 16
		Lepcha 17
		Maori 14
		Papago 15
		Samoans 14
	Alorese 16	Sanpoil 14
	Chamorro 18	Tenino 13
	Dobuans 15	Yakut 13
	Kutenai 14	Zuni 15
Low	Abipone 7	Ontong Java 12
	Andamanese 9	
	Balinese 11	
	Chenchu 9	
	Copper Eskimo 9	
	Ifugao 12	
	Lakher 12	
	Lamba 12	
	Manus 7	
	Marshallese 9	
	Navaho 11	
	Pukapukans 12	
	Tikopia 10	
	Trobrianders 8	

*Numbers indicate rating on severity of aggression training. Relationship between household structure and severity of aggression training: $p = <0.001$ (Fisher exact test).
Source: Whiting and Child, *Child Training and Personality*.

household structure similar to that which occurred in the Zuni society, but in the opposite direction. British culture was characterized by a patrilocal extended family living in an extended household. This type of family brought to America by the early colonists is described by Bailyn:

The family familiar to the early colonists was a patrilineal group of extended kinship gathered into a single household. By modern standards it was large. Besides children, who often remained in the home well into maturity, it included a wide range of other dependents:

114

nieces, nephews, cousins, and except for families at the lowest rung of society, servants in filial discipline. In the Elizabethan family the conjugal unit was only the nucleus of a broad kinship community whose outer edges merged almost imperceptibly into the society at large.

The organization of this group reflected and reinforced the general structure of social authority. Control rested with the male head to whom all others were subordinate. His sanctions were powerful; they were rooted deep in the cultural soil. They rested upon tradition that went back beyond the memory of man; on the instinctive sense of order as hierarchy, whether in the cosmic chain of being or in human society; on the process of law that reduced the female to perpetual dependency and calibrated a detailed scale of male subordination and servitude; and, above all, on the restrictions of the economy, which made the establishment of independent households a difficult enterprise.[16]

A recent study by Alice Ryerson of books written in English from 1550 to 1900 giving advice to mothers shows striking uniformity during the first two centuries. As long as the "Elizabethan family" was the cultural ideal, doctors advised relatively late weaning (two years), self-demand schedules, swaddling, and the use of cradles. The practice of singing and rocking the child to sleep was condoned. Dependence was more valued than independence, and obedience was strictly demanded. The child was believed to be born evil and therefore potentially aggressive, and it was the duty of the parents to control this by stern discipline.[17]

The Elizabethan family fell upon hard times soon after the arrival in America of the colonists. The family heads did not know how to cope with the new and strange environment any better than their children. Furthermore, patriarchs often engaged in the menial labor necessary for survival, with the result that their authority was sharply challenged. For a time, the society attempted to maintain the familiar social structure by legal force. As Bailyn puts it:

There is no more poignant, dramatic reading than the seventeenth century laws and admonitions relating to family life. Those of Massachusetts are deservedly best known: they are most profuse and charged with Old Testament passion. But they are not different in kind from the others. Within a decade of their founding all the colonies passed laws demanding obedience from children and specifying penalties for contempt and abuse. Nothing less than capital punishment it was ruled in Connecticut and Massachusetts, was the fitting punishment for filial disobedience.[18]

Not only was patriarchal authority challenged, but the availability of land and the possibility of westward migration soon made the extended family household nonfunctional and impossible to maintain. This was true particularly for those who, like the ancestors of the Texans, moved westward in nuclear units. The family pattern became more independent, isolated, and nuclear with each step.

> By the middle of the eighteenth century the classic lineaments of the American family as modern sociologists described them — the "isolation of the conjugal unit," the "maximum of dispersion of the lines of descent," partible inheritance and multilineal growth — had appeared. The consequences can hardly be exaggerated. Fundamental aspects of social life were affected. In the reduced, nuclear family, thrown back upon itself, traditional gradations in status tended to fall to the level of necessity. Relationships tended more toward achievement than ascription. The status of women rose; marriage, even in the eyes of the law, tended to become a contract between equals. Above all, the development of the child was affected.[19]

Coincident with these changes in family structure were changes in the literature giving advice and counsel to mothers.[20] After 1750, they were told that they should begin to wean their children between nine months and one year, that they should feed them on schedule, and that they should not swaddle their infants but should permit them to exercise freely so that they might develop more rapidly. Cradles were frowned upon, and mothers were told that singing and rocking the child to sleep was a bad practice. Independence supplanted obedience as a goal of socialization. At this same time there was a dramatic change with respect to ideas about the nature of the child: it was now believed that he was born good, and aggression was considered a normal component of his individualism and independence. The child-rearing practices of modern Texans conform strikingly to this advice: they wean early, value individualism and early independence, and are permissive with respect to aggression.

As shown above, one of the strong constrasts between the extended and nuclear households is that the former are severe in the control of aggression. The contrast between the Elizabethan and the modern Texan homesteader family is an example of this difference. The Texan family has relaxed its pressure on the control of aggression and on the requirement of obedience, and it has substituted an exaggerated and early demand for independence. Whereas Elizabethan parents may have feared that their children would be aggressive and disobedient the major concern of the Texan parent is that the child might be excessively dependent.

To discover whether the difference between the Elizabethan and Texan families is unique or general, let us turn again to our cross-cultural sample. A recent study of child-rearing practices by Bacon, Barry, and Child provides an estimate of the age at which independence training is begun, as judged by the time when there is reduced contact between mother and child.[21] When these scores are correlated with Murdock's judgments of household structure, the median age for the nuclear household is eighteen months, in sharp contrast to the median age of thirty months for all other household structures. Furthermore, cross-cultural evidence indicates that the pressure for independence in the nuclear household in contrast to all others is not only strikingly earlier, but also more severe, as indicated in Table 11. This table correlates the Murdock household scores with the Barry, Bacon, and Child scores of transition anxiety (the anxiety generated in the child during the shift of status from infancy to childhood).

The shift from the historical Elizabethan extended family to the independent nuclear family and household that characterizes the modern Texans is apparently not a unique event but a change in social structure that has general consequences for patterns of child-rearing. What are the consequences of these changes with respect to values? Obviously, we can presume a shift from obedience to independence and from group responsibility to individualism, but we are concerned here with another value which has been shown to follow from the child-rearing practices associated with independent nuclear households — the value of success. Assuming that this value is measured by achievement imagery in folk tales, a cross-cultural study by McClelland and Friedman shows that such imagery is significantly greater in societies with early and severe independence training than in societies which are late and lax in these matters.[22]

Further evidence for a change in values during the eighteenth century is supplied by a study of the relation between "need achievement" and economic development by McClelland. The achievement imagery in drama, accounts of sea voyages, and street ballads in England from 1400 to 1830 was used as an index of need achievement. A striking change in the number of achievement images per

Table 11. Relation between household structure and transition anxiety
in thirty societies. *

Transition anxiety	Households			
	Nuclear		Extended	
High	Rocky Roaders	14		
	Aymara	13		
	Chamorro	13		
	Woleans	12		
	Balinese	12		
	Lamba	12		
	Kaska	11		
	Chenchu	11	Yakut	12
	Pukapukans	10	Winnebago	11
	Navaho	10	Maori	10
	Alorese	10	Hopi	10
Low	Trobrianders	7	Truk	9
	Manus	6	Zuni	9
	Lakher	5	Lepcha	8
			Klamath	7
			Tenetehara	7
			Wichita	7
			Auracanians	6
			Papago	6
			Ontong Java	5
			Samoa	5
			Cuna	2
			Tupinamba	2

* Numbers indicate ratings on severity of transition anxiety. Relationship between household structure and transition anxiety: $p = 0.007$ (Fisher exact test).
Source: Barry, Bacon, Child, "Sex Differences in Socialization"; Murdock, "World Ethnographic Sample."

one hundred lines occurred in the eighteenth century: the average was 2.99 in 1700, 4.23 in 1750, and 6.00 in 1800. McClelland interprets this change as a consequence of the Protestant revival.[23] We would rather interpret it as a consequence of the change in family and household structure to which we have alluded. Although his data refer to Great Britain rather than to colonial America, if our hypothesis is correct, the Elizabethan family was becoming nucleated in England too. Two types of evidence suggest that this was true. First, just as the son of a colonial family could move west from the eastern seaboard, so could the British son emigrate to America. The population increase in America of 750,000 during the period from 1690 to 1745 can largely be accounted for by immigrants from Great Britain. The correlative loss should have put a strain on the Elizabethan family in England similar to that upon its counterpart on the east coast of America. Second, the abrupt change in advice and counsel to mothers was parallel, both in time and content, in England and in America. This change was consonant with the change in family structure that we have posited.

That the Texans are extreme with respect to child-rearing practices that promote a strong drive for success is indicated by the age at which they wean their children, assuming this is the first step in training for independence. Of fifty-two societies reported in Whiting and Child, the onset of weaning was rated as under a year in but two, the Chamorro and the Marquesans.[24] The average age that our Texan mothers began to wean their children was under nine months. Thus, the ancestors of the Texans, like the ancestors of the Zuni, underwent a crisis which resulted in a change in their family structure, which in turn altered both their child-rearing practices and their value system, but in opposite directions.

The Mormon case is especially interesting. During the last two hundred years, they have undergone major crises that have affected their social structure and value system. The first crisis, migration from England to the rigors of frontier life, was identical with that faced by the ancestors of the Texans. The families which later became Mormons, however, were those who refused to accept the independent nuclear household as a solution to the crisis. By 1840, they finally had succumbed to the pressure for change and evolved a modification of the Elizabethan family that was quite different from the one adopted by the ancestors of the Texans.[25] Modeling themselves on the example of the Old Testament, the Latter-Day Saints, led by Joseph Smith, made a valiant and successful attempt to retain some of the essential structure of their ancestral extended family. The Elizabethan pattern of patriarchal authority, subjugated status of women, and complete filial obedience characterized the ideals of the Mormon family from the beginning.

There was, however, one modification of the Elizabethan pattern of great importance — the adoption of polygyny and the concomitant establishment of the mother-child household in contrast to the extended family household. The causes for this change in structure are difficult to determine, and a number of hypotheses have been advanced. One factor which no doubt played a part was the personality of Joseph Smith. From contemporary accounts, he was quite a ladies' man and had liaisons with at least twenty women before polygyny was officially adopted by the Mormon Church. Since other leaders of the Church quickly followed in his footsteps, it is doubtful that the adoption of polygyny can be entirely attributed to Smith's charismatic leadership. Another factor which undoubtedly was responsible was the success with which early Mormon missionaries made female converts in Great Britain, where the lot of women was a hard one and the land of promise alluring. It seems to us, however, that perhaps one of the most important reasons was that the Elizabethan family was breaking up — its sacred and traditional status had been challenged, thus permitting innovations.

Certain features of Mormon polygyny are of particular importance in this chapter. First, it took the form of the mother-child rather than the polygynous household. A Mormon man would build a house for each of his wives and establish her in it as soon as he could afford to do so. Rarely would the wives live under the same roof, and, when this did occur, each wife generally had her own apartment with separate cooking facilities.[26] Second, although a polygynous husband would carefully rotate among his wives, the routine was interrupted if any wife had a nursing infant, since there was, as a matter of church doctrine, a prohibition against sexual intercourse during this time. The practice of the so-called postpartum sex taboo is closely correlated with polygyny the world over and rarely occurs with monogamy. Although we do not have definite evidence, it is probable that the Mormons adopted at this time another feature very closely associated with the polygynous mother-child household, exclusive mother-infant sleeping arrangements. The present-day Rimrock Mormon infant generally sleeps in the parental bed. It is very likely, therefore, that he did so during the period of polygyny.

Several recent studies have suggested that the polygynous mother-child household and exclusive mother-infant sleeping arrangements lead to the unconscious seduction of the male infant by the mother during the time when the mother is deprived of adult sexual satisfaction and the son has exclusive possession of her. They suggest that the control of incest and of sex is the focal problem in societies with such family and household arrangements.[27] Thus, it would be expected that the control of sexual impulses during childhood and adolescence would be a major problem. Since the validity of this assumption is important for our interpretation of the Mormon case, it was decided to test the hypothesis cross-culturally. Table 12 cor-

Table 12. Relation between mother-infant sleeping arrangements and the severity of sex training in eighteen societies.[*]

Severity of sex training	Nonexclusive		Exclusive	
High			Alorese	13
			Arapesh	16
			Chiricahua	17
			Kurtachi	18
			Kwoma	15
			Samoa	13
	Manus	16	Tanala	13
	Navaho	14	Wogeo	16
Low	Baiga	8	Siriono	5
	Hopi	12	Trobriands	9
	Lepcha	6		
	Maori	8		
	Papago	9		
	Pukapuka	5		

* Numbers indicate score on severity of sex training. Relationship between type of sleeping arrangements and severity of sex training: $p = 0.03$ (Fisher exact test).
Source: Whiting and Child, *Child Training and Personality;* Whiting and D'Andrade, "Sleeping Arrangements."

relates the severity of sex-training scores with sleeping arrangements.[28] In the ten cases where the mother and infant share a bed and the father sleeps elsewhere, eight are above the median in the severity with which sex is punished in later childhood, whereas in the eight cases where the father and mother sleep together and the infant sleeps elsewhere, only two are severe in sex training.

As has been shown earlier in this chapter the greatest emphasis of Mormon child-rearing practices was placed upon the control of sex. However, the strong Mormon value statement concerning sex that was cited came from a Mormon tract, not from one of our informants. It therefore represents church doctrine, which was evolved during the period of polygyny. It has persisted as a statement of

121

Mormon ideals even though, as we shall show, it is no longer consonant with their social structure.

The next crisis which the Mormons underwent occurred in 1890 when the United States Government outlawed polygyny. Although many Mormons tried to retain their family and household arrangements — some migrating to Mexico, some maintaining illicit wives secretly, and so on — by the time of our study, none of the Mormon families was polygynous, nor were there any mother-child households. The standard American independent family and nuclear household had been universally adopted in Rimrock village. Along with this change in social structure should go a shift from virtue to success as a dominant value and, along with this, more emphasis on independence and less concern with the control of sex. There is considerable evidence that the Rimrock Mormons were in 1950 moving rapidly in this direction. Approximately one-third of our sample were indistinguishable from the Texans in their child-rearing practices. They weaned their children as early, were lenient with respect to sex, and were egalitarian- and success-oriented. Furthermore, 38 percent of the Mormon children gave responses indicating achievement imagery on the Magic Man test. Therefore, we see the Mormons in a state of transition from their polygynous phase to the general American pattern, and we predict that in another generation, the Mormon and Texan family structure and value system will be indistinguishable. A comparison of Mormon child-rearing practices with those of societies where there is polygyny and a mother-child household suggests that they have already moved a long way toward the dominant American pattern exemplified by the Texans.

Thus, each of the three societies[29] under consideration apparently enjoyed a period, of indeterminate duration, when its culture was relatively stable, before experiencing a sudden dramatic change that gave rise to present child-rearing emphases and their associated dominant values. For the Zuni, the crisis was the invasion of the Apache and Navaho, which led to a shift in household structure from isolated nuclear arrangements to the extended family households and a consequent severe control of the expression of aggression and the emphasis on harmony as a value. For the Texans, the crisis was the break-up of the Elizabethan extended family, due to many factors but particularly to migration to the new world. The result of these events was the adoption of the independent nuclear family household and a consequent shift to exceedingly early socialization, a pressure toward individualism and independence, and an emphasis upon success as a crucial value. For the Mormons, the crisis is assumed also to have been the break-up of the Elizabethan family. It was met with a different solution. They retained the patriarchal features of the Elizabethan family, but adopted polygyny and the mother-child household. This led to a shift in child-rearing practices, exclusive mother-infant sleeping arrangements, and the adoption of the postpartum sex taboo, which in turn led to a strengthening of incestuous feelings between mother and son, countered by strong control of sex in later childhood and adolescence.

Each of the three cultures was characterized by a period of stability in family structure, interrupted by a period of rapid change, followed by another period of stability. This parallels the modern view of biological change as operating in a nonmonotonic manner and suggests that cultural change may often operate in this manner, rather than, as many have presumed, in a steady monotonic drift.

What are the consequences of these child-rearing emphases and the exaggeration of a dominant value when the period of crisis is over? Today, the Zuni need not protect themselves against predatory neighbors, yet they continue to live in extended family households, punish their children severely for fighting, and insist on harmony as a value. The Texans do not have to rely on individual success and isolated nuclearity of their families, but could join a union, get a job in a factory, and adjust to bureaucracy. If they should do this, as Swanson and Miller[30] have shown, early socialization and stress on independence and success would be notably diminished. With the outlawing of polygyny, the Mormons faced a new crisis, and they have not yet reached a stable equilibrium of value system, social structure, and child-rearing practices.

We would like to present the hypothesis here that, when a culture meets a crisis by changing its social structure, child-rearing, and value system, this is done at some psychological cost to the individual members of the society and leads to the development of cultural defenses against the conflicts engendered by the crisis adjustment. Specifically, the Zuni must defend themselves against feelings of must protect themselves against failure; and the Mormons had to protect themselves against strong incestuous feelings.

One of the functions of any culture is to provide its members with a ready-made and culturally acceptable set of defenses, rather than permitting each individual to develop and choose his own idiosyncratic defenses against the crisis-engendered conflict. Certain aspects of the culture of each of the three societies may be so interpreted. The culturally acceptable defensive system for the Zuni consists of the denial and projection of aggression. The Zuni see themselves as peaceful and harmonious, although, as Smith and Roberts have shown, their murder rate is unusually high and they are notorious for their bitter factionalism and malicious gossip. Cultural blinders permit the Zuni to believe that these events are not truly a part of their culture, but that they come from some outside, non-Zuni source, such as foreigners, or sorcerers, or bad Zuni who have been tainted by an external evil force. Here is the classical paranoid defense consisting of the denial of one's own aggression and the projection of one's own hostile feelings onto others, which then permits the expression of justifiable anger. Sorcerers in Zuni are executed with culturally sanctioned sadistic relish.[31]

Texan culture also provides a ready-made defense against failure which employs denial and projection. The principal economic activity — growing pinto beans in this semi-arid area — is not likely to satisfy anyone with a strong need to succeed, and failure is in fact the common lot. Texan culture, however, provides its members with two modes of escape. It permits them to boast of their "metropolis" as "Homestead — Pinto Bean Capital of the World," and it permits them to attribute failure to some external source, such as the weather or bad luck. If the rules of the culture required each individual to admit to himself and to others that failure was due to his own bad judgment, lack of skill, or laziness, life would be intolerable.

The Mormons developed elaborate defenses against the strong incestuous feelings that we have posited to be a consequence of their child-rearing practices and their need to remain virtuous. One of these is sending the adolescent boys away on a "mission," which breaks up, by spatial separation, the warm and intimate relation between mother and son that characterizes the Mormon family during infancy and early childhood. Sending adolescent boys out of the home is a common cultural adjustment as shown by a recent cross-cultural study.[32]

Another way in which Mormon culture protected the virtue of its members was by strong taboos against drinking and smoking, rationalized as pathways to sin. According to our interpretation, these taboos are a means of maintaining their sexual inhibitions and of keeping incestuous feelings under control. Finally, the emphasis of Mormon culture on proselytizing may be interpreted as another method of protecting the virtue of its members. As in the other two societies the conflict is projected outside the group. Proselytizing implies that the Gentiles, not the Mormons, have sinful sexual feelings. If all the world were converted to Mormonism and were virtuous, there would be no dangerous temptations.

In conclusion, to summarize the above thesis, it is hypothesized that certain crises may require a society to modify its social structure — particularly its living arrangements and family organization. These, in turn, may require the extraordinary control of certain impulses such as aggression, dependence, or sex. This leads to the development of child-rearing practices which will insure that these impulses be controlled and the acceptance and elaboration of dominant values — in the present instance, harmony, success, and virtue — to stand against these dangerous impulses. Finally, these child-rearing and value emphases require the development of culturally accepted defenses which enable the individual members of the society to tolerate the conflicts produced by the culture.

Kinship Systems

MUNRO S. EDMONSON

RELATIONSHIP IS THE CORE of kinship[1] in a profound as well as a trite sense. All over the world newborn infants incapable of social or cultural behavior are nonetheless precisely placed from the instant of conception in a complex web of relationships defined by the culture of their parents. It seems surprising that the uniquely personal relevance of these relationships is everywhere recognized by the same mechanism. The terms used to describe and address relatives are always terms of relationship, defining the world of reproduction from the standpoint of a single abstracted individual — a self.[2] Not uncommonly other socially descriptive terms employ the same verbal trick, but no other class of terms does so in all societies. The very nature of kinship systems thus urges us to begin at the beginning, and in the beginning is the person — a self embedded in a biological matrix defined by birth and death, age and sex, marriage and descent. By virtue of kinship relationships the human baby is born a person.

Systems of kinship reach into so many corners of the body social, and have such an important bearing on so many features of social activity, that it is useful to distinguish the things that are more or less purely kinship phenomena from those based on kinship but importantly related to other matters. One cannot discuss kinship systems without discussing both unmixed and mixed kinship, but it is simpler to deal with them separately. In its nuclear or "pure" meaning, kinship consists of the institutional arrangements of a very few biological variables with respect to one another — the variables that flow from the human reproductive cycle. The social arrangement of these variables provides the internal structure of kinship.

Culture imposes two kinds of order on the internal structure of kinship. It defines it conceptually in a systematic terminology, and it controls it behaviorally through the regulation of incest. Both kinship terms and incest taboos are influenced by factors extrinsic to the "internal structure of kinship," but in themselves they deal purely with the basic variables of human biology. Thus, they establish the primary cultural definition of the biological environment of the person. They introduce definitions of space and time, and they define the only purely kinship group that can exist without extrakinship functions, the descent group within which one may not mate.

Exogamy is only a very narrow part of the range of the phenomena of human mating. Examining more broadly the factors which affect marriage — other functions of descent groups or the ramifications and subtleties of kinship terminology — we are confronted by the place of kinship in the whole of social and cultural life. This may be called the external structure of kinship. Its complexity is enormously greater than the internal structure of kinship, and its variability is immense. It concerns marriage rules and preferences that go far beyond biology and involves the fictive extensions of kinship, the kinship factors in social rank, and the relation of kinship to residence.

The broadest view of kinship structure is its bearing on ethnicity. An ethnic culture keeps its traditions distinct from those of its neighbors through the control of crucial kinship patterns, a degree of endogamy, and a distinctive family life; it is always in an important, if partial, sense a descent group. In considering the five kinship systems, we shall follow a survey form that begins with the person surrounded by his admiring relatives and leads through the major institutions of his society to the broadest of his affiliations, his ethnic culture. The systems offer a number of salient contrasts to one another, as well as examples of self-consistency as kinship systems.

Internal Structure

TERMINOLOGY

The immediate biological environment of the person is defined differently by formal Navaho kinship and by European kinship. Navaho kinship reflects social restriction; the small units of the society with their introverted overlaps and identities of kinship positions would not, in a larger society, be the same. Although English and Spanish kinship terms show some correspondences to one another (6 percent, in a strict accounting of consanguineal terms) and have a number of features in common, neither has so much as a single kinship term that is precisely like any single Navaho term in denotation.[3] The same complete disjunction occurs between the European systems and the Zuni one, despite the welter of alternative Zuni usages. On the other hand, Zuni and Navaho kinship terms are quite similar in general features and identical in a few specific ones (17 percent).

A sharp contrast between European and Indian is evident when we regard the kinship terminologies as definitions of time in biological dimension. Navaho and Zuni kinship locate the person in a timeless present, surrounding him with relatives but omitting historical time. Both systems tend toward the recognition of three generations, but these are construed in terms of relationship distance rather than time, and the distance is counted "outward" from the person in concentric circles. Grandparents and grandchildren are remoter relatives than parents and children, but terminological reciprocity equates them with one another, so that generations do not become sequences in a "course" of events or through a "passage" of time. This kinship idea, widespread in the Southwest and represented fully in the Navaho system, is only a tendency in the Zuni.

The Spanish kinship terminology, in common with that of the other Romance languages, some of the older Germanic languages, modern Slavic, and others (including, perhaps relevantly from the historical point of view, Arabic) reflects a sequential, historical concept of time. The person looks "up" to forebears and "down" to posterity in a generationally graded series conceived as lineal. Five generations are distinguished, and these are subject to extension by prefixes. Spanish possesses specific prefixes or roots for distinguishing each of eleven lineal generations. (Latin had the same number.) What may be an old European or Middle Eastern time sense thus manifests itself in the Spanish kinship system more or less in a chronicler's sense: time is like a line or column of indefinitely extended events moving from some obscure beginning to some indeterminate end, and the person is located at a "point" in graded lineal time.

The English kinship system, in common with other systems of northwestern Europe, is simpler and more restricted, and, by the same token, more general and abstract. It recognizes only three kinship tenses or generations, and then allows them indefinite spatio-temporal extension by means of a single simple set of prefixes and qualifiers. English kinship locates the person in a present preceded by an undifferentiated past and followed by an undifferentiated future. Relatives are entirely typed as the parent, sibling, or child.

The Spanish and English terms, which have similar but not identical temporal implications, carry overtones of a spatial conception of kinship as well. Relatives are "close" (*cercanos* or *próximos*) or "distant" (*lejanos*). The words carry a heavy freight of meaning: biological proximity, residential separation, and emotional warmth. The Indian systems do not appear to have this feature. Apart from generation, which carries important implications of "distance," they are little concerned with proximity of relationship as such, and the basic terms of kinship are extended far afield. Only by elaborate circumlocutions could either Zuni or Navaho terms be made to express the idea of precise coordinates in infinite time and space conveyed by the English, "second cousin once removed." [4] The Indian concepts are more categoric and more egocentric and, while the attenuation of "remote" kinship ties is recognized, it is not formally structured in the terminology.

In a general sense kinship terms predicate and formally express the placement of the individual in time and in space. Each of the five cultures differs in some aspect of kinship structure, but at this level Mormon and Texan usage of English is, of course, identical, and both have something in common with Spanish. The two Indian systems stand apart from the three European ones, though they resemble each other closely in some respects. It is quite possible that Navaho kinship reflects considerable Zuni influence in some of its fundamentals, though it is unlikely that this has been direct. Both Navaho and Zuni undoubtedly have been exposed to similar terminological influences from other Pueblo sources, just as they have adopted other social forms and concepts which would lead to terminological similarity, probably from the same sources. It is doubtful that Navaho usage has ever had much influence on Zuni. The similarities between English and Spanish have an analogous history — probably being traceable rather to common European traditions and the diffusion of specific concepts and institutions, perhaps most notably through Latin, than to direct contacts of England with Spain, or Anglo- with Spanish-Americans. This general alignment of the five cultures, the Indian on one side, the European on the other, holds for virtually all aspects of kinship structure.

Both the Navaho and Zuni kinship systems are asymmetrical or dissonant in denotative structure. Both have been puzzling to ethnographers, and the Zuni has been downright controversial. It is not common in ethnography for such easily accessible facts as the terms of kinship to remain long in dispute, particularly in the face of repeated special studies. We may therefore agree with Metzger and Schneider and Roberts that the variability and rich array of alternatives in Zuni kinship usage require special comment.[5] The Navaho system has occasioned less difficulty in the reporting, but perhaps more in the analysis. Terminologically, the details of Spanish and English usage present only minor difficulties.

Navaho and Zuni kinship are patterned and orderly. However, neither system has any discoverable kinship differences that cut cleanly through the whole terminology: the principles of terminological structure do not attain closure but remain restricted to only a part of the field of kinship. Some terms are aligned in this way in most, possibly all, systems, but it is probably more common than not for terminological systems to present *some* measure of general conceptual symmetry.[6]

The lack of symmetry in the Indian systems is of some theoretical interest because it is a feature common to a group of Southwest Indian tribes and lacking in another group of them. Asymmetrical systems of the type found among Southwest Indians are widely distributed among the Indians of North America and perhaps also among other non-Western peoples. (The asymmetry, of course, is only partial. Asymmetry in the sense intended here is associated with various types of "overriding of generations" in the Southwest, but it may occur elsewhere in connection with Crow-Omaha terminology, as well as some other features.)

The basic referential terms of English kinship (affixes and compounds apart) can be almost perfectly described by three principles: (1) distinction of three generations lineally; (2) distinction of collateral relatives from all others; and (3) distinction of all relatives

130

Table 13. English kinship terminology.

Generation	Noncollateral		Collateral	
	Male	Female	Male	Female
Older 2+	father	mother	uncle	aunt
Own	brother	sister	cousin	
Younger 2−	son	daughter	nephew	niece

by their sex. The English system classifies relatives by marriage and decedence, as well as by baptism, with lineal relatives, and distinguishes them all from collaterals. Thus, the English terms for parents, siblings, and children are extended to all noncollaterals by manipulation of a few modifiers: -in-law, step-, half-, great-, grand-, and god-. The only anomaly in English terminology at this level is the lack of separate terms to distinguish male from female cousins. Extended collateral relationships are described by modifiers (great- and grand-) and by numbers (first or second cousin) and "removes" (once or twice removed). These give to English kinship an infinite potential scope for lineal and collateral extension, albeit without much precision. Affinal, decedent, and baptismal kinship is not extended. Alternative forms are restricted to the generic parent and child and the pedantic sibling and spouse; the terms husband and wife are omitted from this characterization.

Spanish kinship terms are more varied but not notably more complex. The principles are: (1) distinction of five lineal and three collateral and affinal generations; (2) distinction of lineal, collateral, and affinal relatives from one another; and (3) distinction of all relatives by their sex. As in English, Spanish lineal terms include step- and baptismal relatives, except that a special alternative term exists for stepchild, *entenado*. Also, as in English, the lineal and collateral terms may be extended, while the decedent and affinal terms cannot be. The modifiers used with the lineal terms are: *re-* (an augmentative), *bis-* (great-), *tatara-* (great-great-), *-astro* (step-), *medio-* (half-), *-ino* (a "diminutive," such as *padrino*, godfather), and *con-* (co-). The collateral terms *tio* (uncle) and *sobrino* (nephew) are apparently extended to great-uncles and grandnephews, without modification, and the cousin term is extended with only a loose numerical quali-

Table 14. Spanish kinship terminology.

Generation	Affinal		Lineal-Decedent		Collateral	
	Male	Female	Male	Female	Male	Female
3+	—		abuelo(a) (grandfather, grandmother)		—	
Older 2+	suegro(a) (father/mother-in-law)		padre (father)	madre (mother)	tío(a) (uncle, aunt)	
Own	cuñado(a) (brother/sister-in-law)		hermano(a) (brother, sister)		primo(a) (cousin)	
Younger 2−	yerno (son-in-law)	nuera (daughter-in-law)	hijo(a) (son, daughter)		sobrino(a) (nephew, niece)	
3−	—		nieto(a) (grandson, granddaughter)		—	

fier, for example, *primo segundo* (second cousin). The etymological derivation of "cousin" (*primo*) from "first sibling" (*primo hermano*) is worthy of remark, though it lacks contemporary significance.

The gender distinctions in Spanish are both more and less fundamental than in English. They are completely consistent, but they are grammatical rather than kinship-linked. Only two sets of terms — *madre/padre* and *nuera/yerno* (daughter-in-law/son-in-law) — make the distinction of sex apart from the mechanism of Spanish grammatical gender. The prefix *con-* creates some interesting, if peripheral, complexities in kinship, notably in the term *consuegro* (co-parent-in-law), an indicator of an important relationship in a culture where parentally arranged marriages are traditional. The prefix recurs in ritual kinship, *compadre* and *comadre* (literally, "co-father" and "co-mother"), and somewhat redundantly in *concuñado* (co-sibling-in-law). Husband and wife, *esposo, marido*, and *mujer*, have been omitted from the Spanish as from the English kinship paradigm.

Simplifying the Navaho terminology is more difficult because of the asymmetry noted. Although the principles are more complex, they are orderly and limited in number: (1) distinction of three concentric generations; (2) parallel-relatives distinguished from

132

cross-relatives (except that patrilineal cross-grandparent and cross-grandchild are equated with patrilineal parallel-grandparent and parallel-grandchild); (3) matrilineal relatives distinguished from patrilineal relatives (except in one's own generation); (4) parallel-relatives distinguished by relative age (except that paternal grandparent is equated with paternal grandchild); (5) child terms distinguished by sex of referent; and (6) completely separate terms used for affinals.

Navaho kinship terminology has been independently recorded by Parsons (described by Spier, but without the terms themselves), Reichard, Opler, Haile, Sapir and Hoijer (reported by Hoijer), and Kaut. The principles summarized describe all the terms on which three of these five sources agree.[7] Discrepancies and variations in the Navaho terminology appear to be due largely to subcultural variations in Navaho usage and the presence of alternative terms. Both present problems in the interpretation of Navaho kinship.

In both the Navaho and Zuni kinship systems, the distinction of cross from parallel relatives traces older relatives in terms of whether the first and second intermediate relatives are of the same or opposite sex; younger relatives are distinguished by the relative sex of ego and the first intermediate relative. The Navaho count all of one's own generation as "older" for this purpose; the Zuni count older siblings as "older" and younger siblings as "younger." The Navaho distinction, which is conceptually much simpler than it sounds in English, is consistently applied, except that -*bijé* is extended alternatively to father's brother, according to Opler, Hoijer, Kaut, and -*tsói* is given by Reichard as the only term for daughter's son and by Opler and Hoijer as an alternative term for the same relative. Kaut does not record the word at all and is the only source of -*čài* for daughter's daughter. The two "majority" usages are listed in the Navaho kinship diagram as alternatives in parentheses, with dotted lines defining their range. An alternative term for mother's sister (-*k'à'i*) is noted in all the sources but is described as definitely rarer than -*má* in that meaning.

The Navaho system assimilates decedent relatives to consanguineal ones. For example, half- and step-siblings are called by the terms that are used for siblings. Half-siblings may have the same (polygynous) father. Stepfather is equated with father's brother (-*bijé*) and stepmother with mother's sister (-*k'à'i*), reflecting the Navaho tradition of

People of Rimrock

the levirate and sororate. No term for stepchild is reported, and there may be none. In its distinction of matrilineal from patrilineal relatives, the Navaho system tacitly emphasizes mother's matrilineage and father's patrilineage, and it differentiates cross from parallel collaterals, merging the latter with the lineage. The coincidence of the two lineages as determinants in sibling and cousin terms accounts

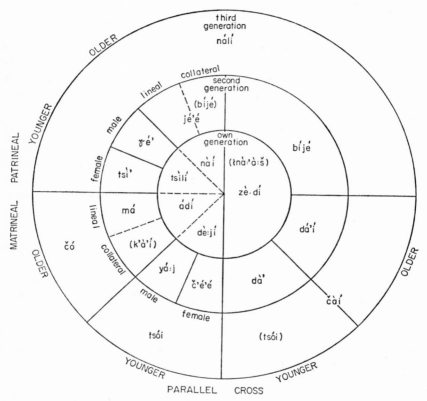

Figure 2. Navaho kinship terminology.

for the equation of these terms in both lines.* A special term (-nà:'à:š) for man's male cross-cousin, a joking relationship, is diagramed as an alternative usage, since Reichard, Opler, and Haile agree that the generic term -zè:dí includes this relationship. The diagrammatic symmetry and simplicity of the terms for cross-relatives

* On this feature Figure 2 is imprecise, since sister and brother terms are extended to both matrilineal and patrilineal parallel cousins.

134

would be even more striking if -*dà'* and -*dà'i* could be merged; it has been suggested that they originated from a single term. Alternative terms for siblings of the same sex, -*k'is,* and siblings of opposite sex, -*làh,* are reported in all the sources except Opler, but there is general agreement that they are archaic. Reichard notes that -*k'is* means no more than "friend" in the central reservation. The same is true at Rimrock. All sources except Kaut agree that some child terms are extended to sibling's child, but no two agree on the actual usage. The common elements in Parsons, Reichard, and Kaut, partially confirmed by Haile and Hoijer, suggest that the Navaho tendency is to consider parallel siblings' children as parallel relatives, thus merging them with own children, as implied in Figure 2. Cross-siblings' children are then called "second generation cross-relatives, matrilineal and patrilineal, younger than myself."

Extension of lineal terms to great-grandparents and great-grand-children can be made specific in Navaho by numerical qualifiers: *na:kidi, tâdi, dî:di ná:náli* (second, third, or fourth grandchild). The Navaho terms for affinal relatives are simple and are entirely distinct from the consanguineal terms listed in the diagram: -*'eszá:,* wife; -*hasti:n,* husband; -*à:dà:ni,* father-in-law or son-in-law: -*γé,* sibling-in-law; and -*jà:á:d,* daughter-in-law. A wife's mother is referred to by the circumlocution *do: yo:'î:ni,* "not to be looked at," referring to the mother-in-law avoidance rule. No term is reported for husband's mother.* A number of alternative terms are reported by Reichard for husband and wife: *yiłire',* co-wife; and *tsatsa ałi'i,* "the one who cooks for me" (jocular); and -*kà',* "male"; and -*'á:d,* "female." (As reported by Hoijer, these terms are considered slang in this usage.) Haile reports the vocative use of -*zâ:ni,* presumably with the force of "my old lady."

Zuni kin terms have a general structure somewhat similar to Navaho, but the differences are highly informative. The principles are: (1) Three concentric degrees of closeness, or quasi-generations, are recognized: "close," "intermediate," and "distant." (These "degrees" are consistently generational, except that the Zuni appear undecided as to whether to count cross-cousins as "close" or "intermediate" relatives, inferable from the fact that they employ the entire range of both sets of usages as alternatives.) (2) Intermediate and

---

* Dr. Clyde Kluckhohn informed me that the referential idiom for "her husband's mother" is *bahasti:n bamá.*

close relatives are distinguished by seniority counted differently for four different sets of relatives: for intermediate relatives it is generational; for siblings it is relative age with respect to ego; for parallel cousins it is the relative age of parent and parent's sibling; for cross-cousins the "Crow" reckoning of lineage relationship applies: matrilateral cross-cousins count as junior and patrilateral cross-cousins as senior. (3) All senior relatives (including the grandparental generation) are distinguished by sex of referent; all junior relatives (including the grandchild generation), by sex of speaker. (4) In the intermediate "generation" all matrilineal relatives are distinguished from nonmatrilineal ones. (A man uses "child" only to nonmatrilineal relatives, a woman only to matrilineal ones.) (5) "Man's close

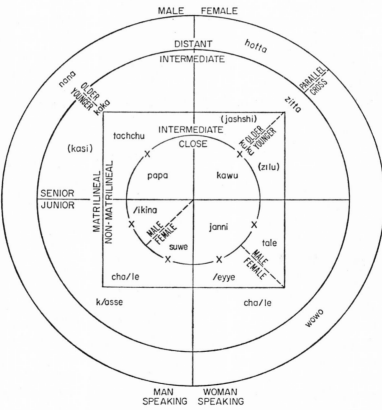

Figure 3. Zuni kinship terminology.
(X = cross cousins are referred to by either of these terms)

136

junior" and "woman's nonmatrilineal intermediate" are additionally differentiated by sex of referent. (Husband and wife, /oyemshi and /o:ye, have been omitted from this account.)

The most striking features presented by Zuni kinship terms in contrast to Navaho are the "Crow" cross-cousin terms and the distinctive treatment of affinals; the two features are related. The Zuni generational distinction appears to reflect, although dimly, the concentric pattern so commonly found in the Southwest; otherwise, the Zuni terms place a heavy emphasis on matrilinearity expressed in distinctions of age and sex. Navahos say they are born *into* their mothers' clans and born *for* their fathers', and the Navaho terms express this conception in a nearly perfect symmetry of matrilineage and patrilineage. A Zuni says he is "of the mother's clan, but the child of the father's," and he pursues this conception to its logical conclusion and expresses it in generational terms. The statement is ambiguous in English. In Zuni one can say simply that he is the *cha/le* of both clans, for the term means one thing to a female and another to a male speaker. The need to know the sex of the speaker in relation to junior relatives is illustrated by a puzzling statement from one of Kroeber's informants: "The objection to marriage into one's father's clan is based on the ground that one is marrying *yam tca'le,* 'one's own child' . . . a woman who has married a member of her father's clan must on certain ceremonial occasions, such as washing the head, behave to her husband as if he were 'her child.' " [8] Kroeber footnotes: "I should have expected the opposite terminology; in this case the husband is the wife's clan father, and she the child of his clan and therefore by extension his child." Kroeber's informant, obviously male, meant this from the standpoint of the "father," who would, of course, be marrying his "child," and the second part of the statement should be amended to read, "as if she were 'his child.' " The head-washing ritual is usually reciprocal and appears in ceremonial adoption between "father" and "child," as well as in the Kokko ritual between "mother" and "child," but a woman's "child" in real kinship is always someone of the same clan as herself and cannot be a patrilateral relative.[9]

Although its general structure is precise enough, the Zuni kinship nomenclature is applied with a flexibility that is at first bewildering. This is particularly marked in relation to cross-cousins, who may be classed either as "close" relatives or as "intermediate nonmatrilineal" relatives, more or less at will. Usage reflects the varying emphasis on closeness, seniority, sex and matrilinearity in different situations.

Other aspects of the Zuni nomenclature present fewer difficulties. The term *wowo,* father's mother, father's mother's sister, woman's daughter's daughter, is exceptional and doubtless reflects a former systematic extension to the grandparental level of the distinction of cross from parallel relatives. The ceremonial term *toshle,* grandson, could have served to complete such a distinctive set of terms. Special terms for mother's older and younger sisters, *jashshi* and *zilu,* are secondary usages at present. Ceremonial terms apply the age distinction to mother's brother, *kaka* and *kasi.* The distinction of older and younger parallel cousins by the relative ages of their parents and one's own further emphasizes the marked preoccupation of Zuni with relative age. Despite the general terms for male and female affinals, */ulani* and *ta: lakyi,* and the existence of a special term for stepmother, *inija,* the primary Zuni usage is to call and to refer to in-laws and step-relatives by consanguineal terms. In view of the multiple dimensions in which kinship is fictively extended at Zuni, the complex and conflicting evidence on nomenclature for distant relatives seems not at all surprising. It may be only rarely that the usage is determined by blood kinship.

INCEST

Kinship terms structure the biological dimensions of relationship in different patterns. Such patterns are elaborated into usages which map biological space, but most of the important behavior that corresponds to various kinship terms is not "biological" behavior. In one case, however, the cognitive map and biological activity are related — mating. In each of the five societies there is a relation between the terminology and the particular application made of the taboo on incest. In none of them is the pattern of mating purely a matter of biological relationship, for it invariably involves religious attitudes, property, considerations of power, prestige, residence, feelings, and other extrakinship considerations. A part of the pattern is nonetheless biologically defined and is thus a matter of internal kinship structure.

The English usage reflects rather precisely the loss of functions of distant relatives and the transitional state of marriage customs. The minimal unit of exogamy is truly minimal — the nuclear family of parents, siblings, and children. The various states in the United States have differing laws on stepdaughter marriage, and on whether to extend the incest taboo to cousins, though they agree that if the taboo is extended it should be extended bilaterally. The equivocal significance of the idea of "family" in English reflects these ambiguities, for it is the principal term by which one refers to both the nuclear unit and the broader bilateral kindred. The extended usage of "cousin" for distant collateral relatives without regard even to generation suggests the schematizing tendency in English kinship that corresponds to this system. The tendency is present in other European languages, but is most marked in English. It has been suggested that the reduction of significant kinship to the nuclear family is old in English history, possibly going back to Anglo-Saxon times, though it is reasonable to believe that the perpetuation of the nuclear kinship system is significantly related to modern economic and social circumstances as well.[10]

The Spanish system is similar to the English one, both typologically and historically, but with less shrinkage or nuclearization. The term *familia* is used in New Mexico today with something of the same ambiguity noted for its English equivalent. Marriage is said to represent the founding of a new *familia*, clearly a nuclear unit. The center of gravity of the Spanish term is still, however, a lineage-and-kindred conception. Because of their Catholicism the Spanish-Americans tend to view first cousins as unmarriageable. However, first-cousin marriages with papal dispensation, by no means infrequent among Hispanic Americans, have occurred in the Rimrock area. The unit of exogamy is thus the bilateral kindred, though it appears to be shrinking. More extended forms of exogamy were known in Catholic Europe as recently as the late Middle Ages, second and even third cousins being bilaterally interdicted. The modern Spanish system of kinship terminology may reflect a long-standing lag in the nuclearization of exogamy, as compared with English. In New Mexico and northern Latin America there are acculturative factors in the reduction of the scope of kinship ties, but the process is also observed farther south and therefore must represent a reaction to general social circumstances that appeared earlier in northern and western than in southern and eastern Europe.

The internal structure of Navaho kinship defines incest as a bilateral kindred system would define it: no first cousin is marriageable, whether cross or parallel. Although, therefore, the Navaho terminology suggests that matrilineage and patrilineage have an important place, they do not appear decisive in defining of the basic unit of exogamy.* Possibly among more distant relatives cross-cousins are maritally more accessible than parallel ones, provided, of course, that they are not of the same clan, but this point is somewhat obscure. There is general agreement that among one's "real" relatives one does not marry into either the mother's or the father's matrilineage at any traceable remove. Navaho usage in addressing patrilateral parallel cousins as siblings suggests that they are not marriageable even when the connection is remote. This leaves matrilateral cross-cousins in the second degree as the nearest likely mates in one's own generation, but whether the Navaho so view them is unclear.

The Zuni do not marry their parents, siblings, or children. And, since they extend these terms to a rather broad group of relatives, by our reckoning both real and fictional, the Zuni incest rule is as simple and as complex as that. Although there are etymological hints of a former preferential cross-cousin marriage system, modern custom does not permit cousin marriage of any type.[11] This taboo apparently extends to the limits of traceable bilateral kinship, possibly including specifically the third cousin degree of consanguinity. In terms of internal structure, then, the Zuni define incest as marriage within a greatly extended bilateral kindred.

The internal structure of the kinship systems of the five cultures of the Rimrock area may be summarized briefly as to terminology and incest. The Texans have a lineal terminology and nuclear family exogamy, with some folkloristic tendency to extend the incest taboo to the bilateral extended family, or kindred. The Mormons are identical, except that the tendency toward extended family exogamy is more marked. The Spanish-Americans have a lineal terminology and bilateral kindred (familia) exogamy. The Navaho have a bifurcate collateral terminology and bilateral kindred exogamy, overlaid with an extended taboo prohibiting marriage within either the paternal or the maternal matrilineage. The Zuni have a bifurcate terminology and a greatly extended bilateral kindred exogamy. The strong em-

---

* According to Dr. Clyde Kluckhohn (personal communication), "The Navaho definitely feel it 'worse' to marry any cousin in one's own clan. Further, in all the statistics at my disposal such marriages are in fact appreciably less frequent."

phasis on matrilineal descent in Zuni appears to have no bearing on mating with real consanguineal relatives of any traceable degree.

EXTERNAL STRUCTURE

The ramifications of kinship involve in some measure all the other institutions of society. Aside from the structuring of mating and descent as such, kinship principles have a patterned relation to property, production, consumption, residence, cult, faction, and social rank. This extension of kinship beyond the purely biological matrix I have called the external structure of kinship.

Three different orders of external structure may be distinguished for clarity of exposition and comparison. First, there is the extension of internal kinship to socially defined descent groups (such as clans or *compadres*), the extended use of kinship terms for nonrelatives, and the elaboration of mating customs beyond the incest taboo. Second, there is the patterning of behavior in relation to religion, economics, politics, rank, and residence as these relate to kinship. And, third, there is the integration of all of these kinship patterns into an ethnic system, defining and maintaining what is for most purposes the primary cultural identification of the group and the individuals within it. Thus, we are concerned with the extension of kinship, its institutional implications, and its bearing on ethnicity.

EXTENDED KINSHIP

The pattern of kinship is typically extended from internal to external contexts in two ways: conceptions of consanguinity and descent are analogically applied beyond the bounds of biological relatedness to create systems of fictive kinship; and the regulation of mating is never just a matter of exogamy or incest but is always subject to subtle and detailed rules of preference. Extended kinship thus has both a consanguineal and an affinal mode.

Extension of consanguineal kinship is most evident in Zuni, among the cultures of the Rimrock area. Kinship is extended to include the members of one's own matrilineal clan, one's father's matrilineal clan, and at least the households and immediate families of one's *kihe*, or ceremonial friends. To all of these individuals and also apparently to members of one's own religious societies, in at least some

141

cases, kinship terms and rules of exogamy are applied.[12] Because these various groupings crosscut one another in some measure, the actual operation of Zuni kinship may be described as a system of sociologically restricted exchange.[13] Zuni has about fifteen clans, with an average membership of around two hundred. If a minimum of four of the clans are interdicted on family or ceremonial grounds and another two hundred people are unmarriageable on grounds of society membership or distant blood relationship, it is obvious that the average Zuni must marry "outside" a rather complexly defined third of the total population. Furthermore, the average size of the clan is not a perfect measure, since the five largest clans comprise about two-thirds of the Zuni population. It is therefore not very surprising that the more extended types of exogamy are taken lightly at Zuni, but, even when they are, the regulation of marriage remains more stringent than in any of the other cultures. For many individuals it begins to approach the rigor of a preferential marriage class system of the Australian type.

Navaho extended kinship is also comprehensive and complex. The taboo on incest theoretically is extended to all members of one's own or one's father's matrilineal clan and to all members of any clan "linked" with either by tradition. Reichard asserts that marriage with a member of the father's clan is not only *not* forbidden but actually preferred. The nine cases she records to document this, however, could as well be interpreted as exceptions to a rigorously exogamic rule, since they constitute less than one-half of one percent of the almost 2500 marriages recorded in her genealogies in which the father's clan affiliation is known.[14] It is certain that the rules of clan and phratry exogamy are broken with some frequency by the Navaho, especially as regards the father's clan and linked clans on both sides, but the situation does not appear to be notably different in this respect from the variability of Anglo-American practice or the use of the papal dispensation by Catholic populations. It may be true that incest constitutes a focus for intense feeling, but this feeling is not generalized rigidly along structural lines. Arizona forbids first cousin marriage; New Mexico permits it; but no one expects a horror of cousin incest to begin at the state line. Something of the same sort is operative in the attitudes toward clan exogamy among both Navaho and Zuni.

Beyond the first cousin degree of kinship the Navaho definition of incest is primarily a function of clan. Thus, the unit of exogamy involves a conception of family of an essentially bilateral type overlaid and extended by a matrilineal clan system. The Navaho count real kinship bilaterally and extended kinship matrilineally on both sides. The effect is the creation of a loose society of weak clans and weaker phratries, both exogamous, combined through affinity into a yet weaker tribal aggregate. Other considerations — the multiple linkage by marriage of local lineages, for example — intensify somewhat the smaller subtribal integration of Navaho society, but these involve other than purely descent factors and will be discussed later.

The Navaho have about sixty clans with an average membership of around 1400 people. Reichard groups them in nine phratries, the last of which is a nonexogamous residual category. These unnamed "clan groups" of "linked clans" are the ultimate units of Navaho exogamy. Since one may not marry within the clan group of either parent, the Navaho incest taboo interdicts mating with about a quarter of the tribe (11 percent in each phratry plus a few real kin not necessarily members of either). This theoretical average represents reality fairly well. Although the clans vary greatly in size (the four largest comprise more than a third of Reichard's large sample and almost half of that given by Carr), there is at least one large clan in each phratry, so that these larger units are relatively homogeneous in size (ranging from 6 to 17 percent of Reichard's sample and 6 to 23 percent of Carr's). Furthermore, despite localization, the clans are widely distributed, and the Navaho travel a great deal, so that the actual circle of a person's acquaintance includes a large proportion of marriageable persons. Of the eight areas sampled by Reichard, Collier, and Carr, only the small community at Navaho Mountain manifested a serious lack of phratry representation, even though only a few clans are typically present in any single small locality.[15] Six of the phratries are represented, albeit thinly, at Navaho Mountain; eight at Shiprock and Klagetoh; and nine at Lukachukai, Keam's Canyon, Ganado, Chinle, and Pueblo Alto.

The Navaho incest rule is less restrictive than the Zuni and stands in marked contrast to that of all the other local societies. The somewhat weak disjunction of the descent groups creates a certain potential for greater solidarity and tighter integration of society, but the relatively open marital choice leaves this potential diffuse and unrealized.[16]

Kinship extension among Spanish-Americans is primarily a function of *compadrazgo,* the godparental relation, but it is of restricted importance today. Exogamy was formerly extended to *compadres* in Europe, but godparents among the New Mexico Spanish-Americans are far less important than they were formerly or are still among many Latin American Indian groups, and their relation is no longer exogamous.

A purely theoretical lineage structure is implicit in the patronymic surname in Spanish as in English, and indeed generally in European culture. Even with the emphasis formerly placed on this in Spanish culture, when laws of entail and primogeniture (*mayorazgo*) seemed about to make it a fundamental institution among the landed classes, the lineage was still embedded firmly in a bilateral structure. The Spanish naming pattern conferred on the individual the surnames of all four of his great-grandfathers. Modern New Mexican Spanish naming customs are identical with English usage.

The kinship pattern of the Texan bean farmers provides for a minimal extension of consanguinity. There is a somewhat loose and slangy use of kinship terms in a variety of contexts but with little or no extension of corresponding behavior. "Brother!" as an expletive has the force of "wow!" or "amazing!" (In Spanish "*¡hijo!*", son, or more rarely "*¡padre!*", father, are similarly used.) "Brother" and "sister" are more formally extended in the religious context of the Baptist church. The latent importance of the patrilineage in English kinship is reflected in one patrilineally extended family in Homestead jokingly referred to as "the clan." But even here there are implications that such solidarity is inappropriate. There is no more than a hint of extended exogamy in Homestead attitudes.[17]

Mormon society lays more emphasis on extended kinship than does Texan. While this has little effect on either kinship terms or marriage customs, it is forcefully represented in social interaction and in ritual. Extensive family reunions are common, and, while these center on a segmental patrilineage with a common surname, they frequently involve married daughters and their descendants, thus expressing the continuing importance of bilaterality. The Mormon religion emphasizes family solidarity to a high degree, "sealing" marriages for all eternity and expecting the ties of kinship to last forever. Family members are enjoined to accept a measure of responsibility for what may be described as joint salvation, and arrangements are made for the consecration of deceased relatives of any known degree. This last provision has led to an unparalleled interest in an elaboration of genealogy by the church.[18] Again the descent conception involved is clearly bilateral. Despite these various extensions of the sphere of kinship, there is no extension of exogamy.

The pattern of exogamy in all the Rimrock area cultures prohibits marriage within the nuclear family; the pattern of endogamy tends in all cases to result in a high proportion of ethnic in-group marriages. Between these limits, marriage is subject in each society to a number of distinctive and often complex influences. All of the groups are monogamous except the Navaho who favor polygyny. Sororal polygyny and stepdaughter marriage are preferred patterns for selecting a second wife. The Mormons were polygynous for about a generation in the middle nineteenth century. Divorce is easy and frequent in both Indian groups; it is not so easy among the Texans, harder among the Mormons, and circumscribed and emphatically disapproved among the Roman Catholic Spanish-Americans. The Navaho practice both the levirate and sororate, customs which are definitely excluded in all the other groups. (The Texan-Mormon case in which a widow married the wartime "buddy" of her deceased husband could be classified as a kind of fictive levirate.) Parentally arranged marriages, formerly the rule for the Navaho, Zuni, and Spanish-Americans, are rapidly disappearing. Among the Navaho such marriages produced an exchange system of multiple alliances between localized lineages which continues to have an important bearing on Navaho social organization. In the other cultures, with or without formal parental intervention, more complex questions of alignment weigh more heavily in the selection of a mate.

Attitudes toward extramarital "affairs" vary from tolerant indifference in the Indian groups through the institutionalized "double standard" of the Spanish-Americans and Texan disapproval without teeth in it, to strong censure by the Mormons. In relation to potestality, there is a spectrum of paternal authority that ranges from a strong patriarchal emphasis among the Spanish-Americans and Mormons, through the nice but precarious egalitarianism of the Texans and the Zuni, to the moderately matriarchal accent among the Navaho.

Attitudes related to endogamy are more diffuse. Marriage within the ethnic group is preferred by all five societies, but the intensity of

145

feeling varies. The Navaho and Spanish-Americans are least insistent on the point. The Mormons and Zunis for religious reasons and the Texans for "racial" reasons are maritally more ethnocentric. There is a tendency toward class endogamy, in sentiment if not in fact, within each of the communities, perhaps weakest among the Navaho and strongest among the Spanish-Americans. In two of the societies there are relics of a slave caste system: in the Texan attitudes toward Negroes (even though there are no Negroes in the area), and to a mild degree in the Spanish-American attitudes toward the Indians (there was a large number of *genizaros,* or Indian slaves, in New Mexico at the time of the Mexican Cession). Contemporary intergroup relations are reflected in the pattern of hypergamy in Texan-Spanish marriages and Spanish-Indian marriages. Navaho-Zuni marriages and Mormon-Texan marriages do not appear to reflect status differentials, and marriages of members of either English-speaking community with Indians are virtually unheard of.

The external structure of kinship and marriage fills out the skeleton of internal structure with the special organs and tissues required for the functioning of kinship in the body politic. Thus, the basic elements of terminology and incest regulation — the use of lineage and the kindred — serve as a foundation for the elaborate forms of kinship-based social solidarity — the clan, the social class, the village, and even the "race," a term with strong and definite meaning in all the European groups. The Navaho system has the effect of a loose and open marital exchange, intensified here and there by local lineage alliances and only weakly integrated at the broader levels of clan and tribe. It might be called a system of "overgeneralized exchange." The Zuni system, though not employing preferential cross-cousin marriage or a marriage class system, has the effects of a system of generalized exchange through the complex overlapping of its incest definitions in relation to a variety of social units. It is as intricate and as tightly organized as a Swiss watch. The European societies, while reflecting in varying degrees what was formerly a more extensive set of controls of marital choice, have come to share a system of marriage hypergeneralized to the point of atomism. The universalizing ideal of romantic love common to these cultures has enhanced enormously the importance of nonkinship factors in the genesis of social solidarity and the maintenance of social order. This is most pronounced among the Texan homesteaders and progressively milder among the Mormons and Spanish-Americans, for whom kinship continues to be an extensively important and even overriding factor in social life.

INSTITUTIONAL INTEGRATION

The nonkinship institutions of Navaho society are fluid and diffuse and are undergoing change. The extended family unit, with a preference for uxorilocal residence, remains the commonest single pattern although it is represented in a minority of households and may affect only a bare majority of individuals. Extended residential groups are formed by various structural rules and in various degrees of intensity. Doubtless a part of this variation results from modern acculturation, but it is likely that Navaho social organization has always been loose and amorphous. Many nuclear Navaho households exist now, as they probably existed formerly, substantially disengaged from larger social units. Larger units are organized on the basis of both residence and kinship. The two criteria correspond precisely to the bilateral and matrilineal tendencies of Navaho society. At least two levels of this organization may be distinguished: the "household" and the "local group" (in Kluckhohn and Leighton[19] called "units" and "extended families," elsewhere called "group" and "outfit"). The household is kinship-based and has primary functions of an economic and religious character. The local group, also kinship-based, has broader economic and religious functions and political ones as well.

Except in relation to a few major economic activities, production is centered in the Navaho household. Traditionally the major property conception with relation to all forms of ownership (lands, stock, houses, tools, knowledge, and names) is that of individualized use-right. Ownership may be alienated freely by the individual by gift or exchange and may be forfeited by abandonment. However, attitudes toward sale and inheritance reveal group interest, and transfer of use-right is for most goods circumscribed by custom and even ritual. An individual may dispose of his own property as he will, and the expressed wishes of a dead man are respected in the distribution of his estate. There is a feeling that property should be kept within the clan, but it appears to be honored mainly in the breach. Livestock operations are the primary productive enterprise, and sheep particularly are likely to be cared for jointly within the household, even though the animals are individually owned. The household is also the primary consumption unit. Proceeds from herding, farming, or wage work are shared within it, whether it is a nuclear or extended unit.

The economic ties to the local group are looser. Members may cooperate for a major enterprise — sheep-shearing, stock-dipping, and the like — and they would extend hospitality and minor economic services freely, but between geographically or biologically distant members of the group such involvements are occasional and episodic rather than constant. The distinction is reflected in ceremonial obligations, where a short "sing" is a household function while a long (nine-night) chant is likely to be supported by an entire "outfit." Larger units of Navaho social organization — the territorial band and the tribe — are little integrated with the style of life of most individuals, though a vague "kinship" is felt among the Rimrock Navaho, and some take an interest in tribal politics. The more rigid clan exogamy governing a considerably smaller population with substantially the same number of clans may have been a factor in the greater solidarity of at least some bands in earlier days. Links of this kind, however, have by now completely disappeared. Instead, the social worlds of the modern Navaho are composed of overlapping, small, loose, local societies.

The Zuni present a marked contrast. The Zuni household is primarily uxorilocal and extended. Although the incidence of various types of residential arrangements at Zuni is unknown, it is almost certainly more consistently uxorilocal than the Navaho households. The units are similar in size, with the Navaho household averaging 7.8 members and the Zuni, 7.5 to 8.4.[20] Property at Zuni is individually held, but title appears to be subject to numerous qualifications as to use, alienation, and inheritance. In cases of disputes, "the maintenance and continuity of the family or household on a sound footing is the major desideratum." [21] To judge from inheritance disputes, a man's sister and her son and his wife and child have the primary equity in his property if he dies intestate. Apparently the balancing of the claims of lineage and household is not thoroughly rationalized, since nine of the twelve known cases of disputed inheritance involve conflicting claims of sisters or maternal nephews and wives or children. Of the claimants of estates before the Zuni council in twelve lawsuits, ten are wives or children of the deceased,

148

ten are sisters or nephews, one is a brother, one a father, and one a daughter's daughter.[22] Although both virilocal and neolocal residence occur, uxorilocal households are the ideal and probably still the typical form. A tendency toward initial uxorilocal and later neolocal residence arrangements may be increasing.

The Zuni household is, then, either a nuclear or, more often, an extended segment of a matrilineage. By tradition it is the primary focus of productive enterprise — farming, stock raising, and handicraft — with the men who have married into the house contributing their labor in the cultivation of fields, maintenance of a house, and care of stock belonging to the women of the household. Parentally arranged marriages and possibly greater marital stability probably gave the system a functional permanency in former times which it no longer possesses. Men who married out of the household preserved an authority in its affairs and managerial as well as proprietary rights to its possessions. The matrilineage and the clan were more important. There is still at Zuni a sentiment that most real property "goes to the woman." Houses and furnishings are believed to belong to the woman. In a legal dispute, fields and herds are likely to be awarded to her if she needs them for support of minor children. But, in case of death or divorce, both a man's lineage and his household may present an enforceable claim to such property. Stock, trucks, and other such movable goods appear to be mainly owned by men and disposable either to the lineage or the household.

Maintenance of the family, that is, lineage, or household is the core of Zuni arrangements concerning ownership and inheritance of property, as Smith and Roberts conclude.[23] However, while a woman's household *is* her lineage, or a segment of it, a man's residential and kinship loyalties and consequently his property rights are necessarily divided. This source of conflict could be eliminated either by vesting all property in women or by giving the lineage a clear priority over the household, and there are some suggestions that both may have been tried at Zuni in former times. Modern custom leaves the issue unresolved, and modern jurisprudence decides conflicts on nonkinship bases, such as need or general morality. Though closely linked in modern Zuni, the household and the lineage are by no means identical.

The ambiguity apparent in production and ownership is manifested also in consumption and in relation to the broader integration of Zuni society. Ceremonially, the lineage is the more important, but exogamy is ceremonially extended to the households of one's "ceremonial friends" and fellow members of the societies, so that community organization extends through a great diversity of social forms which crosscut household and lineage as well as clan. It is here in fact that Zuni society contrasts most dramatically not only with Navaho but with all the other local systems. A minimal description of Zuni social life must take account of: *kivas*, fraternities, priesthoods, orders, classes, villages, the *kachina* society, moieties, phratries, septs, council, factions, and tribe, as well as household, lineage, and clan.[24] The very intricacy of Zuni organization results in the distribution of the roles among the several planes of social activity so as to combine the limited population of the tribe in a wide variety of different sets. The key to Zuni social structure is that it has no key. No single institution is allowed to override the others; none is quintessential.[25]

Two contrasting modes of organization are found in the society of Spanish New Mexico. One is the hierarchical, quasi-feudal system of production and of civic and religious duty associated with the hacienda and represented in New Mexico by the ubiquitous *patrón* system. The other is the egalitarian and fraternalistic pattern linked to the *cofradía* (the *Penitente* Order, forbidden by the Roman Catholic Church but persistent), and the independent and more or less communal land-grant village. The two forms correspond closely to the long-standing coexistence of a double conception of kinship. Lineage and kindred are both structural realities that underlie the ambiguity of the Spanish term, *familia*. Both are present in every village, even in the psychology of every individual, and the general operation of the Spanish kinship system in relation to other institutions can best be understood as a complex adjustment of these quite opposite tendencies.[26]

Even in the absence of great wealth, the lineage system has often become sufficiently rooted in New Mexico to allow an entire village to be dominated and almost exclusively inhabited by a single patrilineage. Los Lunas, Los Chavez, and many similar New Mexican communities derive their names from this kind of structure. Elsewhere a single large *familia* sharing a particular patronymic typically dominates the economic and social life of the Spanish-American village from a position of wealth and importance if not of numerical

150

strength. The patrilineages usually have no great time depth, often having sprung to power three or four generations after the Mexican Cession, but a small number of families can trace their prominence to royal land grants and services to the Spanish Crown. There can be no doubt about the antiquity of the lineage as a system in Hispanic culture.

The countertendency toward bilateral kindred organization is also old and deeply rooted. Every important lineage is surrounded by a host of peripheral relatives, nonpatrilineal or distant, who are a drain on its resources and a brake to its ambitions. Moreover, amassed wealth or prestige positions often are dissipated through multilateral inheritance. Though both primogeniture and ultimogeniture are sometimes approximated, neither has become sufficiently well rooted to prevail over the pattern of subdivision and redistribution of property every generation. The general system remains a balance of lineage and kindred forms.

The ambiguously extended household is the fundamental consumption unit of Spanish-American society in New Mexico. Most important goods, aside from personal articles and clothes, are owned as "community property" by the household and managed in its interest. In very important respects, however, production has always been an extrahousehold function. Both the *rancho,* with its far-flung livestock operations, and the irrigation *pueblo,* with its common pasture and water rights, involve the family in a larger network of economic activities, often though not always organized on a quasi-kinship basis. Until modern times the Spanish-American conception of grazing land was one of use-right rather than individual ownership. This has had a very important bearing on the development of both agricultural and stock-raising villages. The composition of the household reflects these complexities, being sometimes a segmental lineage and sometimes a segmental kindred. Nuclear households, however, have always been common and are becoming more so as new property conceptions and political forms replace the old. Despite the fluidity of the Spanish-American household its position in the social order is clear. Households are grouped together to form a community, usually a *pueblo* or *rancho,* and this affiliation is both stable and important. There may have been some tendency toward village endogamy in former times, and there is a marked tendency toward virilocal residence by village if not by household. Thus, the village itself comes to resemble a greatly extended lineage-kindred. This solidary arrangement is reinforced by the monolithic simplicity of the traditional economic system, the concentration of political power in the hands of a single *patrón,* and the traditional village-unit base of the *cofradía* and the Catholic parish.

In modern times Spanish-American kinship has begun to react to a number of altered circumstances that have disrupted the traditional kinship form of integration of the villages. Class factors have become more important in marriage; wage labor and owner-operation of herds and farms have replaced the village-unit types of economic enterprise; religious orthodoxy has become a social, political, and class issue in the villages; and romantic love and nuclear households are replacing the former system of parentally arranged alliances between extended lineage-kindreds. As it is subjected to more and more of the same influences that have shaped English kinship and as it is influenced acculturatively by continuing intimate contact with Anglo-American culture, the Spanish system comes to resemble the Anglo-American ever more closely. Nonetheless, the forms of its adjustment are still significantly conditioned by factors that have never been present in the Anglo-American case, and the two are still far from identical.

The contrast with Texan social organization is particularly clear. Sprung from an Anglo-American ethnic stratum that has moved westward almost every generation from the middle South, the Texans have developed organizational forms that are mobile, individualistic, and flexible in the highest degree. The household is almost always nuclear: less than 2 percent of Homestead households are in any sense "extended." [27] The ideally conceived unit of production is a "place" farmed by a single household. To a degree this autonomy is extended to other enterprises, especially to small family businesses. The few larger units of society — the school, the cooperative, two informally run Protestant churches, and a number of committees — operate through a fluid factionalism that perfectly reflects the isolating kinship structure. The village unity, such as it is, rests on sentiment and common ethnic origins rather than on kinship. The competitive economic system, the political and quasi-political factionalism, and Protestant sectarianism further emphasize the centrifugal tendencies already inherent in the family structure.

Texan attitudes toward property are thoroughly individualized. The premium placed on individual achievement tempers the desire to give one's children a good start. As in any agricultural community, land is the most important form of property, but agricultural machinery, houses, and farm buildings have considerable value as well. In recent generations Texans of the kind found in Homestead have not remained in any location long enough to regularize inheritance patterns. Hence, Texan culture has never had to confront a land shortage that could not be overcome by migration or economic diversification. Consequently, the Texan family has been reduced to a structure of precisely the small, mobile, flexible character required for the expansive and rapidly changing conditions of general American society. Except in a few atypical families, it retains not even sentimental memories of the timebound lineage structures of the distant eastern South.

While the Texan family is nuclear, isolated, even atomistic, it is in some respects the most highly structured and important element in the social order. It is the center of much of the productive process and virtually all consumption. It is the largest unit that is structurally guaranteed to have some measure of solidarity in political and religious terms as well as in terms of social class. It is thus the rock on which a highly dynamic society has been erected, and it can maintain its unity and fixity even in circumstances requiring rapid adjustments to wholesale change. No other family system in the area has these properties.

Mormon society in many respects falls between the poles represented by the Spanish-American and Texan forms. It holds more important property rights in extended community groups than does the Texan, though fewer than the *pueblo* form of organization. Mormons place more emphasis on individual achievement than do the Spanish-Americans, but temper it with a strong value on cooperative achievement as well. The Mormon household is likely to be larger and more often extended than the Texan. Once the great westward movement was achieved and "Zion" founded, the Mormon family proved more closely bound to its land and its own community than the Texan. Unitary Church membership and political organization, together with numerous cooperative economic activities, give the Mormon village something of the monolithic integration of the

Spanish *pueblo*. Like the *pueblo*, the ward does not involve the tightly ordered kinship patterns of the Indian communities. Multiple intermarriages between two important families in a village may create a certain chance structure of factional solidarity, but there are numerous marriages with people of other communities and in the long run a kind of factional equilibrium results.

Farm land, water rights, grazing land, stock, and agricultural machinery are held both individually and cooperatively in Mormon towns. While there may still be attitudinal traces of the quasi-kinship extension of communal ownership to more personal types of property formerly tried by the United Order, it is a most significant feature of modern Mormon organization that even cooperatively managed property rights are not administered on a kinship basis but on the basis of sound business practice. This is in marked contrast to the traditional economic forms of the Spanish-American village, for both the *hacienda* and the *pueblo* had strong kinship overtones. The pattern of residence is virilocal as to village but most often neolocal as to household. The basic pattern of inheritance is one of multilateral equidistribution. Land holdings are not as fractioned as this would seem to imply, both because of the relative newness of the Mormon settlements and because of the considerable outmigration by reason of marriage, social mobility, and apostasy. Although there are Mormon boom towns and new communities are still being set up, most of the older Mormon communities have rather stable populations.

The ethnic and religious unity of the Mormon village and the mixed tendencies of its political and economic systems create an integrated organization which yet contains the seeds of both change and conflict. The family structure reflects this in a trucelike balance of nuclear and kindred-extension tendencies. Possibly such a balance can be maintained indefinitely, if the complex of forces that have created it remain close to their present equilibrium. The lack of clarity of the structure, however, and the essentially ideological character of its integration would seem to be a point of weakness as well as of flexibility. The maintenance of their way of life is still a firm commitment for Mormons, and the system has survived threats more serious than any now confronting it, precisely through this flexibility. Nevertheless, defense of Mormon family life would be easier if it were clearer just what is being defended.[28]

The creation of a distinct ethnic culture is in large part a kinship phenomenon. A cultural group which freely and randomly inter-marries with outsiders cannot in normal circumstances preserve its way of life from change and eventual absorption into some larger cultural entity. Ethnic endogamy is thus fundamental to the crea-tion and maintenance of ethnic cultures. In a complex society, to be sure, other social institutions can have an importance in the transmission of traditions that is ordinarily reserved for the family in small primitive societies, but kinship is always and everywhere a primary vehicle for such cultural continuity, and the degree to which other forms can replace or substitute for it is still much debated.

Ethnic endogamy can be patterned around a variety of circum-stances, some present in the awareness of the culture groups con-cerned and some not. Geographic barriers and ecological factors play a part; so do the culturally defined self-conceptions of each group. In the last analysis the content of ethnicity — its meaning for each cultural group — is imposed by the distinctive historical experience of the group and is subject to enormous variation. It is therefore useful to distinguish a subjective from an objective level of ethnicity. Many of the "tribes" distinguished by North American ethnography do not conceive of themselves as units at all. For their own purposes and from within their own culture, ethnographers classify on the basis of objective cultural homogeneity: a common language, com-mon technolgy and livelihood, or other shared traits. Cultural iden-tification of one's own group may not correspond to this external view of ethnicity. Most Navahos do not have an ethnic sense of iden-tity, even though they have been treated as a "tribe" for over a cen-tury. The rather vague awareness of kinship with other Navahos is overshadowed by other definitions, ceremonial, residential, and kin-ship-bound. The social worlds in which Navahos appear to locate themselves are the small local ritual and residential units into which their society has divided itself. Subjectively, a Navaho is a member not of a "tribe" or an "ethnic minority" but of his local groups.

It is the subjectively defined ethnicity of each cultural group to which its kinship organization is most closely geared. For the Navaho and the Zuni the fundamental definition of group identification is, in our terms, magico-religious. "They" — the dangerous outsiders —

are witches, not merely people of a different culture. For the Spanish-Americans "we" are the children of God and "they" the powers of Satan. For the Mormons "we" are the Latter-Day Saints and "they" are the Gentiles. The definitions have ethnic overtones, softened somewhat by the ideology of proselytizing. For the Texans "we" is an Anglo-American ethnic concept with racial and political overtones; "they" are the foreigners — ideologically, nationally, and ethnically.

These definitions are reflected in the structure of family life in the various cultures and in the pattern of ethnic or quasi-ethnic endogamy to which each is subject. Ethnic intermarriage, for example, is common among the Indian groups and Spanish-Americans, progressively rarer among the Mormons, and almost nonexistent among the Texans. Religious intermarriage is rare among the Mormons and Spanish-Americans. Navaho marriage choice is restricted by a fear of going too far from home — where witches are to be found. Zunis, who locate witches within the village, have the tightest marriage rules of all, possibly a feature functioning as much for witch control as for family organization.

With a kinship structure as a vehicle of cultural transmission and an ethnic identity capable of being transmitted, each culture can fill these vessels to the full with attitudes, prejudices, customs, and values which are more or less guaranteed survival and preservation. The mechanisms are present for shielding these traits from undue "outside" influence and for communicating them from generation to generation in the subtle intimacy of family life. Strictly, the kinship system is a unique instrument for the transmission of values, for it is difficult, perhaps impossible, to find an institutional parallel for the isolating effects of endogamy or the recruiting capacity of procreation. The Zuni secret societies, for example, are well "protected" from this standpoint, but, like a European type of school, have a more limited opportunity for shaping the next generation. Mormon missionary effort has been highly successful at recruitment, at least in some areas, but it is more exposed to opposition and change.

The choice of forms represented in kinship structure has ramifications throughout the social system. Indeed, it is only by shaping the rest of society in part to its requirements that the kinship system can protect the order it represents and impose the values it enshrines.

In summary, the basic pattern of Anglo-American kinship is highly nuclear; variation in this is probably the only important subcultural difference between Texans and Mormons. The Mormons maintain a more extended kinship unit, including stronger attitudes toward kindred exogamy and consequently a more familistic social organization than the Texans. The minor differences of other types which exist do not affect the structure of formal kinship terminology or the regulation of incest. Mormons and Texans share with other English-speaking peoples a schematic, abstract, three-tense kinship system that places the individual among his relatives much as Newtonian physics places the particle in time and space in relation to other particles.

Spanish-American kinship, though moving toward a similar basic structure, still reflects a tradition that emphasized generational seniority, a chain of tradition transmitted from parent to child and binding them together, and fixed and formal relationships that link the different chains by a classical causality that led one back to first causes, to the laws of our "Grandpa, God," as one Atrisco man described the deity. Compared to the Anglo-American, the person of Hispanic-American kinship is placed in a more populous universe and extends his immediate (incest) solidarity to more people. He is less individual but more personal toward his distant relatives.

The Navaho system places the person in a timeless moment and in a small, safe space surrounded by dangerous nonrelatives (including in-laws) and strangers. The myths that validate custom are honored not because they are old but because they are there. Hence change and improvisation come easily. First causes are not at issue. Even the image of the *Ur*-Mother is Changing Woman. As a map of the environment of the person, the kinship system is almost entirely comprehensive, providing placement for all of the people that one is likely to meet and furnishing a pattern, albeit a loose one, for safe action.

The Zuni system is turned inward upon itself, restricted both spatially and temporally to a strong emphasis on the first two generational "circles" of relatives, and placing the person in a "Middle Place" of intensely concentrated personal relationships of a few simple types. The lack of historicity to Zuni kinship is congruent with a lineage system in which the family lines are related not as measurements of time and space but as precise reciprocals of one another: man is the "child" of woman; paternal links are junior to maternal ones. Time moves inward upon the Zuni "child" and his "mother." While the ramifications of kinship for the Zuni comprise and encompass the universe, they do so by inclusion and enfolding. Even danger is internal and is controlled in a tightly organized synthesis in which the very gods and demons are mothers, fathers, older and younger siblings. Kinship is the philosophy of Zuni.

DETERMINANTS

Among the many determinants of social institutions are values. Other determinants that may explain kinship phenomena include the psychological structuring of socialization, demographic and economic factors affecting residence, potestality, the general level of social confidence, the division of labor, the available technology, and even aspects of linguistic structure.[29] None of these possible determinants of kinship structure has intrinsically a value character. Taken together, however, they determine many traits of kinship organization which might be mistaken for value phenomena. Obviously, an interpretation of the values represented in given structures of kinship rests on some general assumptions about the relevancy and applicability of these other determinants to the case in question. If it is true that all viable societies of a certain complexity must develop the reduced and nucleated family pattern that is now characteristic of Western Europe, it is redundant to say that the society is complex *and* places value on an isolating kinship system. Here is a "chicken-and-egg" problem. It has also been argued that societies become complex precisely when and if their values allow this kind of development. The two phrasings are not necessarily opposed, for the question is not whether values or something else are the unique or even the "most important" determinants of given social phenomena, but whether values can usefully be admitted as one relevant dimension of the apparent determinacy. Kinship analysis is particularly rich in alternative constructions of causation, and it raises correspondingly sharp questions of precision of interpretation.

I have laid particular stress on some features and underplayed others because some aspects of kinship seem to reveal more clearly than others the underlying cultural assumptions — the preferences and choices that give a particular cast to the structure where another might viably have been selected. The relative elaboration of Navaho and Zuni kinship seems remote from value determinacy. Most primitive kinship systems are elaborate in one sense or another. The importance and pervasiveness of kinship patterns in these societies seem equally irrelevant to their values, for this, too, is generic to "the little community." In a sense neither the Zuni nor the Navaho ever had the real option of a reduced, mobile, nuclear family of the Texan type. On the other hand, I know of no other determinant for the Zuni inclusion and the Navaho exclusion of in-laws or for the Zuni extension of kinship to the gods than to say they are dictated by and expressive of value conceptions. The loose and open-ended structure of Navaho mate selection seems value-determined, since a very similar economic structure among many semi-nomads of Asia and Africa may accompany a highly structured lineage system and specific rules of preferential marriage. The concept of concentric generations seems more closely linked to values than to alternative determinants of kinship form; so do the patrilineage emphasis of the Spanish, the hyperindividuality of the Texans, and the group-mindedness of the Mormons.

While these examples may clarify somewhat the role of significant choice in the formation of kinship systems, I do not mean to imply that other choices are not evaluative merely because they involve additional questions of an economic, religious, technological, political, or demographic character. A principal advantage to the value analysis of kinship systems may be the fact that it offers a possible explanation of why changes that might have taken place in these other connections have not occurred. There is no intrinsic reason that any of the cultures of the Rimrock area could not have borrowed any particular kinship form from any other — mais ça n'est pas français. And the definition of what is français — or Zuni or Navaho, Spanish, Mormon, or Texan — is in the last analysis a value definition. It is nowhere so firmly entrenched, so well protected, and so subtly and massively transmitted and preserved as in the kinship structure.

6.

Ecology and Economy

EVON Z. VOGT

with the assistance of CHARLES R. GRIFFITH

THE ECOLOGICAL ADJUSTMENTS which human groups make to the natural environment and the economic systems which they develop to solve their subsistence problems are fundamental features of any culture. Key environmental features — land forms, underlying geological formations, climate, flora, and fauna — establish firm boundaries on the types of ecological adjustment that can be initiated and maintained.

The Rimrock area, in the southern extension of the Colorado Plateau, is part of a physiographic province characterized by high altitudes of from 6000 to over 8000 feet. Erosion has created a dissected land surface, with mesas rising as high as 400 feet above broad, flat, wash valleys and narrow, steam-eroded canyons. Comparatively recent lava flows cover some sections of the land. From the viewpoint of its human inhabitants, it is an area of abrupt and capricious fluctuations in temperature, precipitation, and wind velocity. Within this relatively homogeneous area, however, there are locations that have superior ecological advantage for successful human settlement.

The Zuni Mountains, the highest and most prominent land form, are a natural reservoir of basic elements necessary to the continued existence of the local cultures. Snow accumulating on the slopes during winter and melting during spring provides water for irrigation systems. Timber from the mountains finds a wide variety of use. Wild game, particularly deer and turkey, are hunted each fall in their refuges in the isolation of the mountain wilderness. Each spring the abundance of natural vegetation on the mountain slopes attracts herders with their sheep and cattle from the overgrazed lands at lower elevations.

160

Farming is carried out more successfully in mesa-canyon country. The softer, more developed, and more frequently watered soils are found in canyon bottoms, which are generally refreshed each year by flooding during the spring run-off snow from the mountains and by normal summer rains. The narrowness of some of the canyons has permitted the construction of earthen dams, despite the limited human and material resources of the Rimrock agricultural populations. Of major significance is the lower elevation of canyon floors and the protection against variable winds and temperatures afforded by surrounding mesas. These factors increase the chances for a longer growing season, free of damaging frost and wind erosion.

Due to the complexity of the underlying geological strata, underground water is found at varying depths within the Rimrock area. Subsurface water can be found at relatively shallow depths directly under contemporary drainage troughs or somewhat deeper in drainage troughs following older Tertiary channels. Differential erosion and subsequent redeposition of sands and conglomerates in the Mesa Verde formation during Tertiary times has complicated the water problem. There can be no certainty when wells are drilled whether a ridge of this water-bearing stratum will be reached at a relatively shallow depth or whether it will be necessary to drill deep into one of the ancient channels. Similar conditions presumably characterize other sandstone strata of the region, but detailed information on geological structures is lacking. It would appear that the natural springs in the area flow from exposed sandstone strata or from Tertiary deposits at lower elevations where water from higher elevations has percolated down. A permanent water supply, whether from a natural spring or from a well, is the most consistently sought-after natural resource in the region. The shift to ranching as the basic economic pursuit has been speeded by the continual uncertainty of adequate water supplies for successful farming.

Climatic conditions affect human settlement in at least three major ways. Enough moisture from winter rains and snows must be retained in the soil of the nonirrigated areas to bring the newly planted crops and pasture grasses up in the spring. It is necessary that rains from the Tropical Gulf air mass fall during the critical growing period in summer and be sufficiently sustained to water the maturing crops. In the Homestead community in particular, high winds during the dry period in March and April remove fertile topsoil as they rage over newly plowed fields or fields with no stubble. Last, while the average length of the growing season is 100 to 130 days, killing frosts sometimes occur late in the spring. This necessitates replanting of crops if time for an adequate growing season remains. Frosts early in the fall may reduce the yield and quality of the harvest. A high escarpment on the southern border of the Homestead community shows the effect of topography on rainfall. This 1000-feet-high escarpment, rising abruptly from the valley to the south, has an orographic effect upon the moisture-laden, northward-moving Gulf air masses that results in greater precipitation for the community than would otherwise occur.

The exploitation and control of natural resources is expressed differently in each of the five cultures. Each makes extensive use of at least one important resource and in many cases exploits natural resources to the fullest extent. In general, the more intimate the relation between man and environment, the more entrenched is the culture in a specific style of life.

CULTURAL VARIATIONS IN ECOLOGICAL ADJUSTMENT

While features of the physical environment have offered possibilities for human settlement and use of the land in the Rimrock area, they have also placed constraints upon the development of ecological adaptations that are found in regions with lower elevations, higher rainfalls, or different land forms in other parts of the United States. Within the possibilities and limitations posed by nature, each of the cultural groups has developed and maintained patterns of settlement and land-use which are profoundly influenced by cultural definitions as to the most desirable way to live upon and use the land.

SETTLEMENT PATTERNS

The concept of settlement pattern[1] refers to the characteristic manner in which household and community units are arranged spatially over the landscape.[2] This is one aspect of a widely distributed interest in "territoriality" as a critical feature in the study of animal and human life. Biologists are concerned with territoriality as an aspect of the social behavior of wild vertebrates.[3] Bartholomew and Birdsell discuss the problem with reference to protohominids.[4] Anthropologists have long been actively concerned with discovering the nature of local groups, treating "locality" or "territoriality" as one of two major factors in the study of the basic principles of organization in primitive societies — the other being kinship groupings. Archaeologists are also making increasing use of settlement pattern as a key concept linking environmental and socio-political structure.[5]

The relative amount of clustering or spreading of human habitations over a given landscape has obvious implications for the type of social organization that can or will develop and be maintained. Populations spread thinly are likely to have relatively simple, loosely structured social organizations unless some special integrative feature (such as the Maya ceremonial center) is developed which brings larger groups together periodically to build the centers and carry out the annual round of ceremonials. Populations living in compact villages are likely to have relatively complex and more highly integrated and tightly structured social organizations to handle the basic problems of social and political order which develop with heavier concentrations.

The groups in the Rimrock area have three basic types of settlement patterns (see Maps 2 and 3): compact village — Zuni, Spanish-American, and Mormon; scattered extended family settlement — Navaho; isolated farmstead with service center — Texan homesteader. The compact village patterns of the Zunis, Mormons, and Spanish-Americans vary in detail but have in common the fundamental features of a central plaza and/or church with houses clustered together and fields and ranches located at some distance from the village.

Although the Zuni pueblo has been gradually spreading out from the central plaza during the past thirty years, it still contains almost 2500 persons living within an area the size of a few city blocks, and the houses located at the edge are still within shouting distance of one another (see Map 4). In the heart of the pueblo there are many house units which adjoin others wall to wall. Multistoried structures and wall-to-wall joining of housing units are diagnostic features of the classical Southwestern pueblo architecture found in earlier periods of history, but the multistoried feature is no longer found in modern Zuni. In the outlying farming villages of Nutria, Pescado, and Ojo Caliente, there is somewhat more dispersion. There are also a few outlying Zuni ranch homes occupied for part of every year

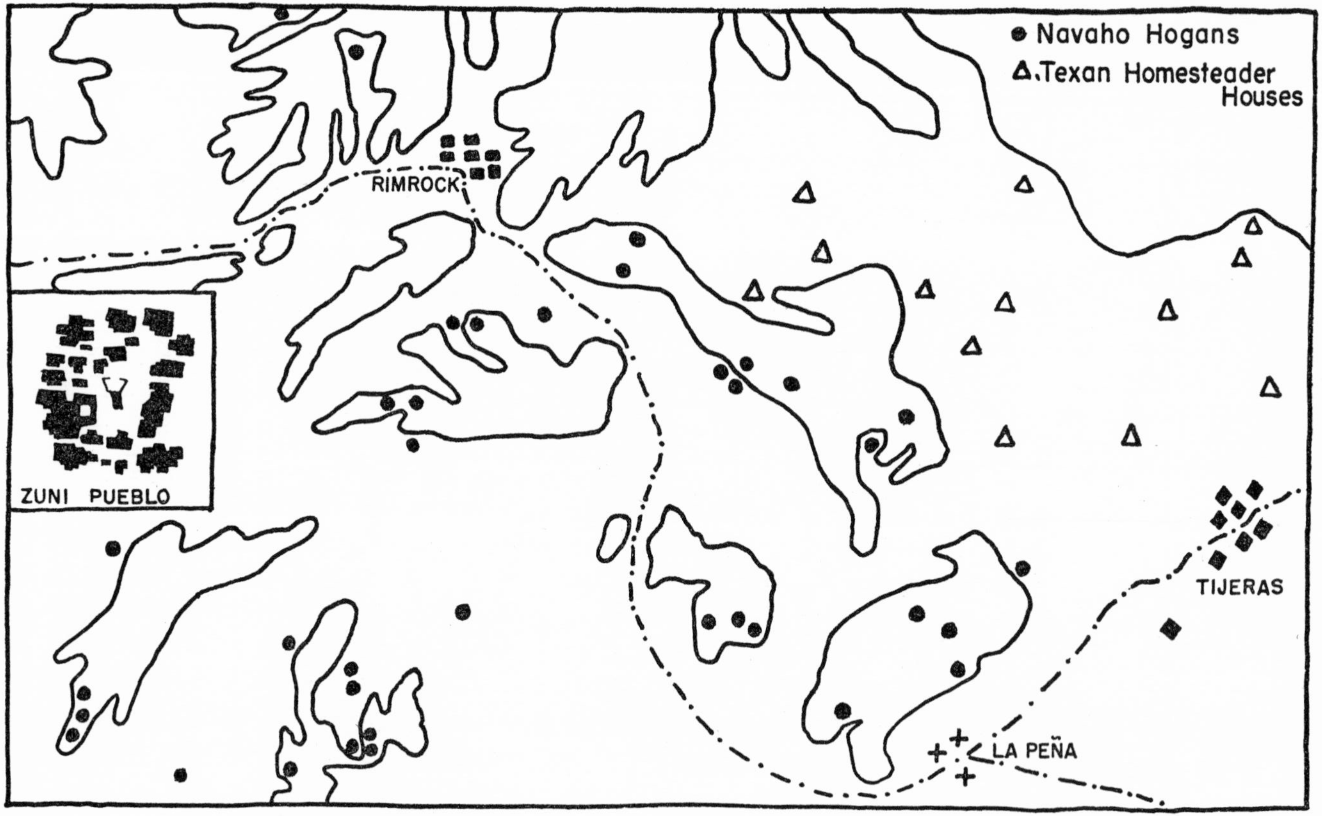

Navaho Hogans
▲ Texan Homesteader Houses

TIJERAS

LA PEÑA

RIMROCK

ZUNI PUEBLO

N ↑

3. Types of settlement patterns

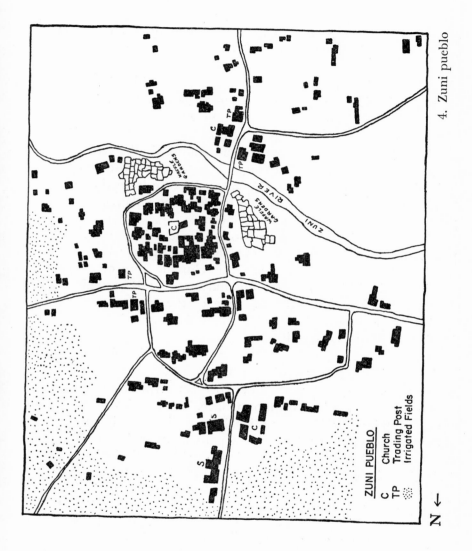

ZUNI PUEBLO
C   Church
TP   Trading Post
⋯   Irrigated Fields

N ←

4. Zuni pueblo

located as far as twenty-five miles from the central pueblo. But the general pattern is still one of a relatively high degree of compactness in settlement, with clustered habitations and with the fields located around the edges of the settlements. Each of the Zuni settlements is located in a valley where there is a permanent water supply and where good agricultural possibilities exist. The Zuni River running past the central pueblo has always been a permanent though small stream; there is now also a dam at Black Rock which in good years collects irrigation water. The farming village of Nutria draws water from springs and run-off from melting winter snows in the Zuni Mountains. There are springs at Pescado and also an irrigation reservoir that collects water from the mountains via the Rimrock Valley watershed, and an excellent large spring at Ojo Caliente furnishes irrigation water for the fields. At some distance from the fields, on top of the mesas and in the valleys between the villages, range-lands provide pasture for Zuni herds of sheep.

The Spanish-American pattern of settlement is also one of compact villages with houses, occupied here by nuclear families, clustered around a plaza with a Catholic church, store or stores, and *cantina,* and with outlying *ranchos* and range-lands located as far as fifteen miles from the villages. Some of the ranch homes are occupied the year round, but most families also maintain a town house in the village. In the villages themselves, the houses are not as compact as in Zuni pueblo; there are no multistoried structures, and there is much less wall-to-wall joining of houses (see "C" on Map 6). But the houses are closer together (typically within a few yards) than they are in a Mormon village. The location of permanent water supplies was important in the selection of village sites for the Spanish-Americans. There is a permanent spring at Tijeras at the foot of the Zuni Mountains that provided a limited amount of irrigation water for small fields near the village. However, in the case of Atrisco, water supply has always been problematic. The first Spanish-American settlement in the vicinity was established in a canyon two miles southwest of the present village, where a large spring provided irrigation water. As a result of a quarrel among the settlers, one large family moved to the present site of Atrisco. There are no springs, and the settlers attempted irrigation agriculture by constructing a dam to collect rain water. The dam washed out after a few years, and the people turned increasingly to livestock raising.[6] Wells drilled in the village produced only brackish water with a high alkali content, so that household water has to be taken from rain-filled pools or stock tanks or hauled from wells either in Homestead Center or on distant ranches.

The Mormon village provides a third variety of compact settlement (see Map 5). The church house is located in the center of

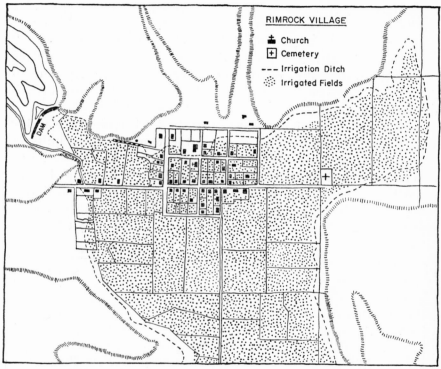

RIMROCK VILLAGE

⛪ Church
[+] Cemetery
--- Irrigation Ditch
∷ Irrigated Fields

N ↓

5. Rimrock village

the community, and most of the houses, occupied by nuclear families, are located on lots making up approximately ten square blocks. The rectangular grid pattern of streets which outline the blocks and the rows of trees and irrigation ditches which line the streets present an orderly arrangement that is lacking in the Zuni and Spanish-American villages. Since garden plots are also located on each lot, the houses are not as close together — though they are within shouting distance of one another — as in a Spanish-American

167

village, where they are a few yards apart. The irrigated fields of the Mormons surround the village on three sides; their dry-land farms and ranches are located on lands as far away as twenty miles to the south and east of the village. A few of the ranch homes are occupied the year round, but most families maintain their residence in the village. In selecting this site for settlement, the Mormon colonists chose one of the best locations for irrigation agriculture in the region. The dam, which collects the run-off from the winter snow-packs in the Zuni Mountains, was built at the mouth of the narrow canyon just above the Rimrock Valley. Two main irrigation ditches, one which circles the valley on the north and west sides and one which circles the valley on the east and south sides, carry water to fields. The village, with its houses and irrigated gardens, was laid out near the center of the valley.

The most scattered settlement pattern is that of the Navahos, who live predominantly in matrilocal extended family units occupying two or more hogans within shouting distance of one another. Associated structures typically include a summer shade, a sweat house, a sheep corral, and a horse corral (see "B" on Map 6). Small fields are found near the hogans. Water for the sheep and horses is provided by stock tanks and/or wells drilled by the Indian

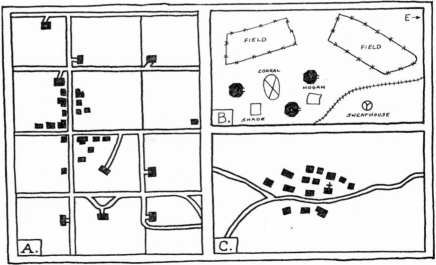

6. Settlement pattern of Texan homesteaders, Navahos, and Spanish Americans

Service. Household water is hauled from these tanks or wells in summer, derived from melted snow in winter. The Navaho extended family establishments are dispersed over the landscape at distances ranging from one to four miles. The lands in between are utilized for grazing and for wood-hauling. The sheep are herded in small flocks owned by members of the extended family, with a consequent tendency for the grazing land in the immediate vicinity of the hogans to become overgrazed. This pattern contrasts markedly with the Zuni and Spanish-American practice in which sheep are handled in large herds kept out on the range at some distance from the villages. The Navaho pattern forces families to shift residence from time to time as water supplies and pasturage are depleted. This movement is not a wide-ranging nomadism, as found in the Near East and Central Asia, but is restricted within a small territory which an extended family owns by the system of inherited land-use ownership.[7] Nowhere in the Rimrock Navaho country is there any clustering of Navaho families larger than three or four hogans, nor is there a Navaho-controlled trading center where larger numbers might live.

The Texan homesteader settlement pattern approaches that of the Navaho in degree of dispersal, but there are important differences. The homesteaders live on isolated farmsteads, predominantly in nuclear family units, which operate a section or more of land (see "A" on Map 6). Each nuclear family lives approximately a mile from its nearest neighbors. But there are crossroad service centers at La Peña and at Homestead which contain stores, schools, and other service institutions, as well as the homes of tradespeople, schoolteachers and, a few of the farm operators whose lands adjoin the service center. At La Peña, at the time of the research, there were only two families, the trader's and the schoolteacher's living at the service center; at Homestead approximately one-fourth of the population lived at the crossroads service center, while the other three-fourths were dispersed on isolated farmsteads.

Comparing these contrasting settlement patterns, the question arises as to what determined the exact locations of habitats within the region at which each cultural group established its settlements, and the types of settlement patterns which emerged and which continue to be maintained. Were the determinants purely geographic, demographic, and economic? Were they a matter of dif-

169

ferential power? Or were certain choices made which reflect variations in value systems? Although the location of each cultural group within the region was determined primarily by geographical, historical, and power considerations (the differential value systems of the cultures having had little to do with the selections made) the types of settlement patterns established were strongly influenced by value systems. The selection of habitats can be explained by a combination of three factors: the availability of permanent water supplies and arable land; the time of arrival in the region; and the differentials in political power among the groups. The Zunis had relatively free choice, being the first group to settle in the region, and they selected habitats which had permanent springs and provided arable land for farming. The early Navaho settlements were established in the Rimrock Valley and in the mesa and canyon country along the southwestern edge of the Zuni Mountains, where there were also some springs and a number of streams which ran for at least part of each year. The later Mormon and Spanish-American entry into the region brought peoples with political power superior to that of the Navahos. They replaced the Navahos in the Rimrock and Tijeras Valleys, pushing them into the less desirable lands to the south. The Atrisco settlement was established on open land to the south of Navaho lands, but here again the availability of a permanent spring and potential dam site were important in the selection of habitat. By the time the Texan homesteaders arrived, the lands with permanent water supplies were all taken and the other four groups were already firmly established with property rights that were supported by the power of state and federal governmental agencies. The only lands left to them were the dry-land homestead tracts in the La Peña and Homestead areas.

Although nature poses important limits, the actual type of settlements — the relative degree of cluster or dispersal that each group established and maintained was significantly related to variations in value systems.* The major contrast is between the compact village plans of the Zunis, Spanish-Americans, and Mormons and the dispersed pattern of the Navaho and Texan settlements. Since the cultural groups with compact villages are also those which practice

* Population density bears no close relation to type of settlement pattern (see Table 15). While Zuni has the highest population density and the most compact settlement pattern, Navaho and Texan are next highest in population density but most dispersed in settlement pattern.

170

irrigation agriculture, one may wonder if the requirements of irrigation have not demanded a compact village plan. The essential historical facts of the development and maintenance of each village plan indicate that this is much too simple an explanation. The compact Zuni village has its roots in the prehistory of pueblo culture and was at least in part a matter of defense against other tribes; the development of irrigation agriculture simply re-enforced it. However, neither considerations of defense nor of irrigation provide an explanation of the continuation of the clustered village, especially since in modern times the Zuni subsistence system has shifted from a focus upon irrigation agriculture to sheep, silversmithing, and wage-work. Rather, it seems clear that Zunis have become town dwellers in a very profound sense, and that their way of life revolves around a compact settlement pattern. They prefer to live in the central village where everything that is important in Zuni life is going on. Those families with lands and houses in the outlying farming villages also maintain houses in the central pueblo that they occupy part of each year, and the herders who care for Zuni sheep out on the range always arrange the herding in such a way as to minimize the amount of time that any given individual spends away from the pueblo.

Defense considerations were also important to the Spanish-Americans in the days before New Mexico became part of the United States and Navaho and Apache raids were stopped by American military power. But the compact village clustered around a church was regarded as the ideal type of settlement by the Spanish crown,[8] and Spanish settlements throughout the New World have conformed to the compact village plan the colonists brought with them from Spain. Like the Zunis, the Spanish-Americans are town dwellers by preference, and most of them maintain town residences even when their ranching activities might suggest that a scattered settlement pattern would be more efficient economically.

The pattern of the Mormon village was neither a direct function of the requirements of irrigation agriculture nor of the need for protection against Indians. The basic pattern was a social invention of the Mormons, motivated by a sense of urgent need to prepare a dwelling place for the Savior at "His Second Coming." The "Plat of the City of Zion" was invented in 1833 for this purpose and has been the basis for the laying out of most Mormon villages, even those established in the Middle West before the Mormons migrated to Utah. Map 4 shows the extent to which the Mormons clustered their houses instead of spreading them out over the valley. Despite shifting of the Mormon subsistence pattern toward cattle raising, the basic village plan is being maintained.[9]

The scattered settlement patterns of the Navahos and Texans reflect quite different concepts of the desirable way to live on the land. The Navaho pattern is closely related to their emphasis upon "familistic individualism," and associated customs of living in extended family units which are typically the largest unit that co-operates on a day-to-day basis in owning and herding sheep and farming the dry-land crops.[10] If their customs permitted the cooperative pooling of sheep in herds of one to two thousand, there is no geographic or economic reason why larger numbers of families could not live together and take turns handling the larger herds, as the Zunis do. Indeed, there is good evidence that herding sheep in larger units that could be kept far out on the range would result in less overgrazing than the practice of bringing the small herds back to the extended family establishments each night.

The Texan homesteader pattern is closely related to a strong stress upon "individualism." The homesteaders brought to the Rimrock area a set of individualistic property arrangements in which it was considered most desirable that each family settle on its own place. Once their communities were established, the individualism permitted by the scattered dry-farming pattern and encouraged by the emphasis upon the small nuclear family reacted upon and strongly re-enforced the value stress upon individual independence. One would not expect farmers whose farms are located fifteen or twenty miles away from the service center to live in town and travel out to work each day, but there is no geographic or economic reason why those families living within two or three miles of the village center could not live in town. But the homesteaders prefer this way of life, as shown not only by the persistence of the pattern but also by their negative remarks concerning the "bunched up" character of a Mormon or Spanish-American or Zuni village. Moreover, a number of families moved "out of town" when they built new houses.[11]

In brief, while the selection of habitats within the region was primarily a matter of compelling geographic, historical, and power factors as each cultural group arrived, the development and maintenance of settlement patterns within each of these habitats are significantly related to variations in value systems that emerged early in the history of each cultural group and continue to influence the residence patterns in each case.

LAND-USE PATTERNS

The particular habitats occupied by each of the cultural groups and the settlement patterns developed are aspects of the ecological adjustment that are intimately related to the economic use each group makes of the land it controls. The land base controlled by each group, the total populations, and the population densities for 1950 are given in Table 15. On these land bases each group engages

Table 15. Population, land bases, and population density of five Rimrock culture groups.

Culture	1950 population	Land bases in sections	Density per township†	Density per section
Zuni*	2486	691.4	129.4	3.6
Navaho	625	240.0	94.5	2.6
Texan	232	98.8	84.5	2.3
Mormon	241	153.0	56.7	1.6
Spanish-American	89	103.5	31.0	0.9
Total	3673	1286.7	—	—
Average	734.6	257.3	79.2	2.2

* Zuni population does not include Zuni families living off the Reservation.
† The density per township is included to make ready comparison possible with population figures calculated on the basis of 100 square kilometers which is only 7 percent more than a township.

in farming, animal husbandry, hunting, and wild-plant gathering, but the focus as to type and amount varies from one culture to another and has undergone important changes in recent years.

In considering the land-use patterns certain hard facts must be kept in mind concerning amounts of land necessary to make a living by irrigation farming, dry farming, or grazing; differentials in risk stemming from geographic features; and differentials in risk stemming from the outside market situation. Whereas a family may derive a subsistence income from 40 acres of irrigated land, it takes at least a section (640 acres) to provide the same kind of income from dry farming, and at least five sections to graze enough sheep or cattle to reach the same income level. With reference to geographic or environmental risk, livestock raising is the most secure, irrigation farming is next, and dry farming is the least secure way of making a living. The reason for this variable risk is that the growing of grass for grazing livestock is least affected by low rainfall and frost. Irrigation farming from permanent springs is a secure economic enterprise, but if one depends upon storage water from winter snows or summer rains, there comes a point in a long drought when irrigation water is exhausted. Dry-land crops are vulnerable both to drought and to frost. The pattern of market risks has shifted since the prewar era. Before World War II the prices on dry-land crops, especially beans, fluctuated enormously, the price of beans having reached a low of two cents per pound during the 1930's and a high of thirteen cents during the war. At that time, therefore, dry-land farming of pinto beans was the least secure way to make a living. Livestock prices were somewhat more stable, and irrigated crops were less affected still, since most of the crops grown on irrigated land in the Rimrock area were subsistence crops, grown for food or livestock feed. However, after World War II, pinto beans were given price support by the federal government; hence this basic dry-land crop involved less market risk than sheep and cattle, the price of which has dropped in the last two or three years of the study. In sum, it appears that, if a family has sufficient land for livestock raising, this type of economic enterprise provides a better balance between the risks posed by nature and the risks posed by the market than does dry-land farming. So livestock raising is a better economic alternative to irrigation farming than is dry-land farming.

Before the arrival of the Spaniards the Zuni land-use pattern was focused upon farming, with secondary emphasis upon hunting and wild-plant gathering. The main crops were corn, beans, and squash grown in the canyon bottoms by a system of dry-land cultivation. There is evidence that some irrigation from the permanent springs was practiced in aboriginal times,[12] but the important shift to irrigation came after the Spanish brought wheat, which could only be cultivated successfully with irrigation. Dams constructed by the United States Government above the central pueblo in 1909 and at each of the farming villages in the 1930's provided a storage capacity of about 20,000 acre feet of irrigation water in good run-off years that could be used for Zuni agriculture. However, by 1940 the capacity of the largest dam above the central pueblo had been reduced by some 12,000 acre feet by silting, leaving only about 8,000 acre feet of storage capacity for irrigation water on the whole reservation.[13]

In 1952, the Zunis owned about 4,095 acres of agricultural land: 2,810 for irrigation farming and 1,285 for dry farming. The rest of the land was used for grazing. Corn is the principal dry-land crop; irrigated crops are alfalfa, wheat, corn, beans, melons, and pumpkins. Peach orchards are maintained near Zuni and at Ojo Caliente, and small crops of chili, onions, and so on are grown in small, terraced gardens, irrigated by hand from the Zuni River, at the edge of the pueblo. The Spanish brought domestic animals to the Zunis; before they had had only the domesticated turkey. Livestock is now a major economic activity with a focus upon sheep (approximately 15,561 head including ewes, wethers, rams, and lambs), and smaller numbers of cattle, swine, poultry, and horses.

The utilization of wild plants has been reduced to the sporadic gathering of a few types of plant foods, especially pinyon nuts in good years, the cutting of pine logs for roof beams and sawing of lumber at a sawmill constructed and supervised by the Indian Service for house roofs and doors, the cutting of juniper posts for fencing fields, and the gathering of wood, particularly pinyon, juniper, and oak, for heating and cooking in all of the villages. Quarrying of sandstone and use of mud for plaster are essential elements for Zuni houses. While the hunting of deer and of smaller game such as rabbits was once important, there is now relatively little hunting. Zuni males do not hunt for sport as frequently as do the Mormons and Texans. Some ritual hunting still takes place, especially the killing of small fawns, the head and skins of which are worn by the *koyemci*, "mud-heads," during the winter dances.

By the time the Navahos settled permanently at Rimrock, their land-use patterns had long since shifted from hunting and gathering as a way of life to dry farming — the crops and techniques of which they are presumed to have borrowed in earlier centuries from the Pueblo Indians — and sheep husbandry, which they acquired later from contacts with the Spanish. A few of the Rimrock

Navahos still go deer-hunting for meat rather than for sport, and many families kill rabbits, prairie dogs, and other small game. Numerous plants, the most important being pinyon nuts and yucca fruit, are gathered for food, and there is intensive use of wild plants for medicines.[14] Pinyon logs for hogan-building and juniper posts for sweat houses are also crucial elements of Navaho material culture. Gathering activities are overshadowed by the food-producing patterns of farming and sheep raising. In good years the Navahos dry-farm approximately 3000 acres, almost half of which is planted in corn, the rest in beans, squash, and other crops. A few Navaho families practiced irrigation in the Rimrock Valley before they were displaced by the Mormons. The balance of the land base is devoted to the grazing of about 6656 sheep, 470 goats, and smaller numbers of horses and cows.

While the original Spanish-American settlers had small irrigated fields at Tijeras and Atrisco, the predominant economic activity soon became stock-raising. During the peak of Spanish-American population and power in the 1920's, numerous large herds of sheep were grazed. Although control of most of the Spanish-American range passed into the hands of the Anglos, the remnant population continued to focus upon livestock-raising, with about 1195 sheep and 378 cattle as of 1952. The farming techniques of the Texan homesteaders provided a model for an increasing amount of Spanish-American dry-land farming in recent years, almost 250 acres of corn, beans, and other crops having been under cultivation in the Atrisco and Tijeras areas. A few wild plants are gathered for food; like the other groups, the Spanish-Americans utilize pinyon and juniper wood for heating and cooking, and juniper posts for fencing. Logs for roof *vigas* are cut from the pines at higher elevations, and sandstone or adobes form the walls of their houses. Deer-hunting is infrequent, but rabbits and other small game are still taken for food.

The Mormon community began with an economic focus upon irrigation farming in the Rimrock Valley. A dam across the canyon above the village was first constructed in 1882–83,[15] and later additions brought its storage capacity up to 13,000 acre feet which irrigated about 1,200 acres of fields, gardens, and pastures.[16] The field crops are predominantly oats, wheat, alfalfa, and potatoes; table vegetables are produced in the gardens, and the pastures provide forage for milk cows. Irrigation agriculture continued to be the predominant land-use pattern until quite recently, when outlying dry-land farms and cattle ranches were established to the east and south. The Mormons dry-farm about 1,000 acres of corn and beans in good years and run about 1,260 head of beef cattle and 950 sheep in 149 sections of range land. Logs for building are cut in the Zuni Mountains, and most of the wood for heating and cooking is hauled from lands near the valley. Sandstone is quarried for building houses and other structures. Juniper posts are used for fencing. Some collecting of wild plant foods, especially pinyon nuts, still occurs. Hunting has become more important to the Mormons than to any other cultural group in the region. Mormon males are enthusiastic hunters, and almost all of them go deer-hunting each fall; some go on successful antelope and elk hunts. Although hunting is carried on for sport, it adds impressive amounts of meat to the family deep freezers.

The Texan land-use pattern is concentrated primarily on the dryland farming of pinto beans. In 1950 Homestead had 11,213 acres under cultivation, 6,417 of which were planted in beans. Corn and winter wheat were the important secondary crops. The balance of the land base of 98.8 sections was devoted largely to the grazing of 1,100 beef cattle. There were also 280 swine, but no sheep. A few families have vegetable gardens watered from wells pumped by windmills. A few wild "greens" and pinyon nuts are collected; corrals are constructed of pinyon or juniper poles and fences built with juniper posts; wood for heating and cooking is gathered locally. Rabbit-hunting is a minor activity, but the Texans are second only to the Mormons as enthusiastic deer hunters. Hunting parties go out each fall, and the majority of families eat at least one buck a year. In good hunting years, probably 10 percent of the total meat supply is venison.

Table 16 compares the differentials in land use classified according to the four major patterns (farming, animal husbandry, hunting, and gathering). This table underscores our statements that the Mormons are irrigation-farmers and cattle-raisers; the Texans dryland bean farmers and cattle-raisers; the Navahos sheep-raisers and dry-land farmers; and the Spanish-Americans sheep- and cattle-raisers. Zuni is in a curious position, for only in the case of sheep-raising is a very important per-capita use being made of the land relative to the other cultures; this large population is supported mainly from

Table 16. Land use classified according to the four major patterns,
arranged according to importance in the five cultures.

Farming (acres per capita)				Animal husbandry (head per capita)			
irrigation		dry land		sheep		cattle	
Mormon	4.9	Texan	48.0	Span.-Amer.	13.4	Mormon	5.5
Zuni	1.0	Navaho	4.8	Navaho	11.4	Texan	4.7
		Mormon	4.1	Zuni	6.2	Span.-Amer.	4.2
		Span.-Amer.	2.6	Mormon	3.2	Zuni	0.2
		Zuni	0.5	Texan	0	Navaho	0.19

Hunting		Gathering	
Mormon	most important	Navaho	most important
Texan		Zuni	
Navaho		Span.-Amer.	
Zuni		Mormon	
Span.-Amer.	least important	Texan	least important

sources other than their land base. There is an interesting pattern
regarding hunting and gathering activities. Mormons and Texans
place relatively great emphasis upon hunting, but little upon gathering. The Navahos and Zunis emphasize gathering activities, but
do not hunt much. The Spanish-Americans do relatively little hunting and make average use of wild plants.

What geographical and cultural factors cause variations in land-
use patterns? In farming it is evident that whether a group engages
in irrigation or dry-land farming is primarily a function of geography, in the sense that Mormons and Zunis control the suitable
dam sites and/or permanently flowing springs that provide the necessary water and the valley bottom land that can be irrigated. This
leaves the Texans, Spanish-Americans (at present), and Navahos
with only dry-land farming possibilities. The relatively greater
amount of Mormon irrigation farming as compared with Zuni is
a geographical and demographic matter, in that the main Zuni storage reservoir has silted in and reduced the total available irrigation
capacity in a period of marked population growth.

The dry-land farming differentials raise more complicated questions, for there are lands controlled by each cultural group that
could be dry-farmed in normal years but are not. A complex com-

178

bination of factors relating to the market, to conceptions of standards of living, to population density, and to value-preferences in the allocation of time and resources are involved. The Texans are outstandingly dry-land farmers. Their farming is largely a commercial operation which produces pinto beans for the outside market and earns money for them to purchase the economic goods they feel they need with their relatively high standard of living. They do not have enough land to go into stock-raising to earn this cash, so they plow and attempt to dry-farm twice as much land as all the other groups together have under dry-land cultivation, goaded on by a strong emphasis upon mastery over nature and a perennial optimism that helps to keep the dry farms operating even in drought years.

The Spanish-American dry farming efforts are definitely secondary to stock-raising as a source of income. They do not farm as persistently or as hopefully as the Texans, feeling fatalistically that, if anything comes of the effort, it is fine and, if there is a drought and the crop fails, it is to be expected in this arid land. The crops raised are utilized much more for subsistence, for household food, and for feeding livestock. Despite the relatively small per capita figure, the Navaho dry-farming activities are of crucial importance to their economy. Dry farming is almost wholly a subsistence, providing food for families and some supplementary feed for livestock, especially horses. Only a few of the Spanish-Americans attempt dry farming, but almost every Navaho family has one or more small fields which it farms. Mormon dry farming differs in that it is done by a few families who have little or no irrigated land in the valley and engage in pinto bean commercial farming as a means of supplementing income from cattle raising. Although there are vast acreages on the Zuni Reservation which in good years could produce dry-land crops, the Zunis have shifted their focus to sheep, which are owned by the richer families, and to silversmithing, which provides income for the poorer families. The market for silver jewelry has drawn economic effort away from the traditional subsistence agriculture.

The decision to raise sheep or cattle is, we think, almost entirely a function of value-preferences within a cultural group. Over a period of time the income from sheep is about equal to that which can be derived from cattle, although sheep provide two marketable products a year (wool and lambs), whereas cattle provide only one (beef). This does not alter the proposition that the total amount of income derived is approximately equal. The choice of the kind of animal to be raised is linked to a whole complex of cultural patterns and values. The Spanish-American is the only group that splits its preferences between the two kinds of animal. This has been true for a long time in Spanish-American history and is continuing in the present, with the same stockmen running both sheep and cattle. The Navahos and Zuni prefer sheep; the Texans and Mormons prefer cattle.*

Sheep have a central position in the Navaho value system. The ideal food is mutton, especially mutton ribs roasted over the coals of an open campfire.† The people sleep on sheepskins in their hogans and the women weave rugs from the wool. The people live close to, and intimately with, their herds. The earliest remembered experiences of young Navahos are of herding sheep. Owning sheep means having wealth and security. Every member of a family (including children) owns some of the sheep. Sacred songs are sung to protect and increase the herds. To the Navahos traditional life would be unthinkable without sheep. The situation is different with the Zunis, although mutton is preferred to beef, and sheep are viewed principally as a source of food and negotiable wealth. The large herds are kept in remote parts of the reservation, where they are herded by adult males, not by the women and children as among the Navahos. Zunis do not weave the wool nor use the skins except in sheep camp. Their attitude is utilitarian — sheep offer a way of earning money to buy goods in the outside market and provide meat for stew.

The Mormon and Texan preference for cattle is due to a liking for beef rather than mutton,‡ to the fact that these groups do not have the social organization to provide sheepherders without hiring them, and to the prestige found in the "cowboy pattern" (stimulated by the Hollywood and comic-book heroes). "Sheepherders" are associated with Mexican and Indian culture, whereas "cowboys" are glamorous figures, as reflected in the style of dress, in rodeo activities, in dancing and music.

* All of the Mormon sheep are owned by two families.
† Even Navaho families who own cattle prefer mutton.
‡ Mutton is sometimes eaten by Mormons, but we have never known a Texan voluntarily to purchase mutton when any other kind of meat was available.

The relative amounts of emphasis placed upon hunting and gathering also has an intimate relation to the value systems of the groups. The Navahos and Zunis have an anciently developed knowledge of the land and its resources and a wholly different attitude toward nature from that of the Mormons and Texans. Their continued gathering activities are linked not only to their economic life, but also very profoundly to their ceremonial life. The Navaho use plants in curing rituals; the Zunis decorate their *katchina* dancers with spruce boughs. On the other hand, hunting has become a male sport of tremendous significance to the Mormons and Texans. It is a time to leave the "women folks" behind and to assert one's manliness in a deer hunt that requires superb skill, much rugged walking and climbing, and carrying back the killed animals. Many Mormons and Texans spend the year looking forward to hunting season.

Operation of the Economic Systems

"Settlement" and "land-use pattern" concern the relations of cultures to their natural habitats; they have more to do with ecological adjustments than with economic relations. Economic systems are linked to the settlement and land-use patterns, but they are basically involved in the social structures of the local cultural groups and are also geared into the larger market situation.

OCCUPATIONAL STRUCTURE

Three major economic occupational categories are found in all five cultures: rancher-farmer, service and business occupations, and wage earners. The rancher-farmer role is filled by those who devote their economic efforts to ranching and/or farming. The service occupations include storekeepers, repair shop operators, service station operators, cafe operators, bartenders, schoolteachers, and postmasters. These occupations are defined by the communities as providing services of various kinds for the families engaged in ranching and/or farming. The business occupations involve both the ownership and management of the small businesses. The schoolteachers and postmasters are appointed by the government. The wage earners are those who have neither ranch, farm, nor a business of sufficient size to support themselves and have to seek employment from others, either within the Rimrock area or, more commonly, in economic enterprises outside the region.

Except for the Catholic priests and Protestant missionaries assigned to work in the Rimrock area (and they are never members of any of the local cultural groups), there are no full-time religious specialists in any of the cultures. There are, however, many part-time religious practitioners in each group (see Chapter 8). There are a large number of other part-time occupational roles: silversmiths among the Navaho and Zuni, rug-weavers among the Navaho, carpenters, plumbers, water-witches, and well-drillers among the Mormons and Texans.

The rancher-farmer role is primary in all the cultural groups; it is the major economic occupation for most men. It is the most prestigeful occupation, and almost all of the men engaged in service occupations and in wage-work are also engaged in ranching and/or farming to some extent. It is significant that in all of these small communities, the rancher-farmers are overwhelmingly owner-operators of their ranch- and farm-lands. This is a recent development in the case of the local Spanish-American group, however, and the kind of ownership varies with the culture. In the 1920's, the bulk of the Spanish-American land base was controlled by a few relatively wealthy ranchers who played the role of *patrón* for their communities. They operated large herds of sheep and cattle on the range-land they controlled and employed the other adult males to care for the livestock. When the bulk of the land passed into the hands of Anglo-American ranchers, the situation changed; in 1951, only two Spanish-American men were employed as herders by the son of the former *patrón*. The others who remained owned some land and were owner-operators of their ranches and farms.

In Zuni, almost all farming and livestock enterprises are operated by the family units defined by Zuni custom as owning the land and the animals. A few of the large sheepmen hire herders, especially Navahos and Spanish-Americans, but there are to our knowledge no cases of tenancy. The same conditions prevail among the Navahos; a few of the large livestock owners occasionally hire herders, but the herding usually is done by members of the extended family or "outfit" unit. Farming is always done by family units who own the land, as defined by Navaho custom.

The same pattern is followed in the Mormon community where

farming and livestock-raising is carried on by the people who own the property. Some of these operations are family cooperatives or larger company cooperatives, but only two families with herds of sheep and a few larger farm operators hire Navahos or others to work in the enterprises. The renting of land to others is very rare.

The Texan homesteader farms and ranches are also predominantly operated by independent owners, but tenant-farming has a higher incidence in this cultural group than in any of the others. In Homestead in 1950, fourteen of the forty-eight farm operators were part- or full-time renters of property owned by others, and these renters farmed 14 percent of the total land under cultivation. However, only six of these farmers rented from absentee-owners; the rest rented from others in the community, mostly close kinsmen. This higher incidence of tenancy among the Texans is closely related to the social structure and value system of this cultural group with its strong stress upon individualistic ownership and management of the farm-lands. Unlike the Mormon, Zuni, and Navaho cultures, in which the larger kinship units operate enterprises cooperatively, the Texans apply the system of tenancy even to those cases in which farms are owned by close relatives of the operator.

In general, the rancher-farmers of Rimrock own their lands and manage their own business affairs, the major axis of differentiation being not between owners and operators of the property but between families owning varying amounts of land and livestock. The differentials in livestock owned by families are especially important in all the cultures. Table 17 provides a comparative profile of the extent to which there is a concentration of livestock ownership by a relatively small number of families in all five groups.

Zuni and Navaho differentials in livestock ownership are being perpetuated in part by Indian Service policy. The Indian Service attempts to control overgrazing through a permit system under which sheep and cattle owners are assigned quotas which they may legally graze on the tribal lands. These quotas are derived by dividing the total carrying capacity of the range among the livestock owners on the basis of the proportionate size of their herds in some selected year. The result is to "freeze" the relative sizes of herds, so that it becomes difficult for small herders to increase their holdings or for nonowners to start in the livestock business.[17]

The most striking fact about the service occupations is that they

Table 17. Ownership of livestock by families in the five cultures in 1952.

Culture	Number of families	Over 1000	501– 1000	401– 500	301– 400	201– 300	101– 200	76– 100	51– 75	26– 50	1– 25	None	Total
					Cattle								
Zuni	600	0	0	0	0	0	0	0	0	4	63	533	541
Navaho	126	0	0	0	0	0	1	0	0	0	5	120	123
Spanish-American	12	0	0	0	0	0	2	0	1	2	6	1	378
Mormon*	54	0	0	0	0	0	3	2	5	6	28	10	1,340
Texan*	61	0	0	0	0	1	1	1	4	5	32	17	1,219
					Sheep								
Zuni	600	2	0	6	7	9	17	39	20	80	9	411	15,561
Navaho†	126	0	1	3	1	5	12	8	10	13	18	55	7,126
Spanish-American	12	1	0	0	0	0	1	0	0	1	0	9	1,195
Mormon	54	0	1	0	1	0	0	0	0	0	0	52	950
Texan	61	0	0	0	0	0	0	0	0	0	0	61	0

* Mormon and Texan cattle figures include dairy cattle.
† Navaho sheep figures include goats.

are performed almost exclusively by Mormons and Texans, insofar as they are filled at all by members of the local groups. There were at the time of writing no traders, service station operators, cafe operators or schoolteachers drawn from the local Zuni, Navaho, or Spanish-American populations. One repair shop was owned by a Zuni in the pueblo; none by Navahos or Spanish-Americans. The Spanish-Americans formerly operated trading posts, but the only service businesses left to them are bars in Homestead and La Peña and the postoffice in Atrisco. Otherwise, the service occupations are filled by Mormons in Rimrock, La Peña, and the Navaho day school; by Texans in Homestead; and by outside Anglos who run the three trading posts, postoffice, and cafe at Zuni. About half of the schoolteachers in Rimrock and Homestead are drawn from the local Mormon and Texan populations, the rest are Anglos sent in by the county school boards. Almost all of the teachers in the Indian schools are outside Anglos.

These variations in the extent to which service roles are occupied by members of the different cultural groups are in part a matter of the access to superior economic resources and education which the Mormons and Texans enjoy as compared to the Indians and Spanish-Americans. But there are also special cultural reasons why the Spanish-Americans have bars (even with their small population), and why the Navahos and Zunis have no stores despite their relatively large populations. The bar, or *cantina*, occupies an important place among the institutions of the village and in the value system of the

184

Spanish-Americans. No Spanish-American village of any consequence is without one or more *cantinas,* any more than it is without a Catholic chapel. The *cantina* is a kind of clubhouse where the men gather each day not only to drink (especially wines), but also to talk and to sing *corridas* to the accompaniment of the guitar. They are especially important during formal *fiestas,* but there is almost no day when at least a small *fiesta* is not going on inside the *cantina.* In contrast, the Mormons have strong religious taboos against drinking and will not tolerate a bar in Rimrock. In Homestead, the strong stand of the women and of some of the men, especially the Baptists, against drinking and bars makes it virtually impossible for a member of one of the Texan homesteader families to own or operate a bar. Until quite recently, Indians were prohibited by federal and state laws from purchasing liquor in any form, much less setting up bars. Only the Spanish-Americans can operate bars with the approval of their communities and without violating federal and state laws. Hence it is no accident that the only two bars in the Rimrock region are owned and operated by Spanish-Americans.

In the past some of the Navahos and Zunis attempted to be storekeepers, but the role is incompatible with two features of these Indian cultures: the operation of kinship obligations and witchcraft gossip. When an Indian attempts to run a trading post, he becomes involved in the problem of extending credit to his kinsmen. If he carries out his reciprocal obligations as a respectable member of the community and extends credit liberally along kinship lines, the trading post goes broke. If he refuses to extend credit, his kinsmen criticize and gossip about his behavior, gossip which can take the extreme form of an accusation that his initial capital was obtained by witchcraft, or more diffusely, of his being a witch.

The problem of extending credit to kinsmen exists also in Mormon and Texan culture, but traders in these groups, where the kinship systems are not as important as in the Indian cultures, are usually able to withstand the pressure more successfully. It now seems fairly certain that at the present stage of acculturation, Navahos and Zunis cannot function successfully as storekeepers, so that these indispensable roles in their communities must be performed by Mormon, Texan, or other Anglo traders.

Some men in each cultural group work for wages, either in local

185

enterprises or in Railtown, Albuquerque, or more distant places. This is a residual category in the sense that the men engage in this form of livelihood only when they do not have enough farm land or livestock or a business of their own, or during drought years when crops fail. There are almost no wage workers in any of the groups who do not also attempt to farm or raise livestock at least on a small scale. Wage-work has its highest incidence among the Navahos, Spanish-Americans, and Zunis, in that order. As of 1952, at least one-half of the Navaho families in the Rimrock area were partly dependent upon wage-work for cash income, predominantly working as section hands on railroads in all parts of the western United States. The dependence is due to three facts: the great increase in Navaho population on the limited land base; the increasing concentration of livestock in the hands of fewer Navaho families; and the increasing indebtedness to the traders who extend credit so that Navahos can purchase food, clothing, and so forth — and then demand that they go to work on the railroad to pay off their debts before any more credit is extended.

Almost one-half of the Spanish-American families are dependent in part upon wage-work. In Zuni only some two hundred men were engaged in wage-work in 1952, despite the relatively low utilization of the land base for agriculture. (Silversmithing as a part-time occupation provides the major source of income for the bulk of families in the pueblo.)

Wage-work is also engaged in by Mormons and Texans, but the incidence is relatively low. Only some twenty Mormons and ten Texans derive substantial amounts of income from wage-work, although the number increases during bad drought years. For example, after the 1950 drought, fifteen families moved away for the winter to engage in wage-work.

The contemporary occupational structure of the five cultures reflects the high value placed upon the role of the rancher-farmer as the most suitable and most appropriate way for males to make a living in all of the cultures. The service occupations are considered necessary to provide services for the primary productive persons, that is, the ranchers and farmers who are actually raising the livestock and growing the crops. Working for wages is a last resort, something one does when ranching, farming, running a small business, or being a schoolteacher is either not possible or does not provide enough income to live on.

SOCIAL MANAGEMENT OF ECONOMIC ENTERPRISES

The occupational roles are embedded in social structural and value system frameworks of each cultural group. These frameworks profoundly affect the manner in which the various economic enterprises function in each.[18] Texan land and business property is individually owned. The members of the nuclear family assist in the operation of farms and businesses. Except for the cooperative which owns and manages the central community well in Homestead center, and a limited amount of exchange work among kinsmen and neighbors, there are no economic enterprises which regularly involve individuals outside the nuclear family. Thus the Texans come close to the classical conception of an individualistic free-enterprise economic system, with a strong emphasis upon competition among individual property owners as the basic regulatory mechanism.

In the Mormon economic system, the concept of individual private property is altered profoundly as a matter of principle. There are several extended family enterprises, and the irrigation, town water, and cattle companies are operated on a cooperative basis. The economic ethic set forth by Joseph Smith in the Law of Consecration is seen in the dual commitment to private individual initiative in the operation of family farms and businesses and to cooperative endeavor in larger communal undertakings. Insistence upon cooperative solutions to problems is supported by strong kinship connections of the Mormons and by the church, which provides the theological emphasis and loans the local community capital to launch communal enterprises such as the cattle company. The cooperative bias of the Mormons is also evident in the operation of the individually owned businesses. For example, there is in Rimrock an informal but effective agreement among the operators of the general store, the repair shop, and the service station that they will not compete with one another. The general store used to sell gasoline, but after the service station was opened, it stopped selling gasoline, and customers had to go to the service station. Similarly, the repair shop used to repair tires and grease automobiles, but with the opening of the service station, it restricted itself to mechanical repairs, sending customers to the service station for greasing and tire repair. This procedure is in marked contrast to Homestead, where it is felt strongly that there should be at least two of every kind of business in a competitive relationship. It is significant that the prices of products and services in the two communities are basically the same — the cooperation in the one case and competition in the other is a matter of economic ethics, not a matter of prices governed by the laws of supply and demand.

Although the Spanish-American community underwent a change from the *patrón* system to individually owned private property in ranches and farm-land, some important vestiges of the *patrón* pattern continued to be operative. These were found largely in the practice of the larger landowners, who functioned as *patróns* for a few Spanish-American herders and a somewhat larger but variable number of Navahos they employed.

The Navaho pattern was originally one of inherited land-use ownership by extended matrilocal family units. In the late 1920's, when the pressure of whites upon Navaho land became intense, the Indian Service began to make allotments of public domain in the Rimrock area to individual Navahos under the Dawes Act of 1877. Almost all of the Navaho group were allotted 160-acre plots by a system of trust patents.* Later, additional lands were leased for Navaho use. By 1941 the individual allotments amounted to approximately 73 sections; about 125 sections were leased or controlled by the tribe, and a few sections were individually leased from the state. Despite the complex legal situation, the extended family group still functions as the significant unit in the control and management of farm-lands and herds and in the production and consumption of foods and services. Even the large livestock operators who control many sections of land for grazing purposes are normally heads of "outfits," and in this role they have economic responsibilities to a large group of kinsmen and other members of the "outfits." They cannot freely accumulate and utilize the land and the herds for their own economic benefit in the same manner that a Texan homesteader can control and dispose of his property with little obligation beyond the limits of taking care of his small nuclear family.

* The trust patent means that an individual Navaho can control the land during his lifetime and can transmit it to relatives when he dies, but he cannot sell the land without permission of the Bureau of Indian Affairs.

188

In Zuni, farm lands are ideally owned and transmitted in the female line by the matrilineal households, although in practice, individual males have come to be regarded as owning certain fields. Grazing land is basically tribal land, and the Zuni Council ordinarily assigns the use of particular areas to individual or family sheep-owners for lambing and shearing purposes. Sometimes the use of specified grazing areas may be assigned to a family or group of families, but more often a family gains rights to grazing land through use.[19] Agricultural produce from farm-lands becomes the property of households and is used to feed the extended matrilocal family unit. The livestock is now owned by individual males. Although the herds are handled cooperatively in large units by groups of male relatives, the products belong to each individual owner, who provides mutton for household use and uses the proceeds of the sale of wool and lambs to purchase goods for his own and for extended family use. Similarly, the income from silversmithing is shared by the extended family household.

Thus, in comparative perspective, only in the case of the Texan homesteaders, though also in recent years to a high degree with the Spanish-Americans, are economic enterprises a matter of individual control and nuclear family management. In the Mormon, Navaho, and Zuni communities, the economic system is embedded in a network of wider cooperative arrangements. These involve the matrilocal extended family unit of the Navahos and Zunis and both extended family and larger communal units among the Mormons. Navaho and Zuni are quite similar in that the large, wealthy livestock owners are, like their less prosperous neighbors, bound by kinship obligations to assume responsibilities well beyond those expected of Texan homesteaders. However, it is among the Mormons that we find the most elaborate community-wide economic enterprises, stimulated by their cooperative values and supported by the formal structure of the Mormon church. This is perhaps somewhat surprising, since Zuni has always been regarded as a highly cooperative culture. But the fact is that, while much Zuni cooperation takes place at the household level and there is cooperative activity involving wider circles of lineage and clan connections in such matters as building houses for the Shalako, there is no community-wide economic enterprise (unless it be organized by the Indian Service) comparable to the irrigation or cattle companies of the Mormons.

Conclusions

Our comparative portrait of selected aspects of the ecological and economic patterns of the five cultures has indicated that these patterns are related to a complex, interacting set of determinants: (1) the limits posed and possibilities offered by the particular niche in the natural habitat occupied by each cultural group; (2) the size of the population relative to the economic opportunities available in this niche; (3) the relative climatic and other risks resulting from different economic uses of these geographic niches; (4) the relative economic risks imposed by the market prices of various goods and services; and (5) the social structure and value systems of the groups. The selection of particular geographic niches, of settlement and land-use patterns, of type of occupation, and of mechanisms for the social management of economic enterprises can be interpreted as resulting from the interaction of these various determinants.

The key economic value-stress in the hierarchy of values in each culture would appear to be upon ranching as a prestigeful way of life. This value-stress is partly a matter of weighing environmental risks against market risks and coming to the decision that cattle or sheep ranching provides the best solution to economic problems, except in the case of those very limited areas where land can be irrigated. But this value-stress has also become highlighted in the various cultures which afford greater prestige to big livestock operators. The operation of this value is especially evident in the cases of the Mormons, Texans, and Spanish-Americans. The Mormons are oriented strongly to ranching values at present, which represents a shift from older farming values. The Texan bean-farmers are ambivalent about the "big ranchers," but there is nevertheless a strong underlying admiration for the rancher who owns vast acres and who is "really wheeling and dealing." The Spanish-American admiration for the *patrón* who was a "big rancher" in this area in the past (and still is in other areas of New Mexico) is quite evident. Zunis and Navahos are less affected by these values, but there is beginning to be some shift in this direction in the case of the Navaho heads of "outfits" and the large Zuni livestock owners. It appears that if ample land were available, most males in all of the cultures would turn to ranching.

Political Structure

GUY J. PAUKER

POLITICAL PROCESSES in the Rimrock area take place in the complex and broad setting of the American polity, but the five culturally distinct communities are more than just parts of the macroscosm encompassing them. Each has its own ways of solving problems. Certain basic needs have to be fulfilled in all societies, but some of the matters requiring collective decisions or coordinated efforts may be peculiar to one group only, others may be similar in several groups. The social mechanisms used to fulfill the needs do not always appear as political in the contemporary Western conception of the term. But relations involving some measure of authority, hence of political organization, are involved in most of the processes which aim at the achievement of certain social goals:

(1) law and order, the administration of justice, defense of the community against internal or external threats — in short, all that gives the individual basic physical security and predictable social environment;

(2) public works such as the construction and maintenance of roads, bridges, irrigation ditches, dams, and various public buildings;

(3) social security and welfare measures, which imply some redistribution or equalization of income in order to provide for public education, public health measures, and aid in various forms to those handicapped by age, disease, or misfortune;

(4) activities giving emotional satisfactions, such as a feeling of belonging and participation, as well as the nonmaterial benefits derived from prestige and influence in the community.

The line between public and private activities which seek to fulfill these social needs is not always easy to draw and may be treated largely as a matter of definition. The manner in which these societal functions are carried out varies through time within a given community, while the comparative analysis of different communities documents a whole range of alternative ways of responding to similar basic social needs. For both historical and comparative analysis, the Rimrock area has the great advantage of permitting at least in part the isolation of certain strategic variables. It can be assumed that in carrying out their political activities the communities living in the area are all affected by factors such as: the dominant influence and the monopoly of power of American government; a pattern of intercultural relations with the other communities; a similar struggle with an arid natural environment; and the specific values and institutions of each group.

In their impact on the five communities, these determinants create different total fields that form the setting of the political process. Obviously, none impinges in exactly the same fashion on all communities; the total field of which they are a part differs for each. The determinants do not seem equally important in explaining a diversity of political structures and processes which can perhaps be expressed, in somewhat oversimplified fashion, by describing Zuni as a city-state, the Navahos as a group relying almost exclusively on informal authority, the Spanish-Americans as feudal, the Mormons as solidaristic, and the Texans as extreme individualists. The first three factors cannot explain these striking differences either historically or analytically. It is at least plausible that the diverse but functionally equivalent political institutions developed by the five groups are the result of efforts to solve problems and fulfill needs in ways compatible with their specific value systems.

To measure the influence of pressures and votes from the Rimrock area on the United States requires a set of equations which we do not have. It would be even more difficult to estimate the impact of the more subtle aspects of the political processes taking place in the area on the larger whole. It can safely be asserted that political power lines to Washington, to Santa Fe, and even to the county courthouse, though not disconnected, carry currents of very low intensity.

The people of Rimrock have strikingly little influence even in county courthouse politics. The state organizations of both major parties in New Mexico are relatively weak, loose, and shifting confederations of strong county organizations which are dominated by leaders deriving influence from wealth, family background, public renown, control of a particular bloc of voters, or prolonged and intensive party work.[1] None of these county leaders has his residence in the Rimrock area, nobody from the area has risen to prominence in state politics, and only the temporarily prosperous *patrón* of Atrisco at one time played a role of some importance in county politics.

The people of Rimrock have very few occasions to familiarize themselves with politics outside their own communities. Few have direct acquaintance with that important aspect of American party politics, the nominating process. Under state party rules, county chairmen are authorized to call precinct meetings for the selection of delegates to county conventions, as first steps toward the nominating process of presidential and other candidates. Each precinct can send one representative to the county convention for each twenty-five votes cast in that precinct at the preceding election for the gubernatorial candidate of the respective parties. In 1952, this rule gave Homestead, Rimrock, and Zuni one delegate each, but Atrisco, with only twenty votes, cast none at the Republican county convention. Only Homestead had cast enough votes in the preceding gubernatorial election to send a precinct delegate to the Democratic county convention. Consequently, only precinct chairmen participated in proceedings at the county level in election years. The experience of others was largely limited to their village.

Electoral participation percentages show no striking deviation from national averages. Spanish-American, Mormon, and Texan voters in the Rimrock area are examples neither of unusual political eagerness nor of particular apathy. Enfranchised in 1948, the Navaho seem to parallel to a remarkable degree the behavior of the other three groups. Only the Zuni strike a distinctive note, firmly rejecting involvement in American politics through electoral participation, probably as part of their efforts to ward off the surrounding world's encroachment upon their affairs. The first impression one gains about the people of Rimrock is that, with the possible exception of the Zuni, they are not unusual components of the immensely complex American political process, although they live pretty much at its fringes.

The Rimrock area is not a distinct political entity. It does not form any special political or administrative unit within the American system. Its five cultural groups are geographically contiguous by the accidents of settlement but in no way united by the habit or the desire to act together.[2] To the extent that goals unite them with people outside their own local community, they lead outside the Rimrock area, beyond the other local groups, which are ignored and bypassed, to the Mormon church, to the Navaho tribe, to the All-Pueblo Council, or to American political parties and pressure groups. Integration into the surrounding political macrocosm, far from following parallel lines, stresses the distinctness of each group.

If monopoly of power is the core of a separate political system, then none of the five groups is more than a segment of a larger whole; yet, within its own boundaries, each has distinct political activities. Each produces, allocates, and sanctions power which is oriented toward the achievement of some common goals. Judging from the historical record, each group would structure and operate its political life quite differently from what it is now were it not for the activities carried out on their behalf and for their benefit by the American polity. Deprived of the legitimate use of force in their own right, these communities are limited in their control over their own members and in their relations with each other. Except for informal social pressures and sanctions, they cannot legally punish delinquents according to their own culture's definition of what is right and wrong. Witches are no longer clubbed to death; horse thieves are not hanged. Neither raiding nor local warfare are available to relieve the tensions generated by intercultural contacts.

Local political activities are not only curtailed by but are also dependent upon the larger American political system. Although, as voting citizens, the people of Rimrock have a share in selecting those by whom they are governed, they are also in a very real sense dependent upon political forces beyond their control. Such dependency is increasing. By 1947 the amount of money New Mexico residents paid into the national treasury in taxes did not equal what the national government expended in carrying on its activities in the state.[3] Through a multitude of administrative agencies, federal, state, and county governments make their presence increasingly felt in the lives of the people. Some "old line" agencies have been at work in the area for a long time: the forest service, the postal service, the internal revenue service. Other federal agencies were established as a result of the New Deal or came and went with World War II.

The people of Rimrock regard some of these activities as beneficial and others as unwarranted and unwelcome interference with their lives. Federal activities concerning conservation of natural resources are most disliked. The Bureau of Land Management, with which the General Land Office and the Grazing Service have been consolidated, administers about one-fifth of New Mexico's land, some fourteen million acres. Its activities generate hostility among the sheep-loving Navaho who are prone to overgrazing, and also among the Texan bean-farmers who see in it the tool of big ranchers against "little people" like themselves. Educational programs, price support measures, and social security legislation are, by contrast, not only accepted but welcomed. Therefore, one cannot speak of one basic attitude toward the government, but of various mixtures of resentment and satisfaction depending upon the way specific interests are affected. Whether the people of Rimrock, even those most integrally members of dominant Anglo-American culture, feel identification at the emotional level with the distant centers of government remains open to question. In other parts of the world the distinction between "we, the people" and "they, the ruling circles" is in most cases a very sharp one, especially in the rural world. To the extent that one can generalize from fragmentary evidence, the impression emerges that in the Rimrock area the basic orientation toward government is neither identification nor outright opposition, but a somewhat utopian longing to be left alone, although there is also strong dependence upon the government as a benevolently paternalistic source of succor.

As everywhere else in the world, the intensity of government is increasing in New Mexico. By 1949 the federal government maintained 10,560 employees in the state. The cost of state government had increased from $5,704,968 in 1912–13, the year following the achievement of statehood, to $102,397,424 in 1949–50. Including 10,749 school employees, New Mexico had 19,336 state and local employees on its payroll in 1949. The presence of state and national government does not affect all groups equally. Although it provides basic guarantees — for instance, with respect to land titles or to the price of agricultural products — the government is in a sense remote from the daily life of the Texan community and interferes little with its way of life. At the other extreme the special relationship of the Indian Service to Navaho and Zuni brings the federal government much closer to their daily routine. But nowhere in the Rimrock area does one sense, in recent years at least, an atmosphere of bureaucratic oppression.

While local mechanisms of control are felt with greatly varying degrees of intensity, national and state governments remain remote, as is to be expected in a thinly settled, distinctly rural area. Divided between Verona County, which had a population of 22,481, and Cleveland County with 27,451, the Rimrock area in 1950 had no urban center whatever. Only the city of Railtown, trading center for the general area and county seat of Cleveland County, was rapidly approaching the population figure of 10,000, set by the United States Census Bureau as the bench mark of urbanism.

Local responsibilities of the state such as collection of revenue, enforcement of criminal law, peaceful adjustment of private disputes, recording of land titles, provision of highways, and care of the poor, are carried out by locally elected county officials; the people of Rimrock hardly participate at all. As county officials must rely on their influence in the state capital to get state funds, the people of Rimrock must court the county officials to have their needs taken into account. To an increasing extent, they have needs and desires that cannot be satisfied by their own means and instrumentalities but by political forces above them. In other words, the area of self-government is shrinking for the people of Rimrock as a whole, though for the Indians, traditionally treated as wards of the national government, the opposite is true as a consequence of a federal policy aimed at broadening the Indians' competence to administer their own affairs.

ZUNI

The political organization of Zuni is only imperfectly understood, despite the existence of extremely rich ethnographic literature. The dominant role of religion prompted Richard Thurnwald to cite Zuni as the extreme example of a sacred state, a theocracy ruled by priests who are the heads of certain preferred or aristocratic families and who govern through civil authorities appointed by them.[4] He compared Zuni political organization with that prevailing in Greece in the sixth century B.C. The Greek state, though tied to the restricted space of the *pólis*, was regarded as an expression of the highest cosmic order, the *nómos*. Similarly, in Zuni philosophy the universe is an all-encompassing kinship system of which Zuni is the Middle Place, the focus of human and supernatural concern.

Its self-reliant ethnocentrism may explain to a large extent why Zuni comes closer to being a total social system than any of the other cultural groups in the Rimrock area (even though the most dependent on the American economy). Zuni cultural resilience is related by John M. Roberts to what he calls their "adaptive conservatism." [5] The label is descriptively apt, but still there is no explanation of how Zuni remain what they are after centuries of submission to the Spanish crown, a century of United States government, and continuous exposure to the impact of Christianity and industrialism.

Judging from the available record, Zuni has only rarely projected itself into political activities reaching beyond the village. According to contemporary Spanish sources, there was concerted action in the Pueblo Revolt of 1680, in which the Zuni acted as allies of the other pueblos. The All-Pueblo Council allegedly organized at that time still meets periodically at Santo Domingo, the instrumentality of a flexible defensive alliance, not of a federation. Its functions usually are restricted to loose coordination of policies toward the American polity and exchange of information and points of view. Zuni has never become, of its own volition, a segment of a larger political entity. Robert Bunker suggests that Zuni was the creation of shrewd leaders who utilized the threat represented by the arrival of the Spanish conquistadors to merge the six or seven legendary cities of Cibola into present-day Zuni.[6] Whatever may have happened in the seventeenth century, Zuni has stood ever since, hedgehoglike, on its own.

Zuni's political system defies analysis, not only because of its intimate connection with zealously guarded religious secrets, but also due to the complexity of the institutional mechanisms through which common goals are achieved. A. L. Kroeber showed that four or five different planes of systematization crosscut each other in Zuni: the clans, the fraternities, the priesthoods, the kivas, and in a measure the gaming parties are all dividing agencies. If they coincided or merged, segregation and fission would be encouraged, and rifts in the social structure would be deep. But, by counterbalancing each other, Zuni social divisions produce segmentations of remarkable complexity, but they never break the national entity apart, thus they actually preserve the integrity of the whole society.[7]

In a social system like that of Zuni, many activities are carried out through the diverse groups mentioned by Kroeber rather than through the instrumentalities of the state. Whether one considers such groups as public or as private organizations is a matter of definition. They have the political function of coordinating action toward common goals. Ruth Bunzel's claim that the clan as such has no social or political functions must be regarded, as Fred Eggan pointed out, as self-contradictory.[8] Bunzel noted that in Zuni each individual feels his closest ties to be with members of his own clan. She noted the practical implications of this attitude: Zunis call on members of their clan for assistance in any large enterprise such as harvest, house-building, and initiations. According to Eggan, the lineage principle, which underlies the kinship system and furnishes the core of the clan organization, provides integration through time, as a mechanism for inheritance of ceremonial duties and obligations as well as for the transmission and preservation of fetishes and other ceremonial paraphernalia. These lineages, within clan lines, he hypothesizes, are determining factors in the selection of the priesthood, which in turn designates the secular branch of the government. The pervasiveness of the conception of kinship in political organization is suggested by the fact that the *ashiwanni*, Rain Priests, are called "fathers" and the governor of Zuni and his wife are called "father" and "mother." [9]

There is no question that Zuni, as described by Eggan, is a theocracy. Political authority is in the hands of a council of priests consisting of three members of the chief priesthood and the heads of three other priesthoods. The "house chief," head of the chief priesthood — that of the North — is at the top of this hierarchy. The *pekwin,* Sun Priest, assists him and acts as spokesman for the priesthood. The executive arm of the system is provided by the Bow Priests. The heads of the *katchina* societies serve as advisors. Besides such cult matters as impersonations of the gods, setting of dates for tribal initiations, and changes in the ceremonial calendar, this council deals with the appointment of secular officers and questions of tribal policy. Too sacred to be involved in secular quarrels and problems, these priests, who have the welfare of the pueblo in their hands, leave the policing of the pueblo to the Bow Priests. Formerly, the latter could torture those suspected of witchcraft to induce confessions and carry out executions. Relations with the outside world, as well as civil suits, quarrels over property, and cooperative work on roads and irrigation ditches were entrusted to a set of secular officials who held office at the pleasure of the priests and could be removed by them at any time. This government, consisting of a governor, a lieutenant governor, and eight councilmen, was generally chosen in such a way that each member belonged to a different clan.[10] If Eggan's reconstruction is accurate, then important changes are taking place in Zuni: the secular branch of the government seems to have emancipated itself from the priests and to find its source of authority increasingly in popular election rather than in appointment.

Kroeber assumed that Zuni's civil government was in substance a native institution, while Eggan concluded that, whatever its origins were, its activities were expanded to deal with the problems brought about by Spanish contacts. More recently, Smith and Roberts, in their study of Zuni law, carefully canvassed the available literature in an attempt to reconstruct the history of secular government in Zuni. Their account shows that the institutions have undergone considerable variation.[11] It may well be that the priesthoods occasionally change the method of selection of the Zuni council, perhaps in order to achieve balance between factions. In the 1920's it became increasingly difficult for the priests to agree on suitable candidates for secular political offices. Part of the complex factional disputes concerned the community's attitude toward Catholic missionaries. One governor had to serve for seven years, since no replacement could be agreed upon. In 1934, a representative of the United Pueblo Agency broke a deadlock by appointing a nominating committee composed of six members, equally divided between the two major factions active at the time. It selected candidates for governor and other civil offices prior to the holding of elections in which adult male Zuni had the franchise. The nominating committee still exists and can be regarded as a device for cushioning the transition from theocracy to democracy. It seems also to have assumed some of the functions of the vanishing Bow Priests, although a recent revival of scalp dances in Zuni suggests that new Bow Priests may have been inducted.

The governor, lieutenant governor and councilmen (*tenientes*) of

199

Zuni have legislative, executive, and judicial functions. In general, the Zuni Council handles all secular cases that are not settled privately. Their tendency seems to be to resist encroachment by American government by dealing with all matters themselves. Cases involving murder, rape, and larceny, which are among the ten crimes over which the United States Congress has specifically conferred power on federal courts, continue to be prosecuted by the Council. Zuni practice has thus made federal criminal jurisdiction concurrent rather than exclusive. The Zuni Council also seems to be actively engaged in the area of public works. According to Smith and Roberts, it supervises dams and irrigation ditches, the distribution of water, work on roads, dealings on behalf of the tribe with officials of American government, the management of certain cooperative enterprises of nonreligious character, and other matters of general public concern.[12] The governor of Zuni may, for instance, raise the matter of the Railtown-Zuni road informally with the governor of New Mexico as the two officials meet at some public function.[13] Or the Council may assume responsibility for repairing fences and maintaining the water supply on Indian lands, as it did when lack of appropriations during World War II prevented the Indian Service from carrying out these activities.[14] The *tenientes* in charge of each village then used local means to maintain the irrigation ditches.

A former General Superintendent of the United Pueblos Agency, Mrs. S. D. Aberle, argues that tightened federal control confused and even paralyzed the Zuni, whereas pueblo government operated effectively when left in complete control over its members. According to her, Zuni in 1943 had an amorphous civil organization, but those in authority were making no satisfactory adjustment to changing economic values. She attributes this stasis within the tribe to strong paternalistic federal control until 1935 which prevented the Zuni from acquiring experience in handling their own affairs.[15] Another member of the Indian Service, Robert Bunker, argued that Zuni and other American Indians should be left to make their own decisions, reflecting his admiration for their political aptitude. It is interesting to note that, while anthropologists are impressed by the strongly organized character of Zuni theocracy, members of the Indian Service find the system either amorphous, if one reads Aberle, or surprisingly democratic, if one follows Bunker, who writes that Zuni government depends on the assumption that the people, in general meeting, will find for each problem some solution that everyone can accept. His image of Zuni is strikingly at variance with most other sources: "The people have no Council but function through general meeting. This, the largest of the Pueblos, is most nearly without 'government.' " [16]

Only the complexity of Zuni government can explain the variety of forms that different people see when they look at this socio-political kaleidoscope. Several dynamic factors keep the pieces of the puzzle in motion: federal paternalism, changing economic values, and a process of secularization causing an erosion of the inner core of religious values. As the theocracy slowly withers away, secular government should assume more power. But it still lacks an independent principle of legitimacy to be strong enough to fill the vacuum left by the shrinking importance of the old mechanisms of social control and political coordination which in the past permeated the whole system.

The Indian Service seems to have backed elected officials against opposition from the theocracy and to have curtailed the powers of the priestly authorities. While at least two main functions of government — welfare and expressional activities — are still carried out through traditional mechanisms, the economically important functions of the secular authorities and their relations with the federal and state law-enforcing agencies may have enhanced their political position and contributed to their emancipation from priestly sources of legitimation.

One of the most intriguing aspects of Zuni politics is the intensity of factional struggle. Whether it originates in the pueblo's religious life is hard to say, but it is present during elections for the Tribal Council and sometimes erupts into the open on other occasions. In May 1955, for instance, there was conflict over an $650,000 public high school. A lease was executed by the Zuni Council and the Cleveland County School Board for the use of seventeen acres of tribal land on which the school was to be built. One faction opposed the school as a threat to the traditional Zuni way of life. Led by two priests (*caciques*), they went to the governor's home and took away the two canes, one dating allegedly from Spanish times, the other given by President Lincoln, which are the Zuni governor's insignia of authority. Then they argued in letters sent to the Commissioner of Indian Affairs that the lease signed by the governor and his *tenientes* after the removal of the canes was void. The governor countered with the argument that, although of old (prior to 1934) the *caciques* had the power to elect and to remove a governor from office, since then action can only be taken by the nominating committee and has to be ratified by a general meeting. The Indian Service upheld the position of the governor. His opponents were left the very modern consolation of writing letters to the editor of the Railtown newspaper, complaining that "the white man still recognizes him as governor but our people do not want him and are forced to take him." [17]

The central question concerns the compatibility of factionalism with the Zuni value premise that harmonious order, construed as control and integration of all beings, is the greatest good and the primary moral imperative. In the past, dissidence was probably effectively controlled by strong directives against excessive self-assertion and in favor of a general attitude of cooperation. Deviance was punished by trials for witchcraft. Becoming a Bow Priest may have given legitimate outlet to special ambition and energy. With the loss of the exercise of ultimate power to the distant and alien federal government, Zuni theocracy has been left in the awkward situation of having responsibility without adequate power sanctioning it. Time will tell whether or not current tensions reflect mainly the difficulties of transition to secular government or a process of tribal disintegration.

NAVAHO

The Navaho tribe is the largest Indian group in the United States, with an estimated population approaching 78,000 in 1955.[18] This spectacular increase from not more than 10,000 in 1868, when the Navaho were released from Fort Sumner, must have had important political implications. In the process of demographic and territorial expansion, some of the traditional formal and informal mechanisms of political coordination may have become inadequate, fostering the adoption of the elaborate modern political organization introduced at the initiative of the United States Indian Service.

Information is lacking on the political organization of the Navaho before they were taken into custody by the United States Army in 1864. The scanty evidence available suggests that in aboriginal times they probably lacked centralized authority and had no sharp divisions of rank, status, or wealth. If the Navaho were not a nation in the political sense of having a territorially based common government, they were culturally a nation by sharing language, values, and traditions which gave them a feeling of distinctness from other people. Their language emphasizes their distinctness even from the closely related Apache tribes, within the Southern Athabascan linguistic family. Before 1864 the Navaho abstained from acts of violence against segments of their own tribe, while constantly raiding all other groups in the Southwest.

The absence of a centralizing political structure among the Navaho accounted for almost constant misunderstanding in dealing with them. In 1785 Governor de Anza tried to enter an alliance with a Navaho chief called Antonio, whom he describes as "very famous" and who promised to get the other chiefs to bring their men along on the next expedition of Spanish troops and settlers against the Apache. Antonio obviously had promised more than he could deliver, and the following year the Spanish governor of New Mexico had to use "gentle and persuasive" exhortations to get the Navaho to agree "to accept the counsel of the old men of greatest judgment and capacity so to be ruled in the future by a single governor, or general, authorized in the manner of the pueblos of Christian Indians so that, excluding from command the multitude of captains raised up among them, the nation might be governed by the single one who would be elected by the universal vote." [19] The Navaho did not prove receptive to this form of government. When General Kearny's Army of the West occupied New Mexico and California some sixty years later, no Navaho authority existed capable of committing Navaho groups. In November 1846 the first of a series of treaties between the United States Government and Navaho chiefs was signed, but for almost two decades the American authorities failed to find any single chief or group of chiefs able to command the obedience of the whole tribe. Finally, after open warfare against the Navaho by the First Regiment of New Mexico Volunteers, commanded by Colonel Kit Carson, a majority were deported to Fort Sumner. Captivity proved a bitter lesson. It is still easy to find in the Navaho country old men who remember hearing from their elders about those terrible years of captivity and who describe the events with intense feeling. The treaty signed with

Navaho chiefs after their release from captivity was never broken again. But it was probably the collective experience of the thousands that had spent some years at Fort Summer rather than the authority of any chief or group of chiefs that kept the Navaho from raiding after 1868. Theirs remained a fragmented society, although very few American observers were perceptive enough to understand it. Almost the only exception was Dr. Michael Steck, for a short time Superintendent of Indian Affairs for New Mexico, who wrote in 1863 to the Commissioner of Indian Affairs:

> The course heretofore pursued regarding these tribes as nations, and treating them as such, is no longer the true and correct one. Not one of them is bound together by any general laws. All are divided into fragments, and these fragments of from ten to fifty men each, headed by some successful warrior, separately act without any consultation with the mass, and recognize in their war raids no law but that of individual caprice. There seems to be no distinguished or national chieftain among them capable of concentrating and leading an undivided tribe to battle, or inspiring their confidence and imparting council in time of peace. With the exception of the Pueblos (an amiable, happy, and law abiding people), the condition will apply to every nation within the jurisdiction of this superintendency.[20]

Did the Navaho have, in the absence of central authority, some alternative mechanism of political coordination for the tribe as a whole? Some authorities mention the existence of an archaic tribal assembly of the Navaho, called *naschid*. It was either a special twelve-day meeting or a lengthy winter camp which gathered either at periodic intervals or in case of tribal emergency, and supposedly lasted until the 1830's. Other authorities doubt the existence of any such institution, and interviews with the oldest and most knowledgeable Navaho leaders in the Rimrock area failed to trace any memory of a *naschid* among them.[21]

In their daily lives Navaho knew only local leaders, the *natani*. War *natani* possessed the "war ritual" assumed to assure the success of raiding parties. As owners of magical skill and perhaps superior leadership qualities, they played a major role on hostile occasions, but probably were not influential otherwise. War *natani* disappeared from the scene when raiding was halted. The civil local leaders, or peace *natani*, are the Navaho's closest aboriginal approximation of political authority vested in any one person or group. Today, as in the past, they are devoid of physical means to impose their will, though they may be able to bring fears of witchcraft to bear. The role of the peace *natani* does not require coercion. His is not a leadership role or a representative function in the Western sense. Rather, it is incumbent upon him to act as preacher, adviser, and arbitrator to the community. The Navaho are less amenable to orders than to persuasion. The *natani* must be able to "make good speeches." What the community expects from them is the benefit of their superior experience and judgment.

Such rudimentary political organization would have to be compensated by unusually strong emphasis on cooperation if more than the simplest common goals were to be achieved. But Navaho mechanisms for the coordination of authority did not develop beyond the local level without pressure from the outside. Lacking village settlements, natural communities beyond the extended family that live within shouting distance of each other cannot easily be identified on a territorial basis or by reference to common leaders. Yet certain groups of related families though scattered sometimes over many square miles cooperate regularly in order to achieve goals that in other societies are directed by more formally structured systems of authority. Clyde Kluckhohn has called these Navaho groupings "outfits." They are fluid entities showing great variation in composition and size. Usually one family forms the nucleus of the outfit. It may be referred to by the name of the principal, usually oldest, man in that family. A dozen such outfits have been counted among the Rimrock Navaho, while four extended families living in the area were not definitely a part of any outfit. More recently, David F. Aberle suggested that the unit which controls its members and aids them in case of need is the "local clan element," consisting of the members of a clan residing in an area, together with any near consanguine members of the clan who reside nearby.[22] There are twenty-one clans represented in Rimrock, but the four largest account for 77 percent and the six largest for 97 percent of the area's total Navaho population. While not necessarily larger in numbers than the local clan element, the outfit seems to be based on a broader principle, including formal ties.[23] There is some indication that routine cooperative efforts draw upon the outfit, whereas in times of crisis the local clan element is called upon for help, but we do not know whether the peace *natani* derive their initial authority from an outfit or local clan element. Traditionally their general recognition comes through election by the community as a whole. Their role is variable in content, and generalizations are apt to be misleading. As Kluckhohn has written: "When the People work together in groupings other than those of kinship it is exceedingly difficult to define the integrating forces or the basis of leadership . . . Decisions as to community policy can be reached only by the consensus of a local meeting. The People themselves are the real authority." [24]

What has been said about general Navaho political organization is applicable to the Rimrock Navaho, but it must not be forgotten that they represent only one percent of the total tribe. However loosely structured the tribe as a whole may be, the Navaho living in the Rimrock area must be viewed in its context. Although they live off the main reservation, they participate in elections for tribal officers and are represented by a delegate in the Tribal Council which meets several times a year in Window Rock, Arizona. The Rimrock Navaho are now under the jurisdiction of the Railtown Area Office of the Bureau of Indian Affairs. Until a few years ago they were separated from the main body of the tribe which was administered by the Navaho Service in Window Rock, Arizona, being themselves dependent upon the United Pueblo Agency in Albuquerque, New Mexico. Living off the main reservation, the Rimrock Navaho are also under the jurisdiction of state and local authorities. The boundary between Cleveland and Verona counties cuts across their homeland, but the county seat of Verona County is too far away to compete with Railtown as "the town" to which they go for trading. Government thus has multiple impact on the Navaho studied here. A whole array of federal and tribal governmental agencies has to be understood and manipulated by them for the satisfaction of needs developed in recent decades.

Facing the perplexing fluidity and diffuseness of the Navaho pattern of authority, the Indian Service found it necessary to create a body legally competent to speak for the tribe. Chief Justice John Marshall had established in 1832 (*Worcester* v. *Georgia*) the legal principle of inherent and unextinguishable tribal authority. But the locus of such authority could not be found among the Navaho, and after 1910 there was a growing need for some type of representative tribal organization empowered to act for and on behalf of the Navaho, especially in connection with mineral and oil leases. This prompted the Commissioner of Indian Affairs in 1923 to establish a Navaho Tribal Council composed of a chairman, a vice-chairman, and twelve delegates. Robert W. Young of the Navaho Agency comments: "Obviously, the early Councils were not democratic functional governing bodies in any sense of the word, nor was the main body of the Navajo people ready for such a radical step at that time. It was a white man's invention." [25]

In 1934 the Navaho rejected by referendum, with 7,992 votes against 7,608, the incorporation which would have permitted the development of self-government in accordance with a tribal constitution. Two years later plans for a larger and more representative Tribal Council were developed by selecting seventy members for a constitutional assembly from among recognized leaders. In the absence of specific Navaho territorial units, Land Management districts were used as bases for apportionment. There was much resistance to the United States Government among the Navaho at that time, as a consequence of a sheep reduction program found necessary for reasons of soil conservation, and no constitution was adopted. In 1938 the Secretary of the Interior promulgated "Rules for the Navajo Tribal Council," which are still the basis for the tribe's governmental institutions.

On September 16, 1938, the first elections for a Tribal Council were held, each candidate being identified by a differently colored ballot. The Navaho elected a chairman, a vice-chairman, and seventy-four delegates apportioned to the Land Management districts. In 1950 a pictorial ballot was introduced, and the requirement of winning a majority of the votes cast was modified to permit election by a plurality. In 1954 responsibility for election procedure was transferred from the Bureau of Indian Affairs to the Navaho themselves, by the establishment of a Tribal Board of Election Supervisors. Apparently, this change and more active campaigning on the part of candidates heightened the tribe's interest in its political affairs. Electoral participation increased from 14,000 in 1951 to 17,000 in 1955.[26]

In 1946, Clyde Kluckhohn found that the Tribal Council had few of the powers of an autonomous governing body. Most action was taken at the initiative of the federal government, and delegates were largely confined to approving or disapproving its proposals. The

207

council's usefulness seemed reduced to the expression of Navaho opinion, and this situation severely limited the delegates' political authority in their own districts.[27]

Impressive changes occurred in the 1940's, and by 1950, many of the seventy-four delegates were responsible representatives. The Tribal Council proved an excellent training ground for learning the basic principles of representative government and parliamentary forms. Increasing revenue from leases and from governmental grants, coupled with the Bureau of Indian Affairs' policy of fostering self-reliance, added continuously to the Council's responsibilities. In 1954, another researcher concluded that it was becoming "an increasingly significant force in Navaho life." [28] However, few delegates were known to the whole tribe; for most Navaho the political horizon was still close to home. But this would not continue much longer. Under the Navaho Rehabilitation Program initiated in 1950 there has been impressive progress toward the objective of universal education and in the field of economic development. In Rimrock a $534,000 dormitory was built to permit Navaho children to attend the public school; by the end of 1955, a total of 24,560 Navaho children were attending school there and elsewhere.[29] It is a fair assumption that their perspective on political as well as other social institutions will be much broader than that of their elders. Even the present generation is likely to increase its understanding of political and governmental processes, as the joint efforts of the Navaho Agency of the Bureau of Indian Affairs and of the Tribal Council have a favorable impact on life throughout the reservation. In all fields of governmental activity — law and order, public works, welfare, tribal affairs — the initiative coming from Window Rock, Arizona, can be seen from even a cursory inspection of *The Navaho Yearbook of Planning in Action* for 1955.

Development from the aboriginal situation in which there was virtually no government toward a political structure with popular roots will be completed when initiative and coordination of action come from the local level. Steps toward this goal were taken in 1927, when local community organizations known as Chapters were organized by agents of the federal government for Indian affairs. Each Chapter was to elect annually a president, a vice-president, and a secretary-treasurer. Within a few years, approximately one hundred Chapters had been created. However, after 1932, during the period of Navaho resistance to stock-reduction measures, the Indian Service reversed its support, and in many places Chapters ceased to exist as District Supervisors failed to initiate new elections. The Chapters still do not occupy an official position in tribal government,[30] but the new emphasis on Navaho self-reliance and initiative has encouraged their development and some eighty were functioning to some degree in the 1950's. Many have meetinghouses built with materials provided by the federal government and by labor contributed by the local Navaho community. Since 1956, Chapter officers have received salaries from tribal funds, and the Tribal Constitution under consideration at that date should give Chapters official status.

The Rimrock Navaho have maintained throughout the years a relatively strong Chapter. They have built a meetinghouse, operated a cooperative store, and maintained a Day School. Local elections have been held quite regularly, and matters of common interest have been discussed at periodic meetings. Serious crises have been weathered without factional lines cutting deeply across the community. But Chapter officers and delegates to the Tribal Council continue to act mainly in the advisory capacity of the traditional peace *natani*, and decisions are still being made in face-to-face meetings by all members of the community.[31] As of the 1950's, the transition to representative government was far from completed.

Spanish-Americans

Descendants of the nation which was for three centuries the paramount power in New Mexico, the Spanish-Americans, although outnumbered by citizens whose origin is different, still play a very important role in the politics of the state. Senators and Congressmen of Spanish-American descent are regularly sent to Washington. Unique among the states, New Mexico prints its ballots in English and Spanish.

Among the five groups studied, the Spanish-Americans are the least numerous: not more than a dozen families, less than ninety individuals, live in or near Atrisco. During the peak of Spanish-American presence in the area, in the 1920's, their predominant economic activity was stock raising, although they also farmed some small irrigated fields. Recently the group's economic and political organization has shifted from the *patrón* system to individually owned private property in ranches and farm-land. Some important vestiges of the *patrón* system are still operative, but they are imbedded in a form of political organization no longer strikingly different from that of the other cultural groups.

Although far removed geographically from its historic origins, the *patrón* system is a product of European feudalism brought to the New World by the immigrants who followed the conquistadores. Habits of subordination and dependence had developed in Europe as a counterpart of the protection that a relation of vassalage provided at a time when no central authority was strong enough to defend the population of Western Europe. What were at first contractual relations, under which obedience was pledged in exchange for protection, became in time, with many local variations, a system under which personal ties establishing a social pyramid of several tiers developed into one under which usage of land carried with it the economic obligations of payment of rent and prestation of services. One of the heritages of the system was a set of attitudes leading to the fusion, perhaps confusion, of wealth and authority. What was taken to the New World was not really the classical feudal system, with its decentralization of political authority. Instead, government was in the hands of governors appointed and recalled at will by the Spanish Crown. The *patrón's* authority over men was also not the result of a military hierarchy, but the carry-over of long-established attitudes of dependence and subordination from and into other sectors of social life. The pattern was reinforced by an economic system for which the correct technical name is seignorial rather than feudal, which gave those who had title to land, granted by the Crown or otherwise acquired, authority over the men working on that land as tenants or *peones*.

It has been suggested that the *patrón* relationship is an extension of the pattern of the dominant father from the small household through the larger *familia* to the village.[32] But authorities such as Marc Bloch point out that feudal societies are not based primarily on lineage, although obligations derived from kinship ties are taken very seriously. Feudal ties are created precisely because kinship ties alone do not provide the necessary protection. Similarly, the failure of lineage or of centralized political authority to provide protection reinforces the seignorial economy and gives a meaningful social role to the *patrón*.[33] Of course, the pattern of submission to a superordinate authority is not the only possible solution to the problems which gave birth to the *patrón* system. Functionally equivalent results are achieved in other cultures by cooperation among equals. Etiological explanations must be postponed until the correlation between political structure and family structure is more fully documented, but it is fair to assume that the Spanish-Americans' conception of the role of the father at least reinforces the orientation toward the *patrón* system. Margaret Mead pointed out that the *patrón's* leadership is achieved through financial status, knowledge of the outside world, or personal power. She noted the system's reproduction of the pattern of family relations, but failed to mention its roots in the feudal and seignorial tradition. She recorded, without drawing any conclusions, that in the more eastern villages of New Mexico, where there are no glaring inequalities of wealth, the *patrón* principle is less clear. She substantiated Bloch's hypothesis about the connection between the origin of feudalism and the lack of alternative mechanisms of social control:

> Throughout the structure [of Spanish-American society in New Mexico], authority and responsibility for leadership, power and obligation for dependents, tend to focus on one person. There are no voluntary associations here, with elected leaders. Society is characterized by already present units: the paternalistic kinship group, the village with which it may prove to be coextensive. Within this, in the appropriate position, the *patrón* rises in authority.[34]

After the annexation of New Mexico by the United States, the *patrón* became also a *jefe político* who could unfailingly deliver the county or precinct vote. The Republican Party machine won elections by subsidizing local leaders to bring in the vote, thus perpetuating its control of the state for many decades. More recently the influx of traditionally Democratic Texans and Oklahomans and the depression which brought in federal welfare agencies changed the balance of power, and the vote is now more evenly divided between the two major parties.

The history of Atrisco exemplifies the working of the *patrón* system. The founder of the village settled in the area in 1882 with less than two score relatives, enriched himself during the boom in the stock business of New Mexico, established a store, made his house the center of local religious activities, and became the local *patrón*. Fifteen years later, when he left the area, his youngest brother became the dominant figure. He leased land from the Santa Fe Railway Company and became, by shrewd entrepreneurship, manipulation, and speculation, a rich man during World War I. In one generation, two sons of a poor sheepherder were thus able to achieve control over a number of dependents and an additional handful of Spanish-American settlers to whom they gave employment, guidance, and protection.

Economic success led to political authority. The *patrón* made himself known as *jefe político* of his district to officials of the predominantly Spanish-American Verona County, by attending conventions and party meetings as the "elected" delegate from Atrisco. In time he became county commissioner and county treasurer. All appropriations for Atrisco were paid to him, with few questions asked as to whether budgeted bridges and roads had been actually built. Florence Kluckhohn stated that the *patrón* was willing to assume paternalistic responsibility but in return demanded submission. Almost everyone in the village was dependent upon him in some way. The people of Atrisco looked to him for food in case of need, for transportation to distant doctors in emergencies, or, at the very least, for advice and guidance. Even those who did not need his help in their daily life relied on him in religious and political matters.[36] In short, the *patrón* fulfilled in some way all the major functions of government mentioned at the beginning of this chapter.

As the scope of the *patrón*'s political ambitions widened, he shifted his major efforts to Railtown. The skills that had brought him success in his village among his dependents did not work in the new setting, where large contributions to the Republican Party did not win him real support. Not given to husbanding his resources, he ultimately went bankrupt, and his ranch holdings passed into Anglo-American hands. Although one might expect the villagers to feel relieved of authoritarian oppression, this was not their reaction. They immediately looked for someone to fill the old *patrón*'s place, but no powerful personality was available. Power became decentralized and village life was disorganized as various groups turned for support to different individuals within or outside the community. Population declined from a peak of 250 around 1920 to 142 in 1936, and a scant 89 in 1949. It is, of course, difficult to assess to what extent this was due to the disintegration of the *patrón* system which had in the past provided employment, guidance, and protection and to what extent the loss of the large ranch-lands was responsible for the depletion.

In the 1930's, following the emergence of contenders for the position of *jefe político,* the political process in the village changed. While the old *patrón* was paramount, routine meetings gave formal sanction to his periodic appearance as delegate to county conventions of the Republican Party. After he had stepped down, a battle between two prominent local men was waged for political control of the village. Characteristically, neither tried to convince the villagers that he was best qualified to represent their interests; instead, each claimed that he was favored by county officials. In other words, they did not seek support from below but invoked authority from above, which carried with it the possibility of controlling the distribution of money and liquor, more meaningful to the Spanish-American voters in those days than political representation.

At the time of our research, in 1950, Atrisco seemed to be without a *patrón*. On matters such as interventions with the Board of Education in Johnson to have a teacher sent to the village, two prominent local citizens would go to town together. One of them was a son of the old *patrón,* the other a successful rancher who did not seem inclined to use his economic position to establish himself as the new *patrón*. Descendants of the old *patrón* still kept closely in touch with Republican headquarters in the county seat and benefited from such perquisites as appointment as election officials, influence on the local work of the county road-grader, or a job as mail carrier. But the village, deprived of its traditional political structure and its land base, was disintegrating.

Mormons

Before the state of Deseret applied in 1850 for admission to the Union and was organized as the Territory of Utah, with the capacity to become a state when sufficiently populous, the Mormons had gone "from near-sect to near-nation." [37] The opening up of the West and President Lincoln's liberal policy toward them created conditions favorable to the incorporation of the Mormons into the American nation. Instead of becoming a theocracy, they accepted the American position on separation of church and state. While not isolated in watertight compartments, church affairs and the politics of civil so-

213

ciety were kept apart, and the central place that religion occupied in the life of the Mormon communities was reflected in their politics.

In the Territory of Utah, the Mormons were organized in the People's Party, while some dissident Mormons in association with Gentiles acted through the Liberal Party. In 1896 polygamy ceased to be an issue in Utah. The Church withdrew its approval of polygamy and the President of the United States pardoned those who had been arrested for plural marriage. The Territory was admitted to the Union. The old political line-up was replaced by the two major American parties, and prominent Mormons were to be found in both the Democratic and Republican parties. At first the Church leadership seemed to favor the Democratic Party, but soon this preference was shifted to the Republican Party. Ever since, although the Church as such does not pronounce itself on politics, its principal leaders have been Republicans.

In the 1860's and 1870's the *Deseret News* argued in its editorials that people disagree only when they are ignorant or wicked, and Brigham Young expounded the theory that the demand for two candidates in the political sphere was a sign of apostasy.[38] But the penetration of values from the larger American culture of which Mormonism is a part into the political life of the Latter-Day Saints has brought about significant changes. The Mormon vote does not go as a bloc to the G.O.P. A two-party system is no longer considered an indication of error and corruption. The freedom of political choice which Mormons enjoy in American politics contrasts with the discipline of their own religious community, though such freedom reduces the danger of conflict between the Mormons' role as Church members and their role as American citizens.

Although less affected by secularization than most Mormon villages in Utah and less assimilated into generalized American patterns[39] the village of Rimrock does not differ significantly from other Mormon villages in the solution worked out in reducing possible conflict between church and state. In its internal organization, Rimrock is a typical Mormon community integrated in authoritarian fashion into the Church, to the seat of which, in Salt Lake City, it is linked through several echelons hierarchically ordered. It is connected with American politics in the peculiarly loose fashion characteristic for our party system through local organizations of the two parties. The description that follows applies principally up to the year 1950, the year of the field research in Rimrock.

As a ward of the Mormon Church, Rimrock is precisely placed in an organization characterized by a distinctive authoritarian structure. The Church hierarchy must be formally accepted by the people, but the initial decisions are made by the authorities and officers of the Church and popular ratification is in practice a certainty. At the top of the pyramid is the President, who is the spokesman of God and who is alone entitled to new revelations binding on the entire Church. His decisions are therefore "right," and opposition to them is in effect a choice of what is "wrong." As a former President explained in a sermon at the beginning of this century:

> I know that the Lord will not raise up "Tom, Dick, or Harry" here there and everywhere, claiming to be Christ, or "one mighty and strong" claiming to be inspired and called to do some wonderful thing. The Lord will not deal with men in that way; that while the organization of the Church exists, while quorums and councils of the Priesthood are intact in the Church, the Lord will reveal His purposes through them, and not through "Tom, Dick, or Harry." Put that in your little note books now, and remember it; it is true.[40]

This elitist principle underlies the authoritarian structure of the Church. At the top is the First Presidency composed of one President and two Counselors. The Twelve Apostles, the Patriarch of the Church, the First Council of Seventy, and the Presiding Bishopric, which together constitute the "authorities" of the Church, are all chosen and ordained by the First Presidency. Mormon consensus and Mormon discipline based on shared views and values are so strong that, once the choice has been made and announced, the required popular approval is for all practical purposes certain. Mormon elitism is mitigated by the absence of a specialized priestly caste. All males over the age of twelve participate in the blessings pertaining to the Priesthood.[41] Thus an authoritarian organization originating in the American democratic milieu safeguards in principle as well as in practice the access of all to the chain of command.

Officials of the lower hierarchy, such as President of a Stake or Bishop of a Ward, are appointed ("receive the keys of priesthood"). They are selected by those in the hierarchy of immediately higher rank, and ultimate approval rests with the First Presidency. A Stake is a "geographical, numerical and governmental division of the

Church," comprising a few or many Wards, depending on circumstances. A Ward usually contains from one hundred and fifty to fifteen hundred members and is presided over by one Bishop and two Counselors. While the Priesthood Quorum of the Ward may be consulted and invited to nominate candidates for the bishopric by secret ballot, more frequently the High Council of the Stake will select the prospective Bishop in closed session, and the recommendation of the Stake President will usually be accepted by the First Presidency. The local community in Rimrock apparently played no substantial role in the nomination of the Bishop, with the possible exception of one local leader who knew the Stake President moderately well and may have had some part in the process of selection.[42] Fully organized Wards have a Relief Society, a Sunday School, a Young Men's and a Young Women's Mutual Improvement Association, a Primary Association and other auxiliary organizations, besides the quorum of High Priests, Seventies, Elders, Priests, Teachers, and Deacons.[43] The system is organized with bureaucratic efficiency. The Wards are kept small enough to enable the Bishop and his counselors to know personally every member of the Ward. There are about seventy offices, from Bishop to Sunday School teacher, in the various Church organizations in Rimrock. A high percentage of the population hold responsible posts. Nominations are suggested by the Bishop and submitted for approval to the members of the respective organizations.

The religious organization of the village is vigorous. In 1950 the Rimrock Ward had 241 members. The incumbent Bishop was the twelfth since the establishment of the Ward, his predecessors having been in office for terms varying from two to fourteen years. The Priesthood had 64 members, the Women's Relief Society had 35 members, the Sunday School 176 members, the Young Men and Young Women's Mutual Improvement Association 60 members, and the Primary 36 children. Average attendance at the weekly sacrament meetings was 94. The tithe, given through the Bishop for general Church purposes, amounted to $8872 during the year.[44]

The solidarity of the Mormon Ward is only mildly disrupted by a measure of factionalism resulting from polarization of village families around two large families, each of which has given Rimrock Bishops in the past. Perhaps its sharpest expression in the life of the community is reflected in the existence of two amateur orchestras.

On serious matters, consensus seems easily achievable, even without authoritarian direction. When returning veterans after World War II found the village lacking opportunities, the Ward formed a Land and Cattle Company. It bought 37 sections of land with the aid of a loan from the Cooperative Security Corporation in Salt Lake City, which also purchased two shares out of a total of 732 in the company. When road contractors were working on the state road near the village, providing an opportunity to have Rimrock streets repaired at a reasonable price, a meeting decided to assess each family twenty dollars to collect the eight hundred needed for the job. This was done in the temporary absence of the Bishop, without "imperative coordination."

In addition to being a Mormon ward, Rimrock is a precinct in the American political system. Both parties have representatives in the village. According to one observer at least, there is no serious break in village solidarity for political reasons.[45] The majority is usually Republican but the Democrats receive more than just a few stray votes. Taking as index the vote for the most important national positions disputed in a given year — President, Senator, or Governor — the Republicans had 28 votes in 1942, 55 in 1944, 49 in 1946, 49 in 1948, 27 in 1950, and 81 in 1952. The last figure includes some twenty Navaho votes, a new development in the precinct. Democrats obtained 18 votes in 1942, 17 in 1944, 14 in 1946, 24 in 1950, and 30 in 1952. There is no pattern of organized control over Rimrock Mormon voting, judging from instances such as the recorded remark of the Bishop on the night of the November 1950 elections that the village had probably gone Democratic "for the first time in its history," when in fact the Republican gubernatorial candidate had obtained 27 votes as against 24 received by his opponent.[46]

Rimrock is not an incorporated village and therefore has no formal civil government. Its only elected local authorities, apart from the Church hierarchy, are the election board and the school board. A deputy sheriff is appointed by the elected sheriff of Cleveland County, but he has more to do with Navahos than with Mormons. No justice of the peace had been elected for some time in the Rimrock precinct, but in 1950 local people were so vague about the existence of this official that they could not tell whether the village had a judge or not.[47]

During the New Deal period, the position of the Democratic precinct chairman was apparently enhanced temporarily by government aid for public works, in one instance a $30,000 grant for the repair and improvement of the dam. But available evidence does not suggest that participation in American politics is an important source of political authority in Rimrock, whereas positions in the church hierarchy are. The Mormons do not allow their roles as American citizens to disrupt the solidarity of the village community.

TEXANS

Homestead has little formal political organization. Each family seems to keep to itself, and what is not the neighbor's business is even less, in these Texans' view, the business of county, state, or federal officials. Most of the things done through community cooperation in Rimrock are either done individually in Homestead or are simply left undone.* The government of the United States maintains the rule of law in the area as a whole, protecting the farmers' land titles against the ranchers and the people against threats that characterized the frontier community in earlier decades — outlaws and Indians. This permits the individualistic Texan farmers to dispense almost completely with government at the local level. Each person, or at best each nuclear family, tends to be a discrete atom in the larger American social and political system.

As an unincorporated village, Homestead has no town officials. In the first years after the community took roots legal conflicts had to be taken to Atrisco; the justice of the peace there soon refused to serve, due to the many demands made upon him by the Texans.[48] In the late 1930's Homestead, as a precinct in Verona County, started to elect its own justice of the peace. This judge not only was unable to maintain law and order, but in fact became involved in various feuds. On one occasion he was taken before another justice of the peace on charges of disturbing the peace. A few years later he left Homestead, and no justice of the peace has been elected by the precinct since. (This is not just characteristically Texan: in numerous

* Although Rimrock took advantage of the presence of a construction company in the area to have the roads of the village graveled by assessing the whole community to meet the costs, the people of Homestead refused any such arrangements. Some villagers made individual arrangements with the construction company and had portions of the street graveled. Homestead rarely if ever acts as a corporate body.

precincts of New Mexico, the position of justice of the peace seems to be an unwanted one, and no candidates appear on the ballots at election time.) The only county official who nominally has existed in Homestead in recent years was the appointed deputy sheriff and game warden, but the only time he attempted to make an arrest he was sent home and told to mind his own business. Hostility to outside, superordinate authority should not be confused with lawlessness. In a community like Homestead law and order are maintained by "hue and cry," to use an obsolete but appropriate legal term. When a job needs to be done, the community organizes spontaneously. Nobody is given permanent authority to be used in cases of emergency.

Reflecting their Southern background, the Texans of Homestead are predominantly Democrats, even at the price of diminished political influence in what was long a firmly Republican county. The two parties are represented by precinct chairmen, but these roles do not carry much weight locally. The Republican precinct chairman at the time of the research was a Spanish-American, son of the former *patrón* of Atrisco.

Local political activities, the coordination of social action for the achievement of common goals, are in theory the province of a multitude of committees. These committees really are ineffectual: unavoidable common action is carried out in informal fashion. In such circumstances, the real "opinion leaders" make their influence felt, whereas committee functions are left to newcomers, to "people who have not learned better yet." Opinion leaders are those who "mind their own business" but are influential for a variety of reasons. These are not always well defined but can be boiled down to brief formulas with local meaning, such as "good farmer." The total informality of Homestead leadership does not mean that the community is completely atomistic. As pointed out by Evon Z. Vogt, there are three types of divisions in the village, related to kinship, to religious belief, and to social rank.[49] Together with the factor of local groupings, or neighborhoods, they create a complicated and constantly shifting factionalism. Thus, Homestead has not a class system but a faction system. As there is no culturally patterned way in which power struggles are controlled, channeled, or kept within reasonable bounds, the major feature of this factionalism is its particularly disintegrative character. Attitudes toward politics are epitomized in the saying common in Homestead: "the best thing to do is to vote your enemies into office."

VALUES AND POLITICS

While the variety of political forms described are found in the common setting of the Rimrock area as part of the American social system, specific action of the various determinant factors on the five groups creates different total fields. Texans and Mormons can and do view themselves as full members of the American community into which they are integrated on a basis of equality, but for the other three groups, Zuni, Navaho, and Spanish-Americans, the relationship is one of subordination to a more powerful but still alien nation. Economic forces also affect the cultural groups differently. Even though they must also rely on other sources of income, Zuni and Mormons, with irrigated farm land, have a firmer basis for survival in the area than the three other groups, which are much more at the mercy of the climate.

The character, elaboration, and intensity of political process within the five groups does not seem determined by the amount of real or seeming freedom from external pressure, political or economic, but by internal factors. Navaho and Spanish-Americans are not strongly organized to defend their interests in a socio-political environment dominated by Anglos, whereas Zuni are. Texans, Navaho, and Spanish-Americans are not organized for community action, although this would seem highly desirable in view of the precarious character of their subsistence economic basis. Situational factors, external to the cultures of all the groups, do not appear to be major determinants of their political processes. Unless one believes that historical accident shaped the political structures and functions of the groups, the diversity of forms must be related to factors within them, to their own cultures and especially their values.

There are striking differences in the orientation of the five groups toward power and authority. These notions seem to be disvalued by Zuni and Navaho, and political office is sought only indirectly; candidates wait to be drafted and show reluctance to assume positions of leadership. In the groups of European descent, political ambition is considered normal and acceptable, with certain reservations in the case of the Texans. In none of the five cultures are power, prestige, or authority explicit, central values; yet they are valued at least implicitly and at least by some individuals, and the cross-cultural differences are real and meaningful. They do not seem mere mannerisms or styles but geuinely different cultural orientations toward the concept of power. Whether the distinctions in orientations to power would be validated by broader cross-cultural comparison remains to be seen, but we can assume that a fully developed political process of the kind found in Western culture requires a power-motive, just as the fully developed economic process of the kind found in Western culture requires a profit-motive. Both may be related to an individual self-assertion which is not a dominant orientation or is negatively valued in the two Indian groups studied.

Conceptions of the individual and the community and conceptions of the order of the universe provide further cross-cultural contrasts. Navaho and Zuni seem to assume that mechanistically conceived impersonal forces dominate the universe, whereas the other groups interpret events by a voluntaristic scheme, probably rooted in their several Christian dogmas. In the latter view events depend on decisions that have to be made by responsible individuals, be they members of a Church hierarchy (Mormons), theoretically equal citizens (Texans), or a *patrón* deciding for the whole Spanish-American community. The Zuni priesthood, acting as mediators between man and cosmic forces, or Navaho *natani,* aided by the community as a whole, are not conceived as making decisions, but as finding out what is fitting in the fixed order of the universe that need only be ascertained and implemented by man.* However traditionalist the Spanish-Americans may be, their *patrón* is expected to make real decisions, not just to ascertain and apply mechanistic formulas.

Possibly related is the difference between Indian and European conceptions of the decision-making process. Navaho and Zuni prefer lengthy and patient confrontation of opinions, carrying on debate until consensus, preferably unanimous consent, is achieved. The mechanism of majority decisions, which leaves one group unconvinced and obliges it to submit to the will of others, seems imperfectly understood and alien. Perhaps majority decisions are not considered adequate to ascertain what course of action is likely to be

* Although there are differences, the distinction is obviously related to Max Weber's view of the working of traditional authority as opposed to rational-legal authority.

successful without disturbing the basic harmony of the universe and optimal social harmony procured through unanimous consent. The making of decisions is also influenced by the different group conceptions of the role of the citizen. By "citizen," I mean not the formal legalistic definition of membership in the community, but the attributes — rights and obligations — which define the full-fledged group member. What is expected of him? How should he behave? The following comparison between Zuni and Navaho was made by a trader who lived all his life in the Rimrock area:

> One of the most important differences between the Zuni and the Navaho was that a lone Navaho would stand up and advance his opinions even if a thousand people were against him and the thousand would respect his right to do this and would hear him out. This was because the Navaho lived such isolated lives. It took real guts to live that way. In contrast a Zuni would seldom advance even a cautious opinion unless he was sure almost everybody agreed with him . . . and if he thought they wouldn't, he'd keep quiet.[50]

There is clearly a difference in emphasis between the Navaho, who enhance the role of the individual in the decision-making process, and the Zuni, who are so sensitive to the pressures of the group that David Riesman considers them the prototype of the "other-directed" personality, guided by the community into which he submerges his individuality.

Basic differences in the decision-making process also appear among the other cultural groups. A Mormon Ward will either accept the decisions of the legitimate leaders, the Church authorities, or will act on its own in the absence of a Bishop and other dignitaries; the political structure and habits of Rimrock make both patterns acceptable. The Spanish-Americans are accustomed to a process of decision-making which leaves responsibility to the *patrón,* and the community finds itself disoriented and paralyzed when left on its own. In sharp contrast, the Texans will not accept any "boss" but will appoint ad-hoc committees for whatever decisions have to be made and then act, if at all, even more informally through such members of the community as happen to be available. In all three groups, the notion seems to prevail that one individual can make decisions for other individuals, although the differences are great between the Spanish-American pattern, where one man can in his own right issue orders to all others; the Mormon situation, where external decision is accepted because it comes from legitimate wielders of authority; and the Texan pattern, where only a committee to which in principle any member of the community could have belonged can make decisions for the group. The most important distinction is that in all groups of European descent, representation is normal, whereas in the Indian groups (even granting the uncertainties created by our insufficient knowledge of Zuni) there seems to be a tendency to accept as valid only decisions made by the group as a whole. The shift from one pattern to the other involves — at a relatively high level of abstraction — some such concept as that a person's will can be determined for him by another person. The relationship may be egalitarian or hierarchical, so that other value-factors also come into play. But once the conception of representation has been grasped and accepted, the road is open for the development of genuine parliamentary institutions. The Zuni Council, the Rimrock Navaho Chapter, the Mormon Ward, and Homestead committees are only superficially similar. A true understanding of their roles requires us to consider to what extent each group accepts the notion of representation and delegated authority, as well as the fundamental orientation of the group toward the problem of the relation between the individual and the community. The individual is obviously not equally valued or similarly defined in all groups.

Related to the presence or absence of the concept of representation is the meaning of voting. The philosophical premises of the electoral process as practiced in the West are found in the conception of free will, permitting and making necessary choices that originate in the citizens' own free volition. It is not surprising that voting was not a highly respected procedure among the Spanish-Americans who were willing to surrender their freedom of choice for a consideration. What is known about Spanish-American fatalism indicates that they do not really believe in freedom of choice in the external world of matter and power, however central volitional freedom is to the inner self as interpreted by their Catholicism. The question of free choice in the Navaho culture is even more interesting. The belief system includes a premise stipulating "automatic-mechanical determinism." It is difficult to see how they could grasp, without major changes in their beliefs about the order of the universe, the notion that they can effectively alter the "nature of things" by political action, by the ultimate repercussions of their individual decisions in the process of selecting leaders and passing judgment on policies. The Navaho may in the course of their political development either acquire voluntaristic conceptions or adapt their notions about man and the universe to a form compatible with the functioning of a political system based on choice and majority rule.

Value-orientations concerning competition also affect the political process. For the Texans of Homestead competition is a normal and desirable aspect of social life. The community wants two stores, two service stations, and so on. The Mormons emphasize cooperation and try to avoid situations that would become competitive. They direct the division of social labor so as to leave repair work to the garage and the selling of gasoline and lubrication services to the service station in the village. Reasoning exclusively from values, the Texan orientation should make competing political parties congenial, but the Mormons might be expected to view them with uneasiness. The impact of political parties on the two Indian groups is still in its earliest stages, but it might be expected that a two-party system would prove more acceptable to the Navaho than to the Zuni. However, the inadequacy of an analysis based only on values as the determining variable is illustrated by the fact that the Texans are, for historical reasons, largely Democrats, while the Mormons, though predominantly Republicans, have a substantial Democratic minority in the village. Similarly, Zuni factions are intensely present in the pueblo, despite the fact that "harmonious order" is supposed to be the greatest good, and, if participation in American politics is accepted, the factionalism pattern rather than harmonious order would conceivably be the basis for political alignments.

Groups rather than isolated individuals are the major actors in politics, coalescing individual wills into meaningful social action. Pressures and counterpressures thus generated may account for the intensity and, to the extent that such forces balance each other, for the stability of the political process. There are few such groups in the communities studied here, with the exception of Zuni, of whom Kroeber says that, "by countering each other they cause segmentations which produce an almost marvelous complexity, but can never break the national entity apart." [51] Whether this circumstance gives

Zuni a better chance for democratic growth in the future must be left unanswered.

The five communities vary also in the way in which they are linked with the American social system. For Zuni and Navaho, the tribe is a barrier to integration rather than a link, and the individual is more likely to find his place in the larger system if his tribal bonds are weakened. Deprived of their *patrón,* the Spanish-Americans find themselves without stable connections outside the family circle. As for the two Anglo groups, Evon Z. Vogt observes:

> Unlike the Mormon village of [Rimrock] which occupies a firm and explicit position in the wider social structure of the Mormon "empire" and has the church to mediate between the local community and the metropolitan world, the [Texan] homesteader must face the American social system unsupported by intermediate organizations. The local Mormon derives a sense of status security from the "concrete community of Zion," while the local homesteader feels he is a peripheral member of American society and is never quite certain that he is being taken seriously by those who are in a more central position.[52]

If the presence or absence of certain values were conceived in terms of a compensatory mechanism striving to create an equilibrium that would permit optimal adjustment of the individual to his environment, the absence of values of the kind that tie the Mormons to their Church would have to be compensated in the case of the Texans by, say, stronger emphasis on the nation as focal value. This does not seem to be the case. Similarly, the weakening of tribal ties among Zuni or Navaho does not seem to lead to a strengthening of their feeling of belonging to the American social system as a whole. Frequently it simply leaves a vacuum. Thus, either the American society as a whole is not a suitable object of group identification, or the theory of a compensatory value mechanism needs refinement.

The relation between values and political institutions cannot be fully elucidated at the present stage of our knowledge. If values are viewed as creating strong need-dispositions seeking fulfillment through a variety of functionally equivalent mechanisms, then the weakening of certain institutions would lead to the appearance of others able to satisfy the same needs. While this frequently is true, it does not always happen. Need for law and order may be assumed as a basic orientation present in all groups. Yet, the curtailment of the prerogatives of the Bow Priests may lead to an increase of covert tension among the Zuni rather than to a strengthening of secular instrumentalities charged with preserving the peace. The weakening of the *patrón* system led or contributed to the disintegration of Atrisco. The people of Homestead have proved unable to provide themselves a judge and learn to live with the constant uncertainty and seeming unpleasantness of factional strife.

In the area of public works, Zuni and Mormons cope with their needs in a variety of ways. Sometimes the community does what is necessary, while at other times it relies on external aid, such as contributions from the Indian Service or other branches of the federal government. The other three groups occasionally seek support for the fulfillment of some of their needs — roads, school buildings, or meetinghouses — but, if there are no results, frustration is accepted. Similarly, there are considerable differences in the degree of initiative shown in meeting social welfare needs. Even those activities through which the group offers its members opportunities for emotional expression and satisfaction show greater variability than would be compatible with a theory of valuations or need-dispositions of equivalent intensity.

In a general way, such central Navaho values as family, knowledge, and enjoyment of life can be suggestively related to an informal political structure in which the "outfit" or "local clan element" is the largest significant unit and *natani* acting in an advisory capacity the only leaders autonomously developed within the culture. Religion and social solidarity are related to the theocratic character of Zuni. Custom, in-group solidarity, and religion are relevant to the functioning of the *patrón* system. Religion, activity, and community are meaningful referents to Mormon political organization. Independence, know-how, and achievement are the kind of focal values one would expect to find in a group with the political characteristics of the Texans. Yet much is left unexplained. Why specific institutions developed as they did must be related not only to values but to other factors as well. "Historical accident" and "the richness of human creativity" can be evoked as stopgaps to fill the wide lacunae in our knowledge of the factors that account for human behavior.

8.

Religious Systems

ROBERT N. BELLAH

RELIGION AS HERE DEFINED is man's attitudes and actions toward his ultimate concern. Ultimate concern, a term borrowed from Paul Tillich, has two aspects, meaning and power — meaning, in the sense of the ultimate meaning of the central values of a society or sub-group of it, and power, in the sense of ultimate, sacred, or supernatural power which stands behind those values. These two aspects, like matter and energy, are mutually convertible under certain conditions. Many religious symbols express this union of power and meaning, just as many religious rituals are concerned with the conversion of meaning into power or the endowment of power with meaning.[1]

With respect to its functions for the social system, religion may be said to be primarily centered in the motivational subsystem of a society. Its primary functions are concerned with personality and the relation of motivation in the personality to the social process. Religion is concerned with the internalization and maintenance of ultimate values in the personality and with the handling by personalities of the ultimate opportunities and frustrations of life. From the point of view of personality, it has both super-ego and id functions. It is concerned with rationalizing and reinforcing with ultimate sanctions the moral norms which have been internalized in the super-ego and with the adequate and therapeutic expression of id forces. These forces are partly regressive, in that they stem from motivational problems left over from earlier stages of socialization — here it is the function of religion to allow them to be expressed in contexts which will not hinder the continued healthy functioning of the personality — and they are partly progressive, in that they motivate the personality toward new levels of integration — here it is the function of religion to provide the symbolic scaffolding for the personality in constructing its new integrations. These functions of religion can, when certain balances are tipped, become very serious dysfunctions. The functions of providing a context of ultimate meaning for moral norms may become the dysfunction of the enforcement of a rigid and compulsive conformity to those norms so that social change is minimized and rigidity and stagnation are maximized. The therapeutic expression of id forces may become the rationalization for the murderous acting out of the aggressive aspect of those forces. The provision of the symbolic scaffolding for personality development may become the provision of the symbolic coffin within which personality development is stultified.

Whereas the family performs most of these functions (or dysfunctions) in respect to the personalities of young children, religion as an independent institutional focus becomes especially important at adolescence and during adult life. It is concerned with the integration of the individual into the moral community which includes but extends beyond the family; it is concerned with the broadest values of the society, not merely with the values of the family. For this reason, religion will always represent universalistic values relative to the values institutionalized in the family, no matter how particularistic the religious values may seem in a broader context. The institutional aspect of religion must therefore be considered as an important part of the institutional system of a society.

Because any existent system of authority is based to some extent on charisma (another word for the sacred power mentioned as one aspect of ultimate concern) of a more or less routinized form, and because the emergence of any new charismatic center in a society almost always has some political repercussions, religion has important implications for and relations to the polity. Finally, the economic ethic of any religion, particularly the relative stress placed on production and consumption, has an important effect on the economy. Thus religion, which functions primarily in the motivational subsystem of a society, also has an important place in the institutional subsystem and important relations to the polity and economy.

Values and Religious Symbols

One function of religion is to provide a context of meaning for the central values of a society on which its morality is based and to relate these values to an ultimate source of power. This ultimate source of power may be considered quite impersonal and amoral, in which case value lies in how to relate to it so that good rather than evil results, and morality is a collection of techniques for so relating; or it may be conceived as the embodiment of morality, so that values are the definitions of its nature and moral norms are its laws of functioning or, if it is conceived personally, its injunctions and decrees. Though the symbolization of the unity of power and meaning as the ultimate source of both is the key to the symbolic world of religion, that world is usually fairly complex and is in part composed of projections from the social structure and personality crises of the people concerned or of their forebears.

In basic religious world view, the Navaho and Zuni may be described as monistic. They conceive of everything in the universe as interrelated and lawful. Men, animals, natural forces, and mythical beings are all "personal," all stand to each other in an "I-thou" relation, all act in accordance with personal motives, but all are subject to control through the working of a mechanistic causation. Nothing stands outside of time or above history. Nothing is by its own nature absolute; everything, including natural forces and mythical beings, is subject to causation, and almost everything can be controlled by man if he has the proper knowledge and performs the proper ritual actions. Neither man, nature, nor mythical beings are felt to be intrinsically good or intrinsically bad in an absolute sense. Almost everything is both good and bad. Powerful beings, human and mythical, are feared as well as respected, because their power may be used for ill as well as good. Nevertheless, there is a clear conception that some people and some mythical beings are more benevolent than others.

The visible and tangible aspect of both people and things is considered at least partly separable from what is usually an invisible aspect, an essence or soul. Many mythical beings are the inner essence or spirit of some natural phenomenon — a mountain, lake, the north wind, and so on — and the spirits or souls of people survive

229

as ghosts or, in the case of Zuni, also as benevolent ancestors. But the more important of the mythical beings, though, like Sun, identi- fied with a natural phenomenon, are not restricted to that phenom- enon but can take various forms. The Navaho Changing Woman and Monster Slayer are not identified with any particular natural phenomenon but are related to many. Further, mythical beings are neither ordered in any rigid hierarchy nor classified in watertight categories. Certain beings, for example Sun in both cases, are more central than others. Some of the Zuni mythical beings are concerned with rain and some with curing, but we must agree with Haeberlin that these beings, "never having undergone a logical specification and systematization, are not clearly definable, are not 'finished' prod- ucts of the human mind, but are rather subject to kaleidoscopic changes due to the shifting angle of apperception of the folk as a whole as well as of its constituent individuals." [2]

To summarize the Navaho and Zuni religious view, power, in the sense of ultimate or sacred power, is widely diffused. Humans, animals, places, and mythical beings all possess such power, some much more than others. Though the sacred and the profane remain conceptually distinct spheres, they are joined in various sorts of combinations at every level of reality. Ultimate meaning derives from the working of these powers, whose workings can explain vir- tually everything — sickness, death, prosperity, drought. When all the powers work together as they should, so that each has its due and none is impinged on, harmony results. Such harmony is the ideal of both Navaho and Zuni religions. When any part of the universe gets out of joint, when norms which are supposed to keep each ele- ment in its proper place are infringed, then friction is produced and harmony is lost. Much of Navaho and Zuni ritual is oriented to keeping such disharmony from occurring or re-establishing har- monious equilibrium when it has. Harmony, balance, equilibrium is the central value of both these cultures and derives its significance from the complex of religious attitudes toward man, nature, and what is more than nature. Morality is not a set of decrees of a Per- fect Being, but a set of rules partly arrived at empirically, partly given by mythical beings possessing superior knowledge, but all designed to maximize harmony and minimize disruption. Acts are bad when bad consequences follow and good when good conse- quences follow. The rules are merely the generalizations of previous generations and wiser beings as to the likely consequences of various acts.

Though sharing a great deal of cultural material in common — for example, the importance of Sun and a complementary female Being, the symbolism of color and direction, the Twin War Gods, the sacred number four — Navaho and Zuni differ in two important respects. Their religious conceptions and ideas of the sacred world reflect their social organizations, which are markedly different, and the types of religious action in which they are engaged are geared to the problems of people living in these two quite different societies.

The Zuni either live in the central pueblo all year or leave it only for relatively brief intervals. It is essentially a single compact settlement unit, self-contained in language, culture, and religion. This is reflected mythologically in the fact that Zuni village is "the Middle Place." All the universe is oriented accordingly. Much of the Zuni origin myth is occupied with the problem of reaching the middle place and ascertaining the correctness of its location. The universe is divided into zones for ritual purposes, and they are always oriented to Zuni as the center. The geography and structure of the sacred world, at least in its general outlines, is relatively clear, as is the relation of its various members to Zuni organization. The sun occupies a place of pre-eminence. He is the source of life and is in this sense "father." Morning prayers to the rising sun are obligatory for all priests and for men engaging in ceremonies, but many others also offer them. Perhaps the clearest sense of the importance of Sun can be derived from Bunzel's description of his peculiar relation to the primary Zuni religious functionary, the *pekwin*:

> . . . the great ceremonies at which the sun father is honored are in the keeping of his special priest, whose title, pekwin, means literally, speaking place. The pekwin is the most revered and the most holy man in Zuni. Even in this society which diffuses power and responsibility until both become so tenuous as to be almost indiscernible, the pekwin is ultimately held responsible for the welfare of the community. He holds his power directly from the Sun Father, with whom he has a very special and intimate relationship.[3]

The Twin War Gods, children of the sun, dwell on the mountain tops and their worship is in the hands of the Bow Priesthood. Historically, this priesthood was both a war society and an organ of religious police. Its powers were derived from the War Gods of mythological times and handed down without break by successive generations.

Another important group of Zuni mythical beings are the *Uwanami,* who, according to Bunzel, are water spirits. She says:

> They live in all the waters of the earth, the four encircling oceans and the underground waters to which springs are gateways. Cumulus clouds are their houses; mist is their breath. The frogs that sing from every puddle after the drenching summer rains are their children. The ripple marks along the edge of ditches washed out by heavy rains are their footprints.[4]

Twelve priesthoods are devoted to the worship of these beings. These priests are second in holiness and importance only to the *pekwin.*

The *Katcina* cult is the heart of Zuni religion, "the most vital, the most spectacular, and the most pervasive of Zuni cults; . . . for the average Zuni it is the focal point of religious, social, and aesthetic experience."[5] The *Katcinas* live at the bottom of a lake some eighty miles to the west of Zuni. There they have a village in most respects like the Zuni pueblo itself, with, for example, their own elaborate priesthood organization. They originated in mythical times from children who were inadvertently dropped into a stream. Since then, many of the Zuni dead have gone to live at the village and have become *Katcinas.* Every Zuni male belongs to one of the six divisions of the *Katcina* society. The *Katcinas,* like most Zuni gods, are primarily bringers of rain. The elaborate dances and ceremonies of the society in which these gods are impersonated play an important part in ensuring the rainfall.

Finally, there are the Beast Gods who dwell in the east at a place called Cipapolima. These are the most violent and dangerous of Zuni gods. Their primary connection is with curing and long life, but they are also associated with witchcraft. Their worship is conducted by twelve societies, each of which is devoted to the curing of special diseases as well as to general medicine.

The world of Zuni mythological beings is relatively well-structured. The sun holds a tenuous primacy over all, the War Gods are patrons of socially approved violence; the *Uwanami* and *Katcinas* are important as bringers of rain; and the Beast Gods are in charge of medicine as well as witchcraft. Much of Zuni society can be understood in relation to the worship of the various gods. Many important activities both sacred and secular are done by their sanction or in order to obtain their favor. They even affect personal attitudes. The *Katcinas* like people to be happy and not have hostile thoughts. Hostile thoughts, especially during important ceremonies, can have severely disruptive consequences, such as drought or sickness. Thus, a great deal of social and personal life is related to the world of the gods and derives its meaning and its sanctions therefrom. That world in turn reflects the orderly complexity of Zuni life, with its atmosphere of benevolent harmony. Certain of the gods — notably the War Gods, the Beast Gods, and the god Kaklo, who presides over the *Katcina* initiation, reflect other, less often mentioned, aspects of Zuni life. They are related to crises of aggression, sickness, and growing up, which might, if not given proper ceremonial expression, break the otherwise tranquil fabric of Zuni life.

Since the Navaho have a markedly different settlement pattern and social organization from the Zuni, it is not surprising that their religious symbolism of place differs also. If the Navaho may be said to have a "middle place," it is the hogan, and there are as many middle places as there are hogans. The construction of the hogan and the placing of its contents are related to mythological imperatives. For example, the door must always face the rising sun, and the dead must be removed through a hole broken in the north wall. The Navaho sings, or ceremonials, take place within the hogan, and many ritual directions depend on the plan of this sacred structure. If this aspect of sacred symbolization of place seems narrower than in Zuni, the other Navaho space symbolization is much broader — the famous four sacred mountains. These roughly bound the territory in which the Navaho live and are over one hundred and fifty miles apart from north to south and at least three hundred miles apart from east to west. We are not surprised that there is no absolute unanimity on which are the four sacred mountains, and they differ somewhat in different parts of the reservation.

The Navaho do not compose a single society in the sense that the Zuni do. Before United States Government rule there were no over-all political offices; even today there are no centralized religious offices. The Navaho are organized in extended families, outfits, and local groups scattered over a large geographical area with little interaction between distant units. Smaller units have considerable freedom of mobility in attaching themselves to larger units. Correlating with this difference from the tight centralized social organization of Zuni is the fact that the religious world of the Navaho is much more loosely organized than that of the Zuni. Reichard has made a case for the centrality of the Sun cult:

> The mutability of the gods, the very difficulty of keeping them in classes, leads me to conclude that a Sun cult is outstanding; that many, if not all, things go back to Sun, although I do not mean by this to indicate a belief in monotheism. If I were to carry my generalization so far it would not be to Sun, but to that ultimately inexplicable term, universal harmony or destiny, monism rather than any kind of theism. Sun is an agent of that monism, a central deity who correlates the nether and celestial worlds with this one, who exists to assist man to his final destiny. Changing Woman may possibly be the female manifestation of Sun. First Man and First Woman seem to be respective manifestations of Sun and Changing Woman in the worlds below this.[6]

Nevertheless, there is no office like that of the Zuni *pekwin* to indicate the central importance of Sun. Reichard's analysis of his centrality is largely as a manifestation of that overriding concept of harmony which is a key concept for both Zuni and Navaho. On a more concrete level, Kluckhohn and Leighton are probably right that Changing Woman, the wife of Sun, is the most important deity:

> Changing Woman is the favored figure among the Holy People. She had much to do with the creation of the Earth Surface People (human beings) and with the meeting at which they were taught how to keep all these forces in harmony with each other. This meeting was a ceremonial of the Holy People and has become Blessing Way, a ritual which occupies a key position in the Navaho "religious system." Changing Woman, ever young and ever radiant in beauty, lives in a marvelous dwelling on western waters.[7]

Of all the Navaho Holy People, Changing Woman alone is consistently benevolent. Kluckhohn and Leighton suggest that there is a relation between this fact and the fact that it is the woman in the hogan, the Navaho mother, who is, if not the strongest, at least the most stable focus of Navaho family life.

After Changing Woman and Sun in importance come their children, the Hero Twins — Monster Slayer and Child of the Water. They are mentioned in almost every ceremonial and are the prototypes of the hero, around whom every ceremonial is focused. They are also, as in Zuni, the Navaho war gods. They are models for conduct in war and for the behavior of young men generally.

Besides the four figures already mentioned there are First Man and First Woman, important mythological persons in the period before the emergence of the people onto the earth's surface, and a number of other figures:

> Another group of Holy People are the Failed-To-Speak People, such as Water Sprinkler, Fringed Mouth, Hunchback, and others who are impersonated by masked dancers in the public exhibitions of the great chants. Still another type are the animals and personalized natural forces like Coyote, Big Snake Man, Crooked Snake People, Thunder People, and Wind People. Finally, there are various helpers of the supernaturals and intermediaries between them and man. Big Fly is "the messenger of gods and of men." He and Corn Beetle whisper omens and advice to Earth Surface People who are in trouble.[8]

The immense number of Holy People do not yield to classification in terms of residence or function in nearly as clear a way as do even the Zuni deities. Ceremonials are not usually oriented to specific supernaturals or groups of them, as in Zuni, but are organized around the adventures of some hero. The role of the hero, semi-human, semi-divine, is in many ways the key to Navaho ceremonialism:

> The line between Holy People and Earth People is not sharply drawn, and in many respects the protagonist of the myth and ritual belongs to both, since he connects the human and the divine. With few exceptions, he starts out as an Earth Person showing no special talent. Often disobedience involves him in supernatural affairs. As punishment for disregarding some admonition, he is led upon adventures. He meets a supernatural who directs him, gets into difficulties, and endures much suffering. Among his tribulations are long, dangerous journeys, which take him to angry deities who say he must be punished but mean he must be taught. Each encounter yields some element of a ceremony which he brings back to his people. He cleanses his family so they will be able to deal with holy things and teaches someone, usually his brother, to sing the ritual. He stays long enough to supervise the brother's first performance, often over a sister, then disappears into the air, sometimes taking a relative with him. He promises to bless and watch over his family and bids them remember him whenever they see some natural phenomenon such as rainbow, rain, sunglow, or growth.[9]

The ceremonies or sings based on such hero myths and supposedly handed down from the hero himself are primarily curing ceremonials. The man who knows such a ceremonial, the singer, has studied it with another singer and had the ceremonial performed over himself four times. Only then is he available to any who can pay his fee and who wish his ceremonial. It is primarily the responsibility of the extended family to see that appropriate sings are given for any family member in need of one. There is no priesthood or centralized organization of singers. Navaho ceremonial life is carried on largely as a result of agreements between extended families and singers. It is not the responsibility of any higher authority.

As in the case of Zuni a great deal of Navaho behavior is sanctioned by supernatural powers and deviance will be punished by them. Those who live in accordance with the Navaho way are most likely to receive the blessings of the good things of life. There is a great deal of ritual which serves to call in the aid of the supernaturals for various purposes: there are war and hunting rituals, rites to be used for salt-gathering and trading with foreigners, as well as songs to be sung so that the corn will grow well. However, there is no calendrical sequence which regulates the ceremonial life of the whole Navaho people to ensure a steady flow of blessings, as with the Zuni. Rites and songs are individually owned and used only for the relevant small groups engaged in hunting, planting, and so on.

The heart of Navaho religion is the curing rituals.[10] These sings are given only when specific persons are in need of treatment, that is, are for some reason physically, mentally, or socially out of harmony with their environment. The prototypes of disequilibrating experiences are those encountered by young men when wandering forth for raiding, hunting, or sexual purposes. There is little doubt that the point of greatest strain in the Navaho life cycle is when a young man must leave his extended family and go forth to make a living and find a wife in some other encampment. The myths reflect the dangers of this period: wild animals, enemy warriors, and witch fathers-in-law. The supernatural aids which the heroes of the past have acquired for meeting these dangers are available for young men in similar disturbing circumstances today through the sings. They are available for the solution of many other problems for young and old, men and women, as well. Ritual knowledge is needed to

236

compel the aid of the various natural and supernatural powers, for in this dangerous world only Changing Woman can be counted on for unfailing benevolence. The structure of the Navaho religious world, with its individual divine-human heroes; Changing Woman, the central and stable mother figure; and a myriad of potentially dangerous supernatural entities who must be placated or controlled if harm is not to result, both reflects certain of the outstanding features of Navaho social life and reinforces conformity to the Navaho way.

The three Christian groups of our study, although they differ among themselves, share certain religious features which fundamentally differentiate them from the Zuni and Navaho. For the latter the answer to the problem of the meaning of life lies in an all-embracing harmony in which natural and supernatural are closely interrelated. For Spanish-Americans, Mormons, and Texans, the answer lies in the idea of salvation. According to their tradition, the world is devalued and all value placed in God. Man is viewed as alienated from this God and therefore in need of salvation. Whereas Navaho and Zuni are almost entirely this-worldly, the Christian groups are to an important extent other-worldly in orientation. They look to life after death for the attainment of salvation and permanent redress of the moral balance of good and evil in this life. None, however, is extreme in its other-worldliness; each group has in important respects revalued the world.

The Spanish-Americans have filled the chasm between the world and God with a host of intermediaries. Still, the Spanish-American concept of God is in important respects the "Wholly Other." He may be influenced; He may never be controlled. God is seen as remote, aloof, and relatively unconcerned with man. What He wills to be, will be, and man can only accept his fate. There is no doubt that this view of God is closely related to the profound fatalism which is a premise of the Spanish-American value system. Man is not, however, entirely alone with his fate. The main significance of religion is as a cushion against this fate. There are certain protective figures among the supernaturals who can be appealed to in case of need. Of key importance is the *Santo*, the patron saint of the village, who is supposed to have the welfare of the villagers at heart. However, other saints may also be appealed to, for example, the *Santo* at Zuni,

237

to whom vows are often made by the people of Atrisco. Both the Virgin and Jesus are important intermediaries who can be appealed to in case of need.

Two roles in the village organization are closely tied into the religious system, those of the *padre* and the *patrón*. In the old days, when the priest was a Spanish-American, he held an especially important place. He had, of course, the power to administer sacraments and to hear confession so that he was directly involved in the process of securing supernatural blessings for his people. Further, he often held the role of *patrón* which gave him a key significance in secular life as well as religious. After the American occupation of New Mexico, it was found that certain of these *patrón*-priests were exercising great secular power and not obeying the vow of chastity. They were replaced by priests of other ethnic origins, and thereafter, the people of Atrisco had priests whose Spanish was hardly understandable to them. Atrisco is too small to support a fulltime priest, so that the priest comes only once a month from the mission at Zuni. Both for this reason and because of language barriers he plays little part in the life of the people. The secular *patrón* also had important religious functions, but in his role of dispenser of benefits and protector against danger or hardship, he is comparable on the natural level to the patron saint on the supernatural level. The patriarchalism and paternalism which make the *patrón* the father of the village family is extended into the realm of the supernatural as well.

Certain behavior, both religious and ethical, is specifically prescribed by the church. Requirements such as confessing periodically and marrying outside of certain degrees of kinship are taken as divine commandments, the church having the authority to interpret and to some extent enforce them. These are the subjects of many of the half-understood sermons in the church. Perhaps more meaningful to the people are the ethical injunctions embodied in custom, the *costumbres*. While these are not seen as given by divine commandment, they have a diffuse religious sanction. One who conforms to them is a *buen Católico*, which implies he is a good member of the community as well as a "religious" person. Spiritual benefits in the life after death as well as in the present life are felt to be more available to the *buen Católico* than to one who is not. Whereas the universalistic divine commandments place the Spanish-

Americans with the Mormons and Texans in regard to the relation between the religious and the ethical spheres, the diffuse religious sanction of a traditional complex of customs place them with the Zuni and Navaho. Particularistic loyalties to family and community are important elements in this traditional complex, and this links the Spanish-Americans not only with the Indian cultures but also with the Mormons.

The religious world of the Spanish-Americans is highly dramatic. Though the underlying fatalism of their religion lessens the possibility of effective human action, it provides rich opportunities for the expression of feelings. Extremes of gaiety and sadness are represented, the two poles being the Fiesta and *Semana Santa*. The happy holiday atmosphere of the fiesta of the patron saint is perhaps the high point of village solidarity during the year, while the ceremonies of Holy Week provide the church and the *Penitente* brotherhood with the opportunity to act out the most anguishing of tragedies, the Crucifixion.

In Mormonism, God is the sole source of morality. Custom per se has no religious sanction, and obedience to divine commandment is the essence of morality. But the conception of God as Wholly Other has been replaced by the idea of a finite God, a God of "body parts and passions," who changes and progresses through the eons in his increasing control over matter, a God who is merely the most advanced of a whole range of spiritual beings in which man is included. "As man is now God once was; as God is now man may become." The God who is the giver of laws and who seems to be the same as the God of Abraham, Isaac, and Jacob, and the God who is the most advanced of a host of spiritual beings (or gods — the Mormons frankly admit to being in a certain sense polytheists), are both integral parts of the Mormon concept of the divine nature.

Mormonism is a religion of the law in the ancient Judaic sense. Just as the law for the ancient Hebrews was revealed by God and written down in the Old Testament, so the law for the modern chosen people, the Mormons, was revealed to Joseph Smith and is contained in the Mormon scriptures, especially the *Doctrine and Covenants*. The office of revelator for the whole church is part of the role of the First President of the church, so that the channel of revelation remains open to the present day. The exact canonical status of revelation after Joseph Smith is not entirely clear, but there are those who believe that all the writings and public utterances of the First Presidents (some even include members of the Council of the Twelve Apostles) are to be considered as revelations. Revelation is not restricted to the highest realm of faith and morals but covers the whole of life. The Mormon village plan and social structure are as laid down in the commandments. The organization of the family and the form of marriage are also subject to such law. Both the establishment and the abolition of plural marriage were in accordance with divine commandment. Together, these commandments form a comprehensive plan, the Gospel Plan, obedience to which ensures salvation and the chance to continue to progress in the afterlife.

The progressive aspect of the Mormon concept of life after death, which separates it from the traditional Christian view, is an important key to Mormon values. There are several realms of glory to which man can attain, depending on his performance in this life: the celestial (the highest), the terrestrial, and the telestial (the lowest). Progress continues within these realms and is unlimited in the highest realm. Activism is pervasive in Mormon life and is an important aspect of life after death:

> If work ended with death, there could be no joy in heaven, no eternal progression. Neither is it all singing and playing of harps. We worship the Lord with deeds even more than with words. Life after death is a period of intense activity. We will pick up our work there where we leave off here, doing the things we love to do and can do best . . . There are no idlers in heaven.[11]

Just as work continues in the life after death, so does the family. Those persons who have been "sealed" in marriage through a proper ceremony in a Mormon temple will continue to be married in the life after death, and children sealed to them will continue to be their children hereafter. Sexuality is an eternal principle and spiritual children will continue to be born. Those who obey the commandments in this life will become gods in the next and will grow in power and glory as they continue to work and have ever greater numbers of progeny. The almost puritan attitude toward work and the almost Hebraic tribal and patriarchal attitude toward social life which are combined in Mormonism are extended to the life after death. Both aspects are reconciled in the concept of planned progression, the absoluteness of God from the point of view of the merely human is relativized by the possibility of similar attainments by men in the future life.

In the comprehensiveness with which social life is religiously sanctioned and in the importance of particularistic ties to family and community, Mormonism seems to resemble the religious symbol systems of the Zuni, Navaho, and Spanish-Americans. The mechanism is, however, entirely different. It is not a question of sanctioning traditional customs, but of obedience to a comprehensive set of divine commandments. Revelation could lead to a drastic change in even the most apparently "sacred" of customs, as when plural marriage was adopted. Further, obedience to commandments is not merely for the sake of the maintenance of a harmonious *status quo*, but to carry out a general plan which has definite directions and goals both on this earth — the establishment of Zion — and in the hereafter.

Of the five communities, the Texan is the least religious. At the time the research was done, there were members of at least ten Protestant denominations or sects represented in Homestead, but only two churches, the Presbyterian (formerly the Community Church) and the Baptist. Only about 20 percent of the community was active in them. In spite of the number of religious bodies, only one major religious tradition is represented, that of left-wing or ascetic Protestantism. However secularized the community is at present, there is reason to believe that elements of the Protestant ethic and the world view of the ascetic Protestant Churches are widespread among the Texans.

In answer to the question, "Do you look at this life as an end in itself, or preparation for the life to come?" one Texan replied, "I don't know. I haven't given it much thought. Sometimes I think maybe we live this life and that's about it. Don't you think?" While this may be the attitude of many in the community much of the time, the ideas of another Texan indicate that this is not the whole story:

> I think most everyone here is a believer when it comes to a showdown. You may not think this when you just look at our actions, when we're making good money and in good health we don't think or talk much about it. But when it comes down to rock bottom and we have to say one way or the other, I think that most people would say they believe.

241

But whatever the conscious religious commitment of the home-steaders, the profound concern with morality which is strong at least among the women and I believe latent among the men (as conversion experiences to be mentioned later indicate), together with the restless energy and initiative directed into the sphere of productive work and technical improvement, are at least in part attributable to the tradition of ascetic Protestantism from which these people come.

In that tradition the absolute Otherness of the God of Calvinism, a God of power and justice, has to some extent been mitigated by the revivalist stress on the love and forgiveness of Jesus. While some moral directives are felt to have the sanction of a God of wrath, capable of inspiring guilt in at least some homesteader minds, the churches stress forgiveness and acceptance for those who repent and honestly attempt to mend their ways. Nevertheless, most Texan morality and customs lack direct relation to divine sanction. Being "good" and "honest" may be seen as conducive to spiritual blessings here or hereafter and being "bad" and "dishonest" may be seen as having the reverse effect, but neither the detailed supernatural sanctioning of custom found among Zuni, Navaho, and Spanish-American, nor the comprehensive set of commandments for daily life of the Mormons are found in Homestead. Most moral norms have purely secular sanction. However, certain specific "sins," such as drinking, are seen as emblematic of general badness and are felt to incur divine sanction.

Concern for salvation, the answer of ascetic Protestantism to the problem of the meaning of life, does not seem very pervasive, but we cannot conclude that life is essentially meaningless to the home-steaders. Certain secular mechanisms that are not so prominent in the other four communities give meaning to life in Homestead. A secular alternative to salvation is provided by the concepts of success for the individual and progress for the group. These concepts give meaning and direction to much of life which in the other cultures would more likely be provided by religion. The goals of success and progress are by no means alien to ascetic Protestantism and are in fact outgrowths of it in important respects. Nevertheless, as an ultimate answer to life, they compete with the religious answer and can only be considered idolatrous by the churches.

Further indication that the Texan is the most secularized of the five communities comes from the fact that it is the only one which is not religiously "centered." Religious symbolism of place makes Zuni village central for the Zuni and the hogan and the land between the four sacred mountains central for the Navaho. The church is central as a physical symbol and an institution in both Rimrock and Atrisco. Moreover, both Mormons and Spanish-Americans look to a religious center beyond the immediate environs of the village in whose orbit they consider themselves — Salt Lake City and Rome. But there is no church at the center, symbolically or institutionally, in Homestead, nor do the homesteaders look to any other religious center. If there is a need for a sense of symbolic centering, it has so far received only a secular fulfillment in the "Pinto Bean Capital of the World."

Competition between sacred and secular ultimate answers to life's problems is probably of importance also to Mormon and Spanish-Americans. In the "harmonious" world view of the traditional Zuni and Navaho religions there is no conflict between sacred and the secular ideals. The one is the expression of the other.

Personality and Religious Action

Religious action in the broadest sense is any action with respect to any part of the world of religious symbols, the "supernatural." One aspect of this action which we may call worship involves the commitment of actors to some part or aspect of the religious world. Worship has the function of internalizing and maintaining in the personality certain religious symbols. In this way it gives a context of power and meaning to the values and moral norms which are related to those religious symbols. A second aspect of religious action may be called therapeutic or restorative. Initiation, rites of passage, and life crisis rituals are primarily of this type. This kind of action occurs in the face of some threat to the personality or social system, such as the death of a near relative, illness, drought, or threats to the personality involved in growing up. Here, religious action involves the acquisition of power and meaning from the religious sphere which can be used to meet the threats, and it also usually involves the expression within limits of the anxieties and regressive behaviors which the threat calls forth. It is this aspect of religious action which accounts for the fact that religion is always and ev-

243

erywhere bound up with the healing function. On the most ultimate level it involves salvation from the threat of alienation from God; on the most concrete level, it involves magical techniques for attaining of empirical ends. The main function of this type of religious action is to help maintain commitment to values and norms in the face of threats which might break that commitment. All concrete religious action involves both worship and therapy but in any specific case, one or the other will probably be primary.

Worship is the dominant activity of Zuni life. Benedict says in speaking of ceremonialism:

> Probably most grown men among the western Pueblos give to it the greater part of their waking life. It requires the memorizing of an amount of word-perfect ritual that our less trained minds find staggering, and the performance of neatly dovetailed ceremonies that are chartered by the calendar and complexly interlock all the different cults and the governing body in endless formal procedure. . . . This preoccupation with detail is logical enough. Zuni religious practices are believed to be supernaturally powerful in their own right. At every step of the way, if the procedure is correct, the costume of the masked god traditional to the last detail, the offerings unimpeachable, the words of the hours-long prayers letter perfect, the effect will follow according to man's desires. One has only, in the phrase they have always on their tongues, to "know how." According to all tenets of their religion, it is a major matter if one of the eagle feathers of a mask has been taken from the shoulder of the bird instead of from the breast. Every detail has magical efficacy.[12]

The function of this kind of religious action for personality is illuminated by a comparison with ritualistic compulsiveness as a type of psychopathology. Without by any means implying that the Zuni as a people are psychopathological, we can assert that the minute attention to detail, the careful regulation of the time and place for formal observances, and the constant reiteration of words, motions, and dance steps give the participants a sense of security and of control over the environment. A key aspect of Zuni ceremonialism is symbolic imitation of supernatural beings and natural forces. Such repeated imitation leads to the feeling that the dancers and the gods are one: good fortune, rain, fertility must be forthcoming.

> The dance, like ritual poetry, is a monotonous compulsion of natural forces by reiteration. The tireless pounding of their feet draws together the mist in the sky and heaps it into the piled rain clouds.

It forces out the rain upon the earth. They are bent not at all upon an ecstatic experience, but upon so thorough-going an identification with nature that the forces of nature will swing to their purposes.[13]

When a man puts on a mask for one of the great *katcina* ceremonials, he "becomes for the time being the supernatural himself. He has no longer human speech, but only the cry which is peculiar to that god." When the Zuni pray to their gods, they say, "We shall be one person." [14] In order to be able to take such a role, the men involved in the *katcina* dances must make a retreat for several days beforehand and must observe continence during the retreat and the ceremonial. During the summer, the Rain Priests or *Uwanami* Priests go into retreat successively, one group going in as another comes out. This ensures that the identification between Zuni and the cosmos will hold and the summer rains will come. There is no question but that compulsive repetition of acts and formulas believed to be efficacious and imitation of supernaturals to the point where there is felt to be identification can give a profound sense of well-being and security to those who participate directly or indirectly. The endless orderly ritual which characterizes this kind of religious action is the essence of the "Apollonian" nature of Zuni. However, this kind of religious action, which is meant to ensure the endless flow of blessings to the pueblo, is peculiarly vulnerable to failure. On the whole, Zuni is a prosperous and successful society; but, when things go wrong, the mechanisms for righting them may prove inadequate.[15] If there is no rain, bitter accusations may be made against the priests. It may be rumored that they were incontinent or broke other taboos. A smallpox epidemic may create witchcraft hysteria. Evil is not something to which much attention is paid in normal Zuni religious thinking, but, when it occurs, it creates intense anxiety and a feeling that it must be someone's fault. The witchcraft persecutions, in the period before the United States Government put a stop to them, were brutal affairs. Bitterness and blame for failures can also lead to the formation of factions, separated by intensely hostile though usually covert gossip. The inability to control such factional hostility adequately is indicated by the fissions which have occurred in pueblos even in historic times.[16] Zuni worship, with its concentration on orderly compulsion of and identification with the supernaturals, is geared to success. Its dominant character leaves little room for the anxieties and explosive hostilities which may be aroused by acute frustration. The "therapeutic" aspect of Zuni religious action, however, gives some outlet for the tensions inhibited by most of Zuni life, though Bunzel has noted its relative weakness:

> The vast wealth of ceremonial elaboration which we have been considering is notably weak on the side of what have been called "crisis rites." In contrast to the ceremonial recognition given to natural phenomena — the solstitial risings of the sun, the alternation of summer and winter, the perpetual dearth of rain — crises in personal life pass almost unnoticed. The ceremonies surrounding birth, puberty, marriage, and death are meager and unspectacular.

There is one striking exception to this rule — initiation. After discussing initiation into the *katcina* societies, Bunzel deals with what is probably the crucial exception:

> Initiations into medicine societies are more clearly ceremonial recognition of personal crises. The initiate is a patient who has been snatched from the jaws of death and his initiation into the group that saved him is the ceremonial assumption of his new status. At his initiation he gets a "new heart," and, as a symbol of the new life he has begun, receives a new name.[17]

The study of psychosomatic medicine indicates that unrelieved anxieties and tensions may build up to the point where they find physical expression as illness. Initiation into the medicine or Beast God societies may serve to express tensions for the "sick" which cannot be handled in the major round of religious life. Toward the close of a famous passage in which she describes the difference between Apollonian and Dionysian cultures, Benedict says, "In Nietzsche's fine phrase, even in the exaltation of the dance he [the Apollonian] 'remains what he is, and retains his civic name.' " [18] This is profoundly true of the great ceremonial dances of the masked gods, performed with an interminable measured tread in which forty or more dancers move as one. It is not, however, true of the initiation into the Onayanakia Order of the Great Fire Fraternity, as described by Matilda Coxe Stevenson:

> . . . the warrior gradually becomes wilder in his gesticulations before the altar, bending until he almost kneels before it, which he leaves every now and then to join the dancers or to heal the sick. A guest from the pueblo of Sia, who belongs to the Fire fraternity of that pueblo, goes to the fireplace and stamps in the fire and literally bathes himself in

the live coals. He then takes a large coal in his right hand, and after rubbing his throat and breast with it he places it in his mouth. Others of the Fire fraternity also play with the coals, rubbing them over one another's backs. As the night wanes, the cries of the theurgists become louder and wilder, and the dance grows faster. . . . The lines of dancers often break into a promiscuous mass.[19]

This is not an isolated instance. The behavior of the Beast God societies is full of radically "Dionysian" elements. Some of them go in for sword-swallowing; one of them, the Cactus fraternity, performs a ritual combat with large pieces of cactus which goes on until the bodies of the combatants are punctured and bleeding and many spines are stuck in the flesh. Perhaps the most extreme behavior is that of the *Newekwe,* who eat feces and drink urine. According to Stevenson,

The one who swallows the largest amount of filth with the greatest gusto is most commended by the fraternity and the onlookers. A large bowl of urine is handed by a Koyemshi, who receives it from a woman on the house top, to a man of the fraternity, who, after drinking a portion, pours the remainder over himself by turning the bowl over his head. Women run to the edge of the roof and empty bowls of urine over the Newekwe and Koyemshi. Each man endeavors to excel his fellows in buffoonery and in eating repulsive things such as bits of old blankets or splinters of wood. They bite off the heads of living mice and chew them, tear dogs limb from limb, eat the intestines and fight over the liver like hungry wolves.[20]

This behavior is supposed to be a "joke." Considering it funny, not to be taken seriously, is one way of limiting and constraining religious action which runs counter to the prevailing type. The Beast God societies as a whole, I think, are controlled means for the expression of emotions which would otherwise be disruptive. They do not represent the dominant mode of Zuni religious life, but should be interpreted as therapeutic mechanisms which drain off potentially explosive tensions and help to maintain the dominant pattern.

In its major emphasis Navaho religion contrasts strikingly with Zuni. It is therapy in a very literal sense: the great ceremonials are almost all curing rites. If Zuni religion is preoccupied with success, one might almost say that Navaho religion is preoccupied with failure. Zuni religion is primarily concerned with seeing that everything stays right; Navaho religion is primarily concerned with righting things when they have gone wrong.

247

Just as Zuni worship has its therapeutic side, so Navaho curing rites have an aspect of worship. Ceremonials and rituals in which worship has primacy are, however, relatively few. Worship tends to be periodic and regular, expressive of the continued devotion of the worshipers to the supernatural; therapy is irregular, depending on situations of need. There is no fixed pattern of worship in Navaho, which is the only one of the five communities without calendrical worship of some sort. An exception to this would be the daily devotion in some households. Kluckhohn and Leighton tell us that:

> The use of the pollen of corn and other plants is very important in maintaining the proper relationship to the Holy People. In old-fashioned households the day still begins with the sprinkling of pollen from one of the little bags and a brief murmured prayer. After the evening meal the members of the family rub their limbs and say, "May I be lively. May I be healthy." More pollen may be offered and a Blessing Way song sung.[21]

Blessing Way is an important Navaho ceremonial and comes closest to being primarily "worship" in the sense intended here. "It places the Navahos in tune with the Holy People — particularly Changing Woman — and so ensures health, prosperity, and general well-being." While not performed at a regular time or interval, it is performed very frequently. "Seldom does a family go for six months without having Blessing Way sung at least once in their hogan. It is held to be peculiarly important that every member of the immediate biological family should be present." [22] Blessing Way functions as a general consecrating rite. It is given for a newly chosen headman and held in a newly built hogan. Songs from it are sung in the girl's puberty rite and in the marriage ceremony. While not a cure, it is skewed in the therapeutic direction by its function as "preventive therapy." It will be sung over a pregnant woman shortly before she is due to give birth, or over a young man who is about to enter the army.

Most Navaho ceremonies are curing rituals performed for a patient or patients. If illness is so central in their religion, what does it mean to the Navaho? It is a much broader concept with them than in other cultures. As Reichard says, "illness is fundamentally the same as disturbance — cosmic as well as human." [23] She goes on to say that any feeling of confusion, bewilderment, frustration, or futility may be interpreted as illness, and the ill person casts about

248

for some explanation. The illness may be attributed to contamination by ghosts, Navaho or foreign, by animals of high supernatural potency such as snake or bear. Concerned with locating the cause, the patient and his family may call in a diviner who will, usually by hand-trembling but also by star-gazing or "listening," discover the source of the disturbance and prescribe the proper chant.[24] A common cause of illness is the breaking of any of the many restrictions which impinge on Navaho life.

> Normally life goes on quietly and satisfactorily enough. A man may observe some of the most obvious restraints or he may not keep any. As long as nothing happens, he is not conscious of breaking them. As soon as misfortune becomes marked — lightning strikes his sheep, his crop is ruined by hail, his wife has a miscarriage and does not regain her strength, his baby coughs — he considers what he might have done to offend the powers. As he thinks over his past, he has no difficulty finding numerous lapses. Further thought makes the accumulation of neglect so impressive that he is impelled to seek a proper cure, a ceremony.[25]

The Navaho sing involves a number of elements which contribute to a therapeutic result. It mobilizes relatives to take responsibility and feel concern for the sick person. The last night of most chants involves singing by a considerable number of people, both relatives and nearby families, who offer "good thoughts" in an effort to make the ceremony successful. This display of interest and concern probably has a very beneficial effect on the "disturbed" person. Further, the singer makes remarks and speeches, aside from the set songs and prayers, in which he encourages and supports the patient and offers moral advice and admonition not only to the patient but also to the relatives and other participants. One of the major themes of the sing is purification. The patient is given suds baths and emetics and must observe continence. Thus, symbolically he is freed from the contaminations which have made him ill and, indirectly, from his own guilt. Through the singer as intermediary, the patient is put in touch with ultimate power and meaning, receiving strength to get well which he did not have alone. "In the height of the chant the patient himself becomes one of the Holy People, puts his feet in their moccasins, and breathes in the strength of the sun. He comes into complete harmony with the universe and must of course be free of all ills and evil." [26] The sing can involve a moral regeneration somewhat analogous to conversion in the Christian tradition, as indicated in a story reported by Kluckhohn: "An English-speaking Navaho who had just returned from jail where he had been put for beating his wife and molesting his stepdaughter said to me, 'I am sure going to behave from now on. I am going to be changed — just like somebody who has been sung over.' " [27]

The Navaho belief in witchcraft[28] shows that their religious symbol system has no better solution to the problem of evil than has the Zuni system. Anxieties and hostilities caused by various frustrations and failures tend here as in Zuni to take a personal reference. A man in difficulty may think, "There are witches around here," or "Someone is witching me." Witching is one source of illness which sings are required to cure. Murders of suspected witches have been reported, but witchcraft belief is probably less disruptive to the Navaho than to the Zuni. While the Zuni often suspect close relatives or important officials, the Navahos usually suspect someone "over there," in Canyon de Chelly or some other distant point. Anxieties about going into crowds of strangers are great but intragroup hostility does not focus on witchcraft.

As in all of the Christian groups, the focus of ordinary religious action among the Spanish-Americans is on church worship. Here the doctrines, dogmas, and moral injunctions are set forth and understood, however imperfectly, by the people. In the sacrament of the Holy Eucharist, the communicants physically partake of and at least spiritually become identified with the divine source of being and meaning. All that is involved in being a *buen Católico* is reinforced by the Mass.

The church also plays an important therapeutic role. Baptism, confirmation, marriage, and last rites can all be interpreted in this light. The yearly round of church festivals and ceremonies provides expression for the joys and tragedies of the people's lives, of which the high point of the religious year is Holy Week. Atrisco is too small to have a full performance of the Holy Week pageant, but we may refer to the description of the dramatizations that are part of the ceremonies as given in the field notes of Munro S. Edmonson for the town of Tome, another New Mexico Spanish-American town somewhat larger than Atrisco. The cast includes apostles, pharisees, Roman soldiers, and so on. Each of the dramatic events is acted out on the day on which it is supposed to have occurred. For instance, on Holy Thursday there is a tableau of the Last Supper. The evening of Holy Thursday, the trial and imprisonment of Christ by the Sanhedrin is commemorated.

> The Cristo was in the center of the church in chains and behind bars. The Virgin and another *santo* representing either Mary Magdalene or the Virgen Dolorosa were on either side of the prison. Roman soldiers and *fariseos* came in and stood in the middle of the aisle . . . the *fariseos* were carrying wooden staves tipped with red.

Good Friday is the climax of the Holy Week ceremonies. In the morning, the trial before Pilate is enacted, with the washing of hands, the freeing of Barabbas, and so on. This is followed by a procession around the plaza; in the observances at Tome in 1950, between one thousand and fifteen hundred people took part. The high point is reached in the afternoon, when the crucifixion is enacted. At Tome, an outdoor stage had been constructed, with a scene of the Holy Land painted on the back wall. There were three crosses. The statue of the *Cristo,* which had movable arms, was placed on the central cross, and two young boys stripped to breech clouts were placed on the other crosses. The whole stage was hidden by a gray curtain. About four thousand people were present in the plaza. According to Edmonson,

> The padre took his place before the stage and preached earnestly and well. Then he prayed briefly and read the scripture on the crucifixion. As he read the line, "The veil of the temple was rent asunder," the curtain of the stage suddenly dropped to reveal the tableau of Christ on the cross. A Roman soldier had his lance at the wound in Christ's side, and a *fariseo* had his staff at Christ's breast. No one stirred. It was indeed a climactic moment. Then the *Cristo* was removed from the cross and placed in the casket. The two thieves were removed and disappeared. The procession was formed in two columns, four abreast and still reached most of the way around the plaza. The centurion now in black, led on his horse. The choir came along singing in Spanish, very slowly and hauntingly.

The ceremonies of Holy Saturday and Easter Sunday, though important, are almost anticlimactic following the intense drama of Good Friday.

The *Penitente* Brotherhood, although it is dying out, observed Holy Week even more intensely than the church. The following is Edmonson's description of the *Penitente* Good Friday:

251

The processions of Good Friday begin . . . with a procession shortly after midnight. At each procession the whips are freely wielded, and the brothers, who have gone without food or rest for as much as two days, suffer genuine agonies. In the afternoon (or sometimes, to avoid publicity, in the evening), the crucifixion is staged, the chosen "Christ" being tied to the cross in cruel torment. Following this is the dramatic ritual of *Tinieblas*, held in total darkness amid the clanking of chains and the rattling of tin.[29]

The *Penitente* Brotherhood, though it never existed in Atrisco, was once an important aspect of Spanish-American religious life. Especially during periods of neglect by the official church, it functioned not only as a mutual benevolence society but also as a means for extreme religious expression. Torture with ashes and whips was part of its ceremonial, and its positive functions, like those of the Beast God Societies in Zuni, may be considered therapeutic tension reduction.

Another religious action in some sense therapeutic is the vow, or *promesa*. In a situation of great anxiety or danger, where not much can be done directly, an individual may promise a saint that, if the desired outcome is granted, he will perform a certain action. Such a vow might be made by the mother of a sick child. The commonest *promesa* in Atrisco is to walk the forty miles to the *Santo* in Zuni. Florence Kluckhohn reports a young couple who walked to Zuni the day after their parentally disapproved marriage.

Although the church sanctions the *promesa* within limits, the *curandero*, a folk curer who uses special herbs and magic spells, is entirely outside church control or approval. The Spanish-Americans may also call upon Indian curers. Although the *buen Católico* is considered immune to witches, belief in the devil, witches, and ghosts is strong in Atrisco, and has much the same function as the belief in witchcraft among the Zuni and Navaho. These beliefs are strongest in women and are in some degree a projection of the fear of possible sexual attack by males.

Worship is an important part of Mormon life. Sunday School and Sacrament Meeting are primarily worship services. Through the sacrament, singing hymns, and giving talks the people of Rimrock express their commitment to God. Worship is not confined to Sunday church meetings. There are also family prayers, prayers spoken at the meetings of the various auxiliary organizations, and prayers to open and close dances and other functions. The affirmation of

Mormon beliefs and values is a dominant theme in this worship, and many talks end with some such phrase as, "I have a testimony of the gospel, and I know that it is true."

The therapeutic function is also well developed in Mormonism. Some important rites of passage are carried out within the Ward, for example, the blessing of an infant, baptism, and funerals. The important rituals of endowment and sealing a marriage for time and eternity are carried out in the temple. (The nearest temple to Rimrock is in Mesa, Arizona.) These ceremonies make a strong impression on the people because of their secrecy, their rich symbolism, and the permanence of the commitment they imply. The moral requisites for having such ceremonies involve conformity to the highest standards of Mormon morality. Being able to "go through the temple" is both a reward for the earnestness of one's religious life and a promise of the blessings which will come in the hereafter. As an explicitly therapeutic technique in case of illness, the Mormons practice the laying on of hands for curing. Joseph Smith instituted this on the strength of New Testament precedent. Prayer is another therapeutic technique, especially in situations of great anxiety. The Mormons of Rimrock believe that disobedience to divine commandments will result in punishment in this life. A good deal of guilt, therefore, has a religious coloration. The Mormon Sacrament Meeting provides an important context for the therapeutic expression of some of this guilt. In the Sacrament Meeting the Bishop, who usually presides, calls on various persons, to whom he may or may not have spoken previously, to make short talks. On the first Sunday of the month, the Sacrament Meeting becomes a Testimonial Meeting in which anyone can speak; no one is called on. Any Sacrament Meeting, but especially the Testimonial Meeting, can be used to express guilt feelings of various kinds. Emotion sometimes runs high and tears are frequent. Intense and tearful expressions of devotion to spouses and parents can be taken as repentance and sorrow for hostile feelings and acts toward them. Direct confessions of wrongdoing are not customary, but generalized statements of failure and inadequacy are common. Such occasions allow the expression of guilt and anxiety in a context which insures forgiveness and love.

Worship in Homestead consists chiefly of the weekly church services for those who attend. Singing of hymns, praying, and listening to the sermon are aspects of the commitment which church attendance implies. As in Rimrock, prayer is a therapeutic technique in situations of anxiety. Like the Mormons, some Texans feel that illness and other misfortunes are divine punishments. There is much less opportunity for the therapeutic expression of guilt than in the case of the Mormons, but it is not entirely lacking. Revivalism offers such an opportunity. At the time of the research, only the Baptists had revival meetings. They enjoyed considerable success, and six conversions occurred in the 1950 revival. The following account of one of the men converted was reported by Vogt:

> He said it certainly gave him a wonderful feeling, that he couldn't describe it very well. All he knew was that he felt a whole lot better after he'd gone down the aisle and given himself up to the Lord. He added that he's always led a pretty bad life and that he never got anywhere and he thinks it's about time he devoted his life to Christ and the church.[30]

Conversion, when it is followed by genuine moral regeneration, is taken by most Protestants to be an indication of personal salvation. It is therefore a critical experience for those who are religious. Even one of the leading Presbyterians, belonging to a church which did not carry on revivals, recounted an experience he had in his youth at a revival meeting. He said that he began to shout and pray and then felt "the burden was gone."

Some Texas males use gambling and drinking to relieve tensions which might in some of the other cultures be handled through religious therapy. This is also true for Spanish-American males to some extent too, and, as far as drinking is concerned, for some of the Navaho. In the three Christian societies magic tends to be separated from the religious complex and is largely secular. Water-witching (dowsing) is the chief example among Texans and Mormons, though other magical techniques exist in connection with farming. Among the five cultures, only the Mormons and Texans do not believe in witchcraft. Tensions and anxieties associated with witchcraft in the others are probably the source of much of the out-group hostility, primarily toward the Indians on the part of the Mormons and toward the Spanish-Americans on the part of the Texans, but also including rather vague categories such as "the government" or "Communists."

Worship serves to commit individuals to the central values of their culture because it commits them to the ultimate power and meaning which lies behind those values. It also motivates behavior which will express those values in the form of moral action. Religious therapy, on the other hand, serves to strengthen commitment and moral action by meeting situations of strain and anxiety in such a way that, while fears and emotions are expressed, the ultimate power of being and meaning is evoked to aid in a successful transition or the re-establishment of a threatened equilibrium. If religion is as important in maintaining commitment to values and managing tension as we have indicated, its ramifications in nonreligious sectors of society should be considerable.

SOCIETY AND RELIGIOUS INSTITUTIONS

The relations between religion and society can be divided into two main categories. One includes the general implications of religious commitments for all sectors of social life, most importantly perhaps for the amount and kind of economic activity which is considered desirable, for the kind of political authority which is considered legitimate, and for the nonreligious solidarities which are considered especially sacred and inviolable. The other important relation results from the fact that persons committed to the same concepts of the divine tend to form temporary or permanent collectivities in which religious action is carried on. These collectivities, especially as they become more firmly established, become complex. They develop authority structures, with differentiated roles for religious leaders and specialists; rules and regulations for the acceptance of members and standards for the maintenance of membership; and some means of meeting the inevitable economic requirements of such an organization. Such a structure may take on political, economic, or integrative functions for the society as a whole and may also direct its activities to pattern maintenance and tension management which, as a religious organization, are its primary functions. Of course, it is possible that in relatively undifferentiated societies, there are structures which handle, say, both political and religious functions. It cannot then be said that a religious structure has "taken over" political functions, but rather that one structure has both functions. It is also possible that nonreligious structures, for example, political parties, may "take over" religious functions.

For the Zuni we may pass over the general relations between religion and society briefly and then deal in some detail with the structural relations. With respect to economic activity, the high evaluation of Zuni religion placed on the things of this life — on corn and children and all good things — is expressed in the religious concern with fertility, and motivates economic effort to attain these goods. A hard worker is a good Zuni. On the other hand, the great amount of effort which goes into ritual activity not only takes time from productive labor but also involves considerable expense for goods. In addition, the hospitality required during great ceremonials may involve the expenditure of virtually all reserves. In this way religion hinders capital accumulation.

With respect to Zuni political authority, we have already noted that in earlier times this was a function of certain priesthoods. Nothing in the religious system legitimizes the right of absolute control of one man over another. The basis of what authority there is resides in general sanctity, in being both moral and holy. Those men most closely identified with the gods deserve to have their opinions most closely followed. While at the present time political authority is becoming increasingly the province of a purely secular governor and council, it is unlikely that men who are very far from the priestly ideal would be elected to these offices.

Zuni religion places the stamp of sanctity on the solidarities of kinship and community. Ancestors of all clans are among the *katcinas* who preside benevolently over the welfare of the village. The harmonious functioning of kin groups and of the total village structure is pleasing to the gods.

There is a sense in which the most important religious collectivity in Zuni is identical with the total Zuni society. In the great ceremonials, such as Shalako, everyone in the village is directly or indirectly involved. Nevertheless, most ritual is carried out by a series of interlocking collectivities organized on different principles, each containing only a limited number of members. The most inclusive religious society is the *Katcina* Society, to which all Zuni males and a very few women belong. The twelve rain priesthoods are composed of from two to six members each and are mostly hereditary in the matrilineal line. It is interesting that two of the key officers, the *pekwin* and the head of the chief rain priesthood, must both be members of the Dogwood clan, the largest in Zuni. Membership in the twelve medicine or Beast God societies is voluntary, usually being the result of a cure by that

256

society. Membership in the Bow Priesthood is restricted to those who have killed an enemy. All these groups have important initiation ceremonies.

Traditionally the rain priesthoods, especially the four major ones, together with the *pekwin,* had the primary political authority. The Bow Priesthood was their executive arm, being used especially in the punishment of religious offenses. The rain priesthoods and the office of *pekwin* were hereditary, emphasizing the importance of kinship as well as religion in the social structure. These sacred groups, however, could not be sullied by responsibility for violence, and it was delegated to a group already involved in that dangerous sphere. In keeping with our analysis of their function, the medicine societies were essentially "private," though they did assume some public responsibilities in the yearly round of ceremonies.

The various religious collectivities have several integrative functions. Perhaps the most important is provision of at least two axes for classifying roles in the community other than kinship. For example, a man has one set of solidarities with his relatives, another with the members of his *katcina* society, another with the members of his medicine society. This prevents cleavages in the community from becoming too serious, because lines of differentiation on one level are bound to be bridged by solidarities on another. The great religious ceremonies symbolize solidarity within Zuni and cement ties with visitors and friends as well.

The economic aspects of the religious collectivities are numerous. Ruth Benedict describes the obligations a man incurs when he assumes responsibility for entertaining the masked Gods at Shalako:

> For this . . . he must build a new house for the gods to bless at housewarming. All that year he must feed the cult members who build for him, he must provide the great beams for the rafters, he must entertain the whole tribe at the final ceremony. There are endless responsibilities he must assume. For this purpose he will plant heavily the year before and increase his herd. He will receive help from his clan group, all of which he must return in kind.[31]

In summary, Zuni is a relatively large and closely settled community with important problems of differentiation and integration which are too large to be solved by kinship groups alone. However, the only structural differentiation beyond kinship in traditional Zuni was effected by the religious collectivities. Various nonreligious func-

257

tions, such as political authority, recreation, and medicine, were provided for the society as a whole by these groups, since there were no secular structures for handling them. The secrecy that is so noticeable a feature of Zuni religious life can in part be explained as a way of keeping a complex and delicate mechanism free from outside tampering.* It may also safeguard internal structural differentiation. Groups that perform vital functions for society, but whose only basis of legitimacy is religion, require secrecy on religious grounds to maintain the boundaries of their structural distinctness and thereby the level of structural differentiation which the community as a whole had attained.

The relation between the Navaho religion and the evaluation of economic activity is the same as that of the Zuni. Religious values support motivation to work for the goods of this world, but ceremonial takes so much time and money that religion effectively prevents capital accumulation. Religious ideas have an important part in the evaluation of the legitimacy of authority. The headman is supposed to embody the values of Navaho religion and is supposed to know Blessing Way. This is not to enable him to serve as a practitioner of curing, but to keep him in touch with the Holy People through this most common and most valued of Navaho ceremonies. The solidarities which are religiously validated are almost exclusively those of kinship.

By contrast with the Zuni the Navaho have no permanent collectivities with a purely religious basis. There are, however, religious specialists who hold key roles, the diviner and the singer. A temporary religious collectivity composed of the singer, the patient, the patient's family, and other friends and onlookers exists for the duration of a ceremonial. This collectivity, while it lasts, has considerable differentiation. The singer has more authority than the leader of virtually any other nonkinship collectivity. The singer regulates the behavior of the patient and of the other participants. This authority is sufficient to empower him to order the summary expulsion of troublemakers from the scene. Some people may be sent to gather herbs, others may help with the sand-paintings, and those who know the songs will be expected to help with the singing. The singer in im-

---

* In this connection the close proximity of Spanish settlements following after intermittent Spanish attempts to stamp out the native religion certainly played an important part in augmenting the importance of secrecy in their ritual.

portant respects stands outside the kinship system. The role is not hereditary; in return for payment, it is acquired from an older singer who may or may not be a relative. The choice of singer is based on medical diagnostic grounds, not on kinship; in fact, a man is not supposed to sing over his wife or close relatives.

There is a sense in which household, extended family, and local group are in part religious collectivities. The household is the unit of daily religious devotions and the primary locus for the performance of Blessing Way. Larger ceremonials are supported by the extended family and attended by a considerable number of the local group. The Girl's Puberty Rite, which symbolizes the fact that the matrilineal extended family is now ready to continue for another generation, is a key extended family ritual. The local group is loosely organized in respect to religious functions as it is in respect to most others. The ceremony of Blessing Way performed over a new headman is the clearest example of a local group ceremony. The initiations which accompany Night Way may be seen as in part local group in their extent and significance, since they involve participants from a number of families. Likewise Enemy Way, with its Squaw Dance, is an important social occasion for the people of the local group. In all these ceremonials, visitors from beyond the local group are welcome, whereas many within the local group do not attend. The local group may be seen as a pool of ritual and ceremonial knowledge. Almost surely someone within it will know war ritual or hunting ritual or salt-gathering ritual and thus local group parties for these purposes will have the requisite ceremonial leadership. It is also likely that the local group will contain singers of a considerable variety of chants, so that for most illnesses the singer can be drawn from the local group.

Although the headman or "peace chief" had to know Blessing Way, the "war chief" was merely a man who knew war ritual and could call up other men to go on a raiding party with him. It was the headman's general reputation of being a fair and good man which gave him the authority to offer judgment in disputes, though he had virtually no way to enforce them. Zelditch has pointed out that the only sanction he could manipulate which approached compulsion was to imply that a stubborn person who would not settle a dispute in the way the headman and the majority of the community thought was fair, was a witch.[32] Since witchcraft involved severe community sanc-

259

tions and, on occasion, violence, this was a potent threat, but it could only be used as a last resort.

Ceremonials have integrative functions for the extended family since they intensify interaction and concern for its members. Also, the larger ceremonials provide the most important opportunity for gatherings of individuals from different extended families, and this interaction helps to integrate the local group.

The economic effects of religious life are numerous.[33] The cost of a major ceremonial is very great and requires the concerted effort of a number of relatives. There is some feeling that wealthy families should give a larger number of ceremonials, which tends to level wealth differentiations. Becoming a singer is an important road to wealth. A successful singer may reach the point where he is almost a full-time practitioner, and his income may therefore be much larger than that of the ordinary farmer-herder. This role provides an opportunity for a poor boy with intelligence and a good memory to rise in the world.

Whereas Zuni ceremonial life has the function of keeping a complex urban mechanism running smoothly, Navaho ritual has a quite different social task. For most purposes, the extended family is the most important functioning group for the Navaho. It is relatively small, undifferentiated, and distant from its neighbors. The contribution of each member is of great importance to its functioning. In this context, the main social function of Navaho religion is to keep each member functioning at full efficiency and to speed the recovery of the sick or disturbed. The singer, as an outside specialist and one close to the Holy People and wise in the ways of the Earth People, is in a strategic position to forward this end. He is not involved in the quarrels and tensions of the family group but devotes his full attention to the recovery of the patient. The temporary religious collectivity which forms during the sing cements ties with more distant relatives and other families in the local group and indirectly contributes to the harmonious functioning of the local group. This is not a closed and secret group as at Zuni. There are no cleavages of structural differentiation to maintain. On the contrary, the more who come, the better it will be for the success of the ceremony. With a professional role to maintain, the singer has his own secrets — there are things he will withhold even from his pupils. But the actual performance of the ceremony is open to all who care to attend. The wonderful and beautiful complexity of Navaho religion is a quality of the myths and the rituals themselves, not of the religious organization.

We may begin our review of the relation between religion and society among the Spanish-Americans by considering what effect their religious orientations have on their economic activity. Neither worldly goods nor work itself has direct validation in the religious symbol system. However, family responsibilities have religious valuation, and these include the obligation to work in support of one's family. The general fatalism and resignation expressed in the idea that whatever comes is as God wills tends to inhibit a strong drive to economic mastery of the world. On the whole, the religious orientation would seem conducive to a traditionalistic economic ethic.

The Spanish Catholic religious orientation favors the acceptance of authority without much question as to the basis of that authority. The important thing is that the individual with authority, the *patrón*, should fulfill the role of caretaker of the people, like the patron saint in the religious system. If authorities fail to take this role, a secondary religious orientation encourages people to help each other. In religion this takes the form of the *Penitente* Brotherhood, where the leader is not "father" but "elder brother."

Ethnic, local, and kinship solidarities have religious reinforcement. The Roman Catholic religion is a symbol of ethnic group solidarity, since it is important in differentiating the Hispanic community from their neighbors, who are largely Protestant Anglos. The local community is a single religious congregation under the care of a single saint. The family is sanctioned by religious symbols and by the injunctions of the priest.

The structure of the parish in so small a community as Atrisco is relatively simple. A missionary priest visits once a month. The *patrón* of Atrisco built its church. In a sense it was "his" church: only his family could be buried within it. Virtually the only other church official is the *mayordomo,* who sees that the church is open and ready for worship on Sunday and has charge of maintaining its facilities. The *patrón* was either himself the *mayordomo,* or else he chose the *mayordomo.* When the *padre* visits town, he stays at the *patrón's* house. The fiesta is under the sponsorship of the *patrón.* If there were a resident priest, authority in the religious sphere probably would be more evenly shared.

The religious structure is complicated by the existence in some Spanish-American communities of the *Penitentes*. This group, partly in reaction to the neglect and exploitation of the Spanish-Americans of New Mexico by the church, established its own rites and ceremonies. It acted as a mutual aid society as well as ministering to the religious needs of the people. It persisted despite condemnation by church authorities. The tendency of the local people to make their own religion is also illustrated by the occasional development of a local cult outside the church's jurisdiction. An image may be discovered in a field, set up in someone's back room, and before long miraculous results are reported by those who have prayed to it.

The church and the *Penitentes* have ceased to play any direct political role in the local area involved in this study. The church does not take away much time or money from the people and so is not an economic drain. Neither does it make any economic contribution to the community. Its integrative role is considerable. It plays a prominent role in the crisis rites which effect the integration of the family. One of its major contributions to community solidarity is the fiesta, held under religious auspices, and to a considerable degree recreational in character. Social ties receive a strong reaffirmation: during the fiesta the population of Atrisco was trebled.

The church provides a focus for the social and emotional life of the traditional Spanish-American village. Its teachings and rituals support the integrity of the family and community, and it reinforces authority at the same time that it provides an outlet for individual tensions. Its primary effort is to maintain the traditional norms of the church in the lives of the people.

Viewing the relation of religion and society among the Mormons, we note that economic effort receives direct valuation. This is not so much because good things are considered desirable, though they are by no means despised, but because work itself is a central religious value. Religious authority is highly valued, and the Bishop has direct religious support for his political functions. In the sphere beyond the church, republican political forms are religiously valued because they provide the most favorable framework for the new dispensation of the Mormon religion. However, the insistence on the freedom of the church and its constituent families leads to a degree of anti-authoritarianism with respect to the national government. Finally, there is a direct religious validation of family and community, especially when the latter is identical with the Ward, because they are both religious units.

The Bishop and his councilors and the officers of the auxiliary societies play important political roles, in fact forming the political structure of the village of Rimrock. Economically, the Church exacts a high contribution in both time and money. It requires attendance at numerous meetings and expects contributions of labor and time to worthy work. It expects every family to tithe. In return the economic contributions of the church to the community have been great. It has made direct loans in support of various cooperative undertakings, has always been ready to lend support in a crisis, and through its organizing power has played a large part in the success of the various cooperative economic ventures. Its integrative contributions are considerable. It provides numerous organizations which cross-cut the kinship factions and thus contribute to social cohesion. The recreational functions which it sponsors also have a valuable integrative role in the community.

The Mormon Church is a coherent, well-planned organization working ceaselessly toward two major goals — aiding its members to attain salvation and preparing the way for the establishment of Zion and the second coming of Christ in the new world. The secrecy of its temple rites is in part a function of its claim to be the sole possessor of certain ordinances which must be performed in order for one to enter the highest realm of glory and which are open only to church members. The church is concerned with every aspect of the life of its members — family, recreational, economic — and seeks to provide an atmosphere conducive to conformity to those commandments which will ensure salvation. At the same time it encourages and motivates its members to the utmost expenditure of energy, not only in the religious sphere, but in the secular as well.

The Texan community shows evidence of the ascetic Protestant orientation to social life, even though religious commitment is not intense at the present time. The high evaluation of productive labor and technical advances, although mitigated by a loafing pattern, is undoubtedly an expression of the Protestant Ethic. The extreme anti-authoritarianism of the Texans developed out of a long religious tradition that goes back to the Reformation concept of the priesthood of all believers. The tendency to reduce particularistic solidarities as nearly as possible to the nuclear family, the so-called individualism of the Texans, stems from a tradition which sought to break every emotional bond except the bond to God and tended to view all other solidarities as idolatrous. The religious rationalization of these basic orientations has been largely replaced by the ideological rationalization centering around the concepts of success and progress, but their religious origin should not be forgotten.

Structurally, religious life in Homestead is fragmented. There has been no resident minister. Only two of the denominations maintained a church, though some of the others, notably the Seventh-Day Adventists, meet in the homes of members. There is a strong tendency for the churches to become focuses of family factionalism, as well as focuses of incipient social stratification among the denominations. The Presbyterians are relatively more prosperous than the Baptists.

While the political and economic functions of the church are virtually nil, it does play some integrative role. It provides one of the relatively few contexts in Homestead for interaction beyond the nuclear family level. Though this tends to be only a clique interaction, the participation in both the Presbyterian and Baptist churches in their more prosperous periods involves members from a number of cliques. The relative unimportance of the church in society corresponds to the relative unimportance of religious action in Homestead personality. The religious situation in Homestead seems unstable, as the ease with which traveling missionaries have been able to attract small followings indicates. The possibility of a significant religious revival in the community should not be discounted. There is much in the values and character structure of the people which would support it.

9.

Expressive Activities

CLYDE KLUCKHOHN

Introduction by Ethel M. Albert

One of the goals of Clyde Kluckhohn's theoretical construction of culture was to identify the human universals of which each culture pattern is a distinctive interpretation.* That expressive activities form a significant, culturally variable human universal is the underlying theme of his chapter.

Even more than other types of value and value-relevant conduct, the aesthetic and recreational have resisted clear and rigorous formulation. There is a large and impressive literature on aesthetics, the arts, and folklore and on play and creativity in human behavior. Yet, little that has been written on these subjects provides theory or methods suitable for cross-cultural description and comparison. The anthropological investigator must start with what he has, the concepts and categories of his own culture. Culture-bound distortion is thus introduced at the outset — in the terms used, in their connotations, and in the concepts and cultural premises they represent. Confronting the problem, however, is sufficient to lead to preliminary redefinition and relocation of the problems.

Classification of Expressive Activities. The major headings used by Kluckhohn are: Arts, Recreation, Aesthetic Standards, and Emotional Expression. Adapting the categories of "arts" and "recreation" to the

* Among the many contributions to knowledge of which we have been deprived by the untimely death of Clyde Kluckhohn is the finished form of the main body of this chapter. Except for minor editorial changes and some rearrangement of the material, it is presented in the original draft from which a completed manuscript was to have been developed. Even in this form, it is characteristically insightful and seminal. For, we are provided with a basis and rationale for conceptualizing, describing, and comparing aesthetic values and expressive activities as integral elements of cultural patterns.

The introduction is an outgrowth of conversations with Clyde Kluckhohn during the period of the Values Study research. It reports as faithfully as possible the intentions of what might have been in the final draft of the paper. Still, coming from a different pen and written a decade after the chapter was drafted, it reflects primarily my own interpretation of the data and recent changes in value theory and methodology.

data on the five cultures of the Rimrock area produces an inventory much at variance with received notions. The attempt to do justice to the role of "aesthetic standards" and the meaning of "emotional expression" in the five cultures requires readjustment of the defining characteristics of these categories and of the relations among them.

Under the heading of arts in the Rimrock area, the subclasses are: music, drama, and verbal arts; graphic arts; and crafts, or practical arts. Summary abandonment of accepted Western distinctions between the fine arts and folk or popular art is imposed by the data. Music includes the ceremonial chants of Navaho and Zuni as well as the secular performances of a Mormon three-piece amateur dance band. The religious music of the American Indian cultures is neither folk music nor music as the specialized arts of composition and performance in contemporary Western culture, nor is it in the same category as church music. Different cultural conceptions of religion and of other institutions related to the arts require modification of denotative as well as connotative meanings of the vocabulary of expressive activities. Verbal art in the Rimrock area includes school plays and Spanish-American performances of classical religious drama, in a local interpretation that would astonish those familiar with the originals. As to plastic and graphic arts in their modern Western forms, there are none. All but a few aberrant members of European-based cultures in the area ignore both the practice and the appreciation of the arts, as defined by the high-flown criteria of Western aesthetic theory. Description of the arts in the five cultures will easily persuade us that only general categories like "music" or "verbal art" can stand the trip across cultural boundaries. Even these entail cross-cultural differences of meaning in comparative study.

Recreation and play are universals of human expressive activities. Kluckhohn's description includes rodeos, sports, games, and dances, but also drinking. Such socially disapproved but much sought-after pleasures as flirting and its possible aftermath might just as appropriately have been listed. Humor, both "dirty" jokes and the kind suitable for mixed company or children, is recreational, sometimes truly creative, and therefore has its place in the inventory. Examination of a few possible additions will indicate the variety and magnitude of changes needed in our categories and conceptions of expressive activities.

Theoretic Significance of Aesthetic-Expressive Behavior. Attention to dress and ornamentation of the person is one of the few truly distinctive characteristics that set mankind off from other animals. Systematic communication, tool-using, even tool-making, we now know, are not peculiarly human. But painting the face or body, plaiting or otherwise doing the hair, and stringing beads around neck or arm or hip, to say nothing of tailored or wrapped body-covering, are pretty much restricted to human beings. Whether baboons or fish have criteria of personal beauty that place individuals of the species into a sharply graded hierarchy has yet to be more carefully investigated. Criteria of feminine pulchritude and of masculine good looks and of elegance of personal adornment, however, are found in all human societies and very much affect the behavior and the lives of individuals.

The notion that direct appreciation of what is pretty or pleasing or beautiful essentially for its own sake is in itself "functional," or significant, or at least is a normal human capacity exercised by most people in most places does not fit in easily with current conceptions of scientific studies of human nature and culture. Studies have been made of cultural differences in criteria of personal attractiveness, of the relation of changes of clothing style to other events, of the psychological and sociological significance of clothing and jewelry. The effect on the chances for marriage and hence on the genetic pool of a community of chance variations of a fraction of an inch in the length of a nose is known to be significant. Generally, studies of this type have tended to concentrate on "functional" explanations, assuming that concern with decoration and personal appearance is, if not frivolous, at best a trivial feature of human behavior, not "functional." Freud reduced art and comparable activities to socially acceptable sublimations of sexual craving. In economics, where rationality and hard facts and figures rule, the presence of aesthetic values among the forces underlying the expenditure of energy for digging, polishing, and controlling the market for precious stones or the annual changes in clothing styles for women is either ignored or deplored; only lately have the notions of planned obsolescence and the affluent society provided some semblance of "rational justification" for waste and display. The profitable returns from entertainment and recreation endow "useless" indulgences with at least fiscal respectability.

Western observers, trained to the textbook ideal of science and to concomitant ideals of utilitarianism and puritanical ethics, could probably study Western societies indefinitely without encountering the theoretic need to deal seriously and at length with aesthetic-expressive values and activities as a nonreducible category.[1] Not even the toughest-minded observer could make much sense of Navaho, Zuni, or Spanish-American culture without becoming actively concerned with beauty and ugliness, enjoyment and avoidance. These and other elementary aesthetic-appreciative categories appear indispensable to a meaningful description of their life-ways.

In all likelihood, the impress of Western culture explains the theoretical complexities contrived to avoid confronting aesthetics as an irreducible and naturalistic area of behavior and values. Dress is not and probably never has been merely for warmth, let alone merely for decency. It is subject to judgment as attractive and pleasing or not, and satisfaction with it depends on whether it is pleasing or not. Decoration of the body, like decoration of baskets or cooking pots or houses, is not and perhaps never has been purely functional. Decoration of the body may be directed to attracting a satisfactory mate, or it may serve to display wealth and hence enhance social status, but at the same time it is intended to be aesthetically

267

pleasing. Prices of luxuries and necessities in the American market reflect aesthetic preferences: not only jewelry and clothing, where it would be expected, but also "attractive" packaging and advertising of common household goods are consciously directed to appeal to taste or even to elevate "status symbols" above merely practical values. Changes in American automobile design are directed to the eye and the feelings, rarely to improvement of engine efficiency.

In the history of social-behavioral science theory, the influence of negative evaluations of aesthetic factors is patent. Perhaps awareness of their role in other cultures will enable us to see it more clearly in our own and to develop relevant method and theory, free from the distaste of puritanism, the distrust of utilitarianism, the sentimentalism of the opposing romantic tradition of art, and the snobbishness of the ultra-refined humanistic tradition.

Variable Loci of Expressive Values. Variations of the boundaries and contents of the aesthetic-expressive category can be evaluated by an extension of Kluckhohn's discussion of expressiveness in responses to death in the five cultures. Studies of death, funerals, rituals, and beliefs related to death and of emotional-expressive cultural differences and behavioral norms for survivors and others do not ordinarily treat the aesthetic aspects of the complex. Yet, funerals and attendant ceremonials and rituals are in some cultures — the Spanish-American notably among the five of this study — an occasion for both aesthetic and emotional expression. Church rites, the solemnity of demeanor appropriate at funerals, expressing sympathy for the bereaved, and also intense suffering and release of the full flood of grief in bereavement are intentionally and necessarily aesthetic in Mediterranean culture and its New World off-spring. Grief and suffering are not ugly or to be concealed or avoided, as in Anglo culture. They are considered ennobling, therefore both good and beautiful. The prime example is Jesus' suffering, literally in com-passion with suffering humanity. The sight of suffering is expected to evoke compassion from onlookers. The emotive, the ethical, and the aesthetic are inseparably commingled.

In a quite different way, death in Zuni is given strong positive meaning by aesthetic transformation. The departed in due course and on condition of the performance of appropriate rites become friendly ancestors, senders of rain. The reliance of the Zunis on the beauty of their religious rites as a direct antidote to unhappiness or "bad thoughts" is well documented. The cultural system lets no opportunity pass to put its elaborate and beautiful ceremonial resources at the disposal of the community to overcome evil. Grief and other deep emotions are not suppressed, as in Anglo culture, nor allowed expression, as in the His-panic. They are dissolved by a social-ceremonial treatment that assumes the power of beauty to affect human behavior favorably.

The strong, pervasive aesthetic aspect of Navaho values and culture is comparable to the emphasis on beauty in the Zuni and Spanish-American cultures. However, it does not reach as far as death and burial in Navaho culture. The four-day ceremonial to send the feared shade on its way out of this world at best removes the sharpest edge from the intense Navaho fear of dead bodies and their contaminating power. The ragged hole torn in the hogan wall to signify that the dwelling was deserted because a death occurred within its walls is a chillingly apt symbol of the meaning of death in Navaho culture. Avoidance of the ugly and dangerous is the best resort available.

Anglo-American culture deals with the mixed and deep emotions normally evoked by a death through moral rather than aesthetic devices and through control rather than expression of emotions. Mormon religious belief and Texan homesteader secularism, as antidotes to the effects of death, share these characteristically Anglo-American views and values. The relevant value judgments reflect cultural standards for "bearing up well" that are as much aesthetic as ethical. Comforting the bereaved is a social "art" in which good taste figures along with moral obligation. Proper behavior of all concerned has a dual value aspect: "unseemly" behavior violates both ethical and aesthetic rules. The mortician's art and that of the memorial stone-carver, though it is not in accordance with Anglo-American canons of good taste or delicacy to mention them, are additional evidence of aesthetic criteria relevant to death. Americans like their corpses nicely dressed and rouged, their caskets handsomely lined as well as sturdily and elegantly built, their graves neat and well-planted, their memorial monuments handsome and appropriate as well as durable.

Kluckhohn's use of the term, expressive activities, in view of the data to which it refers, has the neutrality needed for at least a first approximation in comparative study to the universal core concept and the cultural variation of interpretation. It is evident that a customary category like "arts" cannot contain all that is properly called aesthetic, and the line between arts and recreation or between aesthetic and other values is rarely sharp.

The impracticality of identifying the expression of aesthetic values exclusively with the arts has a complementary defect in a tendency to define aesthetic expression as purely emotive, and the emotive as irrational or nonrational. Plato's banishment of the artists from the ideal republic has, no doubt unwittingly, been duplicated in much contemporary social-behavioral science. Psychological definitions of the "normal" personality are virtually a parody of Plato's image of the rational man, purged of the impurities of the emotions. Fear of death, hysterical weeping at a funeral — even at the funeral of an only child or a beloved spouse or parent — would seem to indicate a need for psychotherapy. But, if the model of the well-adjusted, optimistic, rational man, so common in modern Western thought, were applied universally, all the world would be mad.

The relativity of psychological adjustment to cultural norms needs amplification, but we have sufficient evidence to be confident that emotions are differently interpreted, evaluated, and expressed in different cultures. Equating aesthetic with emotive expression therefore leaves much to be desired. As a catch-all category, "emotive" cannot identify the varieties of responses and experiences that constitute aesthetic and other expressive behavior. It is also wholly unsuited to cross-cultural study. For a Spanish-American, a tranquilizer and a nap in a darkened room is no substitute for the traditional pattern of grief at a death in the family. The deprivations involve both aesthetic and other emotive expression, for example, shame and dishonor for failure to give the dead their due and lack of needed reassurance from compassionate and equally grief-stricken and grief-expressing relatives and friends.

Active awareness of the role of intellect in art may diminish the prominence of emotive connotations to the aesthetic, produced by cultural habit rather than by data. Aesthetic expression could then be freely linked to whatever other values are relevant, such as the rationality of designing, the technology of producing, and the intellectual-aesthetic combination necessary to appreciation, as well as the aesthetically oriented ethics of the Spanish-Americans and the highly utilitarian and religious aesthetics of the Navaho and Zuni.

Scientific Study of Expressive Activities. The pronounced mutual disesteem between the Texan homesteaders and the Spanish-Americans in the Rimrock area is a curiously faithful reproduction of the centuries-old conflict between a rationalist-ethical world-view and an aesthetic-emotive one and between "science" and "humanism" in the Western tradition. In their own vocabularies, homesteaders find Hispanos excessively emotional, improvident, and extravagant in every way; the Hispanos see the *Tejanos* and *Anglos* generally as cold, lacking in sensibility and drama, mere grubby materialists. Kluckhohn's observation that the homesteaders are by comparison with the other cultures of the Rimrock area very poor in aesthetic values strengthens the suspicion that Western scientific observers are not neutral but are, consciously or otherwise, perpetuating the same tradition, including its stereotypes.

In the pragmatic philosophy of John Dewey, which had a strong influence on Clyde Kluckhohn's thinking about values, there is a plea to regard "art as experience." Bringing art and the aesthetic, and, by extension, the overlapping category of recreation, within the purview of ordinary human experience is a step in the direction of redefinition. The actual procedure, however, is extremely difficult. "Expressive activities" tends to be a residual category, related to observable behavior but comprising only that part or those types that do not fit into familiar functional categories.

Maintenance of a rigorous, quantitatively-oriented approach is entirely compatible with an interest in aesthetics and expressive activities. Accurate analysis is not within our reach at this time. Still, even a casual inspection of the expenditure of resources — money, time, and energy —

in the five cultures suggests the manifold significance of expressive activities and of their cross-cultural variability, quantitative and qualitative. We cannot figure the costs to the penny, but we know that much time, money, and energy go into rodeos, fiestas, and dances; ceremonials and sings; decisions by shoppers requiring or allowing choice from a variety of available jewelry, clothing, or other objects; funerals and the accompanying concerns with mourning dress, feeding or feasting the funeral party, presenting gifts, and doing services for the bereaved.

Quantitative studies can reveal cross-cultural differences in the allocation of resources among aesthetic and utilitarian activities only on the condition that the boundaries that separate them are correctly drawn for each culture. The Zuni Shalako and the Navaho sing, for example, involve a complex of values and definitions of the situation of ceremonial action not characteristic of European-based cultures. Examination of the consequences of comparative cultural study will further reinforce the view that a radical change is needed in the conceptualization of the nature, relations, and functions of aesthetic, emotive, recreational, and expressive values and activities. That religion, economics, ethics, psychology, and other factors are present together with the aesthetic and recreational in various degrees and proportions does not change but only redirects the exploration of expressive activities. We need to know that we must look for aesthetic and recreational components, and we need to know where to look for them — in effect, in the midst of everyday activities as well as of special occasions.

Comparison: Descriptive, Functional, and Relational. The theory of human universals expressed in unique cultural patterns is a hybrid, its viability still open to question. The critical problem is raised briefly by Kluckhohn when he cites Vogt's query as to the cross-cultural validity of the "dance" as a category for comparison. The same question can be raised for music or graphic art or religion, or for virtually any other component of culture patterns. There seems to be an intrinsic incompatibility between faithful description of a culture pattern and of its constituents in their correct cultural context and trustworthy universalization of the categories of culture and concomitant comparative study. Some way out of the impasse is needed that will avoid the extremes, that is, descriptions so distinctive that no two cultures can be compared in any respect whatever, and comparisons so superficial that significant contextual differences are ignored for the sake of presenting cross-cultural similarities.

If the description of a culture is to be adequate and faithful to the data and if the theory of culture is to provide an exhaustive inventory of categories of culture, a place must be made for what Kluckhohn has called expressive activities. If we begin a comparative study from specific content categories such as music or the dance we must be prepared for cross-cultural differences in their functions and interpretations. If we start from functional categories such as aesthetic enjoyment or recreation we must be prepared for different specific contents in different cultures.

271

People of Rimrock

As Kluckhohn approached the problem, it could be phrased as the question, when we classify together the dances of the five cultures of the Rimrock area, what have we accomplished? For homesteaders a dance means recreation, fun, and drinking. In Rimrock village alcohol is taboo, but a dance is recreation, but recreation that is virtually obligatory. Shy men are literally dragged out onto the dance floor, for recreation is good and wholesome, as well as community-wide and mandatory. For Spanish-Americans, dancing is excitement, part of the ritual of courtship, and often a great emotional strain for both sexes. Navaho and Zuni traditional dances are for groups, not mixed couples. There are few dances of purely recreational value. Although enjoyment is one of the values of dances, the principal motive for most of them is ritual and aesthetic, not recreational. Particularly in Zuni, dancing for the dancers themselves is hard work, a religious duty for the benefit of the community, preceded by self-denying rituals of purification and governed by anxious supervision of every detail of gesture, word, and costume. For the onlookers, although enjoyment is evident, religious participation is also strong, and sharp eyes seek out any departure from prescribed procedures. It is not only the rhythms that are unlike those of the polka or varsoviana. The purposes and the relevant values — including the aesthetic-expressive — vary greatly.

We can treat the dance as a single category, if we place the necessary limitations on our procedures and objectives. From the point of view of form — the conscious attention to rhythm, the invariability of social-cultural definition of dancing as distinct from walking or other bodily displacements, and the existence of criteria by which better and worse performances are discriminated — there is a valid basis for defining dance as a class of activities. The potential for enjoyment, aesthetic or recreational or both, is probably universally present. The distinction between the performer or direct participant and the relatively inactive spectator is part of our definition, but we must also be prepared for a whole spectrum of values and functions in a cross-cultural study of this single descriptive category.

The legitimacy of comparative examinations of art forms, recreation, humor, and other such categories need not be questioned. There is confusion only if such content-specific, descriptive categories are expected to do work for which they are not suited, namely, to serve as analytic variables of equal unit value that occur in identical relations with other uniform units of culture. Dancing at weddings is sacred in some places and purely secular in others; decoration of pottery or basket designs may or may not have religious implications; games may be recreational only or recreational and religious. Comparison of descriptive categories, then, while fruitful and interesting, is limited in theoretic potential.

Similarities of form of the kind represented by the arts or recreation do not predict similarities of function. By the same token, if cultural functions are the point of departure for a classification, it is a virtual certainty that descriptively heterogeneous activities will be included in the categories. Recreation is a universal culture category, but dancing is not universally recreational. For the Zuni rain priests or for a footsore chorus girl dancing is not primarily recreational; it is work. Vogt's discussion of intercultural relations in Chapter 3 presents some of the different cultural views of rodeos, the chicken pull, and other activities in which the communities are jointly involved. Heterogeneity in the specific contents of functional categories is also characteristic of systems of kinship, economics, religion, and politics. The interrelations of these institutional foci with each other and with expressive activities are highly variable from one culture pattern to another. Again, the comparative study of institutions and actions from the point of view of their functions is itself a worthy and useful enterprise. Like the study of content-specific categories, it has its limitations as well as its uses.

The likelihood of multivalence of any concrete object or specific activity suggests a direction for exploring the potentiality of the aesthetic, recreational, and expressive as analytic rather than as descriptive categories and of examining their relations to other analytic variables. So, for example, dress and personal ornamentation may be viewed as simultaneously aesthetic and socio-biologically functional, or dancing and music as simultaneously religious and aesthetic, or as recreational and aesthetic. Aesthetic values remain significant even when they are, as we find them to be in most cultures, only one of a number of cooperating functions or variables. Moreover, they must be taken into account even when their role is very small by comparison with other elements of behavior or culture. The aesthetic value of cave paintings does not cease to exist because they were primarily for hunting ritual. Navaho blankets and Zuni turquoise jewelry are not less valuable aesthetically for being also an important source of cash income; on the contrary, their cash value is a function of their aesthetic value. A bright red geranium in a rusty tin can in a dusty adobe house in Atrisco, pathetic though it may seem to those who can afford to patronize florists or raise flowers in their gardens, functions as a thing of beauty to bring joy to the beholder in a culture where life without beauty is hardly conceivable. Or, the immense collection of seashells, pretty pebbles, picture postcards, and whatnots in the living room of an ancient Mormon grandmother should be seen for the aesthetic-emotive value they have to the collector: "I know they are not much, but they are real pretty. And they remind me of things that happened long ago . . . that's from my oldest boy when he was in the war in Europe . . . And that's just an old piece of rock from around here, but it sure is real pretty." [2]

For a focal point in studying aesthetic-expressive culture, we may look with profit at the different interpretations of aesthetic values in the Rimrock area. In the Zuni pueblo, aesthetic qualities are explicitly elaborated as indispensable to moral and social well-being, individual and social. "Happiness" is a moral obligation. An unhappy man is wicked; he has "bad thoughts," and these lead to witchcraft. The gorgeous costumes of the gods, the quantities of turquoise jewelry, and the tinted holiday bread are explicitly intended to make men feel happy, so that morality may be kept at a high level. That hard work, altogether in the spirit of the "Protestant ethic," is also a remedy against "thinking too much" is especially interesting in the context of a contrast with Anglo-Protestant culture, where for so long beauty has been associated with evil, immorality, and temptation to sin, and where plainness or outright ugliness have been comforting tokens of "utility" and insurance against the temptations of the flesh.

The Mormon emphasis upon good looks, the positive value of physical intimacy between the sexes, attention to recreation as a wholesome thing, and a positive evaluation of "joy" have no fundamental similarity to the Zuni aesthetic-expressive category. It is only a minor departure from standard Anglo-Protestant criteria. Good looks are presumably the reward of good health, good health the reward of respect for the taboos imposed by the Word of Wisdom; all the joys, pleasures, and recreations are "wholesome," and "wholesomeness" is a peculiarly Protestant notion, decidedly moralistic in orientation. Fun for its own sake is not countenanced in Zuni or Rimrock village, although the individualistic, "secular" Navaho and Texan homesteaders can and do permit it, albeit in markedly different ways. While the homesteaders are poor in aesthetics, they keep themselves well suppiled with recreational activities, as Kluckhohn's account will show. The Hispanic-American emphasis upon beauty is, in the context of the five cultures under examination, distinctive, for not only is aesthetic value very high, probably at the apex of the value hierarchy, but also it is involved with deep and often painful emotions and is the keystone of the value system.

Kluckhohn's initial hypothesis — that aesthetic-expressive values and activities are culturally variable human universals — in the light of the data of the Values Study comes to mean that every culture pattern has a distinctive aesthetic-expressive spectrum of values and related activities. We do not find anywhere in the annals of human behavior a people totally without aesthetic expression in at least several media. We may find here and there a statement that in a certain group there is no literary art, or in another no music to speak of, or in another a blank in some other place. In secular Western culture, the arts are so specialized as to form a separate category, potentially pursued exclusively "for art's sake," and sports and recreation are profitable occupations and businesses. At present it would be difficult to make a case for a distinctively aesthetic response or expressive drive; but it is not possible to do justice to data, particularly to cross-cultural data, if expressive activities and the governing values and norms are not treated as seriously as data reporting other types of human behavior and values.

Expressive Activities

CLYDE KLUCKHOHN

Some forms of recreation and some forms of art are valued in all cultures. In general, our information on expressive activities in the five Southwestern cultures of this study is less comprehensive than for many other behavior spheres. On the other hand, some topics, large and small, have been dealt with very intensively. McAllester has written extensively on one aspect of Navaho music and has unpublished notes on Mormon, Zuni, and Spanish-American music. Mills has studied four Navaho art media in detail and has made some comparisons with Zuni. Bradley has investigated Navaho and Mormon children's drawings. Edmonson has investigated Spanish-American humor very thoroughly and made comparative notes on humor in the other four groups. There is excellent detail for individuals from four cultures in Roberts.[3] The expressive side of religious behavior has been dealt with by Rapoport and by Kluckhohn. Vogt has published a microscopic study of one multicultural recreational (and economic) pattern. Lenneberg and Roberts are concerned mainly with the cognitive features of language, but Edmonson presents excellent material on expressive features of New Mexican Spanish, and there is some material on Navaho in Kluckhohn and Leighton and in Kluckhohn. Spencer has supplied a thorough analysis of Navaho chantway myths, with some Zuni comparisons. Geertz, in an unpublished study of the different cultural patterns associated with drought, death, and alcohol, has, in the process of discussing the psychological, social, and cultural aspects of these crises, uncovered data significant for a study of expressive-aesthetic activities and values.[4] With the exception of these studies, the data for this chapter, while rich and varied, are fragmentary and unsystematic. Nevertheless, some knowledge can be detailed, some comparisons and contrasts noted, and some generalizations formulated. Of the latter, the most significant is the appearance of cultural variations in what we presumed to be the human universals of expressive activities. Categories for this aspect of behavior are not definite or exhaustive, but this preliminary survey can be addressed to the specific types of activity that make up the familiar general headings, art and recreation.

THE ARTS

The original meaning of aesthetics was "pertaining to the senses." But in all cultures the realm of the arts to some extent overlaps the realm of values. To state only the extremes: in some cultures entities are moral because they are beautiful, whereas in others the reverse tendency prevails, and moral values are considered antithetical to aesthetic values. Art, as Franz Boas has pointed out, arises from two sources: technical pursuits, and the expressions of emotions and thought as soon as these take rather fixed forms. Whether or not, as Kant maintained, there can be a science of sensitivity (aesthetics) as well as a science of understanding (logic), hence the possibility of establishing universal laws, it is certainly true as a cross-cultural generalization that art always involves discipline, the control of established forms over the random and idiosyncratic responses of individuals.[5]

MUSIC

In Homestead, music other than in the high school and listening to radio is attached to the dances. " 'Good music' is provided by local 'fiddlers' and guitar players who always play 'Western' or 'Hillbilly' tunes." [6] This type of music is also preferred on the radio over American "popular" or "jazz" music.

Music is an important expression of the Mormon doctrine that "man was that he might have joy." In Rimrock in 1950 there were four parlor organs and sixteen pianos. The piano and organ are played mainly by women, while the violin is considered a masculine instrument. In 1950 there were sixteen persons who played the violin and thirty-five who played the guitar. There were two local orchestras, organized along family lines, which played both in Rimrock and elsewhere.[7] Two local men have written "Western" type popular music. The partial text of one is:

> We're coming, we're coming, Leo
> So Leo, don't despair.
> While you are in the cave-in hopin'
> We are up above you gropin'
> And we soon will make an openin', Leo
> We're closer, we're closer, Leo
> And soon you'll breathe fresh air,
> So while you're in the Devil's prison,
> Keep that spark of life a-fizzin'.

The last line has a distinctively Rimrock Mormon flavor.

Dr. McAllester has kindly given me some unpublished material on music in Rimrock.[8] The Bishop's wife commented that an interest in music helped to keep the young people at home and away from Railtown. Musical skill is highly valued, and remarks such as "he played the guitar very pretty last night" are frequently heard. McAllester was struck by the fact that Mormon hymns are usually lively, not dreary like many Protestant hymns. They are often sung — and well sung — without instrumental accompaniment. They have dash and a lyric quality. The instructions in the hymn books, even for hymns the Mormons consider "sad," read "cheerfully," "with martial spirit," "vigorously," "joyously." Mormons also sing secular folk music, some of it, such as "The Brooklyn Theatre Is Burning," going back to the period when their ancestors migrated from the East. Mormons like Spanish-American music, and the varsoviana is played at Rimrock dances. Mormon reactions to the content of the songs are, expectably, quite different from those typical of Spanish-Americans. Thus, they love a Spanish-American song which deplores the irresponsibility of a man who wouldn't hoe his corn. Characteristic Mormon reactions to Navaho music are: "Just a lot of whooping and hollering" or "Navaho music was all right until tunes was invented."

The Spanish-Americans of Atrisco love music. There used to be informal singing in the evening, preferably to the accompaniment of an accordion. The guitar and violin were also played. The songs are in part New Mexican, in part Mexican in origin. Edmonson has recorded the verses of a very large number of Spanish songs sung in

Atrisco and San Martin. Some additional verses to the famous Mexican song, "La Cucaracha," were improvised in Atrisco. One well-known New Mexican *corrida,* a song form that starts from interesting current events, is said to have started in San Martin. At the *bailes* (dances) music consists of guitar, accordion, violin, and drums.

Secular music at Zuni formerly was limited to a few lullabies and children's play songs.[9] There were work songs for the grinding of corn, but everything connected with the handling of corn is sacred activity. In more recent times younger Zunis have created erotic ballads of a type not dissimilar to those sung at Navaho Enemy Way. The text of one recorded by McAllester contains these phrases: "I don't care if I have you . . . I can get another girl, a juicy, greasy, one." [10] Zuni sacred music varies considerably in style but has not yet been described technically. McAllester observed that the Zunis were very interested in and receptive to foreign music and that they manifested a keen aesthetic enjoyment of what they liked.

Navaho culture also places music almost completely in the religious area. Today, however, some Enemy Way songs and other songs sung by men and boys while riding horseback are sung in an essentially secular atmosphere. Navaho women in the Rimrock area do little singing, though the culture permits any woman who knows the songs to join in ritual singing, and, indeed, a woman past menopause may herself become a "professional" singer. Men derive a great deal of pleasure from singing both in formalized and informal situations. A typical statement is "I like singing. It makes me feel happy. I sing when I am happy." Navaho musical instruments were the flute, the whistle, the pot-drum, and rattles. The last three survived but are employed exclusively in ceremonials. In the old days women sang, as they ground corn, to the accompaniment of flute music.

Navaho ceremonial music exhibits many styles and varieties. Most of it must be carefully learned, but in connection with two rites there is provision for self-expression by free composition. McAllester notes the following "principles" of Navaho music:

(1) tonality should be consistent;
(2) a good voice is somewhat nasal, the vibratto is rather wide; the voice should be as high as possible, it should be capable of sharp emphases, and there should be an easy and powerful falsetto;
(3) a striking contrast may be drawn between the discipline of Zuni group singing and the wild freedom that characterizes group singing among the Navahos;

278

(4) Navaho rhythms are characteristically fluid. The syncopations, the interrupted double beat, and the intricate variations in beat from one measure to the next evoke a gratified rhythmic motor response from native listeners — the rhythm is not a steady background for the melody, as in the case of most Western European music, but is as keenly perceived as melody for its combinations and permutations. In the chant music where the melody may be limited to two or three notes, the rhythm may be even more complex.

(5) There seems to be no *largo* in the scheme of the Navaho esthetic. Moreover, the note values are strikingly limited . . . It is tempting to think of this speed and restriction of note values as an expression of the Navaho value on action and motion.

Among other cultural values associated with music, McAllester lists competition between localities, guarded quietness, and reticence in complementary distribution with the singing,[11] prestige brought by musical knowledge, individualism, "provincialism," and formalism.

DRAMA AND OTHER VERBAL ARTS

In Homestead there are high school plays, in Rimrock school plays, operettas, and occasional community plays. In Atrisco the religious drama of *Las Posadas* survived until about 1940, and *Los Comanches* has been danced only once in Atrisco but several times in later years at Las Norias. It is performed in honor of the Holy Child on Christmas Eve. The rosary and Christmas hymns precede the dance by boys and girls dressed as Indians and wearing much jewelry. The dance proceeds until the *Santo* has been stolen by a thief or thieves. The "Indians," guided by two *padrinos,* go after the *Santo,* bring it back home, and deal out punishment to the thieves. The whole performance is quite dramatic. As Edmonson remarks, drama is pervasive and intense in all Spanish-American fiestas and other religious rituals.[12] In recent times, Zuni youngsters have participated in plays in English at school. Zuni and Navaho ceremonials are dramatic spectacles. Wilson says of the Zuni Shalako:

> The kind of thing one sees in the Shalako dance must be something like the kind of thing that was revived in the Russian ballet — not brought to the point of refinement to which Dyaghilev was able to carry it, but, in its color and variety and style, in the thoroughness of the training involved and the scrupulous care for detail, a great deal more accomplished and calculated than one could easily conceive without seeing it.[13]

279

Reading in Homestead, Rimrock, and Atrisco is about what one would expect in American rural communities generally: newspapers, church periodicals, and popular magazines. This pattern is also followed today by some of the younger Zunis and a few of the younger Navaho. The Bible is read by Mormons and by devout Christians in Homestead, and the Book of Mormon is read in Rimrock. There are a few individuals in Homestead and still more in Rimrock who give some time to literature. A number of Rimrock homes contain sophisticated books, particularly in the field of poetry, and some of the women compose poetry. The Women's Relief Society devotes certain meetings to the discussion of literary classics, such as Milton.

Little "literary" reading is done in Atrisco. Indeed a number of villagers could not read, even in Spanish. On the other hand, verbal skills are appreciated, especially those of political oratory where, again, the Spanish sense of drama comes to the fore.

The Zuni and Navaho have an extensive corpus of oral mythology, ritual poetry, and folklore. In both cultures prestige and some measure of economic reward accrue to those who know these materials for ritual purposes and for reciting them — partly for instruction and partly for entertainment — on winter nights. Wilson speaks of the "highly developed and vividly imagined" Zuni mythology as "a great thing to hold a people together and to inspire them with confidence in themselves." [14] With this statement one can heartily agree. But it is worth pointing out explicitly that the cohesive force of the mythology may rest in part upon the very fact that it supplies an outlet in fantasy for expressions forbidden in daily life. The Zuni code requires control of expressions of personal emotion and especially of hostility toward other Zunis. In fact, gossip at Zuni — as in most small towns — is rife and frequently malicious. This is a form of social control as well as of release of hostility. Social controls are almost completely externalized rather than internalized. A Zuni definition of a witch is "a person who has no shame." A psychological analysis of the mythology reveals free and abundant expression of hostile impulses.[15]

Spencer's comparisons of Zuni and Navaho mythology are very instructive. "Navaho chantway myths appear to be remarkably controlled by comparison with the bizarre imagery and unrestrained violence characteristic of the Zuni tales." [16] In Zuni mythology such themes as the desertion of children by their families, the children's ultimate shaming of and triumph over the wicked parents, and the

280

young man's seduction and attack by threatening female figures are central and recurrent, whereas they are only incidental in Navaho mythology.[17] The two mythologies differ in other ethnographically significant respects. Zuni mythology lacks accounts of warfare, supernatural encounters, acquisition of power, father-in-law tests.

Bunzel says that Zuni prayers are:

> . . . highly formalized in content and mode of expression. Nearly all prayers are requests accompanying offerings. They have three sections which always appear in the same order: a statement of the occasion, a description of the offering, and the request . . . Events are always described in terms of . . . stereotypes, which are often highly imaginative and poetic. These fixed metaphors are the outstanding feature of Zuni poetic style. There are not very many of them; they are used over and over again, the same imagery appearing repeatedly in one prayer . . . The short lines are declaimed slowly and with marked emphasis, the long lines are spoken rapidly, unaccented syllables are slurred or elided, and the word accents pile up on each other. The two types of lines are like the booming of the surf and the rushing of the brook.[18]

Here are two examples of Zuni poetry. The first is recited on the eighth day of an infant's life when it is presented to the sun:

> Now this is the day
> Our child,
> Into the daylight
> You will go out standing.
> Preparing for your day,
> We have passed our days.
> When all your days were at an end,
> When eight days were past,
> Our sun father
> Went in to sit down at his sacred place.
> And our night fathers
> Having come out standing to their sacred place,
> Passing a blessed night
> We came to day.
> Now this day
> Our fathers,
> Dawn priests,
> Have come out standing to their sacred place.

This is the prayer of a priest on going into retreat:

> This day
> Desiring the waters of our fathers,
> The ones who first had being,

In our house
Having prepared prayer meal,
Shells,
Corn pollen,
Hither with our prayers
We made our road come forth.
This way we directed our roads.
Yonder on all sides our fathers,
Priests of the mossy mountains,
All those whose sacred places are round about,
Creatures of the open spaces,
You of the wooded places,
We have passed you on your roads.[19]

GRAPHIC ARTS

A former resident of Atrisco became an art teacher and was a semi-professional painter. There is at least one painter in San Martin, and in Homestead one woman paints. In Rimrock, there are both men and women who are painters in a naturalistic and somewhat romantic style. There are some painters at Zuni, but we lack systematic information about them and their work.

The substance of this section must be drawn primarily from Mills.[20] He deals with four Navaho media: drawings, weaving, sandpainting, and silversmithing. Two features, "full but not crowded treatment of format" and "movement," appear in all four, and "outlining" and "expansion" occur in three. Perhaps more interesting is his finding that there are four pairs of traits that are about evenly balanced in the Navaho arts: carefulness-casualness, expansion-containment, fixity-variability of patterning, and restricted-liberal use of color. From this and from mythological and other materials Mills infers a "bipolarity of Navaho outlook and insight." This he links to their spatial orientation which does not, as does the Zuni, emphasize the center but rather "the successive boundaries of their life-space." Thus he interprets characteristically incomplete Navaho designs as relating "not so much to lack of means of defense as to necessity for control over exchanges between the inner space of the design and the space which lies outside it." [21] Mills finds Navaho arts generally mirroring the most fundamental Navaho values:

The Navaho aim is to transform this life-space within the circle into a manageable space, a zone of safety. For this, control, in all its forms, is necessary because good in Navaho dogma is control . . . If knowledge is power and power is control, to lack or lose knowledge is to fail in understanding and control . . . If the life-space represents a potentially controllable space, the region beyond (the alien) is less controllable and therefore more dangerous . . . Although their efforts are directed at control, the Navaho recognize that . . . life, being complex, involves us in good as well as evil and for that reason a constant exchange between the life-space and its enveloping space is necessary . . . While the Navaho recognizes that movement outward through a series of concentric life-spaces is dangerous, he also recognizes that such movement is necessary and that it may bring rewards . . . Excess as lack of control is identified with the alien which may be beyond control. The excessive and uncontrolled and alien come together in the figure of Coyote . . . Harmony is not merely a quality of a particular life-space; rather it is a function of the relationship between native and alien life-spaces and powers, however they may be defined at any moment. The effort for harmony is an effort to keep these two worlds in balance within the Navaho cosmos.[22]

These premises are reflected as much in subject matter as in formal features. Many art values deal with the disruption of harmony: the arresting of natural law and the disintegration of natural relationships; physical deformities; the alien; conflict of men and animals; loneliness; violence; and every form of disorder. The scenes and subjects portrayed as well as those omitted indicate that, while Navahos believe in action and especially in ceremonial action to restore harmony and are not paralyzed by the world pressing in upon them, they are nevertheless, as Geertz says, "ceremonially nonconfident" in contrast to the "ceremonially confident" Zunis.[23]

Mills asked both Navaho and Zuni subjects to do three drawings each: one "pretty," one "ugly," and one according to the subject's own taste. The comparisons inform us greatly on expressive and other values. Zuni "pretty" drawings emphasize not merely abundance and well-being as such, but abundance and well-being that are the fruit of labor. "Ugly" drawings highlight the difficulties inherent in providing food and housing and the carelessness and maliciousness of human nature. Rimrock Navaho "pretty" drawings present "a vision of green and summery landscape able to support its animal and human life." Considerable interest is shown in the individual. In "ugly" drawings the disruption of the natural order — enduring hardship, arid land, illness, accident, and aliens — is most prominent.

Navaho "pretty" pictures have much movement, but these are "ugly" by Spanish-American standards; for them "pretty" drawings are static. Helen Bradley found that more Navaho than Mormon children drew figures full of motion and flexibility.[24] Navaho children also covered more space and oriented their figures to one another in the drawings much earlier than did the Mormons. Finally, the Navaho adapted their designs to the shape of the paper more readily.

A long essay could be written on Zuni and Navaho color symbolism in the graphic and plastic arts, but it would have to be highly technical and complicated.[25] Color preferences in European civilization — apart from some fixity in the Christian Church — appear as relatively isolated values; the only way to link them to a larger system of values is through study of their effective implications. The Zuni and Navaho, however, systematically relate color to the sexes, to the six directions, to some animals, and to many elements of ritual. The Zuni system is more completely standardized than the Navaho; for example, yellow stands for the female and is "the leader," and blue stands for the male and is "the vice-president."

CRAFTS — THE "PRACTICAL ARTS"

Silversmithing is of considerable economic importance at Zuni but of minor importance among the Rimrock Navaho in recent years. Adair has compared the techniques, aesthetic standards, and economic aspects of silverworking among the Zuni and the Navaho.[26] The chief distinguishing feature of Zuni silver is the prominence of turquoise sets. Compared to Navaho, it is characteristically lighter, and die-work is rarer.

Weaving has or had a place in each group except Homestead. As late as the early part of this century there were spinning wheels and looms in many Rimrock Mormon homes. Wool was bought from the Navaho and colored with homemade dyes. Clouded yarns were fashionable. Shawls, dresses, and carpets were woven. Two Atrisco women learned to weave in the arts and crafts school for adults in the 1930's, and one continued to weave for some time thereafter.[27] Most adult Navaho women can weave, and two or three produce quite good rugs. Most of the weaving, however, is of saddle blankets and rugs of inferior grade. Only two men in this area are known to have attempted weaving, and neither became a serious craftsman. Zuni

284

weaving has been described by Spier. *Mantas,* women's belts, and other items are still made there.[28]

Pottery and beadwork are of some significance at Zuni. Beadwork is also done by the Rimrock Navaho, but pottery has lapsed, and basketry almost so. Moccasins are made by both Zuni and Navaho. There is a saddle shop in Rimrock where rather fine work in leather is done. One Atrisco man is a leather craftsman and taxidermist.

Silverwork, weaving, leatherwork, pottery, and beadwork are by no means hobbies of the "arts and crafts" variety in the communities. They are decidedly economic enterprises. The business of making a living by these crafts, however, is not only tempered by aesthetic values of the individuals engaged in them, but also make the chief difference between the more and the less successful. To the extent that the market determines preferred designs, the native aesthetic values in each culture may well be given inferior place. Nevertheless, the outside market exists in virtue of an appreciation for Indian jewelry or blankets, and the local market for these and for the other products of craftsmen is also much determined by aesthetic preferences, conjoined with utilitarian considerations. Generally the ambiguous status of crafts in industrialized Western culture cannot be projected upon the Indian or Spanish-American cultures where beauty is valued in many kinds of expression and where aesthetic values are included with others, not mutually exclusive with ethical or economic or practical use values.

RECREATION

The ways of "having a good time" overlap a great deal in the five cultures. Although there are distinctive cultural variations, all five peoples, for example, enjoy dancing and watching dancing. The people of Homestead learned to dance only after they moved into this area. In the two Indian cultures the native context is primarily ceremonial rather than social, and Mormon dances are opened and closed with prayer. All cultural groups either participate in the rodeo complex or attend as spectators. With the partial exception of the Mormons, all are involved to varying degrees in the *fiesta* system. Vogt's description of the Laguna Fiesta may well stand as a kind of paradigm of much of the multicultural recreational patterns in the Rimrock area.[29] Navaho, Spanish-Americans, and Anglos attend the

285

public portion of the Zuni's Shalako. Members of all five groups are seen at the annual Inter-Tribal Ceremonial in Railtown. The same is true for Mormon Day in Rimrock and was true for the Saint's Day in Atrisco during the period when the Spanish-American population in that region was larger. At a "Squaw Dance" of the Rimrock Navaho, one almost always sees at least a few Anglos — though none from Homestead — and a few Zunis; Spanish-Americans are seen only rarely.

To be sure, as Vogt points out, the definitions of the situation and the roles played vary.[30] The Shalako is a religious experience only for the Zuni, though it has religious overtones for the Navaho. But it is also a spectacle and an occasion for sociability and for trade. Members of the other groups come for "the show" and sometimes to look for herders or other workers among the Indians. For Mormons, Mormon Day commemorates a decisive date in the history of the church; others are drawn to compete in or watch the rodeo and to attend the dance. Zunis are only rarely seen at the social dances of the Mormons, Homesteaders, or Spanish-Americans, but Navahos are often shyly present on the sidelines, and in recent years a few have actually entered the dance floor. Rimrock, Atrisco, and Homestead dances are, however, usually multicultural both in participation and in the dance figures used. La raspa and the varsoviana are danced in Rimrock and Homestead, and in recent Atrisco *bailes,* the polka and schottische and other steps favored by Mormons and Texans have been as prominent as the paso-doble, raspa, and varsoviana.

While the meaning of these occasions and the parts played in them vary for members of the five groups, some of the experience is fundamentally similar: travel to the location, social visiting,* seeing and being seen, exchange of news of mutual interest, and spectatorship at cowboy sports and at dances. Some of the implicit values are obviously those common to people who live in somewhat isolated rural circumstances all over the world: getting together, special food,

---

* "Social calls" within each group are also culturally patterned. For example, F. Kluckhohn ("Los Atarqueños," p. 125) says of Atrisco: "as a rule the women do not visit with anyone other than relatives except on Sunday. Sunday is a day devoted to the calling on friends. The calls are of a semi-formal nature as far as etiquette is concerned, and no woman would make such calls without being dressed in her best clothes. Even the men are apt to 'dress up' on Sunday."

seeing and doing something a bit out of the ordinary. The distinctive thing about these activities in the Rimrock area is their multicultural character. This provides much common content and, in some respects, a common framework. Yet the meaning of "the same" recreational activity alters with cultural context, cultural values, and with the images each group has of the others. So, Navaho (and to a lesser extent, Zuni) behavior at a rodeo inevitably is regarded by members of the three Christian groups as having a "barbaric" or "heathenish" quality because Indians are defined as "uncivilized" or inferior. Casual remarks at any rodeo bear out this generalization. And in some instances something is added to "the same" activity which documents the "savage" dimension. For example, at major Navaho rodeos there is ordinarily a "chicken pull" at which horsemen grab for the head of a chicken buried up to its neck in the sand. Actually, this was introduced into the Southwest by the Spaniards, but today it is identified as a feature of "Indian" rodeos.

Let us look at a more complicated illustration: drinking. The use of alcoholic beverages is forbidden to Mormons by the Word of Wisdom, and is disapproved by conservative Zuni culture and by orthodox Christianity at Homestead. The remaining two cultures do not condemn drinking as such but only drunkenness that leads to violence and economic waste. Nevertheless, some members of each of the five groups drink on occasion, and Geertz's study examines the hypothesis that their patterns of drinking behavior follow structural strain, cultural disharmony, and psychological conflict.[31] So far as Homestead is concerned, he is convinced that the hypothesis is at least plausible in the light of the evidence. Only men drink or, at any rate, only men drink openly. "The woman's patterned reaction is to become 'mad,' and to threaten to leave, never to come to another dance and the like. The men react, usually, with more drinking to protect themselves in the eyes of their fellows and themselves, and so a complementary schismogenesis occurs in which men on the one side and the women on the other tend to crystallize into factions around the (ostensible) issue of drinking." Drinking, in other words, is a badge of masculinity and of freedom from female domination.

Geertz thinks that the dominance of women and intersex hostility, which he considers a central strain in the Homestead community, is present also among the Spanish-Americans, particularly those who are highly acculturated. These latter do not follow the traditional patterns in approaching women, and there are shy men who will not even dance with a girl unless they are drunk. "Drinking now replaces the formal structuring of courtship patterns in the reduction of *vergüenza* [shame, propriety] and supports the poor male as he travels through the terrors of establishing inter-sex relationships." In the less acculturated situation there is more intermale hostility in drinking at the *baile*. This centers on a strain not found at Homestead — the "succession problem," entailing the relations between older and younger brothers and the hierarchical relation of all men to the *patrón*. There is some evidence that in the more stable families older sons drink less frequently than younger ones.

Drinking by "Jack Mormons" is interpreted by Geertz as essentially a reaction to the restrictions placed by Mormon culture on behavior in all areas of living. Indeed, for a Mormon, to drink is to define his status as at best marginal to his group or more likely as an "outgrouper." In the Rimrock area Mormons who drink are usually men who either have married non-Mormon wives or who had especially close and long-continued social and economic relations with non-Mormons.

Navaho drinkers are the most aggressive and the most openly sexual. In part, this is a consequence not of Navaho culture and personality but of the simple fact that Indians until recently had to drink covertly and were often sold liquor that was poor in quality. Hence the Navaho idea of drinking is dominantly that of becoming inebriated rather than of social drinking. It is also true, however, that the Indian groups have had fewer outlets for aggression and that the suppressed hostility within small groups becomes released under the influence of alcohol. The observation that Navaho drinking results, on the whole, in more violence than does Zuni drinking may be related to the circumstance that acculturation has penetrated deeper among the Navaho at least in the sense that native social controls and native social organization as a total felt entity have further dissolved.

Geertz feels that the sparse data on Zuni drinking present an unclear picture. This is true, but also, Zuni culture provides systematically for orgiastic behavior (the feces-eating and urine-drinking, sword-swallowing, and the old War Dance ceremony), whereas Navaho culture, in theory, always demands control. Coyote is the figure he is in Navaho mythology and folklore precisely because he lacks control.

SPORTS AND GAMES

Baseball, basketball, and other American school sports are prominent at Rimrock and Homestead and participated in by members of the other three groups who attend schools. Younger Zunis continue to play basketball after they have left school, and in Atrisco, while there is no team play, boys and men amuse themselves with a basketball. The favorite male pastime in Atrisco, however, is pitching dollars or washers; this is also enjoyed by the Texans. Horseshoes are pitched by Mormons and Texans. Navaho go in for horse- and foot-races; Zunis likewise race both in their own and in "American" fashion (that is, competitively). In recent years the track meet has drawn a larger crowd of Zunis than most of their ceremonial dances. The kickstick race as a ceremony became obsolescent about 1950, but is still practiced by small boys. The Indians do not swim to any extent, but there is some swimming — especially by younger people — in Rimrock Lake, and in the stock tanks of the Atrisco-Homestead area. The rodeo is the only sport that is genuinely common to all five cultures.

Native Zuni and Navaho games for adults have disappeared or are obsolescent, except perhaps for string figures ("cat's cradle"). The Navaho moccasin game has not been played at Rimrock for some years, and the stick dice and hoop and pole games disappeared much earlier. Rimrock Navaho play cards only when Navahos from other areas are present. Navaho and Zuni children still play games that derive from the aboriginal culture. Clay dolls are — or were — made by or for Zuni and Navaho children; at Zuni they had a ceremonial use as well as in children's play.[32] Zuni adults gamble at cards but are said to play "only Zuni card games." Acculturated Zunis frequently play pool in Railtown.

There are no distinctive games in Atrisco. Boys stand around a campfire at night, visiting as their fathers do. "Sometimes they play games — most of which have been adopted from the *Anglo* culture — but these games are not played with much fervor."[33] There is some gambling among the men in poker, crap-shooting, and cock-fighting. At mixed social gatherings, a game (introduced in the thirties by an Anglo schoolteacher) called "who went where with whom?"

is often played. *Rifas* (lotteries) or "raffles" are held at the school and at *bailes*. Spanish-American men like to play pool in San Martin or Railtown.

In Homestead a domino game ("42") is unique in this area. There is also a bridge and canasta club, and some men and women play poker. Good Mormons do not play card games, but some of the local Jack Mormons play poker. Good Mormons do, however, play "authors," checkers, and similar games.

HUMOR

Correct classification of humor is as difficult as correct analysis of its bases and functions. Enjoyment is, however, an obvious and permanent feature, at least for the humorist and his audience if not always for the butt or object of a joke. Verbal and practical joking, neither art nor craft, can most conveniently be classed as a form of recreation. This form of expression is in some ways, as Edmonson points out, strikingly tied to cultural context.[34] I shall here review briefly only those aspects of humor that are thus culture-bound. The joke the Spanish-Americans found funniest was one on a *patrón* in which sexual and authority symbols were juxtaposed. The next most favored situation involved the ties and frustrations of kinship. There is also a pattern of flirtatious joking. Navaho humor focuses on sex and on drinking, and McAllester was particularly struck by its defensive quality.[35] The two incidents observed by Edmonson which provoked the most laughter by Zunis involved the *koyemshi* ceremonial clowns. In one instance these clowns gave a not-too-veiled insult to the Navahos present; in the other, they ridiculed in pantomime a major Zuni ceremonial and perhaps, by implication, their own culture. The Zunis also relish ribald sexual humor in many forms. Mormon humor tends to center upon lusty sexuality and male virility, with some attention to the contrast between behavior expected of Mormons (for example, taboo on drinking) and that customary with other groups in the area. Favorite Texan jokes concern "the preacher," "the city slicker," and "the country cousin." There is also some rough joking, both about and between husbands and wives.

Edmonson makes the following comparisons of the general patterns of humor:

Hispano humor as a whole is anecdotal and situational. It involves little physical aggression, even on the fantasy level, and where it is concerned with sexuality the most outstanding mode is genital . . . Navaho culture presents us with a pattern quite strikingly different . . . Where *Hispano* culture seems to inhibit humor in relation to the death theme of Christian ritual, Navaho culture inhibits it in two entirely different contexts: the Corn Pollen prayer toward the close of a ceremonial, and the first menstruation rite . . . Among the more rigid patterns of Navaho humor are those represented in nicknames, coyote stories, the cross-cousin joking relationship, the ceremonial clown, mother-in-law jokes, and . . . puns. As is the case in *Hispano* humor, anecdotes figure more largely than jokes.

Joking about the clown or more generally about the dances appears with some regularity in the small collection of *pueblo* jokes obtained. Otherwise there are only hints of patterns: two or three jokes about drinking, suggesting that the liquor prohibition has a similar effect on Navahos and Pueblos: jokes about Eisenhower, the Japanese, money, the boss, women, smoking, and infantile sexuality. Of 10 "intergroup" jokes by Pueblos, 8 concerned Anglos and 2 Navahos.

The patterns of humor among the Texans and Mormons . . . represent two rather distinctive sub-cultural types which are yet within the framework of a single language and general culture . . . There is a considerable increase in the importance of jokes, as opposed to anecdotes, when we shift from the *Hispano* to the "Anglo" materials . . . Two Mormon patterns which seem to be unrepresented in the Texan data are those revolving around "participation" and around "virility" or "fitness" . . . a recurrent and slightly aggressive theme in Mormon humor is "kidding" reluctant people (especially boys and men) into dancing every dance, attending every function, and "enjoying themselves." It is probably significant of the difference in family structure that it is the men in [Rimrock] and the women in [Homestead] who have to be coaxed to attend community affairs.

A general pattern of aggressive scapegoatism appears to be fairly clear in . . . intergroup jokes. The Texan aggression is still channeled against the mythical Negro, the hypothetical Indian, and the Anglo city slicker, a pattern which probably emerged in Texas rather than New Mexico. The Mormon aggression attaches to "dudes" and Navahos. *Hispano* humor attacks *gringos, Navajoses,* and *tejanos.* For the Navaho the "White man" is the overwhelmingly popular object of humor, with *Hispanos* and *Pueblos* strictly secondary. The scanty Pueblo data suggest a similar alignment, with *Hispanos* ignored entirely and Navahos as an important secondary object of humor.[36]

Aesthetic Standards

The Texans are the most poverty-stricken group from the point of view of aesthetics. One can only enumerate dancing, the singing of hymns and hillbilly music, the high school play, one man who does a puppet act, and a few women who either paint or make lamp bases or colored felt figures. Moreover, while there is some variation among individuals and families, the general aesthetic standard is a not very high-grade version of rural-middle-class or lower-middle-class American life. To some extent, this may be related to the negative evaluation of expressions of emotion. "Beauty" is far lower in the scale of values than economic success, education, and other forms of achievement or recreation. In Atrisco, there is equally little articulateness about "beauty," and the villagers say that goodness is more important than beauty. Yet one must infer that even the conception of "goodness" has a dimension that can properly be described as aesthetic, partly because of the emphasis upon "being" as opposed to "doing." "What a man *is* can be known, but what he may *do* is uncertain." [37] And, while the majority of the objects in Atrisco houses would not please the professionally trained observer, there is nevertheless always something or some arrangement which evidences an aesthetic sensitivity or "taste" that is almost completely lacking in Homestead. Wooden *Santos* have been replaced by plaster, but there is still some grace. Similarly, no one could witness a *baile* or a *fiesta* without concluding from their elements of gusto, drama, and restraint-delicacy that the Spanish-Americans have aesthetic sense and experience aesthetic pleasure, however little they may talk about these matters in abstract terms.

In Rimrock there is explicit belief, flowing from Mormon teachings, that the aesthetic as well as the intellectual sensibilities should be cultivated. Much of the expression will strike the contemporary sophisticate as old-fashioned or quaint or even crude. Rimrock living rooms are either bare or full of "clutter." However, it remains a fact that the proportion of people in this isolated rural village who have musical and literary and other aesthetic skills and interests is surprisingly high, compared to the general Anglo rural norm. Moreover, it is clear from what is said and done that, while these are mainly part of the "joyous recreation" complex, they are likewise "aesthetic," in Santayana's meaning of "intellectualized and objectified pleasure."

Nevertheless, most observers would agree that the aesthetic life is richest and most varied in the two Indian groups. Their religious dramas with attendant dances and music please almost everyone who attempts to understand and who is not determined to label them as "savage." Their mythology and poetry are filled with images and incidents of universal appeal. The best of their arts and crafts delights connoisseurs from many lands. Their own costumes are not merely exotic but colorful in a truly aesthetic sense. Their wearing of jewelry strikes some from our culture as too heavy or garish or overdone, but the effect usually is pleasing.

Many or most visitors with background in European or Asiatic civilizations find the arts of the Zuni and Navaho meaningful and sometimes exciting. But this of itself tells us nothing as to whether the Indians themselves have experiences that we would be prepared to term "aesthetic." Some writers have stressed the economic motivation in weaving, silverwork, and the rest. As far as "efficient cause" is concerned, the primacy of the economic motive today is hardly open to question. Yet, no one who has been at the side of weavers and smiths for hours on end and been able to understand their remarks in their own language would challenge the assertion that, whatever the instigation of their activities, most Indians manifest both an "instinct of workmanship" and "aesthetic satisfaction" in the actual performance and design.

One must not align oneself with the romantic sentimentalists about Indian arts and crafts; but in evading this trap one should not go to the other extreme. The Santa Fe aesthetes are right, as Wilson says, in recognizing that the Indians have known how to sustain "vitality and self-sufficiency" in their arts.[38] And one should always be aware of the mistakes in discourse that may arise from differences in vocabulary, in the basic categories. Western thought in recent centuries has tended to segregate intellective, emotional, asthetic, economic, and other activities, motivations, and functions as if they were disparate entities. Zuni and Navaho speech tends to use categories in which two or more of these are blended, though there may be a stress upon one or another.[39] As McAllester says of the Navaho, the "good" and the "beautiful" do not seem to be separable.[40] And, although art for art's sake, or beauty for beauty's

293

sake, is not commonly expressed in clear-cut form by Zunis or Navahos, neither is its expression entirely absent. I remember seeing a
Navaho of about fifty years of age with his family in a wagon some
miles off course between his hogan and the Rimrock trading store.
When I asked him what he was doing there, he replied: "This is a
beautiful spot where my family used to live. Sometimes I come here
just to look at it." J. M. Roberts has obtained from Zuni informants
lists of the ten most beautiful spots on their reservation. Or, one
may take the Zuni remark recorded by Bunzel: "The children do
not mind being whipped by the Salimpia. They are such pretty
dancers." Utilitarian and aesthetic criteria are distinguished in the
same frequently heard Zuni remark: "Pretty, but not strong." [41]

Nothing is more typical of both Zuni and Navaho thought than
the juxtaposition of explicitly aesthetic terms with "functional" ones.
A Zuni, speaking of an admired relative, said, "A pretty personality;
he's happy all the time and always joking." When asked about the
happiest time of her life, an old Navaho lady replied: "one summer
when it rained a whole lot, the grass was very tall, seen a lot of birds,
seen a lot of different kind of flowers, seen a lot of livestock, they
all got fat, and I remember a lot of people like it the same way I
did." I suspect that European language usage of the same terms
("good" and "bad") for moral and aesthetic values is an echo of a
period when our ancestors likewise failed to make a sharp segregation between the two categories. At any rate, while the Zuni and
the Navaho show both in their verbal and their nonverbal behavior
that they are sensitive to the beautiful as such, the following represent reliable generalizations for both groups: what is considered to
be morally good tends to be assimilated also to the aesthetically good;
whatever promotes or represents human survival and human happiness tends to be felt as "beautiful"; anything that is nonfunctional
(worn out or failing somehow to promote the satisfaction of needs*)
is considered "ugly." [42]

EMOTIONAL EXPRESSION

Over and above the more generalized forms of personal expression
in recreation and the arts, there is a question as to how each culture

---

* A Zuni explained that an old horse was ugly because, among other reasons, it was
no longer able to function sexually.

defines emotional outlet in its cultural codes. It is not possible to treat this subject exhaustively, but two studies made by Values Project collaborators contain interesting cross-cultural comparisons on certain aspects.

Geertz considers reactions to death.[43] Among the Spanish-Americans, death and the preceding illness tend to become dramatized. Death is seen as tragedy. Men by and large attempt to maintain an acceptance of whatever comes, but a more open display of grief is permitted women, and in fact seems to be encouraged. The ghosts of the newly dead are feared, especially by women. Texans minimize ritual and emotional display. Much overt grief is regarded as a sign of weakness or instability, though more tolerance is extended to women than to men in this respect. With Mormons also, extreme emotionality is neither expected nor valued. Death is held to be just an incident in the eternal progression toward godhood. Zunis die quietly and are quietly mourned. The Zunis are unhappy when someone dies — dying is not a good thing — but they are not terribly grief-stricken, for neither is dying a terrible thing. The Navaho fuses a relatively calm acceptance of his own death with a tremendous fear of others who are dead. Navaho mourning practices call for considerable, often "hysterical," expressions of grief.

Untereiner has compared conceptions and expressions of emotions among the Texans and Zunis.[44] The former regard emotional phenomena as different and separate from the more objective values and thoughts. For the Zunis emotions are not distinct and separate. They merge with the thoughts and values in the more unitary and less personalized self. Being neither so separate nor so different, the possibilities of inner conflict are not so accentuated. Not only control of emotions but also harmonious cooperation with other "inner" elements is asked of Zunis. For Texans, in ordinary daily life situations, the lack of control is more important from a self rather than from a social point of view.

Texans have much more generalized conceptions of happiness or pleasure than the Zunis. Happiness is conceptualized as a condition of the self. To the Zunis, it is more a consequence of certain kinds of events. For the Texan, the stress is on the happy person or his state of mind; for the Zuni, it is on the happy situation. Also, there seems to be less emotional immediacy for the Texan. Data on the Zuni suggest more vivid emotional involvement and also physical involvement: they do not distinguish, in effect, between "psychology" and "physiology." The Zuni emphasis is on the present, whereas the Texan more often looks to the future. Nine out of ten Zunis said, "I am more interested in what makes me happy now than in what might make me happy in the future." Only one out of six Texan adults answered a similar question about temporal aspects of happiness affirmatively.

The Zunis in Untereiner's sample showed much more awareness and verbalization of violent and disruptive impulses. These were considered "bad" both for the individual and the group. Untereiner suggests that the Zunis, being more oriented to others, are more in the habit of talking about impulses as if they were external. Also, the self is more dependent on others for impulse control, hence its impulses can be blamed on others. Texans, on the other hand, think of impulses as being personal, inside themselves, and as their own responsibility to control. The Zunis talk more frequently and freely of their emotions because their main area of secrecy is religious and socially valuable information rather than the self and its feelings. The lists of things they liked or feared or were disgusted by were longer than those of the Texans, and their likes and dislikes attached more to the concrete and tangible: appearances, possessions and property, behavior, outer stimuli, and events, whether natural, cultural, or social. Texans spoke more of inner stimuli and states, personal qualities, intentions, underlying meanings. The most frequent Zuni response to questions about unpleasant feelings was "pain and sickness," but the Texan was "moods of depression." Emotionality is not valued by the Zuni — yet feelings, like everything else, have "a place." They play their part in the orderly scheme of things and do not have the mysterious and unexplainable quality they have for Texans.

Spencer has dissected out some of the less conscious aspects of Navaho emotion. She points out that Kaplan (personal communication) and Vogt find considerable emphasis on the search for nurturant older male figures in personal fantasy. She links this to the image of the protagonists of chantway myths as a "passive, suffering hero, who is drawn into punishments, ordeals, trials, and conquests, rather than of an active conqueror who undertakes feats of strength, a prolonged quest for a high goal, or subjection of rivals by cleverness and wits." [45]

Conclusion

Not by any means have all expressive activities been mentioned or commented upon. Each culture has its unique recreational and aesthetic features. The "42" game at Homestead has been mentioned. At Rimrock one could instance the marshmallow roasts and the all-night hikes sponsored by the Mutual Improvement Association. Courtship is culturally styled in all five groups, but among the Spanish-Americans and the Zunis it is patterned in a quasi-aesthetic way. The making of objects for the home is an important means of expression, particularly in Zuni and at Rimrock. Some members of all groups now take photographs, and their subject matter and composition tend to be culturally distinctive for each people, in ways that are difficult to verbalize.

The preceding sentence is but one special case of the simplest but most significant generalization that can be made. There is much common content in the expressive activities of this rural area, but "the same" content has varied styles and fits in different places into each total way of life. Dancing is a completely secular activity for the Texans, and the dances bring out tensions relating to religion, intergroup conflict, and, especially, hostility between the sexes. For the Spanish-Americans dancing is primarily secular though often part of a religious fiesta. The *baile* has aesthetic overtones in itself and encourages aesthetic expression in the courtship patterns and of social formalities.[46] The Mormon dance is sanctified by the church as a manifestation of community solidarity, the joy of life, and other Mormon values. As O'Dea points out, recreation is viewed as "a lighter form of education," both an end in itself and a valued means.[47] In the five groups, as with country folk the world over, the oral word is of great importance. But in Homestead, the climax of this activity is the story told in loafing groups, in Rimrock the testimonials in religious meetings loom largest, among the Spanish-Americans it is political oratory, in Zuni perhaps the ritual words spoken in kivas, and among the Navaho the speeches given by leaders at weddings and at "Squaw Dances." There are also, of course, many differences in verbal style and in the sheer intensity of verbalization.

Themes, explicit or implicit, may be carried through various kinds of expressive activities that reflect either core values or situational

297

pressures. As illustrations of the former, one can mention the recurrent stress upon the group in Zuni and Rimrock, contrasting with the familism of the Navaho, and the individualism of the Texans. Or one could instance repeated Navaho attention to motion and action. The Navaho supply striking examples of the effects of situational pressures: McAllester finds preoccupation with loneliness a central theme in music, Mills in art, and Spencer in mythology. And the Rimrock Navaho in recent years, beset by economic difficulties and by the difficult transitions of rapid acculturation, appear to a striking degree to equate "pleasure" (whether recreational or aesthetic) in some sense with "escape." In the five cultures generally, and doubtless in all human groups, expressive-aesthetic values are interwoven in numerous activities with other elements. Extensive study of aesthetics beyond the rather narrowly defined province of the fine arts in Western culture should in time enable us to understand the full scope and functions of expression as a human universal, characterized by individual and cultural variation.

Appendix I

PUBLICATIONS OF THE "COMPARATIVE STUDY
OF VALUES IN FIVE CULTURES" PROJECT

I. PUBLISHED OR IN PREPARATION

ALBERT, E. M.

"Causality in the Social Sciences," *The Journal of Philosophy*, 51:695–706 (1954).

"The Classification of Values: A Method and Illustration," *American Anthropologist*, 58:221–248 (1956).

Cultural Value Systems: A Comparative Study of Five Cultures of Rimrock, New Mexico. In preparation.

"Values Sentences and Empirical Research," *Philosophy and Phenomenological Research*, March 1957, pp. 331–338.

"Value Systems," *International Encyclopaedia of Social Sciences*, in progress.

ALBERT, E. M., AND J. CAZENEUVE

"La Philosophie des Indiens Zunis," *Revue de Psychologie des Peuples*, 2:3–12 (1956).

ALBERT, E. M. AND CLYDE KLUCKHOHN

A Selected Bibliography on Values, Ethics, and Esthetics in the Behavioral Sciences and Philosophy, 1920–1958. Glencoe, Ill.: Free Press, 1959.

BAILEY, W. C.

"Cotton Center, Texas, and the Late Agricultural Settlement of the Texas Panhandle Community," *The Texas Journal of Science*, 4:482–486 (1952).

"The Status System of a Texas Panhandle Community," *The Texas Journal of Science*, 5:326–331 (1953).

EDMONSON, MUNRO S.

Los Manitos: A Study of Institutional Values. Middle American Research Institute, Publication No. 25. New Orleans: Tulane University Press, 1957, pp. 1–72.
"Value Systems," in Evon Z. Vogt, ed., Essays in Anthropology in Memory of Clyde Kluckhohn. In preparation.

HOBSON, RICHARD

Navaho Acquisitive Values. Cambridge, Mass.: Papers of the Peabody Museum of American Archaeology and Ethnology, vol. 42, no. 3, 1954.

KAPLAN, BERT

A Study of Rorschach Responses in Four Cultures. Cambridge, Mass.: Papers of the Peabody Museum of American Archaeology and Ethnology, vol. 42, no. 2, 1954.

KLUCKHOHN, CLYDE

"Abstract: On Values in Cross-cultural Perspective," *Proceedings of the Fifteenth International Congress of Psychology, Brussels, 1957.* Amsterdam: North Holland Publishing Company, 1959, pp. 82–84.
"An Anthropological Approach to the Study of Values," *Communication: Bulletin of the American Academy of Arts and Sciences,* 4:2–3 (1951).
"A Comparative Study of Values in Five Cultures," in E. Z. Vogt, *Navaho Veterans:* A Study of Changing Values. Cambridge, Mass.: Papers of the Peabody Museum of American Archaeology and Ethnology, vol. 41, no. 1, 1951, pp. vii–xii.
"Cultures, Values and Education," *Bulletin of the Research Institute of Comparative Education and Culture,* English edition, no. 1, March 1957, pp. 44–61. Published simultaneously in Japanese translation, Kyushu University, Fukuoka, Japan.
"Ethical Relativity: *Sic et Non,*" *Journal of Philosophy,* 52:663–667 (1955).
"The Evolution of Contemporary American Values," *Daedalus,* 87:78–109 (1958).
"Have There Been Discernible Shifts in American Values During the Past Generation?" in Elting Morison, ed., *The American Style.* New York: Harper & Bros., 1958, pp. 145–217.
"Implicit and Explicit Values in the Social Sciences Related to Human Growth and Development," *Merrill-Palmer Quarterly,* 1:131–140 (1955).
"Navaho Morals," in Vergilius Ferm, ed., *Encyclopedia of Morals.* New York: Philosophical Library, 1956, pp. 383–390.
"The Scientific Study of Values," *Three Lectures.* University of Toronto

Installation Lectures, 1958. Toronto: University of Toronto Press, 1959, pp. 25–54.

"The Scientific Study of Values and Contemporary Civilization," *Proceedings of the American Philosophical Society*, 102:469–476 (1958).

"Some Navaho Value Terms in Behavioral Context," *Language*, 32:140–145 (1956).

"The Special Character of Integration in an Individual Culture," in *The Nature of Concepts, Their Interrelation and Role in Social Structure*. Proceedings of Stillwater Conference Sponsored by Fundation for Integrated Education and Oklahoma A. & M. College. Stillwater, Okla.: Oklahoma A. & M. College, 1950, pp. 78–87.

"Toward a Comparison of Value-Emphases in Different Cultures," in Leonard D. White, ed., *The State of Social Sciences*. Chicago: University of Chicago Press, 1956, pp. 116–132.

"Universal Categories of Culture," in A. L. Kroeber, ed., *Anthropology Today*. Chicago: University of Chicago Press, 1953, pp. 507–523. Translated into Arabic by Farwq Abd-il-qadir, for *Readings in the Social Sciences*, 1:9–34 (Winter 1958–1959). Published by the UNESCO Middle East Science Corporation Office, 1959. Reprinted in Frank W. Moore, ed., *Readings in Cross-cultural Methodology*. New Haven: HRAF Press, 1961, pp. 89–105.

"Universal Values and Anthropological Relativism," in *Modern Education and Human Values*; Pitcairn-Crabbe Foundation Lecture Series, vol. IV. Pittsburgh: University of Pittsburgh Press, 1952, pp. 87–112.

"Values and Value-Orientations in the Theory of Action" in Talcott Parsons and Edward A. Shils, eds., *Toward a General Theory of Action*. Cambridge, Mass.: Harvard University Press, 1951, pp. 388–433. Translated into Chinese in *Contemporary Philosophy and Social Sciences* (Hong Kong), 1:65–79 (October 1957). (This contains an amplification requested by the editor of *Contemporary Philosophy and Social Sciences* on the subject of "Conscience," and is printed as a letter from Clyde Kluckhohn to the editor.)

KLUCKHOHN, CLYDE, AND EVON Z. VOGT

"The Son of Many Beads, 1866–1954," *American Anthropologist*, 57:1036–1037 (1957).

KLUCKHOHN, FLORENCE AND FRED L. STRODTBECK

Variations in Value-Orientations: A Theory Tested in Five Cultures. Evanston, Ill.: Row, Peterson and Company, 1961.

LADD, JOHN

The Structure of a Moral Code: A Philosophical Analysis of Ethical Discourse Applied to the Ethics of the Navaho Indians. Cambridge, Mass.: Harvard University Press, 1957.

LANDGRAF, JOHN L.

"Cultural Anthropology and Human Geography," *Transactions of the New York Academy of Sciences,* series II, 15:152–156 (1953).

Land-Use in the Ramah Area of New Mexico: An Anthropological Approach to Areal Study. Cambridge, Mass.: Papers of the Peabody Museum of American Archaeology and Ethnology, vol. 42, no. 1, 1954.

LENNEBERG, ERIC H.

"Cognition in Ethnolinguistics," *Language,* 29:463–471 (1953).

LENNEBERG, ERIC H., AND JOHN M. ROBERTS

The Language of Experience, a Study in Methodology, supplement to *International Journal of American Linguistics,* vol. 22, no. 2. Indiana Publications in Anthropology and Linguistics, Memoir 13, 1956.

MC ALLESTER, DAVID P.

Enemy Way Music: A Study of Social and Esthetic Values as Seen in Navaho Music. Cambridge, Mass.: Papers of the Peabody Museum of American Archaeology and Ethnology, vol. 41, no. 3, 1954.

MC FEAT, T. F. S.

"Some Social and Spatial Aspects of Innovation at Zuni," *Anthropologica* n.s., vol. 11, no. 1, 1960.

MICHAEL, DONALD N.

"A Cross-cultural Investigation of Closure," *Journal of Abnormal and Social Psychology,* 48:225–230 (1953).

MILLS, GEORGE

Navaho Art and Culture. Colorado Springs, Colo.: The Taylor Museum, 1959.

O'DEA, THOMAS F.

"The Effects of Geographical Position on Beliefs and Behavior in a Rural Mormon Village (with a commentary by Lowry Nelson)," *Rural Sociology,* vol. 19, no. 4 (1954).

"Mormonism and the American Experience of Time," *Western Humanities Review,* 8:181–190 (1954).

"Mormonism and the Avoidance of Sectarian Stagnation: A Study of Church, Sect, and Incipient Nationality" *American Journal of Sociology,* November 1954.

The Mormons. Chicago: University of Chicago Press, 1957.

APPENDIX I. PUBLICATIONS

PAUKER, GUY J.

"The Study of National Character Away from that Nation's Territory," *Studies in International Affairs,* 1:81–103 (1951). Committee on International and Regional Studies of Harvard University.

RAPOPORT, ROBERT N.

Changing Navaho Religious Values: A Study of Christian Missions to the Rimrock Navahos. Cambridge, Mass.: Papers of the Peabody Museum of American Archaeology and Ethnology, vol. 41, no. 2, 1954.

ROBERTS, JOHN M.

Four Southwestern Men: A Study in Culture, Cultural Control, and Values. Lincoln, Neb.: University of Nebraska Press, In press.
"Kinsmen and Friends in Zuni Culture: A Terminological Note," *El Palacio,* Summer 1965, pp. 38–43.
Zuni Daily Life. Behavior Science Reprint. New Haven: Human Relations Area Files, 1965. (Reprinted from Notebook No. 3, Laboratory of Anthropology, University of Nebraska, No. 2, 1956.)

SCHNEIDER, DAVID M., AND JOHN M. ROBERTS

Zuni Kin Terms. Behavior Science Reprint. New Haven: Human Relations Area Files, 1965. (Reprinted from Notebook No. 3, Laboratory of Anthropology, University of Nebraska, No. 1, 1956.)

SMITH, WATSON, AND JOHN M. ROBERTS

"Some Aspects of Zuni Law and Legal Procedure," *Plateau,* 27:1–5 (1954).
Zuni Law, a Field of Values. Cambridge, Mass.: Papers of the Peabody Museum of American Archaeology and Ethnology, vol. 43, no. 1, 1954.

SPENCER, KATHERINE

Mythology and Values: An Analysis of Navaho Chantway Myths, Journal of American Folklore, Memoirs, vol. 48, 1957.

STRODTBECK, F. L.

"Husband-wife Interaction over Revealed Differences," *American Sociological Review,* 16:468–473 (1951).
"The Interaction of a 'Henpecked' Husband with his Wife," *Marriage and Family Living,* 4:305–308 (1952).

TELLING, IRVING

"Coolidge and Thoreau: Forgotten Frontier Towns," *New Mexican Historical Review,* 29:210–223 (1954).

"Ramah, New Mexico, 1876–1900: An Historical Episode with Some Value Analysis," *Utah Historical Quarterly*, April 1953, pp. 117–136.

VOGT, EVON Z.

"American Subcultural Continua as Exemplified by the Mormons and Texans," *American Anthropologist*, 57:1163–1172 (1955).

"The Automobile in Contemporary Navaho Culture," *Selected Papers of the Fifth International Congress of Anthropological and Ethnological Sciences*. Philadelphia: University of Pennsylvania Press, 1960, pp. 359–363.

Modern Homesteaders: The Life of a Twentieth-century Frontier Community. Cambridge, Mass.: Belknap Press of Harvard University Press, 1955.

Navaho Veterans: A Study of Changing Values. Cambridge, Mass.: Papers of the Peabody Museum of American Archaeology and Ethnology, vol. 41, no. 1, 1951.

"On the Concepts of Structure and Process in Cultural Anthropology," *American Anthropologist*, 62:18–33 (1960).

"A Study of the Southwestern Fiesta System as Exemplified by the Laguna Fiesta," *American Anthropologist*, 57:820–839 (1955).

"Water Witching: An Interpretation of a Ritual Pattern in a Rural American Community," *The Scientific Monthly*, 75:175–186 (1952).

VOGT, EVON Z., AND THOMAS F. O'DEA

"A Comparative Study of the Role of Values in Social Action in Two Southwestern Communities," *American Sociological Review*, 18:645–654 (1953).

VOGT, EVON Z., AND JOHN M. ROBERTS

"A Study of Values,'" *Scientific American*, 195:24–31 (1956).

VON MERING, OTTO

A Grammar of Human Values. Pittsburgh: University of Pittsburg Press, 1961.

ZELDITCH, MORRIS, JR.

"Statistical Marriage Preference of the Ramah Navaho," *American Anthropologist*, 61:470–491 (1959).

II. THESES (UNPUBLISHED)

CHASDI, ELEANOR HOLLENBERG

"Child Training among the Zeepi with Special Reference to the Internalization of Moral Values," unpub. diss., Harvard University, 1952.

APPENDIX I. PUBLICATIONS

EDMONSON, MUNRO S.

"Los Manitos: Patterns of Humor in Relation to Cultural Values," unpub. diss., Harvard University, 1952.

FAIGIN, HELEN

"Child Rearing in the Rimrock Community with Special Reference to the Development of Guilt," unpub. diss., Harvard University, 1952.

MC FEAT, T. F. S.

"Values Patterns in a Design for Learning: A Study in Contextual Shifts," unpub. diss., Harvard University, 1957.

MILLS, GEORGE

"Navaho Art and Culture: A Study of the Relations Among Art Styles, Art Values, and Cultural Premises," unpub. diss., Harvard University, 1954.

STRODTBECK, F. L.

"A Study of Husband-wife Interaction in Three Cultures," unpub. diss., Harvard University, 1950.

TELLING, IRVING

"New Mexican Frontiers: A Social History of the Gallup Area: 1881–1901," unpub. diss., Harvard University, 1952.

UNTEREINER, WAYNE W.

"Self and Society: Orientations in Two Cultural Value Systems," unpub. diss., Harvard University, 1952.

VON MERING, OTTO

"Individual and Cultural Patterns of Valuation," unpub. diss., Harvard University, 1956.

ZELDITCH, MORRIS, JR.

"Authority and Solidarity in Three Southwestern Cultures," unpub. diss., Harvard University, 1955.

Appendix II

Advisory Committee
John O. Brew
Clyde Kluckhohn
Talcott Parsons

Research Fellow
Katherine Spencer (1949–50)

Research Associate
Ethel M. Albert (1953–55)

Co-ordinators
John M. Roberts (1949–53)
Evon Z. Vogt (1953–55)

Office Co-ordinators
Edward I. Fry (1950–51)
Irving Telling (1949–52)

Field Workers (1949–55)

Ethel M. Albert
Helen Faigin Antonovsky
William Arnold
Barbara Chartier Ayres
Wilfrid C. Bailey
Robert N. Bellah
Mary Louise Bensley
François Bourricaud
Eleanor Hollenberg Chasdi
David De Harport
Munro S. Edmonson
Clyde Kluckhohn
Florence Rockwood Kluckhohn
John Ladd
John Landgraf
Edgar L. Lowell
Harmon D. Maxson
David P. McAllester
Tom F. S. McFeat

Robert C. Mendenhall
Donald N. Michael
George Mills
Thomas F. O'Dea
Guy J. Pauker
Robert N. Rapoport
John M. Roberts
A. Kimball Romney
Marion St. John
Paul Sears
Watson Smith
Margaret Sperry
Fred L. Strodtbeck
Irving Telling
Wayne Untereiner
Evon Z. Vogt
Otto von Mering
Morris Zelditch, Jr.

Data Analysis (1949–55)

Ethel M. Albert
Malcolm J. Arth
Victor Ayoub
Eugene P. Banks
June Nettleship Barnes
Jane Ferguson Blanshard
Edward I. Fry
James Gazaway
Clifford J. Geertz
Charles R. Griffith
John Gulick
Herbert R. Harvey
Richard Hobson
Eric Lenneberg

Tom F. S. McFeat
Robert C. Mendenhall
Kaspar D. Naegele
Anne Parsons
Norman M. Prentice
Elizabeth Clark Rosenthal
Clarissa Hall Schnebli
Katherine Spencer
Nan Stoller
Irving Telling
Jane Cushman Telling
Arthur Vidich
Otto von Mering
Morris Zelditch, Jr.

Bibliography

Aberle, David F. "Navaho," in David M. Schneider and Kathleen Gough, eds., *Matrilineal Kinship*. Berkeley and Los Angeles: University of California Press, 1961, pp. 96–201.

—— "Navaho Kinship: A Trial Run," unpublished memorandum, Social Science Research Council Summer Seminar on Kinship, Harvard University, 1954.

—— *The Psychosocial Analysis of a Hopi Life-History,* Comparative Psychological Monographs, 21, no. 1 (serial no. 107). Berkeley, Los Angeles: University of California Press, 1951.

Aberle, Kathleen Gough. "Constants and Variables in Matrilineal Systems." Paper read at the annual meeting of the American Anthropological Association, Chicago, December 28, 1957.

Aberle, S. D. *The Pueblo Indians of New Mexico, Their Land, Economy, and Civil Organization*. American Anthropological Association, Memoir No. 70.

Adair, John. *The Navaho and Pueblo Silversmiths*. Norman, Okla.: University of Oklahoma Press, 1946.

—— and Evon Z. Vogt. "Navaho and Zuni Veterans: A Study of Contrasting Modes of Culture Change," *American Anthropologist,* 51:547–561 (1949).

Albert, E. M. "The Classification of Values: A Method and Illustration," *American Anthropologist,* 58:221–248 (1956).

—— "Cultural Value Systems: A Comparative Study of Five Cultures of Rimrock, New Mexico." In progress.

—— and Clyde Kluckhohn. *A Selected Bibliography on Values, Ethics and Esthetics in the Behavioral Sciences and Philosophy, 1920–1958.* Glencoe, Ill.: Free Press, 1959.

Astrov, Margot. "The Concept of Motion as the Psychological Leitmotif of Navaho Life and Literature," *Journal of American Folklore,* 63:45–57 (1950).

Bailyn, Bernard. *Education in the Forming of American Society*. Chapel Hill, N.C.: University of North Carolina Press, 1960.

Bancroft, Hubert Howe. *History of Arizona and New Mexico, 1530–1888.* San Francisco: The History Company, 1889.

Bandelier, A. F. "Documentary History of the Zuni Tribe," *Journal of American Ethnology and Archaeology,* III, 1892.

Barry, Herbert A., Margaret K. Bacon, and Irvin L. Child. "A Cross-cultural Survey of Some Sex Differences in Socialization," *Journal of Abnormal and Social Psychology,* 55:327–332 (1957).

Bartholomew, George A., Jr., and Joseph B. Birdsell. "Ecology and the Protohominids," *American Anthropologist,* 55:481–496 (1953).

Beale, E. F. "Wagon Road from Fort Defiance to the Colorado River," Washington: U.S.G.P.O., 1858 (U.S. Congress, House, Executive Document 124, 35th Congress, 1st session, pp. 82–83).

Bellah, Robert N. *Apache Kinship System.* Cambridge, Mass.: Harvard University Press, 1952.

Benedict, Ruth. *Patterns of Culture.* Boston: Houghton Mifflin, 1934.

Bennion, M. Lynn, and J. A. Washburn. "The Restored Church at Work," *Deseret Sunday School Union,* 1951.

Berlin, Brent, and A. Kimball Romney. "Descriptive Semantics of Tzeltal Numerical Classifiers," in A. Kimball Romney and Roy Goodwin D'Andrade, eds., *Transcultural Studies in Cognition, American Anthropologist,* 66:79–98 (1964).

Bloch, Marc. *La Société Feodale.* I and II. Paris: Albin Michel, 1949.

Bradley, Helen. "Cultural Differences in Drawings by Children from a New Mexico Region," unpub. diss., Radcliffe College, 1942.

Brew, J. O. "Comments on Erik K. Reed, 'Transition to History in the Pueblo Southwest,' " *American Anthropologist,* 56:559–602 (1954).

Broom, L., B. J. Siegel, E. Z. Vogt, and J. B. Watson. "Acculturation: An Exploratory Formulation," The Social Science Research Council Summer Seminar on Acculturation, 1953, *American Anthropologist,* 56:973–1002 (1954).

Bullen, Adelaide. "Archaeological Theory and Anthropological Fact," *American Antiquity,* 13:128–134 (1947).

Bunker, Robert. *Other Men's Skies.* Bloomington: Indiana University Press, 1956.

Bunzel, Ruth. "Four Papers on Zuni Religion," *47th Annual Report of the Bureau of American Ethnology,* 1932, pp. 467–1086.

——— "Introduction to Zuni Ceremonialism," *47th Annual Report of the Bureau of American Ethnology,* 1932, pp. 467–544.

——— *The Pueblo Potter.* New York: Columbia University Press, 1929.

——— "Zuni Katchinas," *47th Annual Report of the Bureau of American Ethnology,* 1932, pp. 837–1086.

Burt, W. H. "Territorality and Home Range Concepts as Applied to Mammals," *Journal of Mammalogy,* 24:346–352 (1943).

Caldwell, Gaylor L. "Mormon Conceptions of Individual Rights and Political Obligations," unpub. diss., Stanford University, 1952.

Carr, Malcolm, Katherine Spencer, and Doriane Wolley. "Navaho Clans and Marriage at Pueblo Alto," *American Anthropologist*, 41:245–257 (1939).

Chang, Kwang-Chih. "Study of the Neolithic Social Grouping: Examples from the New World," *American Anthropologist*, 60:298–334 (1958).

Chasdi, Eleanor H. "Child Training among the Zeepi with Special Reference to the Internalization of Moral Values," unpub. diss., Harvard University, 1952.

Colby, B. N. "Manual for the Use of the Clyde Kluckhohn Value-Categories" (revised and expanded). Mimeographed paper, 1961.

Collier, Malcolm Carr. "Local Organization among the Navaho," unpub. diss., University of Chicago, 1951.

Conklin, Harold C. "Lexicographical Treatment of Folk Taxonomies," *International Journal of American Linguistics*, 28:119–141 (1962).

Cushing, F. H. "Outlines of Zuni Creation Myths," *13th Annual Report of the American Bureau of Ethnology*, 1896, pp. 321–447.

——— *Zuni Breadstuff*. Indian Notes and Monographs, 8. New York: Heye Foundation, 1920.

David, Paul T., *et al. Presidential Nominating Politics in 1952, The West*, vol. 5. Baltimore: Johns Hopkins Press, 1954.

Donnelly, Thomas C. *The Government of New Mexico*. Albuquerque: University of New Mexico Press, 1947.

Dorroh, J. H., Jr. *Certain Hydrologic and Climatic Characteristics of the Southwest*. Albuquerque: University of New Mexico Press, 1946.

Durkheim, Emile. *Les Formes élémentaires de la Vie religieuse*. Paris, 1912.

Edmonson, Munro S. Field Notes, Values Study Project, 1949–50. Harvard University Laboratory of Social Relations.

——— "Kinship Terms and Kinship Concepts," *American Anthropologist*, 59:393–433 (1957).

——— *Los Manitos: A Study of Institutional Values*. Middle American Research Institute, Publication No. 25. New Orleans: Tulane University Press, 1957, pp. 1–72.

——— "Los Manitos: Patterns of Humor in Relation to Cultural Values," unpub. diss., Harvard University, 1952.

——— *Status Terminology and the Social Structure of North American Indians*. Seattle: University of Washington Press, 1958.

Eggan, Fred. *Social Organization of the Western Pueblos*. Chicago: University of Chicago Press, 1950.

Faigin, Helen. "Child Rearing in the Rimrock Community with Special Reference to the Development of Guilt," unpub. diss., Harvard University, 1952.

Fenneman, Nevin M. *Physiography of Western United States*. New York and London: McGraw-Hill, 1931.

Ferguson, Erna. *New Mexico*. New York: Alfred A. Knopf, 1951.

Firth, Raymond. *Elements of Social Organization*. London: Watts and Co., 1951.

Forrest, E. R. *Missions and Pueblos of the Old Southwest: Their Myths, Legends, Fiestas, and Ceremonies, with some Accounts of the Indian Tribes and Their Dances; and of the Penitentes.* Cleveland: Arthur H. Clark Co., 1929.

Fortes, M., and E. E. Evans-Pritchard. *African Political Systems.* London: Oxford University Press, 1940.

Foster, Roy W. *Scenic Trips to the Geologic Past* (no. 4): *Southern Zuni Mountains.* Socorro, N.M.: State Bureau of Mines and Mineral Resources, a division of New Mexico Institute of Mining and Technology, 1958.

Frake, Charles O. "Cultural Ecology and Ethnography," *American Anthropologist,* 64:53–59 (1962).

——— "The Diagnosis of Disease Among the Subanan of Mindanao," *American Anthropologist,* 63:113–132 (1961).

——— "The Ethnographic Study of Cognitive Systems," in Thomas Gladwin and William C. Sturtevant, eds., *Anthropology and Human Behavior,* Anthropological Society of Washington, 1962, pp. 72–85.

——— "Notes on Queries in Ethnography," in A. Kimball Romney and Roy Goodwin D'Andrade, eds., *Transcultural Studies in Cognition, American Anthropologist,* 66:132–145 (1964).

Geertz, Clifford. "Drought, Death and Alcohol in Five Southwestern Cultures." Harvard. Laboratory of Social Relations. Values Study Project, 1951. Manuscript.

Ghurye, G. S. *Family and Kin in Indo-European Culture.* University of Bombay Publications, Sociology Series No. 4, Bombay, 1955.

Goodenough, Ward H. "Componential Analysis and the Study of Meaning," *Language,* 32:195–216 (1956).

——— "Cultural Anthropology and Linguistics," in P. L. Garvin, ed., *Report of the 7th Annual Round Table Meeting on Linguistics and Language Study.* Monograph Series on Languages and Linguistics, No. 9. Washington, D.C.: Georgetown University Press, 1957.

Haeberlin, H. K. "The Idea of Fertilization in the Culture of the Pueblo Indians," *Memoirs of the American Anthropological Association,* vol. 3, no. 1 (1916).

Haile, Berard. *Learning Navaho,* vol. 1, St. Michaels, Ariz.: St. Michaels Press, 1941.

Hald, A. *Statistical Tables and Formulas.* New York: John Wiley & Sons, 1952.

Haskett, Bert. "History of the Sheep Industry in Arizona," *Arizona Historical Review,* 7:19 (1936).

Havighurst, Robert J., and Bernice Neugarten. *American Indian and White Children.* Chicago: University of Chicago Press, 1955.

Hill, W. W. "Comments on Ruth Underhill, 'Intercultural Relations in the Greater Southwest,'" *American Anthropologist,* 56:657–658 (1954).

Hodge, Fredrick Webb. "History of Hawikuh," *Publications of the Fredrick Webb Hodge Anniversary Publication Fund*, 1:1–155 (1937).
———— "The Six Cities of Cibola 1581–1680," *New Mexico Historical Review*, 1:478–488 (1926).
Hoijer, Harry. "Athabaskan Kinship Systems," *American Anthropologist*, 58:309–333 (1956).
———— "The Chronology of the Athapaskan Languages," *International Journal of American Linguistics*, vol. 22, 1956.
———— "The Sapir-Whorf Hypothesis," in Harry Hoijer, ed., *Language in Culture*. Chicago: University of Chicago Press, 1954, pp. 128–134.
Hymes, D. H. "More on Lexicostatistics," *Current Anthropology*, 1:338–345 (1960).
Ivins, Anthony W. "Journal." Typescript copy in possession of Stanley S. Ivins, Salt Lake City. A microfilm copy of the original Ivins Journal, on which the elaborated typescript above referred to was based, is in the library of the Utah State Historical Society.
Kaplan, B. *A Study of Rorschach Responses in Four Cultures*. Cambridge, Mass.: Papers of the Peabody Museum of American Archaeology and Ethnology, vol. 42, no. 2, 1954.
Kaut, Charles R. *The Western Apache Clan System: Its Origins and Development*. University of New Mexico Publications in Anthropology, No. 9, 1957.
Keleher, William A. *Turmoil in New Mexico 1846–1868*. Santa Fe, N.M.: The Rydal Press, 1952.
Kirk, Ruth. "Little Santu of Cibola," *New Mexico*, 17:16–17, 35–36, 38 (1940).
Kluckhohn, Clyde. "A Comparative Study of Values in Five Cultures," in E. Z. Vogt, *Navaho Veterans*. Cambridge, Mass.: Papers of the Peabody Museum of American Archaeology and Ethnology, vol. 45, no. 1, 1951, pp. vii–xii.
———— "Myths and Rituals: A General Theory," *Harvard Theological Review*, 35:45–79 (1942).
———— "A Navaho Personal Document with a Brief Paretian Analysis," *Southwestern Journal of Anthropology*, 1:260–283 (1945).
———— *Navaho Witchcraft*. Cambridge, Mass.: Papers of the Peabody Museum of American Archaeology and Ethnology, vol. 22, no. 2, 1944.
———— "Participation in Ceremonials in a Navaho Community," *American Anthropologist*, 40:359–369 (1938).
———— "The Philosophy of the Navaho Indians," in F. S. C. Northrop, ed., *Ideological Differences and World Order*. New Haven: Yale University Press, 1949, pp. 356–384.
———— "Some Personal and Social Aspects of Navaho Ceremonial Practice," *Harvard Theological Review*, 32:57–82 (1939).
———— "Toward a Comparison of Value-Emphases in Different Cultures,"

in L. D. White, ed., *The State of the Social Sciences*. Chicago: University of Chicago Press, 1956, pp. 116–132.

——— "Values and Value-Orientations in the Theory of Action: An Exploration in Definition and Classification," in Talcott Parsons and Edward A. Shils, eds., *Toward a General Theory of Action*. Cambridge, Mass.: Harvard University Press, 1952, pp. 388–433.

——— and Dorothea Leighton. *The Navaho*. Cambridge, Mass.: Harvard University Press, 1946.

Kluckhohn, Florence R. "Dominant and Substitute Profiles of Cultural Orientations: Their Significance for the Analysis of Social Stratification," *Social Forces*, 28:376–393 (1950).

——— "Los Atarqueños: A Study of Patterns and Configurations in a New Mexican Vilage," unpub. diss., Radcliffe College, 1941.

——— and Fred L. Strodtbeck. *Variations in Value-Orientations: A Theory Tested in Five Cultures*. Evanston, Ill.: Row, Peterson and Co., 1961.

Kroeber, A. L. "Zuni Kin and Clan," *Anthropological Papers of the American Museum of Natural History*, 18:41–204 (1917).

Kubler, George. *The Religious Architecture of New Mexico in the Colonial Period and since the American Occupation*. Colorado Springs, Colo.: Taylor Museum, 1940.

Ladd, John. *The Structure of a Moral Code: A Philosophical Analysis of Ethical Discourse Applied to the Ethics of the Navaho Indians*. Cambridge, Mass.: Harvard University Press, 1957.

Lambert, W. W., L. M. Triandis, and M. Wolf. "Some Correlates of Beliefs in the Malevolence and Benevolence of Supernatural Beings: A Cross-cultural Study," *Journal of Abnormal and Social Psychology*, 58:162–169 (1959).

Landgraf, John L. *Land-Use in the Ramah Area of New Mexico: An Anthropological Approach to Areal Study*. Cambridge, Mass.: Papers of the Peabody Museum of American Archaeology and Ethnology, vol. 42, no. 1, 1954.

Lenneberg, Eric H., and John M. Roberts. *The Language of Experience, a Study in Methodology*, supplement to *International Journal of American Linguistics*, vol. 22, no. 2. Indiana Publications in Anthropology and Linguistics, Memoir 13, 1956.

Lévi-Strauss, Claude. "Language and Analysis of Social Laws," *American Anthropologist*, 53:155–163 (1951).

——— *Les Systèmes élémentaires de la Parenté*. Paris: Presses Universitaires de France, 1949.

Lincoln, Jackson S. *The Dream in Primitive Cultures*. London: Cresset Press, 1935.

Lorenz, Konrad. *King Solomon's Ring*. New York: Crowell, 1952.

Lounsbury, Floyd G. "A Formal Account of the Crow- and Omaha-Type Kinship Terminologies," in W. H. Goodenough, ed., *Explorations*

in Cultural Anthropology: Essays in Honor of George Peter Murdock.
New York: McGraw-Hill, 1964, pp. 351–393.

———— "Semantic Analysis of the Pawnee Kinship Usage," *Language,*
32:158–194 (1956).

———— "The Structural Analysis of Kinship Semantics," in Horace G.
Lunt, ed., *Proceedings of the Ninth International Congress of Linguistics.* The Hague: Mouton & Co., 1964, pp. 1073–1093.

McAllester, David P. *Enemy Way Music: A Study of Social and Esthetic
Values as Seen in Navaho Music.* Cambridge, Mass.: Papers of the
Peabody Museum of American Archaeology and Ethnology, vol. 41,
no. 3, 1954.

McClelland, David C. *The Achieving Society.* Princeton, N.J.: Van Nos-
trand, 1961.

———— et al. *The Achievement Motive.* New York: Appleton-Century-
Crofts, 1953.

———— and G. A. Friedman. "A Cross-cultural Study of the Relationship
between Child-training Practices and Achievement Motivation Ap-
pearing in Folk Tales," in G. E. Swanson, T. M. Newcomb, and
E. M. Hartley, eds., *Readings in Social Psychology* (rev. ed.). New
York: Henry Holt, 1952, pp. 243–249.

Mead, Margaret. *Cultural Patterns and Technical Change.* New York:
Mentor, 1955.

Metzger, Duane. "The Formal Analysis of Kinship: Special Problems as
Exemplified in Zuni." Paper read at the annual meeting of the
American Anthropological Association, Chicago, December 28, 1957.

———— and Gerald Williams. "A Formal Ethnographic Analysis of Tenejapa Ladino Weddings," *American Anthropologist,* 65:1076–1101
(1963).

———— and Gerald Williams. "Procedures and Results in the Study of
Native Category Systems: Tzeltal Firewood," Anthropological Research Papers 12. Stanford University, 1962.

———— and Gerald Willaims. "Tenejapa Medicine I: The Curer," *Southwestern Journal of Anthropology,* 19:216–234 (1963).

Michael, Donald N. "A Cross-cultural Investigation of Closure," *Journal
of Abnormal and Social Psychology,* 48:225–230 (1953).

Milgroom, Bernice. "The Reflection of Zuni Personality in Zuni Mythology," unpub. diss., Radcliffe College, 1948.

Miller, Daniel R., and Guy E. Swanson. *The Changing American Parent.*
New York: John Wiley & Sons, 1958.

Mills, George. "Art, Life and Death: The Navaho Pattern," Harvard
University, Laboratory of Social Relations, Values Study Project,
1955. Manuscript.

———— *Navaho Art and Culture.* Colorado Springs, Colo.: The Taylor
Museum, 1959.

Mischel, Walter. "Delay of Gratification, Need for Achievement, and

315

Acquiescence in Another Culture," *Journal of Abnormal and Social Psychology,* 62:543–552.

Murdock, George P. *Social Structure.* New York: Macmillan, 1947.

—— "World Ethnographic Sample," *American Anthropologist,* 59:664–687 (1957).

Nelson, Lowry. *The Mormon Village: A Pattern and Technique of Land Settlement.* Salt Lake City: University of Utah Press, 1952.

Nice, Margaret. "The Role of Territoriality in Bird Life," *American Midland Naturalist,* 26:441–487 (1941).

O'Dea, Thomas F. "Mormonism and the Avoidance of Sectarian Stagnation: A Study of Church, Sect, and Incipient Nationality," *American Journal of Sociology,* November 1954.

—— *The Mormons.* Chicago: University of Chicago Press, 1957.

—— "Mormon Values: The Significance of a Religious Outlook for Social Action," unpub. diss., Harvard University, 1953.

Opler, Morris E. "The Kinship Systems of the Southern Athabaskan-Speaking Tribes," *American Anthropologist,* 38:620–633 (1936).

Parent and Child. (Written by the Mormon Church and used in parents' Sunday School class.)

Parsons, Elsie Clews. "The Franciscans Return to Zuni," *American Anthropologist,* 41:337–338 (1939).

—— "The Kinship Nomenclature of the Pueblo Indians," *American Anthropologist,* 34:377–389 (1932).

Parsons, Talcott. "The Kinship System of the Contemporary United States," *American Anthropologist,* 45:22–38 (1943). Reprinted in Talcott Parsons, ed., *Essays in Sociological Theory Pure and Applied.* Glencoe, Ill.: Free Press, 1949, pp. 233–250.

—— and Neil Smelser. *Economy and Society.* Glencoe, Ill.: Free Press, 1956.

Rapoport, Robert N. *Changing Navaho Religious Values: A Study of Christian Missions to the Rimrock Navahos.* Cambridge, Mass.: Papers of the Peabody Museum of American Archaeology and Ethnology, vol. 41, no. 2, 1954.

Reed, Erik K. "Transition to History in the Pueblo Southwest," *American Anthropologist,* 56:592–595 (1954).

—— "The Western Pueblo Archeological Complex," *El Palacio,* 55:9–15 (1948).

Reichard, Gladys A. *Navaho Religion* 2 vols. New York: Pantheon, 1950.

—— *Social Life of the Navajo Indians.* New York: Columbia University Press, 1928.

Roberts, Frank H. H., Jr. "The Village of the Great Kivas on the Zuni Reservation New Mexico," *Smithsonian Institution, Bureau of American Ethnology Bulletin III,* 1932, pp. 158–169.

Roberts, John M. *Four Southwestern Men: A Study in Culture, Cultural Control, and Values.* Lincoln, Neb.: University of Nebraska Press, in press.

—— *Zuni Daily Life.* Behavior Science Reprint. New Haven: Human Relations Area Files, 1965. (Reprinted from Notebook No. 3, Laboratory of Anthropology, University of Nebraska, No. 2, 1956.)

Roheim, Geza. *Psychoanalysis and Anthropology: Culture, Personality and the Unconscious.* New York: International Universities Press, 1950.

Romney, A. Kimball. "The Formal Analysis of Kinship: General Analytical Frame." Paper read at the annual meeting of the American Anthropological Association, Chicago, December 28, 1957.

—— and Roy Goodwin D'Andrade. "Cognitive Aspects of English Kin Terms," in A. Kimball Romney and Roy Goodwin D'Andrade, eds., *Transcultural Studies in Cognition, American Anthropologist,* 66:146–170 (1964).

Ryerson, Alice. "Medical Advice on Child Rearing, 1550–1900," unpub. diss., Harvard Graduate School of Education, 1959.

St. John, Marion. "Three Southwestern Non-Anglo Economies: Values Study," unpub. ms., Harvard University Laboratory of Social Relations, 1952.

Schneider, David M., and George Homans. *Marriage, Authority and Final Causes.* Glencoe, Ill.: Free Press, 1955.

—— and John M. Roberts. *Zuni Kin Terms.* Behavior Science Reprint. New Haven: Human Relations Area Files, 1965. (Reprinted from Notebook No. 3, Laboratory of Anthropology, University of Nebraska, No. 1, 1956.)

Schroeder, Albert H. "Comments on Reed, 'Transition to History in the Pueblo Southwest,'" *American Anthropologist,* 56:597–599 (1954).

Sears, Robert R., Eleanor E. Maccoby, and Harry Levin. *Patterns of Child Rearing.* Evanston, Ill.: Row, Peterson and Co., 1957.

Shepardson, Mary. "Leadership and Culture Change: A Case Study of the Navaho Indians," unpub. diss., Stanford University, 1956.

Smith, Watson, and John M. Roberts. *Zuni Law, a Field of Values.* Cambridge, Mass.: Papers of the Peabody Museum of American Archaeology and Ethnology, vol. 43, no. 1.

Spencer, Katherine. "Mythology and Values," unpub. diss., University of Chicago, 1952.

—— *Mythology and Values: An Analysis of Navaho Chantway Myths,* Journal of American Folklore, Memoirs, vol. 48, 1957.

Spier, Leslie. "The Distribution of Kinship Systems in North America," *University of Washington Publications in Anthropology,* 1:69–88 (1925).

—— "An Outline for a Chronology of Zuni Ruins," *American Museum of Natural History Papers,* vol. 18, pt. III, pp. 207–331.

—— "Zuni Weaving Techniques," *American Anthropologist,* 26:64–85 (1924).

Spuhler, James N., and Clyde Kluckhohn. "Inbreeding Coefficients of the Ramah Navaho Population," *Human Biology,* December, 1953.

Stephens, William N. *The Oedipus Complex: Cross-cultural Evidence.* Glencoe, Ill.: Free Press, 1962.

Stevenson, Matilda Coxe. "Ethnobotany of the Zuni Indians," *30th Annual Report of the Bureau of American Ethnology, 1908–1909,* 1915, pp. 31–102.

———— "The Zuni Indians: Their Mythology, Esoteric Societies, and Ceremonies," *23rd Annual Report of the Bureau of American Ethnology, 1901–1902,* 1904, pp. 1–634.

Strodtbeck, F. L. "Husband-Wife Interaction over Revealed Differences," *American Sociological Review,* 16:468–473 (1951).

Sturtevant, William C. "Studies in Ethnoscience," in A. Kimball Romney and Roy Goodwin D'Andrade, eds., *Transcultural Studies in Cognition, American Anthropologist,* 66:99–131 (1964).

Talmage, J. E. *A Study of the Articles of Faith.* Salt Lake City: The Church of Jesus Christ, 1924.

Telling, Irving. "New Mexican Frontiers: A Social History of the Gallup Area, 1881–1901," unpub. diss., Harvard University, 1952.

———— "Ramah, New Mexico, 1876–1900: An Historical Episode with some Value Analysis," *Utah Historical Quarterly,* April 1953, pp. 117–136.

Thomas, A. B., ed., *Forgotten Frontiers: A Study of the Spanish Indian Policy of Don Juan Bautista de Anza, Governor of New Mexico 1777–1787.* Norman, Okla.: University of Oklahoma Press, 1932.

Thurnwald, Richard. *Werden, Wandel und Gestaltung von Staat und Kultur.* Berlin: Walter de Gruyter, 1935.

Tillich, Paul. *Systematic Theology,* vol. 1. Chicago: University of Chicago Press, 1950.

Titiev, Mischa. *Old Oraibi.* Cambridge, Mass.: Papers of the Peabody Museum of American Archaeology and Ethnology, vol. 22, no. 1, 1944.

Twitchell, Ralph E. "Spanish Colonization in New Mexico in the Onate and DeVargas Periods," *Historical Society of New Mexico,* 22:1–39 (1919).

Untereiner, Wayne W. "Self and Society: Orientations in Two Cultural Value Systems," unpub. diss., Harvard University, 1952.

———— Field Notes, Values Study Project, 1950–51. Harvard University Laboratory of Social Relations.

United States Indian Service. *United Pueblos Irrigation Division, Table 5.* Washington: U.S.G.P.O., 1941.

Van Valkenburgh, Richard. "Navajo Common Law I — Notes on Political Organization, Property and Inheritance," *Museum Notes, Museum of Northern Arizona,* vol. 9 (October 1936).

Vestal, Paul A. *Ethnobotany of the Ramah Navaho.* Cambridge, Mass.: Papers of the Peabody Museum of American Archaeology and Ethnology, vol. 40, no. 4, 1952.

Vogt, Evon Z. "American Subcultural Continua as Exemplified by the

Mormons and Texans," *American Anthropologist,* 57:1163–1172 (1955).

———— "An Appraisal of 'Prehistoric Settlement Patterns in the New World,'" in G. R. Willey, ed., *Prehistoric Settlement Patterns in the New World.* Viking Fund Publications in Anthropology, No. 23, New York, 1956.

———— Field Notes, Values Study Project, 1949–55. Harvard University Laboratory of Social Relations.

———— *Modern Homesteaders: The Life of a Twentieth-century Frontier Community.* Cambridge, Mass.: Belknap Press of Harvard University Press, 1955.

———— "The Navaho," in Edward H. Spicer, ed., *Perspectives in American Indian Culture Change.* Chicago: University of Chicago Press, 1961.

———— *Navaho Veterans: A Study of Changing Values.* Cambridge, Mass.: Papers of the Peabody Museum of American Archaeology and Ethnology, vol. 41, no. 1, 1951.

———— "A Study of the Southwestern Fiesta System as Exemplified by the Laguna Fiesta," *American Anthropologist,* 57:820–839 (1955).

———— "Water Witching: An Interpretation of a Ritual Pattern in a Rural American Community," *The Scientific Monthly,* 75:175–186 (1952).

———— and Thomas F. O'Dea. "A Comparative Study of the Role of Values in Social Action in Two Southwestern Communities," *American Sociological Review,* 18:645–654 (1953).

Von Mering, Otto. *A Grammar of Human Values.* Pittsburgh: University of Pittsburgh Press, 1961.

Wallace, Anthony F. C., and John Atkins. "The Meaning of Kinship Terms," *American Anthropologist,* 62:58–80 (1960).

Whiting, John W. M. "The Cross-cultural Method," in G. Lindzey, ed., *Handbook of Social Psychology.* Boston: Addison-Wesley Publishing Co., 1954.

———— "Sorcery, Sin and the Superego: A Cross-cultural Study of Some Mechanisms of Social Control," in *Symposium on Motivation,* University of Nebraska Press, 1959, pp. 174–195.

———— and Irvin L. Child. *Child Training and Personality: A Cross-cultural Study.* New Haven: Yale University Press, 1953.

———— and Roy Goodwin D'Andrade. "Sleeping Arrangements and Social Structure: A Cross-cultural Study." Presented at American Anthropological Association Annual Meetings, Mexico City, December 1959.

———— Richard Kluckhohn, and Albert S. Anthony. "A Cross-cultural Study of Initiation Rites at Puberty," Paper read at the annual meeting of the American Anthropological Association, Santa Monica, California, December 19, 1956.

———— Richard Kluckhohn, and Albert S. Anthony. "The Function of

Male Initiation Ceremonies at Puberty," in E. E. Maccoby, T. M. Newcomb, and E. M. Hartley, eds., *Readings in Social Psychology.* New York: Henry Holt & Co., 1958, pp. 359–370.

Widtsoe, John A. *Priesthood and Church Government in the Church of the Latter-Day Saints.* Salt Lake City: Deseret Book Company, 1950.

Willey, Gordon R. *Prehistoric Settlement Patterns in the Viru Valley, Peru.* Washington: U.S.G.P.O., 1953 (Smithsonian Institution, Bureau of American Ethnology B 155).

Wilson, Edmund. *Red, Black, Blond and Olive.* New York: Oxford University Press, 1956.

Wittfogel, Karl A., and Esther S. Goldfrank. "Some Aspects of Pueblo Mythology and Society," *Journal of American Folklore* (1943), pp. 17–30.

Woodbury, Richard B. "The Antecedents of Zuni Culture," *Transactions of the New York Academy of Sciences,* ser. II, vol. 18, no. 6, pp. 557–563 (April 1956).

Young, Kimball. *Isn't One Wife Enough?* New York: Henry Holt, 1954.

Young, Robert W., ed. *The Navajo Yearbook of Planning in Action.* Window Rock, Ariz.: Navaho Agency, 1955.

Zelditch, Morris, Jr. "Authority and Solidarity in Three Southwestern Communities," unpub. diss., Harvard University, 1955.

——— Field Notes, Values Study Project, 1953–54. Harvard University Laboratory of Social Relations.

Notes

CHAPTER 1. THE "COMPARATIVE STUDY OF VALUES IN FIVE CULTURES" PROJECT

1. C. Kluckhohn, "Comparative Study of Values," pp. vii–viii.
2. *Cf.* Albert and Kluckhohn, *Selected Bibliography.*
3. Ralph Barton Perry, *The General Theory of Value,* New York: Longmans, Green, 1926. Wolfgang Kohler, *The Place of Value in a World of Facts,* New York: Liveright, 1938. Max Weber, *The Theory of Social and Economic Organization* (translation), New York: Oxford University Press, 1947. John Dewey, *Theory of Valuation,* Chicago: University of Chicago Press (International Encyclopaedia of Unified Science 2, 4), 1939.
4. C. Kluckhohn, "Values and Value-Orientations," p. 395. See also Charles W. Morris, "Axiology as the Science of Preferential Behavior," in Ray Lepley, ed., *Value: A Cooperative Inquiry.* New York: Columbia University Press, 1949.
5. Albert, "Classification of Values," pp. 221–222.
6. Albert and Kluckhohn, *Selected Bibliography.*
7. Albert, "Classification of Values," p. 223.
8. *Cf. ibid.,* p. 225.
9. *Ibid.,* p. 223.
10. F. Kluckhohn and Strodtbeck, *Variations in Value-Orientations,* pp. 3, 10.
11. C. Kluckhohn, "Toward a Comparison of Value-Emphases," pp. 16, 117–119.
13. Colby, "Manual for Kluckhohn Value-Categories."
14. See, for example, Bunzel, "Zuni Ceremonialism," p. 483.
15. Personal Communication. Roberts will explore this distinction in his contribution to the series, Case Studies in Cultural Anthropology, edited by George and Louise Spinder.
16. Hymes, "Lexicostatistics," p. 343.
17. See, for example, Lounsbury, "Semantic Analysis of the Pawnee Kinship Usage," "Structural Analysis of Kinship Semantics," and "A Formal Account of the Crow- and Omaha-Type Kinship Terminologies"; Goodenough, "Componential Analysis and the Study of Meaning," and "Cultural Anthropology and Linguistics"; Conklin, "Lexicographical Treatment of Folk Taxonomies"; Frake, "Diagnosis of Disease among the Subanan of Mindanao," "Cultural Ecology and Ethnography," "Ethnographic Study of Cog-

nitive Systems," and "Notes on Queries in Ethnography"; Metzger and Williams, "A Formal Ethnographic Analysis of Tenejapa Ladino Weddings," "Procedures and Results in the Study of Native Category Systems: Tzeltal Firewood," and "Tenejapa Medicine I: The Curer"; Romney and D'Andrade, "Cognitive Aspects of English Kin Terms"; Berlin and Romney, "Descriptive Semantics of Tzeltal Numerical Classifiers"; Wallace and Atkins, "Meaning of Kinship Terms." A paper by Sturtevant, "Studies in Ethnoscience," summarizes these methodological developments up to 1964.

18. Frake, "Cultural Ecology and Ethnography," and "Notes on Queries in Ethnography," and Metzger and Williams, "A Formal Ethnographic Analysis of Tenejapa Ladino Weddings," and "Tenejapa Medicine I: The Curer."

CHAPTER 2. GEOGRAPHICAL AND CULTURAL SETTING

1. Fenneman, *Physiography*. Technical details on the geographical setting may be found in Foster, *Scenic Trips*; C. Kluckhohn and Leighton, *The Navaho*; Landgraf, *Land-Use*; Vestal, *Ethnobotany*; Vogt, *Navaho Veterans*; Vogt, *Modern Homesteaders*. We have drawn freely on these earlier publications in preparing this summary of the geographical features of the Rimrock Area. See also Chapter 6, "Ecology and Economy."

2. Vestal, *Ethnobotany*.

3. Dorroh, *Hydrologic and Climatic Characteristics*.

4. Telling, "New Mexican Frontiers."

CHAPTER 3. INTERCULTURAL RELATIONS

1. Reed, "Western Pueblo," pp. 9–15. See also Reed, "Transition"; Roberts, "Great Kivas"; Woodbury, "Antecedents."

2. The question of whether there were six or seven villages inhabited in 1540 has been a controversial one. Bandelier, "Documentary History," Stevenson, "Ethnobotany," and others say seven. Eggan, *Social Organization*, Hodge, "Hawikuh," "Six Cities," Reed, "Transition," and Spier, "Zuni Ruins," say there is evidence for only six.

3. This summary derives from Bandelier, "Documentary History," and Hodge, "Six Cities."

4. Legends about the 1680 Rebellion and reconquest are still a part of the Zuni oral tradition. Stevenson ("Zuni Indians," pp. 286–289) has a published account of versions she obtained from two informants. Vogt obtained substantially the same account of the rebellion from two middle-aged Zuni men (Gaspar and Chavez).

5. Reed, "Transition," pp. 594–595.

6. Stevenson, "Zuni Indians," pp. 285–286. For divergent opinions on the date and builder of the church at Zuni, see Kubler, *Religious Architecture*, pp. 95–97.

7. Parsons, "Franciscans Return," pp. 337–338. Bandelier, "Documentary History," p. 103.

8. Reed, "Western Pueblo"; Schroeder, "Comments on Reed"; Brew, "Comments on Reed," pp. 597–602; Hill, "Comments on Underhill," pp. 657–658; Hoijer, "Athapaskan Languages"; Vogt, "The Navaho."

9. Bandelier, "Documentary History," pp. 106–107; Hodge, "Six Cities," p. 126.
10. Beale, "Wagon Road."
11. Vogt, *Navaho Veterans*, p. 9.
12. Bancroft, *Arizona and New Mexico*, pp. 419–422.
13. Haskett, "Sheep Industry," p. 19; Telling, "New Mexican Frontiers," pp. 29, 30; F. Kluckhohn, "Los Atarqueños."
14. Kirk, "Little Santu"; Parsons, "Franciscans Return."
15. Cushing, *Zuni Breadstuff*, pp. 534–535.
16. F. Kluckhohn, "Los Atarqueños," pp. 239–240.
17. *Ibid.*, pp. 240–241.
18. Telling, "Ramah," pp. 117–136.
19. Ivins, "Journal," p. 25.
20. Landgraf, *Land-Use*.
21. The concept of "intercultural roles" was developed by the SSRC Summer Seminar on Acculturation in 1953 in which Evon Z. Vogt was a participant.
22. Rapoport, *Navaho Religious Values*, pp. 980–981.
23. Vogt, *Navaho Veterans*, p. 20.
24. Broom, Siegel, Vogt, and Watson, "Acculturation," pp. 981–982.
25. Vogt, *Navaho Veterans*, pp. 18–19.
26. According to one Zuni informant, Gaspar, the "Mexicans" don't want to see Zuni katchina dances because, "When we first came out from the ground, the Mexicans came with us. And one of the katchinas came with us and the Mexicans didn't want to see it because they were afraid. So that's the reason the Mexicans don't come around to see our katchinas." You mean the Mexicans are afraid to come? "Yeah." Will anything happen to them? "Well, when they see the katchinas, later on they get sick and in some kind of trouble and might die." Which katchina? "It's the dance with the crown. And that katchina could talk Mexican too. The Zunis still dance this one sometimes." A second informant, Wyaco, added the information that "the katchina which spoke Mexican couldn't qualify for any of the other katchina societies, so he had to be taken care of by the Newekwe Society. The Newekwe volunteered to take care of him." Which katchina is it? "There are two different ones. The female has feathers like the Shalako, and the male has a long stick coming out of his head. The one with the stick is Mitotaca; the other one is A·wan koko ana. They are the ones that speak Mexican." Bunzel, "Zuni Katchinas," p. 908 and plate 58.
27. The typical visit to pay respects to the *Santo* is a local manifestation of the widespread *promesa* (promise) pattern. A Spanish-American will pray to the *Santo* for some favor (e.g., to cure an illness or bring a relative safely back from the war) and make a *promesa* to undertake a pilgrimage to pay homage to the *Santo* after the favor is granted.

   In the Spanish-American view, this *Santo* is the *Santo Niño*, the Infant Jesus. But the Zuni view is that the *Santo* is a female. The following mythological account of the origin was given by an informant in 1952: "Long time ago the *Santo Niño's* mother was raised south of here and she traveled around and came to Ojo Caliente. When she was girl, the sun do something to her and she got a baby. And finally her father find out and he asked her who gives her the baby, because she didn't go outside. Just stay inside all the time. She don't know how she get the baby. And her father told her go out and live outside someplace. She walk out and went West and just travel around and sun take care of her and finally she got to Ojo Caliente. They call the place Hawiku. And she moved to Zuni. She told those Zuni people to make a church for her. Then everybody worked on the old church and when people finished the church and then she born that *Santo Niño*. After the *Santo Niño* born, everybody came around to dance for her. And finally those Acoma people came around to dance for her. And this *Santo Niño*'s mother liked the Acoma dance, so they want to go back home and she wanted to go with them. So they took her mother and her little daughter is kind of lonesome and finally she turned into rock. Sometimes has eyes open if feel good; sometimes closed if not feel good. Sometimes rosy cheeks and sometimes cracked all over. That's why the Mexicans come around to pray for her. Sometimes if Mexican very sick and promise to come and pray and when they come and pray then they get well. No matter if they come from Santa Fe or Albuquerque. When they get someplace in mountains they have to walk. Nobody took care of her in church, so have to take her in house. She have everything little bells and little horns. And also big bell they keep in house. In grandmother' day in November have to take out and make big noise with bell. Make announcement four days and then take out and ring bell and all the villages have to cook everything and nighttime feed our mothers who have passed away." Offerings? "Yes, leave shoes, dresses, and money." What happens to money? "People who live there take it, sometimes buy clothes for her." Zunis pray too? "Yes, they go too. Some years ago some Mexican from Atrisco, stay all night, and try to steal that doll. Put in wagon at night. Go up there that mesa and stay overnight. He put it in a box. Next morning open the box and nothing in there. She came back. Lot of Mexicans steal money and go someplace and then look in pocket and nothing there. Mexicans kind of afraid of her." This version is substantially the same as that given by Ruth Kirk, "Little Santu."

28. Vogt, *Navaho Veterans*, pp. 18–19.
29. Talmage, *Articles of Faith*, p. 260.
30. Rapoport, *Navaho Religious Values*.
31. Vogt, "American Subcultural Continua."

CHAPTER 4. THE LEARNING OF VALUES

1. In 1950 the team consisted of Eleanor Hollenberg Chasdi, Helen Faigin Antonovsky, and Margaret Sperry Lawrence. In 1951 Barbara Chartier Ayres replaced Margaret Sperry Lawrence on the team. Although the senior author had some responsibility for the research design, much of it was worked out in detail by the field teams, particularly Eleanor Hollenberg Chasdi and Helen Faigin Antonovsky, for whom this research was the basis of doctoral theses in the Department of Social Relations. They and Dr. Ayres were also responsible for the major part of the organization and analysis of the materials, such as coding the interviews, developing scales, and rating both the mothers and children on certain dimensions.
2. Roberts, *Zuni Daily Life*, p. 9.
3. *Ibid.*, pp. 91ff.
4. *Ibid.*, pp. 45–53.
5. *Parent and Child.*

6. Whiting, "Cross-cultural Method"; Sears, Maccoby, and Levin, *Patterns of Child Rearing*, p. 15.
7. Roberts, *Zuni Daily Life*, pp. 45 ff.
8. *Ibid.*, p. 61.
9. *Ibid.*, p. 93.
10. *Parent and Child.*
11. Mischel, "Delay of Gratification"; McClelland *et al.*, *Achievement Motive.*
12. Whiting, "Sorcery, Sin and the Superego."
13. Chang, "Neolithic Social Grouping," p. 319.
14. Whiting and Child, *Child Training and Personality;* Murdock, "World Ethnographic Sample."
15. Hald, *Statistical Tables.*
16. Bailyn, *Education in the Forming of American Society*, pp. 15–16.
17. Ryerson, "Medical Advice on Child Rearing."
18. Bailyn, *Education in the Forming of American Society*, p. 23.
19. *Ibid.*, pp. 24–25.
20. Ryerson, "Medical Advice on Child Rearing."
21. Barry, Bacon, and Child, "Sex Differences in Socialization."
22. McClelland and Friedman, "Child-training Practices and Achievement Motivation."
23. McClelland, *The Achieving Society.*
24. Whiting and Child, *Child Training and Personality.*
25. During the same period, a large number of Utopian movements (such as the Shakers, Owenites, and Fourients) appeared, most of them advocating a modification in the family household and structure.
26. K. Young, *Isn't One Wife Enough?*
27. Stephens, *Oedipus Complex;* Whiting, Kluckhohn, and Anthony, "Male Initiation Ceremonies"; Whiting, "Sorcery, Sin and the Superego."
28. Whiting and Child, *Child Training and Personality;* Whiting and D'Andrade, "Sleeping Arrangements."
29. In the following discussion, the Mormons will be considered as though they were still in their classical polygynous phase.
30. Miller and Swanson, *Changing American Parent.*
31. Smith and Roberts, *Zuni Law.*
32. Whiting and D'Andrade, *Sleeping Arrangements.*

CHAPTER 5. KINSHIP SYSTEMS

1. The pattern of formal kinship relates to inclusive "cultures" larger than the local communities studied by this project. Reliably reported variants are highly occasional and relate to informal rather than formal structure. With the exception of Zuni, therefore, the larger cultural units are the locus of the interpretation. Both the kinship features and the values to which they are related are relevant to Navaho culture in general, the Spanish-American culture of northern New Mexico and adjacent areas, the Texas subculture of west Texas and vicinity, and the culture of rural Mormon populations in Utah and other parts of the Southwest. I am indebted to Drs. Clyde Kluckhohn and John L. Fischer for a critical reading of this chapter and for helpful comments and suggestions.

2. Absolute rather than relative kinship statuses are found in many societies: mother (as opposed to one who has not had a child), first-born son, father of a male child, married man, and so on.

3. The figures given here and below represent the total number of terms compared, divided into the sum of the number of terms in each system which denote precisely the same relatives as some term in the other system, irrespective of linguistic form. See Edmonson, "Kinship Terms and Kinship Concepts."

4. Navaho uses numerical qualifiers for lineally extended relationships. Zuni, Dr. Stanley Newman informed me in a personal communication, does not. Such qualifiers do not appear for collaterally extended kinship in either language.

5. Metzger, "Formal Analysis of Kinship"; Schneider and Roberts, "Zuni Kin Terms."

6. The formal analysis which follows pursues a method previously applied to Zuni by Romney, "Formal Analysis of Kinship," and to Navaho, Zuni, English, and Spanish by Edmonson, "Kinship Terms and Kinship Concepts." It is here carried somewhat further by examining the configurational symmetry of the "ranges" of individual terms more intensively for each system.

7. Spier, "Distribution of Kinship Systems"; Reichard, "Social Life of the Navajo"; Opler, "Southern Athabaskan-Speaking Tribes"; Haile, *Learning Navajo;* Hoijer, "Athabaskan Kinship Systems"; Kaut, "Western Apache Clan System." I have also had the opportunity to examine W. W. Hill's terms, reported by Aberle, "Navaho," in Schneider and Gough; these terms are also discussed in Bellah, *Apache Kinship Systems.*

8. Kroeber, "Zuni Kin and Clan," p. 92.

9. *Ibid.,* p. 164.

10. Edmonson, *Los Manitos;* Parsons, "Pueblo Indians."

11. Opler, "Southern Athabaskan-Speaking Tribes."

12. Eggan, *Western Pueblos.*

13. This and subsequent suggestions of the operation of kinship as an exchange system derive from Lévi-Strauss, *Systèmes élémentaires.*

14. Reichard, "Social Life of the Navajo." See also Carr, Spencer, and Woolley, "Navaho Clans and Marriage," p. 254, where an incidence of 0.8 percent is noted in 241 marriages.

15. Reichard, "Social Life of the Navajo"; Collier, "Local Organization among the Navaho"; Carr, Spencer, and Woolley, "Navaho Clans and Marriage."

16. For a very interesting discussion on the consequences of weak disjunction in unilinear kin systems, with special reference to the Navaho among others, see K. Aberle, "Constants and Variables in Matrilineal Systems."

17. Vogt, *Modern Homesteaders.*

18. O'Dea, *The Mormons.*

19. C. Kluckhohn and Leighton, *The Navaho.*

20. Kroeber, "Zuni Kin and Clan."

21. Smith and Roberts, *Zuni Law,* p. 99.

22. *Ibid.,* pp. 86 ff.

23. *Ibid.,* p. 99.

24. Edmonson, *Status Terminology.*

25. Kroeber, "Zuni Kin and Clan," pp. 183 ff.

26. Edmonson, "Los Manitos"; F. Kluckhohn, "Dominant and Substitute Profiles."

27. Vogt, *Modern Homesteaders,* p. 150.
28. O'Dea, *The Mormons,* pp. 222–263, and *passim.*
29. Spier, "Distribution of Kinship Systems"; D. Aberle, "Navaho"; Lévi-Strauss, "Social Laws"; Schneider and Homans, *Marriage;* Lévi-Strauss, *Systèmes élémentaires;* Durkheim, *Vie religieuse;* T. Parsons, "Kinship System."

CHAPTER 6. ECOLOGY AND ECONOMY

1. See Landgraf, *Land-Use,* for further details of the settlement patterns of Spanish-Americans, Navahos, Mormons, and Texan homesteaders.
2. Vogt, "Prehistoric Settlement Patterns," p. 174.
3. Burt, "Territoriality"; Lorenz, *King Solomon's Ring;* Nice, "Bird Life."
4. Bartholomew and Birdsell, "Ecology and the Protohominids."
5. Willey, *Prehistoric Settlement Patterns.*
6. F. Kluckhohn, "Los Atarqueños."
7. C. Kluckhohn and Leighton, *The Navaho,* pp. 7–8, 46, 59–62.
8. Twitchell, "Spanish Colonization," pp. 4–5.
9. Vogt and O'Dea, "Two Southwestern Communities," p. 652; Nelson, *The Mormon Village,* pp. 28–38.
10. C. Kluckhohn, "Philosophy of the Navaho," p. 367; Adair and Vogt, "Navaho and Zuni Veterans," pp. 558–560.
11. Vogt and O'Dea, "Two Southwestern Communities," p. 653.
12. Wittfogel and Goldfrank, "Pueblo Mythology," pp. 21–23.
13. U.S. Indian Service, *United Pueblos.*
14. Vestal (*Ethnobotany,* pp. 57–60) discovered that of the 456 uncultivated plant species he collected in the Rimrock area, the Navahos had names for all but three species and could describe some medicinal or dietary use for all but two species. This fact is a striking index of the profound knowledge Navahos have of wild plants and the use they make of them.
15. O'Dea, "Mormon Values," p. 422.
16. O'Dea ("Mormon Values," p. 423) estimates that some 800 additional acres could be brought under irrigation with this storage capacity, if adequate precipitation fills the reservoir each year and if more irrigable land could be acquired by the community.
17. Twitchell, "Spanish Colonization," pp. 7, 16–17.
18. Firth, *Elements,* pp. 122–154.
19. Smith and Roberts, *Zuni Law,* pp. 78–81.

CHAPTER 7. POLITICAL STRUCTURE

1. David *et al., Presidential Nominating Politics,* p. 122.
2. See also chapter 3, "Intercultural Relations," by Evon Z. Vogt, with the assistance of Malcolm J. Arth.
3. Donnelly, *Government of New Mexico,* p. 179.
4. Thurnwald, *Werden, Wandel und Gestaltung,* pp. 169, 186.
5. Smith and Roberts, *Zuni Law.*
6. Bunker, *Other Men's Skies,* p. 194.
7. Kroeber, "Zuni Kin and Clan," p. 153.

Notes to Chapter 7

8. Bunzel, "Zuni Ceremonialism," pp. 467–544; Eggan, *Social Organization,* p. 197
9. *Ibid.,* pp. 217, 187.
10. *Ibid.,* p. 210.
11. Smith and Roberts, *Zuni Law,* pp. 28–35.
12. *Ibid.,* pp. 36–37.
13. Vogt, *Field Notes.*
14. S. D. Aberle, *Pueblo Indians of New Mexico,* pp. 19, 27, 65.
15. *Ibid.*
16. Bunker, *Other Men's Skies,* pp. 115, 138.
17. *Gallup Independent,* 9, 11, 13, 17, 24 May 1955.
18. R. Young, *Navajo Yearbook,* p. 143.
19. Thomas, *Forgotten Frontiers,* pp. 260, 346.
20. Keleher, *Turmoil,* p. 411.
21. Van Valkenburgh, "Navajo Common Law," p. 17; Zelditch, *Field Notes.*
22. C. Kluckhohn and Leighton, *The Navaho,* pp. 62–63; Rapoport, *Navaho Religious Values,* p. 7; D. Aberle, "Navaho Kinship," p. 9.
23. Spuhler and Kluckhohn, "Inbreeding Coefficients," p. 301; D. Aberle, "Navaho Kinship," pp. 12–13.
24. C. Kluckhohn and Leighton, *The Navaho,* p. 69.
25. R. Young, *Navajo Yearbook,* p. 115.
26. R. Young, *Navajo Yearbook,* pp. 112–114; Shepardson, "Leadership and Culture Change."
27. C. Kluckhohn and Leighton, *The Navaho,* p. 102.
28. D. Aberle, "Navaho Kinship," pp. 12–13.
29. R. Young, *Navajo Yearbook,* pp. 2–4.
30. *Ibid.,* p. 113.
31. C. Kluckhohn and Leighton, *The Navaho,* p. 103.
32. F. Kluckhohn, "Los Atarqueños," p. 98; Thurnwald, *Werden, Wandel und Gestaltung,* p. 154.
33. Bloch, *Société Féodale,* p. 244.
34. Mead, *Cultural Patterns,* p. 158.
35. Ferguson, *New Mexico,* p. 224.
36. F. Kluckhohn, "Los Atarqueños," pp. 94–95.
37. O'Dea, "Avoidance of Sectarian Stagnation," p. 292.
38. Caldwell, "Mormon Conceptions," p. 124.
39. Widtsoe, *Priesthood and Church Government,* p. 647.
40. *Ibid.,* p. 48.
41. *Ibid.,* p. 44.
42. Caldwell, "Mormon Conceptions," p. 122; R. Young, *Navajo Yearbook.*
43. Caldwell, "Mormon Conceptions," pp. 286–287, 301–302.
44. O'Dea, "Mormon Values," p. 331.
45. *Ibid.,* p. 489.
46. *Ibid.,* p. 456.
47. Zelditch, *Field Notes;* O'Dea, "Avoidance of Sectarian Stagnation."
48. F. Kluckhohn, "Los Artequeños."
49. Vogt, *Modern Homesteaders.*
50. Untereiner, *Field Notes.*
51. Kroeber, "Zuni Kin and Clan," p. 183.
52. Vogt, *Modern Homesteaders,* pp. 134–135.

CHAPTER 8. RELIGIOUS SYSTEMS

1. This chapter is dependent on the work of a number of other persons, some connected with the Values Study Project. I am primarily indebted to Stevenson ("Zuni Indians"), Bunzel ("Zuni Ceremonialism," "Zuni Katchinas") and Benedict (*Patterns of Culture*) for Zuni; C. Kluckhohn ("Myths and Rituals," "Navaho Personal Document," *Navaho Witchcraft*), Spencer (*Mythology and Values*, Memoirs), Rapoport (*Navaho Religious Values*) and Reichard (*Navaho Religion*) for Navaho; F. Kluckhohn ("Los Atarqueños") and Edmonson ("Los Manitos") for Spanish-Americans; O'Dea ("Mormon Values") for the Mormons; and Vogt (*Modern Homesteaders*) for the Texans. The theoretical statement of the functions of religion in society is based on an unpublished set of categories for the analysis of social systems devised by Talcott Parsons. This has appeared in part in Parsons and Smelser's *Economy and Society*. Paul Tillich (*Systematic Theology*) has influenced both my general orientation and some of my terminology.
2. Haeberlin, "Fertilization," p. 16.
3. Bunzel, "Zuni Ceremonialism," p. 512.
4. *Ibid.*, p. 513.
5. Bunzel, "Zuni Katchinas," p. 843.
6. Reichard, *Navaho Religion*, pp. 75–76.
7. C. Kluckhohn and Leighton, *The Navaho*, pp. 123–124.
8. *Ibid.*, pp. 124–125.
9. Reichard, *Navaho Religion*, pp. 65–66.
10. Katherine Spencer, *Mythology and Values*, Memoirs, has provided a definitive treatment of this aspect of Navaho religion on which I have leaned heavily.
11. Bennion and Washburn, "Restored Church," pp. 14–15.
12. Benedict, *Patterns of Culture*, pp. 54–55.
13. *Ibid.*, pp. 84–85.
14. *Ibid.*, pp. 62, 117.
15. This interpretation is based on the very interesting analysis which David F. Aberle, "Hopi Life-History," has made with respect to the Hopi, especially pp. 123–125.
16. Titiev, *Old Oraibi*.
17. Bunzel, "Zuni Ceremonialism," pp. 540, 541.
18. Benedict, *Patterns of Culture*, p. 72.
19. Stevenson, "Zuni Indians," p. 495.
20. *Ibid.*, p. 437.
21. C. Kluckhohn and Leighton, *The Navaho*, p. 141.
22. *Ibid.*, p. 149.
23. Reichard, *Navaho Religion*, p. 89.
24. This treatment of Navaho religious action has been influenced by Robert N. Rapoport, *Navaho Religious Values*. Readers interested in the effect of Christian missions on the Rimrock Navahos should refer to this work.
25. Reichard, *Navaho Religion*, p. 80.
26. C. Kluckhohn and Leighton, *The Navaho*, p. 165.
27. C. Kluckhohn, "Myths and Rituals," p. 76.
28. See C. Kluckhohn, *Navaho Witchcraft*.

329

29. Edmonson, "Los Manitos," p. 129.
30. Vogt, *Field Notes.*
31. Benedict, *Patterns of Culture,* p. 70.
32. Zelditch, "Authority and Solidarity."
33. C. Kluckhohn, "Navaho Personal Document."

CHAPTER 9. EXPRESSIVE ACTIVITIES

1. In her account of the people of Alor, for example, Cora DuBois was led by the cultural data to discuss "Finance and Aesthetics," in recognition of the role of wealth in the composition and performance of verse and music. (Cora DuBois, *The People of Alor.* Minneapolis: University of Minnesota Press, 1944, pp. 136–143.)
2. E. M. Albert, Field Notes, 1954.
3. McAllester, *Enemy Way Music;* Mills, "Art, Life and Death"; Bradley, "Cultural Differences in Drawings by Children"; Edmonson, "Los Manitos"; Roberts, *Four Southwestern Men.*
4. Rapoport, *Changing Navaho Religious Values;* C. Kluckhohn, "Myths and Rituals," "Participation in Ceremonials," and "Some Personal and Social Aspects of Navaho Ceremonial Practice"; Vogt, "Study of the Southwestern Fiesta System"; Lenneberg and Roberts, "Language of Experience"; Edmonson, "Los Manitos"; C. Kluckhohn and Leighton, *The Navaho;* C. Kluckhohn, "Some Navaho Value Terms"; Spencer, "Mythology and Values," and *Mythology and Values;* Geertz, "Drought, Death and Alcohol."
5. Not even a summary of the vast literature on the arts of the Zuni, Navaho, and Spanish-Americans is possible here. Instead, only a brief survey of the arts in the five groups will be attempted with a slightly more extended treatment of the materials and analyses developed by the Comparative Study of Values Project. A sketch of symbolism in the arts alone would take us to too great length. Navaho dream symbolism has been reviewed by Lincoln, *Dream in Primitive Cultures,* and some Rimrock Navaho dreams are analyzed by Roheim (*Psychoanalysis and Anthropology,* chapter 8). Texan and Zuni "daydreams" are dealt with by Untereiner ("Self and Society," pp. 252 ff). Many technical details of Zuni and Navaho symbolism will be found in such sources as Adair (*Navaho and Pueblo Silversmiths*), Bunzel ("Zuni Religion," *Pueblo Potter*), and Mills ("Art, Life and Death").
6. Vogt, *Navaho Veterans,* pp. 117, 181.
7. O'Dea, "Mormon Values," pp. 402–403.
8. Personal communication, September 1956.
9. Bunzel, "Zuni Religion," p. 496.
10. McAllester, *Enemy Way Music.*
11. Cf. the "bipolarity" found so important by Mills ("Art, Life and Death) in his discussion of Navaho aesthetics.
12. Edmonson, "Los Manitos," p. 183.
13. Wilson, *Red, Black,* p. 39.
14. *Ibid.,* p. 67.
15. Milgroom, "Zuni Mythology."
16. Spencer, "Mythology and Values," Memoirs, p. 226.
17. Spencer, "Mythology and Values," thesis, p. 188.

18. Bunzel, "Zuni Religion," pp. 617–618, 620.
19. *Ibid.*, pp. 635–643.
20. Mills, "Art, Life and Death."
21. Experiments by Michael ("Cross-Cultural Investigation") with the Navahos and Texans gave no statistically significant results on *perception* of closure in the two groups.
22. Mills, "Art, Life and Death," p. 412.
23. Geertz, "Drought, Death and Alcohol."
24. Bradley, "Cultural Differences." Additional material on free drawings of Rimrock Navaho and Zuni children will be found in Havighurst and Neugarten, *Indian and White Children,* chapter 7.
25. On color as a perceptual and cognitive category at Zuni, see Lenneberg and Roberts, *Language of Experience.*
26. Adair, *Navaho and Pueblo Silversmiths.*
27. F. Kluckhohn, "Los Artequeños," p. 189.
28. Spier, "Zuni Weaving Techniques."
29. Vogt, "Southwestern Fiesta System."
30. *Ibid.*, p. 837.
31. Geertz, "Drought, Death and Alcohol."
32. Bullen, "Archaeological Theory"; Mills, "Art, Life and Death," p. 155.
33. F. Kluckhohn, "Los Artequeños," p. 216.
34. This section is based almost entirely on Edmonson, "Los Manitos."
35. McAllester, *Enemy Way Music,* p. 71.
36. Edmonson, "Los Manitos," pp. 245–261 *passim.*
37. F. Kluckhohn, "Los Atarqueños," pp. 203, 281.
38. Wilson, *Red, Black,* p. 68.
39. See C. Kluckhohn, "Navaho Value Terms."
40. McAllester, *Enemy Way Music,* p. 71.
41. Bunzel, *Pueblo Potter,* pp. 89, 86.
42. For example, disease and ugliness and improper or indecent behavior are all grouped together in Navaho. C. Kluckhohn, "Navaho Value Terms, p. 145.
43. Geertz, "Drought, Death and Alcohol."
44. Untereiner, "Self and Society," pp. 231 ff.
45. Spencer, *Mythology and Values,* Memoirs, pp. 222, 20. And see Vogt. *Modern Homesteaders,* p. 80.
46. Edmonson, "Los Manitos," p. 183.
47. O'Dea, "Mormon Values," pp. 101, 103.

Index

Aberle, David F., 205
Aberle, Mrs. S. D., 200
Absolutism, 5
Acoma, 37, 49
Activity, Expressive. *See* "Expressive activities"
Adair, John, 284
Aesthetics, 265–266, 273–274, 292; theoretic significance of, 266–268; of Texans, 270; and expressive activities, 270–274; and arts, 276; standards of, 292–294
Agencies, federal administrative, 194. *See also* U.S. Government; names of specific agencies
Aggression, 29. *See also* Zuni, control of aggression
Agriculture, 23; growing season, 43, 161–162; and settlement pattern, 171; Zuni, 175, 189; dry-land, 178
Albert, Ethel M., 10, 12, 15, 20, 33
Albuquerque, New Mexico, 44, 45, 186
Alcohol. *See* Liquor
All-Pueblo Council, 194, 197
Amarillo, Texas, 44
American Indians, 62; education of, 74. *See also* specific tribes
Anasazi, 46
Animal life. *See* Rimrock, flora and fauna
Anthropology, 1, 17
Antonovsky, Helen Faigin, 9
Anza, Juan Bautista de, 203
Apache Indians, 46–47, 50, 51, 112, 122, 203. *See also* Jicarilla Apache; Western Apache
Arizona, 25, 38, 41, 43, 142; and early Mormons, 55–56
Arts, 32, 265–266, 269, 276–285, 293; music, 32, 266, 271, 276–279; drama, 266, 279;

verbal, 266, 280, 297; graphic, 266, 271, 282–284; and aesthetics, 276; practical, 284–285; loneliness theme, 297
Athapascan Indians, 51, 203
Atrisco, 1, 38, 44, 45, 166, 176, 184, 218, 278; early settlement of, 47, 53–54, 170; and Homestead, hostility between, 59–61; Spanish-American culture of, 78, 209, 238, 261; history of *patrón* system in, 211–213
Authority, 84; household, 86–87; Mormon, 86, 102, 262; political, 191, 220–223, 256–257; and Spanish-American, 210, 261–262 (*see also* Spanish-Americans, and *patrón* system); and religion, 229–230, 258–259, 263
Ayres, Barbara Chartier, 9

Bacon, Margaret K., 117
Bailyn, Bernard, 114, 115
Bal, Fray Juan de, 49
Bandelier, A. F., 50, 51
Barry, Herbert A., 117
Bartholomew, George A., Jr., 162
Baseball. *See* Recreation, sports and games
Basketball. *See* Recreation, sports and games
Basket Maker periods, 46, 112
Bellah, Robert, 31–32
Belonging and participation, 191
Benedict, Ruth, 244, 246, 257
Binary oppositions, 18–21
Birdsell, Joseph B., 163
Black Rock, 166
Bloch, Marc, 210, 211
Bluewater, New Mexico, 76
Boas, Franz, 276
Book of Mormon, 69, 280. *See also* Church of Latter-Day Saints; Mormons
Bradley, Helen, 275

333

INDEX

hos, 188; relationship to Navaho and Zuni, 195–196, 206; and Zuni theocracy, 201; in factional struggles, 202; and Navaho political structure, 202, 208; and creation of Navaho Tribal Council, 207; Navaho Agency, 208; and Navaho Chapters, 209; and public works, 226

Infant Christ of Our Lady of Atocha, 53, 66

Initiation, religious, 243, 246. *See also* Socialization, and religion

Inscription Rock. *See* Morro, El

Intercultural relations, 25–26; hierarchy of, 80–82; and Rimrock political activities, 192

Interior, U.S. Department of, 207

Intermarriage, 154, 156; Texan–Spanish-American, 60; Zuni–Navaho, 63, 64–65; Zuni–Spanish-American, 65, 66; Indian–Spanish-American, 66, 67–68; Mormon–Indian, 70, 72–73; Texan–Mormon, 76; Spanish-American–Mormon, 77; Spanish-American–Texan, 78, 79; and intercultural hierarchy, 81–82

Irrigation. *See* Water

Jicarilla Apache, 51
Johnson, New Mexico, 44, 45, 213
Jose Pino Canyon, 37
Justice, administration of, 191

Kansas, 38
Kant, Immanuel, 276
Kaplan, B., 9, 296
Kaut, Charles R., 133, 135
Keam's Canyon, 143
Kearny, Stephen Watts, 203
Kinship, 7, 30, 126–159; terminology, 21, 126–138; Zuni, 30, 67, 86–87, 99, 128–130, 133, 135–138, 140–142, 148–150, 157–158; Navaho, 30, 127–130, 132–135, 137, 139–140, 142, 147–148, 159; external structure of, 127, 141–159; fictive extensions of, 127, 141–154; in social rank, 127, 141, 146; and residence, 127, 141, 147–154; Spanish-American, 128, 131–132, 139–140, 144, 150–152, 157; Mormon, 129, 140, 144–145, 153–154, 157; Texan, 129, 140, 144, 152–153; asymmetrical Indian, 130, 132; English, 130–131, 139, 152, 156; and cultural continuity, 155; and transmission of values, 156; determinants of, 158–159

Klagetoh, 143

Kluckhohn, Clyde, 1, 12, 147, 205, 206, 234, 248, 250, 275; defines values, 1–3, 6, 22; and "dimensions" of values, 13; and binary oppositions, 18–19, 21; and value change, 30; and expressive activities, 32, 265–266, 268, 274; on Navaho Tribal Council, 207–208

Kluckhohn, Florence, 9, 12, 53, 252, 275; value-orientations theory, 15–18; on *patrón* system, 212

Köhler, Wolfgang, 6

Kroeber, A. L., 137, 197, 198, 199, 224

Kwiayalane. *See* "Twin Mesas"

Ladd, John, 8, 11–12

"Lamanites," 56, 69–70

Land, 160; use-pattern, 30, 162, 173–181; early distribution, 55, 59, 170; and Mormon–Indian relationship, 69; and Texan–Spanish-American relationship, 79–80; and Zuni use-pattern, 174–175; Navaho use-pattern, 175–176; Spanish-American use-pattern, 176; Mormon use-pattern, 176–177; geographical and cultural factors in use-patterns, 178; allotments for Navaho, 188; administration of New Mexico's, 195

Land and Cattle Company (Mormon), 217

Landgraf, John, 10

Language, 7, 203, 275; and cultural diffusion, 25; and Indian–Spanish-American relationship, 66; and Mormon–Indian relationship, 70; and Mormon–Spanish-American relationship, 77, and Spanish-American–Texan relationship, 78

Latter-Day Saints. *See* Church of the Latter-Day Saints

Leadership, 31; Navaho, 204–205. *See also* Spanish-Americans, and *patrón* system

Leighton, Dorothea, 147, 234, 248

Lenneberg, Eric, 9, 275

Letrado, Fray Francisco, 49

Lincoln, Abraham, 201, 213

Linguistics, 18–19

Liquor, 58–59, 75, 185, 275; and Indian–Spanish-American bootlegger–customer relationship, 66–67, 77, 288; and Mormon attitude toward Texan, 75–76; and barkeeper–customer relationship, 78; crosscultural reaction to, 287; and inter-sex relationships, 288

Little Colorado River, 37

Los Chavez, New Mexico, 159

Los Lunas, New Mexico, 150

Lubbock, Texas, 44

INDEX

Sociology, 1, 16–17

Spain, conquests of. *See* Conquistadores, Spanish

Spanish-Americans, 13, and water supply, 23–24, 166; cultural affiliations of, 25, 44; self-image, 26, 220; patrilinealism, 30, 131–132, 140, 150–152, 211; and dancing, 32–33, 272, 297; and neighboring towns, 44; early settlement of in Rimrock, 47, 52–55; and Zuni, 53–54, 65–69; and Navahos, 54–55, 65–69; and Mormons, 56–58, 77; and Texans, 58–60, 77–80, 270; tolerance of, 78; political affiliation of, 80; and religion, 80, 237–239, 250–252, 260–262 (*see also* Catholicism); value-orientation, 80; in intercultural hierarchy, 80–81; kinship system, 128, 131–132, 139–140, 144, 150–152, 157, 211, 238; and divorce, 145; and group identification, 156; settlement pattern, 163, 166–167, 170–171; land-use patterns, 176, 179; as rancher-farmer, 182; as wage worker, 186; economic system, 188–189; political structure, 192, 209–213, 220, 226; electoral participation, 193; and *patrón* system, 210–213, 222, 224, 226, 238, 261; and decision-making, 222; and curers, 252; and death, 268, 270, 295; and aesthetics, 274, 292; and music, 277–278; and drama, 279

Spencer, Katherine, 9, 275, 280, 296, 297

Spier, Leslie, 133

Sports. *See* Recreation, sports and games

Steck, Dr. Michael, 204

Stevenson, Matilda Coxe, 246

Strodtbeck, Fred L., 9

Success, 29, 30; as Texan value in child-rearing, 105–106, 111, 117, 119; as Mormon value, 122

Sunset, Arizona, 56

Swanson, Guy E., 123

Symbols, religious, 227–243

Taboos, 7; Zuni, 50, 53, 63; Mormon, 76, 104, 120, 123, 290; and incest, 127, 139–140

Talmage, J. E., 69

Teenagers, 76. *See also* Child-rearing

Tejanos. See Texans

Television, 45

Telling, Irving, 10

"Territoriality," 162–163

Texans, 44, 224; and water supply, 24, 170; cultural affiliation of, 25; self-image, 26, 156, 220; cultural shift, 29, 113–114, 122–123, 124; hyperindividuality, 30, 58, 159, 172, 242, 263, 297; decision-making process, 31, 222; religion, 32, 80, 97, 98, 219, 237, 241–243, 253–255, 263–264; and dancing, 32, 78–79, 272, 276, 298; and neighboring towns, 44; early settlement by, 48, 58–61; and Mormons, 58, 74–76; and Spanish-Americans, 58–60, 78–80, 270; and Navaho, 58–59, 73–74; attitude toward Indians, 58; and Zuni, 73–74; and Mormonism, 75; political affiliation of, 80, 219; value-orientation of, 80, 219; in intercultural hierarchy, 80–81; child-rearing, 83–84, 87–88, 89–92, 93, 94, 105, 111; housing, 85; authority pattern of, 86–87; early marriage age, 102; attitude of toward premarital sex, 104–105; and Magic Man Test, 106–108; and conflict and anxiety test, 108–110; and affirmative values test, 110–111; early history of, 113–119; and cultural defenses, 124; kinship system, 129, 140, 144, 152–153, 219; and divorce, 145; settlement pattern, 163, 169, 170, 172; land-use pattern, 177, 179; and cattle-raising, 180, 183; and service occupations, 184; as storekeepers, 185; as wage workers, 186; economic system, 187, 189; political structure, 192, 218–220, 226; electoral participation, 193; and federal agencies, 195; hostility of to outside authority, 219; local political activities, 219; and social rank, 219; and Protestant ethic, 241–242, 263; and death, 269, 295; and aesthetics, 274, 292; and music, 276; and drama, 279; and emotional expression, 294–296

Texas, 38. *See also* Homestead

Thurnwald, Richard, 196

Tiguex, New Mexico, 49

Tijeras, 37, 44, 47, 166, 176; early settlement of, 52, 54; and early trading, 53; and early Mormons, 55; Valley, 170

Tillich, Paul, 227

Time, 16–17; and kinship systems, 128–130, 157; and Zuni ceremonialism, 244

Tome, New Mexico, 250–251

Towayalane. *See* "Corn Mountain"

Towns, 43–45

Toys, 94

Trading: intergroup, 53, 57, 59; and Mormon–Indian relationship, 71–72; and Texan–Indian relationship, 74

"Twin Mesas," 37

340